Leading, Managing and Developing People

Fourth edition

Edited by Gary Rees and Ray French

The Chartered Institute of Personnel and Development is the leading publisher of books and reports for personnel and training professionals, students, and all those concerned with the effective management and development of people at work. For details of all our titles, please contact the publishing department:
tel: 020 8612 6204
email: publishing@cipd.co.uk
The catalogue of all CIPD titles can be viewed on the CIPD website:
www.cipd.co.uk/bookstore

Leading, Managing and Developing People

Fourth edition

Edited by Gary Rees and Ray French

Chartered Institute of Personnel and Development

Published by the Chartered Institute of Personnel and Development
151 The Broadway, London SW19 1JQ

This edition first published 2013

Designed and typeset by Exeter Premedia Services, India

Printed in Great Britain by Bell & Bain, Glasgow

British Library Cataloguing in Publication Data

A catalogue of this publication is available from the British Library

ISBN 978 1 84398 318 7

The views expressed in this publication are the authors' own and may not necessarily reflect those of the CIPD.

The CIPD has made every effort to trace and acknowledge copyright holders. If any source has been overlooked, CIPD Enterprises would be pleased to redress this in future editions.

Chartered Institute of Personnel and Development
151 The Broadway, London SW19 1JQ
Tel: 020 8612 6200
Email: cipd@cipd.co.uk
Website: www.cipd.co.uk
Incorporated by Royal Charter.
Registered Charity No. 1079797

Contents

List of figures and tables

Acknowledgements

Leading, Managing and Developing People is underpinned by some classical insights and findings developed over many years, but at the same time it is a fast-moving area, strongly influenced by the wider economic and social context. This fourth edition contains new research findings, case studies and other examples to reflect topicality and enhance relevance for readers.

Chapter authors have had to work within a short timeline in order to achieve the book's aims and we would like to thank them all for their professionalism.

Thanks are also due to Katy Hamilton and Heidi Partridge at CIPD Publishing for keeping us on track in an efficient and always pleasant way. We wish to thank, finally, reviewers of draft chapters for their constructive feedback and trust that we have responded to their observations in this fourth edition of our textbook.

Gary Rees
Ray French
University of Portsmouth Business School
May 2013

List of contributors

Derek Adam-Smith
Gill Christy
Richard Christy
Ray French
David Hall
Liza Howe-Walsh
Margaret Mackay
Charlotte Rayner
Gary Rees
Sally Rumbles
Simon Turner
Alex Tymon

All the contributors work at the University of Portsmouth Business School, Portsmouth UK.

CIPD qualifications map

Leading, Managing and Developing People

The content of this CIPD module is covered as follows:

Leading, Managing and Developing People learning outcomes		Leading, Managing and Developing People chapters
1	Review and critically evaluate major contemporary research and debates in the fields of HRM and HRD.	Chapter 1: Introduction Chapter 2: The Scope and Nature of HRM and HRD Chapter 3: HRM Contributions in Different Settings Chapter 13: Summary Themes and Future Trends
2	Evaluate major theories relating to motivation, commitment and engagement at work and how these are put into practice by organisations.	Chapter 5: Leadership Chapter 7: Flexibility and the Psychological Contract Chapter 11: Managing the Employment Relationship Chapter 12: Performance Management, Motivation and Reward
3	Debate and critically evaluate the characteristics of effective leadership and the methods used to develop leaders in organisations.	Chapter 5: Leadership
4	Contribute to the promotion of flexible working and effective change management in organisations.	Chapter 6: Managing Change Chapter 7: Flexibility and the Psychological Contract Chapter 8: Organisational and Job Design Chapter 9: Recruitment and Selection
5	Critically discuss the aims and objectives of the HR function in organisations and how these are met in practice.	Chapter 8: Organisational and Job Design Chapter 9: Recruitment and Selection Chapter 10: Developing Employees Chapter 11: Managing the Employment Relationship Chapter 12: Performance Management, Motivation and Reward

Leading, Managing and Developing People learning outcomes		Leading, Managing and Developing People chapters
6	Assess the contribution made by HRM and HRD specialists in different types of organisation.	Chapter 8: Organisational and Job Design Chapter 9: Recruitment and Selection Chapter 10: Developing Employees Chapter 11: Managing the Employment Relationship Chapter 12: Performance Management, Motivation and Reward
7	Promote professionalism and an ethical approach to HRM and HRD practice in organisations.	Chapter 4: Professionalism and Ethics in Managing People Chapter 11: Managing the Employment Relationship Chapter 13: Summary Themes and Future Trends

Walkthrough of textbook features and online resources

LEARNING OUTCOMES

After reading this chapter, you should be able to:

- appreciate how HR practices may differ across sector types: private, public and third sector
- recognise that delivering HR services in smaller organisations differs from those in larger organisations
- consider the ways in which the HR function may change as an organisation grows in size
- understand the concept of global HRM and its implications for practice in terms of policy and practice for localisation and control from head office
- explore the notion of strategic international HRM; variegations in practice for staffing overseas.

LEARNING OUTCOMES

At the beginning of each chapter a bulleted set of learning outcomes summarises what you can expect to learn from the chapter, helping you to track your learning.

CASE STUDY 12.2

TOTAL REWARD AT ARUP

Arup is a global design and engineering consultancy. The company employs around 10,500 people in 37 countries, around half of whom are based in the UK. At Arup, which is employee-owned, the reward package includes a global profit-sharing scheme as well as a range of other benefits.

Although the organisation did not formally publish a total reward policy until 2007, Arup has been practising a total reward strategy for much longer, and offers online total reward statements to its employees around the world. Tony Hatton-Gore, director,

afterwards, Arup decided to adopt this approach.

There were three key reasons behind the decision to introduce total reward statements:

- total reward statements were seen as an effective way to ensure staff understood the make-up and the value of their employment package
- in line with its values of honest and fair dealings with staff, and in the interests of transparency, Arup wanted people to understand what was available within the organisation as an employee-owned firm

CASE STUDIES

A number of case studies from different sectors and countries will help you to place the concepts discussed into a real-life context.

REVIEW QUESTIONS

1. Do you think HR professionals at all levels can demonstrate value-added, or is this an issue only for people at the top?

2. What would you see as the challenges of someone changing job from being an HR business partner in the private sector to one in the public sector? How would you suggest such an individual prepares for their new role?

3. Assuming there are financial gains for providing an outsourced HR service, what other parameters would you consider when evaluating this issue?

4. Why is adding an international dimension to one's operation so challenging for HR? Use the example of a UK organisation setting up a sales office in Canada to illustrate your ideas. In this operation some local Canadian staff would be employed, but need head office assistance during the set-up period.

REVIEW QUESTIONS

These review questions are aimed at reinforcing what you have learned in the chapter.

REFLECTIVE ACTIVITY 3.1

Consider the example of Surrey Police provided above.

Questions

1   In what ways do you think the relationship between line managers and HR may have changed as a result of the new approach?

2   How would staff in your HR department react to enabling more managerial discretion?

3   Discuss the strengths and weaknesses of devolving power to the line manager in the public sector.

REFLECTIVE ACTIVITIES

Questions and activities throughout the text encourage you to reflect on what you have learned and to apply your knowledge and skills in practice.

KEY LEARNING POINTS

- The HR function adds value to the organisation in a number of ways through delivering business strategy.
- The HR function adds value, but how it does so, and who is perceived as adding value, is complex and sometimes a function of internal politics and the perceptions of line managers.
- The way in which HR adds value changes as the organisation grows, and also between sectors.
- Outsourcing aspects of HR is common, but needs to be done carefully to ensure the organisation does not lose competitive edge.
- Internationalisation is a current issue for those who recruit, and for those involved in mobilising staff between countries.
- The degree of control from the parent company in the area of international HR presents a challenge which needs to be balanced depending on the context.

KEY LEARNING POINTS

At the end of each chapter, key learning points consolidate your learning.

EXPLORE FURTHER

Becker, B. and Huselid, M.A. (2006) Strategic human resource management: where do we go from here? *Journal of Management*. Vol. 32, No. 6, pp898–925. This article is a very effective overview of the strategic issues within HR. Their application of business strategy into the undertaking of HR roles is both thought-provoking and holds a list of key texts, should readers wish to pursue the forms of HR delivery within organisations.

Boselie, P., Brewster, C. and Paauwe, J. (2009) In search of balance-managing the dualities of HRM. *Personnel Review*. Vol. 38, No. 5, pp461–471. This paper provides an excellent overview of strategic HR issues and constructs in contemporary thinking with an excellent reading base for further exploration. This can be compared to the CIPD-sponsored research (Sears 2010), which is drawn from large organisations where the notion that practice outstrips thinking and academic work is put forward.

EXPLORE FURTHER

Explore further boxes contain suggestions for further reading and useful websites, encouraging you to delve further into areas of particular interest.

ONLINE RESOURCES FOR STUDENTS

Visit www.cipd.co.uk/sss

- Annotated web links
- Glossary to support understanding of terminology

ONLINE RESOURCES FOR TUTORS

Visit www.cipd.co.uk/tss

- Lecturer's guide – practical advice on teaching the Leading, Managing and Developing People module using this text.
- PowerPoint slides – build and deliver your course around these ready-made lectures, ensuring complete coverage of the module.

LEADING, MANAGING AND DEVELOPING PEOPLE: AN OVERVIEW

CHAPTER 1

Introduction

Ray French and Gary Rees

LEARNING OUTCOMES

After reading this chapter, you should be able to:

- identify important themes within the area of leading, managing and developing people through an analysis of two case studies

- complete case study exercises which explore generic leading, managing and developing people issues

- familiarise yourself with the learning features within this book

- understand the structure of the book in relation to the CIPD Leading, Managing and Developing People unit (7002)

- locate or map the Leading, Managing and Developing People unit (7002) learning outcomes to particular chapters in the text.

OVERVIEW

Leading, managing and developing people forms a key part of everyday life in work organisations. While topics and issues covered in this book may fall within the formal remit of a specialist human resource management (HRM) function, there is equally a strong sense in which leading and managing employees infuses all aspects of working life. Aston (2013), in identifying the 'tough times' facing organisations, notes the important role occupied by line managers – those people who directly manage people within a chain of authority – and the need to support those managers. Aston *op cit*, notes that:

> Now more than ever it's about doing more with less and creating a work environment that proactively manages pressure so that it doesn't turn into stress. Line managers are essential to achieving this through nurturing the people they manage to prevent burn out and attrition. However, line managers are being squeezed from top to bottom and it's important they also receive the support they need to do the best job possible.

We hope that insights contained within this book will help you both to manage people effectively and support other managers with people responsibilities.

Individual chapters within this book identify and discuss the core topics that make up the study and practice of leading, managing and developing people. We have organised the chapters into discrete areas – for example leadership, managing the employment relationship and performance management. However, managing people is a broad area of work and day-to-day events and challenges are best understood and acted on by taking an overview which goes beyond any one sub-division of HR work. This can be seen in Case Study 1.1 below, which deals with a single theme but one that has broader ramifications in leading, managing and developing people.

CASE STUDY 1.1

TREAD CAREFULLY BEFORE SAYING 'BAH! HUMBUG!'

As Christmas approaches thoughts turn to the annual office bash. But given the tough economic climate, it is not surprising that many organisations look to cut costs. We consider whether an organisation that has always paid for a staff Christmas party, covering the cost of the venue, meal, entertainment and bar, can suddenly forego paying for this and instead ask employees to make an individual contribution.

If the employees of an organisation have received a fully subsidised Christmas party for many years, then it could be argued that it has become an implied form of the contract of employment (see Chapters 7 and 11) through custom and practice. Although it might seem a rather strange thing to become an implied term, many employees will see the Christmas party as a valuable benefit, particularly given their own outgoings at this time of year.

In this situation, the organisation may wish to consult with employees about ways of reducing Christmas party costs, by using a less expensive menu or some other cost-saving measures.

When the organisation really cannot afford to pay for it at all, it will need to consult with employees as this will be a variation of contract. Such a variation can only be achieved through mutual agreement. Employers should also be aware that imposing the change without agreement might lead to an employee resigning and then claiming constructive dismissal (where a worker resigns due to perceived breaches of contract). This scenario is unlikely and any claim may not succeed, but is possible nonetheless.

Source: HR-inform (2012)

A survey conducted on Christmas and New Year working arrangements in 2012/13 identified other implications of special events at that time of year. These included the following questions:

- Do you have a behaviour policy for the work Christmas party?
- Do you give advice on getting home after the Christmas party?
- Did any problems arise at the last work party/meal and, if so, what were the consequences of these?
- Can employees opt out of arranged celebrations if they do not celebrate Christmas?
- Can members of non-Christian faiths mark their own religious festival in the workplace?

Source: XpertHR Survey (2012)

We see here how Christmas parties can legitimately be viewed as a people-management issue. As a result it may be that work organisations decide to devise a robust policy covering such events. Even if there is such a policy managers will need to exercise discretion and there are unlikely to be many right answers. Managers should be prepared to be subtle and creative in seeking solutions: managing people is rarely viewed as a hard science. In this book we will show that in many topic areas, one size definitely does not fit all. At the same time, there is a need to be fair and equitable and policies can act as a useful way of working towards these aims.

Finally, HR managers wish to nurture their talented or key workers (whether we believe this term applies to everyone who makes a contribution, ie *all* workers, or just to a named sub-group of workers). Employees will often seek to work for a 'good employer' and being treated shabbily – at least in their own perception – might adversely affect their *psychological contract*; this is a term we go on to explore in Chapter 7, but is essentially the mental picture a worker has of how their input in an organisation relates to what they receive from it. If employees experience negative feelings (in this case about Christmas parties) they may come to see this as a sign that they do not, after all, work for a good employer, with all the consequences that such a feeling can lead to.

Questions

1   Summarise arguments for and against holding work Christmas parties in the context of people management. On balance, would you recommend they take place? Give reasons for your conclusion.

2   How would you seek to avoid talented workers of non-Christian faiths becoming disaffected by Christmas work celebrations?

INTRODUCTION

This chapter introduces the purpose, content and structure of the book. This fourth edition has been adapted to meet the requirements of the Leading, Managing and Developing People Unit (7002). We have updated the book to include new research and survey report findings and have also devised newly relevant and topical reflective activities and case studies.

A consistent rubric has been developed for each chapter which includes the following key features:

- a set of learning outcomes
- an overview
- an introduction
- short reflective activities
- critical reflection
- a conclusion
- case studies
- key learning points
- review questions
- explore further (suggested further reading and references).

The text introduces a balance of theory and practice, drawing upon major research work, including theoretical and conceptual models through to major survey research findings. A combination of learning activities, including reflective activities, case studies, *vignettes* and links to relevant articles, are intended to bring the subjects to life and offer you scope for self-reflection. The structure of the text is set out more fully on page 12.

Leading, managing and developing people is fundamentally a topical area. We will provide many examples of the need for those who manage people to keep abreast of trends and developments in the environment – and to respond to them. The death of former UK Prime Minister Baroness Thatcher in 2013 prompted much retrospective comment on her governments' legacy, and many media reports highlighted the significant impact of the Thatcher governments' policies on managing people at work. Many of the topics examined in this book have a strong political and/or ethical component, and the working life of HR professionals changes in line with the prevalent political orthodoxy. Holbeche (2013) summarised a number of trends which followed on from the neo-liberal economic policies put forward in the UK after 1979 (the year in which Thatcher rose to power), which had at their heart an advocacy of free markets and flexible labour. These trends included:

Trends after 1979.

- deregulation of business and reduction of trade union power
- industrial and organisational restructuring with much manufacturing and 'back office' work migrating to parts of the developing world
- free market principles and managerialism applied to public sector institutions
- within organisations, a closer relationship between HRM and the needs of business, with HR increasingly being required to demonstrate commercial value.

There is certainly a need to locate leading, managing and developing people within an economic and social context. Following a period of industrial unrest and economic crises, the 1990s and early years of this century saw a period of economic expansion, based on knowledge-based work. This was coupled with major changes in work design and practices underpinned by major advances in information and communication technologies (ICT). Significant inward migration to London and other UK cities resulted in an increasingly diverse workforce in many sectors (French 2010). All of these trends posed challenges for HR professionals and impacted on the nature of their work. Since 2007 leading, managing and developing people has been framed within a predominantly gloomy economic backdrop. Case Study 1.2 below (regrettably still topical in 2013) outlines the impact of a recession on HR. However, interestingly, the author advocates taking a longer-term perspective in difficult times and points to some enduring good practice in managing people.

London workforce

MANAGING THE WORKFORCE IN A RECESSION

CASE STUDY 1.2

David Fairhurst, senior vice president, chief people officer at McDonald's Northern Europe, knows a thing or two about HR. Recently voted as HR's most influential practitioner – one of many accolades over the last few years – he has been responsible for a number of achievements at the fast food chain, including the development of a pan-European talent management programme and its highly successful training programme in which employees can be awarded nationally recognised qualifications.

Fairhurst is therefore extremely well placed to advise on HR's role in the current recession, especially when it comes to employee engagement.

'You do have to continue to engage with employees because they are going to be with you at the end of a recession and you have to maintain that engagement – so this needs to be thought through,' remarks Fairhurst. 'Think of engagement at its most simple level, which is creating a mutual value between the employer and staff – you do things for me and I do this for you. However, as we ride through the recession we have to refocus on engaging employees and what we do to engage them will be different and will take some thinking about.'

A different view on engagement

The question is, then, how will it be different? 'Well, for example, is there more financial support that you need to give your employees during this time? Do you need to be more paternal, making sure they don't dip out of pension schemes and that they themselves become too short-term in their outlook? We have to think about all these sorts of things, but the principle is that you have to keep engaging,' he advises.

Equally, HR must also think about the employees that are being 'disengaged' from the organisation, and must ensure it is done in such a way that is perceived to be fair and compassionate by others, he says.

'But there is one challenge I put out there for HR directors: when you look back at the end of this recession, will you be a case study of role model behaviour, values and best practice as an organisation? Will people say, "Remember what that business did?"'

This challenge comes back to what Fairhurst dubs as a 'new way' of doing things, in terms of engagement. 'We must not take our eye off this continual experimentation and delivering the results,' he comments.

However, he warns there is a danger that employers can become short-sighted in the current downturn. 'It's too easy to stop doing all these things like engagement, creativity, and experimentation, and go right to the other end and say, now is the time to make sure that people have a desk and you don't bark at them – that's very short-sighted. If the profession as a whole can really hold together and focus and help them keep their nerve and remain creative in difficult times, then I think some good can be done in times of recession.'

Managing talent

Another function that can come under stress during a recession is talent management. Fairhurst points out that there are all types of misconceptions about talent management at the moment, but emphasises that talent needs managing, no matter what the market conditions are.

'Organisations that are proactively managed as opposed to "let happen" are the ones that have been more successful, and it's no surprise, if you look at the top priorities from all the research coming out from Harvard and places like that, the key issues are reputation, and the CEO's credibility, and talent has gone right to the top of the CEO's agenda as they have figured out that organisations are about talent and how you manage that talent.'

Fairhurst adds that talent is an organisational resource that needs to be managed in a way that suits the current and future needs of the organisation's strategy, regardless of the economic climate. 'Of course, the fact that we are talking about the lives and livelihoods of individuals here makes this a particularly difficult management challenge – but that is the HR challenge for the 21st century and we have to rise to it.'

HR departments also need to think about their strategic initiatives within the organisation, and must not just view talent management as another term for 'succession planning'. 'Strategic talent management these days is all about projecting the operational income of an organisation – where the business is going to make money, what the talent implications and the gaps are from that, how things need to evolve and where you are going to get it from,' he says.

So, it is not just about 'bums on seats' and who fills what job anymore, comments Fairhurst, it is about keeping up with the fast-moving changing skill set – which leads him on to the subject of the war for talent.

'Some have said the war for talent has eased, but this is misleading as talent supply is dictated by the rate of change in business and the economy – change has never been faster so the war for talent is as alive as it has ever been,' he remarks.

What is McDonalds' secret?

So how does Fairhurst himself ensure that staff morale, engagement and productivity levels stay buoyant at McDonald's during the downturn?

'First and foremost, McDonald's is one of the organisations that has enjoyed positive growth during the current downturn and there are strong business reasons for this. At the same time, we have continued forward momentum with initiatives such as apprenticeships, degrees and local enterprise partnerships (LEPs). Maintaining this momentum at a time when it might be argued we could "take our foot off the gas" has undoubtedly enhanced morale, motivation and productivity levels.'

And for HR in general, Fairhurst states that the current recession is the ideal time for HR to step up to the challenge. 'HR has for years wanted the top table position, and if ever there was a time to show what values can be created at the top table, it is now. I like the old joke that leadership is like a teabag – you only know how good it is when it's in hot water. It's the same with HR – you only know how good your HR function is when they show how they adapt and how they maintain focus in the toughest times, and now's the time to step up to the function.'

Fairhurst's top tips

What should HR focus on during a recession?

- Doing what is right for the business – short and long term.
- Engage those who will ride out the recession with you to ensure they are aligned with what the organisation needs to achieve.
- Treat those who may have to leave the organisation with compassion and fairness.
- If we are judged in hindsight to have done the right things for our organisation, in the right way for our people, we will have done ourselves and our profession an enormous amount of good.

Source: Mitchell (2009)

Questions

1   To what extent is McDonald's doing anything different during a recession from what organisations should do during times of prosperity? Give reasons for your answer.

2   What are the fundamental messages that David Fairhurst espouses in terms of HR adding value in practice?

Earlier in the chapter we highlighted the changing nature of the UK public sector following policies introduced by the Thatcher and subsequent governments, which stressed free market principles and managerialism, not to say a renewed preoccupation with performance given declining resources. Case Study 1.3 examines leading, managing and developing people issues in a public sector organisation. Once again, the case study and accompanying questions raise generic leading, managing and developing people issues which can be analysed at this point, before you delve further into the book.

EMPLOYEE ENGAGEMENT AT WYCHAVON DISTRICT COUNCIL

Introduction

In 2008, Wychavon District Council was awarded top place in the *Times*' 'Best Councils to Work For' awards, a ranking that is judged through independent submissions from council staff. This was achieved despite difficult circumstances for employees, who were at the time experiencing the effects of a pay and grading review (part of a nationally negotiated agreement affecting all local authorities).

Internal research also points to consistently high engagement levels. In 2006, when the council's most recent staff survey was carried out, 70 per cent of employees said they were proud to work there, and 93 per cent said they enjoyed their job.

Having staff who are happy and engaged is not an aim in itself at Wychavon District Council, but it has been a vital ingredient in achieving the organisation's overall goals, according to Jack Hegarty, managing director of the council, and Fiona Narburgh, head of strategy and communications.

'We have learnt the lesson that you can't deliver well for the residents unless your staff are on board with what you are trying to do, so [our view on staff engagement] is really pragmatic. It hasn't really been to do with a major policy,' explains Narburgh.

Hegarty, who has worked in public sector management for 20 years, adds: 'If you aspire to be a high-performing organisation you won't do it unless your staff are engaged; you just won't do it. You can put processes in, you can put money in, but unless you are working with your people, it won't happen. I've seen this.'

From mediocrity to high performance

Since Hegarty took over the leadership role at Wychavon District Council in April 2004, he has helped take it from what he describes as 'mediocrity' to what has been judged as an outstanding organisation. In 2007, it won the *Local Government Chronicle* (*LGC*) 'Council of the Year' award, which recognises excellence in councils who take their work beyond the normal level of service provision.

Hegarty describes the challenge he faced when he first took on the leadership role: 'If you are a small, lean council where everyone has got two or three jobs, not just one, how do you get staff to go the extra mile? If staff don't go the extra mile, you remain a mediocre, middle-of-the-pack organisation. There was no chance of us being a failing council, but there was no aspiration at one stage for us to be successful. And that was our starting point.'

Engaging staff

Hegarty says that in order for staff to perform at their best, they have to be heavily engaged with the organisation, feel proud to work for it, and 'feel that they and the organisation are one and the same thing'.

As Narburgh and Hegarty explain, there is no one factor alone that has helped to motivate staff at Wychavon District Council, but a number of elements have helped to shape the way people work, including:

- an open, strong, non-hierarchical leadership style
- a culture where staff are rewarded, supported and listened to
- teamworking as the norm
- clearly communicated, straightforward, shared goals, with a clear focus on customers

- performance management that is clear-cut and confrontational when required
- clear, engaging communications that help promote a sense of pride, fun and shared values.

Leadership style

Hegarty has a naturally open, accessible style of management, which, coupled with his 'open door' policy helps staff to feel they can bring ideas or issues to him at any time. The style appears to work, as he was ranked 'best leader' in the *Times*' 'Best Councils to Work For' special awards.

Hegarty communicates with his staff through regular updates posted on the intranet; briefing sessions for all 420 employees; and – unlike some chief executives (as council leaders are usually known) – he is not afraid to mingle with staff at their desks.

This non-hierarchical style is shared by the Wychavon councillors (or members), who also prefer dealing with employees directly, instead of communicating through management. Staff names are displayed on desks to help facilitate this.

Managers throughout the council are also expected to work in a similar style with their teams by involving all staff, listening, and sharing information on a regular basis. Team meetings are a regular part of working life. A recent initiative saw several leaders, including the deputy managing director, shadow employees such as traffic wardens (known as civil enforcement officers) and waste disposal workers, while some non-management staff shadowed managers.

Teamworking

All managers have access to a shared set of 12 management principles, which are as follows:

- We will continually develop and challenge to remain excellent.

- We will continue to adopt an entrepreneurial not municipal culture.
- We will focus on resident and customer satisfaction as a principal objective and adopt customer insight techniques.
- That the council will run core services very well and invest in them accordingly – maintain the 'don't fail to succeed' approach.
- Value for money principles will be applied to all policy initiatives and services.
- That application of good performance management will be a cornerstone of the management of the council.
- That efficiency gains will be driven out by our own actions as an organisation rather than a disproportionate reliance on others.
- We will retain a positive approach, partnership working/joint working with other public and private sector organisations where it improves quality, reduces cost and builds on the council's reputation.
- We will, where they add value, be engaged in partnerships to help deliver more than we could do above.
- That the approach of 'don't grow the establishment unless you grow the business' be maintained, as will a culture of using skills flexibly within the organisation.
- We will 'invest to save' where there are robust cases to do so.
- We will maintain good officer [staff] and member [councillor] relationships and the 'Team Wychavon' approach.

According to Narburgh, managers consider these principles to be an accurate reflection of how managers work at the council, as opposed to a remote set of ideals.

The 'Team Wychavon' approach has been a crucial aspect of the council's success. 'We have learnt that you can't deliver well externally without your staff being part of a team,' says Narburgh. 'And we have to work hard at the "one team, one council" feel,' she adds.

A document that summarises the council's strategy for the year is central to the ongoing team-building exercise, as it ensures that all staff know what the council is trying to achieve each year, and keeps the focus clearly on the common aim of helping the residents in the community. This document, known as the Clear Priorities Paper, has been created by the leadership team and is used on a day-to-day basis by all departments.

Within the strategy document, the priorities focus on the improvement of the local area. They remain the same each year and act as headlines (Safer, Greener, Healthier, Stronger and Successful). The text beneath each priority, known as the 'promises', changes each year. Copies of the document are displayed on office walls to help focus team planning, and it is used as a basis for each staff member when setting priorities in their performance development reviews.

Employee involvement

A key feature of working life at Wychavon District Council is the involvement of staff in decision-making and new initiatives and, because it is a small council, acting on suggestions can happen quickly. Involvement is encouraged in various ways, including through an employee forum known as the 'sounding board'.

The sounding board was used to shape a new annual staff competition, Wychavon Outstanding Service & Colleague Awards–known now as the WOSCAs. Nominations include best-dressed employee, manager and team of the year, and most positive role model.

An initiative known as the Big Ideas Scheme encourages employees to pass on ideas that are 'bigger than the routine issues'. Narburgh is currently working on a feedback initiative so she can let employees know how the organisation has responded to the large number of ideas that have been submitted so far.

Snap surveys are also carried out over the intranet to find out how people feel about particular issues. These are well received, averaging a 60 per cent response rate. As an example, the electronic survey is being used to find out which day employees would prefer to have as an additional day off over Christmas.

Employee motivation

According to the 2006 staff survey, the two most important motivators for staff are a sense of personal achievement and a good work–life balance (both voted as 'very important' by 76 per cent of employees). In third place, 'opportunities for flexible working' was considered a high priority by 68 per cent; while 55 per cent cited pay and benefits.

Flexible working at the council differs from the public sector norm in that there are no core hours when every employee needs to be present in the office, although each team must make sure that there are enough people available to provide the required service for residents. Using an automated clocking-in system, which is backed up with automated timesheets, each individual can organise their own hours, having liaised with the team, so long as there is cover provided during published office hours.

This means, in practice, that individuals are free to attend school functions and caring appointments, and keep up with other commitments outside work, so long as they make up the time. Conversely, if they work extra hours one week, they can take time off in lieu later. Narburgh believes that flexibility is a two-way process.

Additional reward schemes, including health insurance and employee assistance programmes, were introduced after 2007.

Performance management

'You can't have good staff engagement if people are working under poor management,' says Narburgh. 'It is impossible, which is why leadership is the most important aspect [of employee engagement], and by that I mean inspiring, open, authentic leadership. You just can't say you want to be a brilliant council and then tolerate poor management.'

This view is at the root of the tough, focused attitude to performance management at Wychavon District Council. Narburgh continues: 'We are motivating hearts and minds, and so on, and we are training and developing, but actually there is also a hard edge. We are managing performance in a much, much stronger way. We are setting objectives, looking at our targets, being clear about what our strategy is, and a whole host of things.'

Performance development reviews

As part of the ongoing performance management process, all employees are expected to have one formal, annual performance development review meeting with their manager, with two follow-up conversations to chart progress later in the year. This is valued by employees, according to staff surveys, and provides an opportunity to meet the line manager and work through objectives, look at career progression, and assess what help is

needed through training. Approximately 1.5 per cent of the staff budget is allocated to each service unit to support performance development.

Culture and communication

A 'values' poster sets out five, simple pointers to help employees understand the shared culture, and to communicate some of the key points about working at the council. These are:

- brilliant customer service
- great services every time
- value for money
- fun, motivated and positive
- innovative, always improving.

Conclusion

Narburgh believes that there is no single factor that makes staff feel good about working for an organisation. However, an organisation that fosters an open, honest style of working will encourage employees to do a good job. This involves management listening and being clear about its expectations; and a simple strategy that fits on to one side of an A4 sheet of paper.

Source: Wolff (2008)

Questions

1   Consider the extent to which Wychavon's employee engagement approach may make them an employer of choice.

2   In what ways can Wychavon's 12 management principles be used by HR to add value to the organisation?

THE STRUCTURE OF THE BOOK

The learning outcomes and content for the Leading, Managing and Developing People unit can be subdivided into three particular areas, namely contextual factors, core themes and effective practice. As we have already stressed, readers need to appreciate the context within which HR operates and how HR can directly or indirectly affect the leadership, management and development of employees. Three core themes of leadership, change and flexibility assist in understanding how the HR function can add value to organisations, whilst the effective practice section addresses how functional aspects of HR can make a direct impact upon organisations and organisational performance.

The text is therefore presented in five parts: (see Figure 1.1)

1   **Part 1** provides the introduction and setting the scene of the text.

2   **Part 2** addresses the contextual factors which have shaped the nature of HR, and considers the aims, objectives and contribution of HRM across the public, private, third sectors and across small, medium, large and multinational organisations.

3   **Part 3** addresses the core themes that run through the process of leading, managing and developing people. Leadership, managing change and flexibility form the bulk of these core themes.

4   **Part 4** considers how HR practitioners and managers can turn relevant and valid theory into practice and use research findings to add value in terms of worker and organisational performance.

5   **Part 5** comprises the conclusion to the book and makes suggestions about the future of HR by drawing upon various research findings and reports.

Chapters 1 and 13 allow for the text to be introduced and concluded through the use of integrated arguments, case study illustrations and contemporary thinking and research.

Figure 1.1 The structure of the text

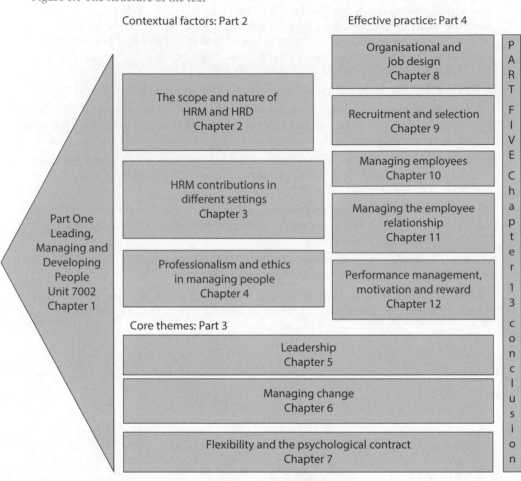

Contextual factors: Part 2 — Effective practice: Part 4

Part One Leading, Managing and Developing People Unit 7002 Chapter 1

The scope and nature of HRM and HRD Chapter 2

HRM contributions in different settings Chapter 3

Professionalism and ethics in managing people Chapter 4

Organisational and job design Chapter 8

Recruitment and selection Chapter 9

Managing employees Chapter 10

Managing the employee relationship Chapter 11

Performance management, motivation and reward Chapter 12

Core themes: Part 3

Leadership Chapter 5

Managing change Chapter 6

Flexibility and the psychological contract Chapter 7

PART FIVE Chapter 13 conclusion

CONCLUSION

The nature of leading, managing and developing people makes this is a highly complex area: challenging and integrative, but also a very rewarding one. Having a good grounding in leading, managing and developing people is core knowledge for those working in HR. We trust that you find the following chapters informative, thought-provoking and a useful framework for understanding leading, managing and developing people.

At this point it is appropriate to introduce brief clarification on terminology. As we will see in Chapter 2, tasks involving leading, managing and developing people often fall to specialist HR managers within work organisations. In an important sense, however, general or line managers need to be involved in managing people too in their day-to-day work. The term 'HR manager' therefore denotes anyone who takes a role in leading, managing and developing people. In some cases HR work is outsourced to specialist providers. In view of this complex picture some writers use the term 'human resource practitioner' to encompass anyone whose work touches our subject area. For our purposes, though, the terms 'human resource manager' and 'human resource practitioner' are sufficiently close for both to be used interchangeably and you will find examples of both terms throughout the book.

THE AIMS, OBJECTIVES AND CONTRIBUTION OF HRM

CHAPTER 2

The Scope and Nature of Human Resource Management and Human Resource Development

Gary Rees

LEARNING OUTCOMES

After reading this chapter, you should be able to:

- have an appreciation of the role and function of HRM and HRD

- explore approaches to, and models of, HRM and HRD

- be aware of and evaluate models of strategic HRM and HRD

- consider the links between organisational strategy and HR strategy

- understand the interrelationship between line management and HRM/HRD

- identify recent research findings about how HR equates into practice

- assess the value and contribution of HRM and HRD.

OVERVIEW

In Part 2 of this book, we examine some of the factors influencing the nature of human resource management (HRM) and human resource development (HRD). The aim is to lay the groundwork for subsequent sections in which we firstly identify core themes in leading, managing and developing people (Chapters 5–7), and then go on to examine effective practice in selected areas (Chapters 8–12). In Chapter 3, we will highlight the ways in which leading, managing and developing people may vary across different types of organisational settings. In this chapter we will discuss some even more fundamental questions, including how HRM and HRD are defined, who does – and who should – take responsibility for leading, managing and developing people, and whether HRM and HRD can be regarded as strategic activities. Underlying these questions is the concept of HR practitioners adding value, possibly by taking on the role of business partner.

It is useful at this stage to clarify the relationship between the two terms HRM and HRD. They could be considered separate aspects of an overall HR function, while one of these sub-functions may take precedence over the other at any one point. Within academic models, HRD is typically subsumed within HRM when functional aspects are taken into consideration. In this chapter we will explore the HR function in terms of HRM and HRD, without making judgements as to how these two areas converge or separate themselves. Dependent upon the context, some organisations may combine the HRM and HRD functions into an HR function, while other organisations may have a predominance of HRM within the HR function.

HR requires the collaboration of line and senior management. We look at this long-established notion and find support in recent research evidence within the UK. In the teeth of a global economic recession in the period after 2007/08, measurement of contribution and accountability were issues of heightened importance for many business functions, including HR. We attempt to pinpoint the value of HR and, within the overall aims of our book, look at key research findings from recent research, which inform current debates.

INTRODUCTION

Robert Townsend, former CEO of Avis (1981), likened the HR function ('personnel' as it was typically known then) to a malignant growth. Townsend claimed that if personnel people were left unchecked, they would multiply and ultimately take over the company. His controversial and, we can assume, provocative analogy is that of serious and possibly terminal disease. Personnel is therefore by definition, abnormal and pathological, thus requiring treatment. One important task of an organisation, according to Townsend, is to stem the growth of the personnel function and, if necessary, cut it out altogether. Denigrating Townsend's notion of personnel should be an easy task, and we might also question whether such an unpleasant and, for many of us, distressing analogy is appropriate at all. It does shine a light, though, on the negative reputation that HR or personnel has sometimes had, and points to the need for HR practitioners to demonstrate clear valued contributions to an organisation.

REFLECTIVE ACTIVITY 2.1

Despite the change of name from 'Personnel' to 'HR', it could be argued that the HR function is still suffering from a lack of status and, like Cinderella, does not get invited to the ball (or top table). Why is it that HR, on the whole, lacks the reputation to make strategic contributions to organisations and establish a strong reputation for itself?

We will argue that the role and function of HR has transformed itself over the last 40 years or so. However, there will no doubt be examples of the full span of traditional Personnel and modern HR in contemporary UK organisations. To what extent can HR be pigeonholed into structural or functional compartments, thereby limiting its scope and impact?

Ulrich, quoted by Brockett (2010, p11), stated that, 'I think that HR people should see themselves as a professional services group within their own organisation, being a key account manager for the most important clients. Their job is to assess the resources available and use their knowledge to determine how best to transfer those resources to client productivity.'

However, before we look at contemporary HR roles, some historical perspective is useful and it is important to consider the transition from personnel management to HR, and to address definitions in order to make appropriate contrasts.

DEFINITIONS OF PERSONNEL MANAGEMENT, HUMAN RESOURCE MANAGEMENT AND HUMAN RESOURCE DEVELOPMENT

PERSONNEL MANAGEMENT

We begin by considering a widely used definition of 'personnel management' from several decades ago: 'Personnel management aims to achieve both efficiency and justice, neither of which can be pursued successfully without the other. It seeks to bring together and develop into an effective organisation the men and women who make up an enterprise, enabling each to make his/her own best contribution to its success both as an individual and as a member of a working group. It seeks to provide fair terms and conditions of employment, and satisfying work for those employed' (IPM, quoted in Hendry, 1995, p10).

As we can see here, personnel management is perceived as occupying a neutral position, placed between employers (in the form of management), and other rank and file employees. Its role was reinforced by the development of policies and procedures indicating professional independence and objectivity. An emphasis upon standardisation and equal treatment would often underlie such policies.

HUMAN RESOURCE MANAGEMENT AND HUMAN RESOURCE DEVELOPMENT

Any brief consideration of definitions of HRM elicits a set of definitions which differentiate HR from personnel, in academic terms at least.

Storey (1995, p5) defines HRM as: 'a distinctive approach to employment management which seeks to achieve competitive advantage through the strategic development of a highly committed and capable workforce, using an integrated array of cultural, structural and personnel techniques.'

However, definitions of HRM are by no means identical, or even especially similar. Boxall and Purcell (2000, p184) argue that 'HRM includes anything and everything associated with the management of the employment relationship in the firm. We do not associate HRM solely with a high commitment model of labour management or with any particular ideology or style of management.'

Whilst a universal and generally accepted definition of HRM is lacking, the same could be said for defining HRD.

HRD has been defined by Stewart and McGoldrick (1996, p1) as follows: 'Human resource development encompasses activities and processes which are intended to have impact on organisational and individual learning. The term assumes that organisations can be constructively conceived of as learning entities, and that the learning processes of both organisations and individuals are capable of influence and direction through deliberate and planned interventions. Thus, HRD is constituted by planned interventions in organisational and individual processes.'

Whilst defining HRM and HRD may prove to be a tricky task, the nature, scope and objectives of HRM and HRD may change considerably in differing contexts. The historical background, senior management philosophy and practice, external forces and internal forces may shape different outcomes as far as what HRM/HRD actually does within the organisation.

In terms of what HR typically 'does', we could include the following as typical: HR planning, job and organisational design (covered here in Chapter 8); recruitment, selection and induction (see Chapter 9); training and development (see Chapter 10); managing the employment relationship (see Chapter 11); pay, reward and performance management (see Chapter 12); ethical treatment of people including equal opportunities and diversity management (see Chapters 4 and 11); health and safety; knowledge management; mentoring; and disciplinary and grievance-handling, to name just some.

Perhaps the most logical argument that determines what HR does in an organisation may be traced back to its historical roots. Who actually started the HRM process in an organisation (eg a CEO deciding that due to growth of the organisation, an HR function and HR manager needed to be brought in) can be important in tracing its subsequent development. The question of why the HR function was started (perhaps with specific goals in mind, such as identifying training gaps, dealing with increased specialist recruitment, etc) is also highly relevant. Following this, identifying key milestones in the development of the HR function may provide further understanding of how HR has evolved (eg the introduction of a performance management system). Whilst each organisation evolves in its own inimitable fashion, generic models of the goals of HRM can, nonetheless, be considered.

HRM GOALS

Whilst the academic debate surrounding the defining of HRM goals continues, Boxall and Purcell (2008, p20) suggest that there are four underpinning motives in HRM:

- *Cost-effectiveness* – maintaining stakeholder loyalty and trust is essential here, and this may mean running the business within budgetary constraints or maximising profits.
- *Legitimacy* – in essence, the allocation of moral legitimacy and ethical standing in society (see Chapter 4).
- *Flexibility* – in order to cope with change, organisational flexibility is vital for survival. It incorporates both short-term responsiveness and long-term agility (see Chapter 7).
- *Autonomy* – particularly managerial autonomy and the power to act. The political context may bring about change in managerial behaviour which may need some regulation in terms of corporate social responsibility.

The goals of HRD could be defined simply as developing and improving the performance of individuals and organisations, and we might also include team performance at this point.

In addition to this, 'the most obvious role HR has to play is as the expert on ethical employment practices (which is a core strand of corporate responsibility)' (CIPD 2013a, p5).

Whilst the various goals of HR may differ across private, public and not-for-profit sectors (see Chapter 3), there will also be some similarities. Current UK public sector HR goals may tie in with strategic initiatives linked to the Gershon Efficiency Review (2004) and any other key governmental initiatives; for example, Agenda for Change, commissioning, private finance initiatives and best-value-type initiatives. Ultimately, efficiencies (savings) are sought, with the stated goal of maintaining, or even increasing, service-level quality, which means that employees will ultimately have to work harder or, more euphemistically, to work 'smarter'.

Managers in the private sector will already be familiar with the imperative for efficiency gains and, as we will note in the next chapter, the third (or not-for-profit) sector is also facing pressures in this regard.

REFLECTIVE ACTIVITY 2.2

To what extent can an organisation exercise duty of care to all its employees and at the same time drive towards the highest level of cost efficiency? How can HR balance these potentially conflicting goals?

In order to move HR from a mere internal function, we need to analyse the broader strategic context within which it operates to consider whether HR can be strategic in its intent, actions and contribution.

STRATEGY AND HR

Strategy in its most basic sense is a plan of where the organisation would like to go. Although a strategy may take the form of a statement, it is also likely to be supported by strategic plans and imperatives that make up the building blocks required to meet its planned destination. A strategy should not be envisaged as an end in itself, as there may be a requirement to change course, or to embark on several journeys. One metaphor for business strategy is that of travel. So your strategy might be to travel in a northerly direction. At some points in time people might observe you travelling toward the south. However, your long-term strategic intent is still to move northwards and your apparent change of direction might be a short-term retreat or tactical manoeuvre.

De Wit and Meyer (2004, p50) define strategy as 'a course of action for achieving an organisation's purpose'.

Taken in its broadest sense, this may not automatically mean profit generation and maximisation, or market domination. Strategy could be determined from more of a bottom–up approach, eg in a workers' collective, than a purely top–down approach; or alternatively a range of key stakeholders/shareholders can be involved in making strategic decisions.

There may also be a vision or mission statement to accompany a strategy. The vision is sometimes a means of providing employees with a notion of where the organisation is heading and the values associated with it. The mission statement should reinforce to employees where the company is intending to go, but is often directed at shareholders or customers.

Possessing an organisational strategy and HR strategy is not enough. Strategic fit between HR strategy, HR practices and organisational strategy is paramount (Wang and Shyu 2008). So how is such strategic fit accomplished? One method is to consider the vertical and horizontal integration of HR policies and procedures. The vertical fit is important in terms of achieving organisational goals through ensuring the alignment of HR activities to strategy. Horizontal fit plays an essential role in making use of these resources. Horizontal integration of HR activities includes aligning different HR activities such as recruitment and selection, performance management and reward so that each activity supports (rather than contradicts/interferes with) other HR activities. Vertical integration includes the way in which these activities fit into and support overall organisational activities, including the organisational vision, mission, etc.

In order to assess the extent to which HR as a function can be strategic in its thinking and actions, we need to consider the various approaches/models of HR and the extent to which these align with strategic intent.

MODELS OF HRM AND STRATEGIC HRM

Hall (in Gilmore and Williams 2009, p144) defines strategic HRM as 'not any one particular HR strategy, but is a framework for shaping a number of people management strategies.'

Figure 2.1 The hard model of HRM

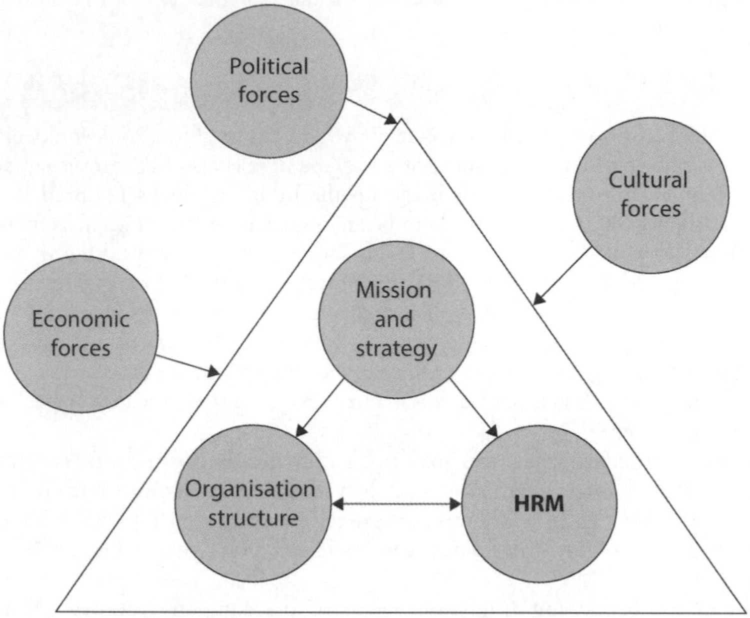

Source: Fombrun *et al* 1984, p35

While the analysis of the employment relationship and context is important, Beardwell and Claydon (2010) argue that two other issues affect the definition of HRM. First, the significance of HRM is variable, sometimes with emphasis upon people, strategy, employment relationships, etc. Secondly, HRM is derived from a range of antecedents, and depends on the stance and philosophy of the analyst.

These definitions also ally themselves to the hard and soft models of HRM (Fombrun *et al* 1984, Beer *et al* 1984). Hard models emphasise using employees to gain competitive advantage and focus on business and employment strategies by linking HR to business systems. Soft models, contrastingly, emphasise employee commitment and engagement, and attempt to align the interests of employees and management (see also Chapter 11).

Devanna *et al* (1984) suggest that within the organisation there needs to be an alignment of mission/strategy, the organisational structure and HRM. External to the organisation are forces (eg political, cultural and economic) impacting upon the organisation. This approach assumes that HR emerges from the other factors, with strategy as the primary driver, and that HR needs to seek a 'best fit' within this context.

Another approach found within the field of HRM is the resource-based view of the firm; namely one 'that focuses on the resources and capabilities controlled by a firm as sources of competitive advantage' (Barney and Hesterly 2008, p74).

Figure 2.2 The soft model of HRM

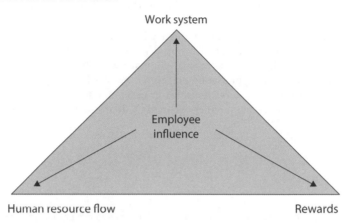

Source: Beer *et al* (1984)

Another approach used in HR is that of the 'best practice' model, often referred to as 'high commitment' or 'high involvement' HRM, in which managers consider how bundles of effective HR practice merge together.

CRITIQUE OF BEST FIT AND BEST PRACTICE MODELS

A major criticism of the best fit model is that it may ignore employee interests, and be ignorant of some of the important aspects of the psychological contract (see Chapter 7). The focus of the best fit model may be the pursuit of economic performance to the detriment of everything else. There may also be academic criticisms when addressing the measurement of various HR practices. How do we assess the validity of best fit practices? The transient nature of strategy and the need for constant change also makes alignment of current and future needs difficult.

When considering the best practice model, it is difficult to argue that HRM can apply across all organisational settings at all times. To what extent do HR practices transfer from the United States to Eastern Europe or the Indian sub-continent, for example? Another central concern is the extent to which organisations can adopt a long-term approach in reality.

BALANCED SCORECARD

Another model that helps to assess the contribution that HR makes to a business is that of the balanced scorecard. The CIPD Human Capital reporting survey (2004a) argues that the central focus in this model is upon vision and strategy, with four key supporting elements that require targets and measure taken, namely:

- *Learning and growth* – relating to how we sustain our ability to change and improve (see also Chapters 6 and 12).
- *Customer* – how we should appear to our customer (see also Chapter 4).
- *Financial* – how we should appear to our shareholders.
- *Internal business processes* – to satisfy shareholders and customers, what business processes must we excel at?

This model assumes planned and effective communication (internally and externally) to be a key imperative. The question arises then as to what level HR can become involved in developing and measuring the balanced scorecard.

THE BATH MODEL OF HRM AND INNOVATION

The concepts of human, social and organisational capital are not new. The Bath model adds extra understanding by providing contextual issues such as: climate, trust and culture as the platform from which innovative outputs can then emerge. Where traditional human capital approaches have addressed inputs and outputs, the context is often overlooked. There is now an appreciation that employees work within teams and contexts, relying upon successful working relationships in order to add value to the organisation, with less emphasis upon the measurement of an individual's performance (CIPD 2012a).

CASE STUDY 2.1

MANAGERIAL PERCEPTIONS OF THE ROLE OF THE HR FUNCTION IN SRI LANKA

Mammam *et al* (2006) investigated the extent to which HRM plays a significant role in organisational strategy processes in Sri Lankan export-oriented clothing manufacturing companies. It was claimed that typically Sri Lankan companies have short-term financial objectives which override long-term HRM objectives. Complementary to this are line managers' perception of the low importance given to the HR function and its contribution. The HR function derives its direction from corporate plans instead of influencing those plans. Three primary reasons were given for this:

- HR managers failed to provide a quality service
- HR is unable to operate as effectively in delivering services needed at the standard expected
- the HR function suffers from structural and managerial limitations, resulting in lack of delivery of quality of service and contribution to individual and organisational performance expected of them.

The key findings of this report are:

- Participation by HR in the decision-making process did not equate to favourable perceptions given to the HR function in the company. Hence, their role was more symbolic than important.
- When comparing local companies and multinational corporations, the transfer of HRM practices is primarily attributed to international buyers demanding high-quality practices and good management practices (the avoidance of a 'sweat-shop' reputation being a driving force).

Question

1   Despite the limitations of the survey (primarily managers' perceptions), what practical steps can the HR function take in order to reduce or possibly eliminate the concerns expressed in the findings?

HRD AND STRATEGIC HRD

However, as we noted at the start of this chapter, 'mainline' HR may not necessarily include HRD and strategic HRD. HRD may be considered to be a sub-set of HR, and strategic HRD a sub-set of strategic HR. But the field of HRD has grown rapidly in the last 30 years and 'development' as a theme cuts through many traditional HR areas. The current heightened interest in talent management (see Pilbeam and Corbridge 2010) includes a great deal of debate and research around talent development; see also Martin (2012).

The definition of development carries with it a series of different connotations and meanings. Thomas (2001, p184) defines development as 'a process of competency attainment and of self-differentiation in the sense of progressively distinguishing oneself from the environment and from other people in order to create a unique self-identity'.

Gubbins and Garavan (2009) argue that the primary responsibility of HRD professionals traditionally focused on identifying, selecting and evaluating training programmes. In effect this equates to transactional HR. However, Gubbins and Garavan contend that the role of HRD includes the consideration of environmental forces, and how the development of employees can add to competitive advantage.

Beer and Spector (1989, p25) define strategic HRD as 'a proactive, system-wide intervention, linked to strategic planning and cultural change. This contrasts with the traditional view of training and development as consisting of reactive, piecemeal interventions in response to specific problems.'

Perhaps the question of where HRD sits as a discipline is a moot point. On a micro level, can HRD be aligned to adult learning and associated psychological theories? On the other hand, at a macro level, where national policy and HRD will be linked, the influence of educational policy and societal impact should be investigated. Wang and Sun (2009) argue that economics, psychology and system theory constitute foundations of HRD.

McCracken and Wallace (2000) devised a model depicting nine key characteristics of strategic HRD. Underpinning these characteristics are a strong learning culture, strategic change focus and a highly mature organisation in HRD terms. These nine characteristics bear similarity with the strategic HR theory outlined above. The first characteristic that McCracken and Wallace identify is that of shaping organisational missions and goals. Secondly, there is top management leadership (including support). Thirdly, the environmental scanning by senior management is in HRD terms. Fourthly, there are HRD strategies, plans and policies in place. Fifthly, strategic partnerships exist with line management. Following that, there are strategic partnerships with HRM. The seventh key characteristic is that trainers act as organisational change consultants. The penultimate characteristic is the ability to influence corporate culture. Lastly, there is emphasis upon cost-effectiveness evaluation.

To what extent are skills, knowledge and core competencies the drivers of innovation and the key sources of competitive advantage (Gratton 2000)? If core competence leads to organisational capability and competitiveness, then developing employee competence will be a strategic priority.

REFLECTIVE ACTIVITY 2.3

Think of an organisation, and consider the following questions:

Questions

1   What makes this organisation distinct?

2   What precisely is the organisation good at doing (core competences)?

3   What has led to the organisation being successful?

4   How has any HRD intervention assisted its current competitive position?

The HRD function can play an important part in developing an organisation's culture to learn and aspire to be a 'learning organisation'. However, caution needs to be adopted here, in that we need to continually strive to link learning with performance (Henderson 1997).

The interplay of HRD and HRM will continue to prove challenging to organisations. In some cases there are obvious structural divides in organisations, for example, an HRM and HRD department that don't particularly work well together, and deliberately separate out the functional aspects. In other cases, there is a strong synergy of activities that seamlessly integrate with organisational practices, and add value, and are seen to be adding value.

THE SHAPE OF HR

Harrison (2009, p297) provides a useful framework when deciding the shape of the learning and development function, which can then be extended to HR more generally.

Firstly, the line-managed function, where line managers are handed the main responsibility for HRD/HRM. Secondly, the HR and HRD function could be outsourced. Thirdly, there is the three-legged stool model proposed by Ulrich (1997).

Within the line-managed function, there is very much a devolved approach, handing over the majority of responsibility to line managers. The outsourced model may work well for specific aspects of HR and HRD; for example, assessment centres, competence development. Some of the key determinants in deciding whether to outsource include cost-efficiency, added value, control and partnership.

Previous work by Harrison (2005) cited three other shapes that HRM/HRD could adopt: as a cost or profit centre; as a consultancy; or the traditional centralised function.

Operating as a profit centre may prove more attractive to an organisation than viewing HR as a cost centre, which does not necessarily generate its own revenue and therefore is a drain on corporate budgets. The argument of accountability may be less profound if a profit centre is generating sufficient funds. It could be argued that an HR function that can 'sell' its services successfully exhibits a level of professionalism within the market. However, the converse argument could also be true. HR operating as a consultancy service may bring into question the internal/external fit, and to what extent the 'consultancy' aligns with corporate culture and values.

In a recent CIPD survey (2013b), just over half of HR professionals reported that their departments outsource some activities. This recent trend offers another perspective on the shape of HR and shows again the importance of contextual factors, eg developments in technology which enable activities to be outsourced, possibly to another country.

HR BUSINESS PARTNER MODEL

Perhaps one of the more talked-about current models is that of the HR business partner. Ulrich's original work in 1997 emphasised four key roles that HR need to adopt:

- strategic partners
- administrative experts (shared services)
- employee champions
- change agents.

If HR adopts a more business-focused approach, as advocated by Ulrich *et al* 2008, then the emphasis upon customer focus, cost efficiencies, innovation and the ability to respond quickly to changes is highly important.

Business partnership describes the relationship between HR managers (partner) and line/functional managers within an organisation, with an emphasis upon outputs and performance measures, and a view to increasing effectiveness and efficiency of the organisation as a whole.

A research report produced by the CIPD (2007a) found that less than 30 per cent of respondents had introduced the model in full, with another 30 per cent having partially introduced the Ulrich model.

Perhaps larger organisations are more likely to adopt the Ulrich model, commonly known as the 'three-legged stool', whereby three functional areas of HR include (CIPD 2010a):

- Shared services handling transactional services, such as absence monitoring, payroll, etc. The emphasis here is upon low-cost and effective HR administration.
- Centres of excellence, consisting of small teams of HR experts with specialised knowledge of leading-edge HR solutions. Competitive advantage is sought through HR innovations, such as reward, learning, engagement and talent management.
- Strategic business partners working with business leaders to influence strategy formulation and strategy implementation. Some activities include organisational and people capability building, resource and talent planning, intelligence gathering, etc.

A recent report from Henley Business School looks at the factors behind successful HR departments and asks how others could do better. The Henley report found that the majority of non-HR professionals believed that getting the operational side of HR right was more important than the function understanding business strategy; and while chief executives and board-level colleagues valued strategic skills more than operational, this was never as much as HR did. It also suggested that: 'Some functions operate in victim mode, which isn't conducive to securing investment or confidence in the function' (*Personnel Today* 2012).

 HR BUSINESS PARTNERING IN WHITEHALL

CASE STUDY 2.2

HR business partners in the Civil Service will undergo new training to brush up on their skills ahead of looming budget cuts.

Jacquie Heany, deputy director of the Civil Service's HR professionalism team, reported that Whitehall departments were set to launch a development scheme for all 1,459 Whitehall business partners in order to help create a consistent approach to the change agenda and meet business needs.

In early 2010, the Labour government revealed plans to slash public sector budgets by £15 billion by 2013/14. The Conservative Party, in opposition at that time, pledged to cut Whitehall budgets by 10 per cent if they won the election in 2010.

Hundreds of jobs would be cut across back office roles, including HR, to protect front-line services. Heany

added that the changes would present 'the leadership challenge of a generation', but Whitehall HR functions had the capability to deal with the task and had been preparing for this over the past 18 months.

'We have some business partners that are fantastic, we have some that are good at some things, but not others – it's like any workforce,' she said. 'So what we are trying to do is make sure that, when we know what the [change] agenda is, we have a consistent programme to make sure that the business function is ready, willing and able to cope with it.'

'As we go forward, and there are so many challenges, I think business partners will really be at the forefront of those challenges.' The new programme launched in January 2010 across the Civil Service.

The then Business Minister Ian Lucas added that private and public sector HR professionals had a 'very demanding agenda' ahead of them. He stated that, 'HR people need to look for and identify good leaders. They need to find and identify good practice within their sector and work together, and communicate with other HR directors in different organisations about what works.'

Meanwhile, Heany reiterated that civil service HR teams – totalling 8,823 people – would inevitably shrink as

budget cuts took effect. She refused to be drawn on the size of the scale-back expected.

She said: 'The numbers in HR will go down, there's no question of that, just as the numbers in the Civil Service will go down.'

Source: Baker (2009)

www.XpertHR.co.uk

Question

1   Discuss some of the challenges that HR business partners might face.

WHY DO ORGANISATIONS ADOPT THE BUSINESS PARTNERING MODEL?

The key drivers identified by CIPD (2010a) included:

- *Cost–efficiency* – smaller teams of HR have to demonstrate their cost-efficiency or face being cut back.
- *Accelerating competition* – with HR central to business competitiveness, delivering skilled, motivated, creative, flexible and creative employees (see Chapters 7, 9, 10 and 12).
- *Rising expectations of HR* – with an expectation that HR contributes towards strategy, the execution of business plans and delivering tangible commercial benefits.

 BUSINESS PARTNERING AT THE AA

CASE STUDY 2.3

The Automobile Association has undergone significant change since 2004, having passed between three different owners within this time period. The overriding strategic imperative was to increase profitability. The HR function developed a strategy and HR business partner model to support the new business targets and help drive commercial success. In order for Hazel Lee, the HR manager, to grow profits from £100m in 2005 to £300m in 2008, she had to dovetail HR and business strategy.

HR business partners were appointed and made responsible for planning the people strategies for the AA's business units. Three senior business partner

roles were set up to cover the following:

- corporate, policy and reward
- insurance, driving school, publishing and signs
- road operations.

In addition to this, a communications section was set up to integrate the different functions, which all reported to the HR director.

A new competency framework identifying key behaviours and experience requirements to operate at business partner level, including commerciality, influencing, operational decision-making and facilitating change, was introduced.

The new-look HR function was a leaner department, now operating with 60 employees rather than the previous 85.

The strategic business themes were:

- business focus (more profitable business)
- operational efficiency (lower operating costs with industry-best quality of service)
- brand differentiation and scale (by leverage of strategic advantage driving sales and market share).

The HR department looked at how it could deliver value to the business in each of these three areas.

In practice, this meant that Lee and her fellow business partner colleagues were automatically invited to operational management team meetings within their specialist area. In effect, this changed the emphasis towards a much more proactive role for HR, and the expectation from the operational team that HR would make a continuous contribution. The learning curve for all HR business partners was a steep one.

HR's expertise with managing human capital meant that the types of roles and competencies required to meet the

business strategies could be created by HR.

According to Lee, some of the critical success factors included:

- HR seizing the business strategy quickly through buy-in
- strong leadership within HR
- business partners having sound commercial knowledge and focus on the right organisational issues
- HR strategy developing alongside business strategy
- performance measures to demonstrate the tangible benefits of having business partners
- some quick wins, and the ability to deliver quickly, then focus on longer-term projects
- a seat on the board for the HR director.

Source: Suff (2008)

www.XpertHR.co.uk

Question

1 Despite the AA being a highly unionised organisation, why did the HR business partner model appear to be an appropriate choice in terms of improving the value of HR?

BUSINESS PARTNERING: THE COUNTER ARGUMENTS

Pitcher (2008) argues that the business partner model had not resulted in strategic thinking, and was primarily only a change in title. He cites the example of Elizabeth Arden, where the HR director, Gabriele Arend, disagreed with any model that split HR professionals into recruiting, training and employee relations experts. Her company is moving towards a traditional structure, where HR employees are trained to develop generalist knowledge.

A CIPD Factsheet (2010a) recommended exercising caution when adopting the business partner model and suggests that partnering should mean a paradigm shift for most HR functions, resulting in changes to HR's values, operation and skills, and not simply a repackaging of good HR practice.

Perhaps the key question comes down to credibility and contribution, summed up succinctly in a Deloitte report (2009, p8): 'The business partners' greatest failing has been their inability to convince senior managers that they have the necessary business acumen to contribute to the strategic debate.'

CASE STUDY 2.4

HR PARTNERS AT CHRISTIAN AID

Bentley (2008) quotes Higgins, a CEO of a human capital company, arguing that: 'role fulfilment can only happen if the requisite talent is there'.

This point is picked up by Jane Clark, senior HR business partner at aid agency Christian Aid. She says HR business partners require a whole different skill set compared with traditional HR generalists, and in some organisations HR has been expected to make this transition without adequate support.

'If you re-badge people without giving them training and awareness, you are setting them up for failure,' she says.

For Clark, a strategic HR business partner must be focused on looking forward, 'anticipating change, understanding its impact on the people side of the business and managing this change'. She says they must be comfortable working with senior people from the business on an equal footing and acting as an internal consultant within the business.

Outside experience

But many HR practitioners who have spent all their working life solely within the function will struggle to tick all these boxes, according to Clark. She believes her experience of working

outside of HR in an international development role for many years has helped her develop her strategic focus.

She recommends giving HR business partners secondments to other functions in the business as a way of expanding their strategic and commercial nous.

For Jane Clark, strategic HR business partners, who have developed commercial skills, have a choice of career paths.

She says: 'They are well-positioned to move into an HR director's role, but equally could make the step into a senior management position on the top table, and even the chief executive role. Consultancy work is also another option.'

Source: Bentley (2008)

www.XpertHR.co.uk

Question

1   With reference to the comments made by Jane Clark, to what extent could it be argued that the strategic HR business partner is more of a generalist role, incorporating change and strategic decision-making?

For further discussion regarding the future implications for HR, see Chapter 13.

The shape of the HR/HRD function may evolve through historical developments, or may be deliberately changed to meet the needs of key decision-makers. Perhaps the important factor here is how HR can constantly adapt its HRM and HRD activities, services and interventions to suit critical needs in that particular situation. Flexibility, adaptability and survival of HR remain the key determinants of HR's ability to transform itself to differing contexts. HR does not operate in isolation and requires management support – sometimes senior management support, but more often, line management support and engagement.

LINE MANAGERS AND HR: EVIDENCE FROM RESEARCH FINDINGS

The question of how much line managers are expected to contribute towards implementing people management activities and practices is a moot one. What is the level of intervention from HR's perspective when they spot errors and mistakes in the way in which line managers operate? If HR is purely acting in an 'advisory' capacity, whereby managers can ignore advice, then by definition, does this not spell the denigration of the HR function?

In an IRS survey (2009), it was found that in some cases HR took the lead (eg specialist knowledge or expertise surrounding a tribunal claim). In contrast, policies that needed to be applied across every individual employee in the workforce involve greater focus on the role of the line managers (eg performance appraisal reviews). The survey found that in 87.3 per cent of tribunal claims, HR took the main responsibility compared to 5.5 per cent who reported a shared responsibility between line managers and HR. The other two areas where HR took on a significant role were equal opportunities and employee relations (see also Chapters 4 and 11). It may be presumptuous to assume that the three key areas avoided by line managers could be considered to be 'dirty work', ie tricky areas that can be drawn out, complex and potentially damaging to the reputation of the individuals concerned. In the IRS 2008 survey on line managers' roles in people management, the key findings included:

- Line managers are increasingly expected to implement people management policies, with duties ranging from managing flexible working requests to handling disciplinary and grievance procedures.
- HR practitioners are not always impressed with the way that line managers carry out these responsibilities, and assess their performance as poor in some areas. Line managers are judged ineffective in training and development, absence management and maintaining personnel records.
- HR practitioners believe that training for line managers should be compulsory, and that levels of training and support on offer are inadequate.
- Two-thirds of organisations predict the role of line managers to change further in the next three years, and this means taking on more HR functions.

Despite the IRS survey finding that HR use a number of techniques to support line managers in their people management role, such as coaching, meetings advice and support, training and posting information on various channels, the attitude that line managers possess can sometimes inhibit outputs. Some of the problems here may be quite simple, eg the line manager is taking on too much, which may detract from what they perceive as their core function or contribution.

REFLECTIVE ACTIVITY 2.4

Consider how a formal arrangement can be made so as to secure a strong working relationship between HR managers and line managers. What key aspects would this arrangement include and how could they be evaluated?

HR IN REALITY: RESEARCH FINDINGS IN THE UK

So what does HRM and HRD actually involve in practice? The following section considers some of the more recent major research findings in the UK over the last couple of years.

XpertHR survey research findings (2012) revealed some interesting findings with regards to HR strategy and planning:

- The HR planning process is often informal, yet the majority of respondents believe it has had a positive impact on the performance of their organisation.
- Two-thirds of employers without an HR strategy believe that their organisation would perform better if they had one.
- Whereas senior managers outside of the HR function are involved in the HR planning process at three-quarters of organisations, senior HR staff are only involved at two-thirds.
- HR line managers are involved at just 18 per cent of organisations – indicating that, in many cases, people management priorities are set without the valuable input of those with relevant, first-hand experience.

Managing performance remains a key area for HR to show contribution, evidenced by the CIPD HR Outlook survey (CIPD 2012b), which showed that 68 per cent of respondents focused upon performance management, in the areas of managing change and cultural transformation, workforce planning, employee well-being and organisational restructuring. The survey further demonstrated that this was prevalent in the public sector and the private sector and focused on engagement, staff retention and talent management.

A Knowledge Pool survey (2010, cited in IRS 2010), based on responses from 10,000 managers, found that where learners receive line manager support, 94 per cent go on to apply what they learned. The role that the line manager plays cannot be underestimated, and line managers' actions may inhibit or enhance employees' performance. The boss may be the biggest stress factor to an employee, or the strongest motivator to perform.

Findings from a recent survey on learning and development (CIPD 2013c) found that the proportion of organisations using e-learning (74 per cent) has not changed significantly from the previous research in 2011. However, e-learning is being offered to an increasing proportion of employees within those organisations. The proportion completing courses remains low at just 31 per cent, although this is a slight improvement on 2011 figures (23 per cent). In the same survey, talent management activities were undertaken by nearly three-fifths of organisations. Echoing findings from the previous 2012 survey in this area, talent management activities cover all or most employees in two-fifths of organisations, while still more focus on high-potential employees and senior managers. As in previous years, growing future senior managers/leaders and developing high-potential employees remain the key objectives of talent management activities.

In addition to these findings on people management practices, research related to HRD and employee skills (National Employer Skills Survey 2012) has highlighted the following trends.

- Although only a small minority of businesses reported vacancies unfilled because of skill shortages, nearly all businesses with a skills shortage (93 per cent) found it had an impact on the operation of the business. The survey also finds concentrations of these skills shortages in particular industries and occupations (such as skilled trade occupations), concentrations which have been reported in previous English surveys.
- Whilst the proportion of businesses with vacancies has risen since 2009, it has not risen to the levels observed in 2007. Overall, the proportion of all vacancies which are skill shortage vacancies has remained stable since 2009, but this masks variation by size, sector and region. For example, mid-sized establishments (employing between 25 and 199 people) reported an increase in the proportion of vacancies which are linked to skill shortage, in contrast to larger or smaller establishments.
- Over 1.3 million employees did not have the skills required to perform their job role. Looking back at previous surveys in England, there are persistent pockets of concentration of these skills gaps, to which training is often a response.

- Just over a half of employees (53 per cent) received training in the previous year, a slight decline on the 56 per cent reported in 2009. As in previous years, training rates varied significantly between occupations, with 44 per cent of those employed as managers receiving training compared to 70 per cent of those employed in caring and leisure services.
- Around a third of businesses (30 per cent) had recruited someone straight from education in the last two to three years. The majority of these were satisfied with the work-readiness of education leavers, and this satisfaction rises with the age of the education leaver

Whilst the picture presented demonstrates that HRD makes a contribution to business needs, evidence provided in the CIPD Learning and Talent Development survey (2013c) found that perceptions of the economic situation and training spend was similar to 2012, with only a minority (8 per cent) reporting that their organisations' economic/funding circumstances have improved over the past 12 months. The situation is particularly difficult for the public sector, two-thirds of whom report their funding situation has got worse over the last year. The HRD function as pictured here attracts the same sort of challenges that faces the HRM function, necessitating a need to 'come out of its corner fighting'.

HR SHOWING ADDED VALUE

For HR to maintain its credibility, it not only has to be seen to be *doing*, but needs to provide evidence through appropriate measurements that it is adding value. The use of HR metrics and other indices like human capital management measures continue to be an aspect of HR. Warech and Tracey (2004) believe that HR is far more than a cost centre, and that being able to communicate assertively affects HR's collective impact on the company's bottom line.

The role of the line manager cannot be overplayed, and both HR and HRD specialists need to engage with line managers in order to establish and maintain a successful business partnership. Cantrell and Benton (2007, p360) state that their research 'shows that the more involved managers are in employee development, learning and performance appraisals, the better the financial performance of the organisation'. These authors also emphasise the important role that line managers have in active involvement with selection and development of employees.

If we consider the results of the IRS survey (2010, p5) on HR roles and responsibilities, 'most employers measure the effectiveness of their HR functions, with 72 per cent rating their HR function as very effective or above average based upon their evaluation.' Here HR has contributed towards managing cost-cutting exercises, an increased role in developing strategy (with senior managers) and reorganising and restructuring work (in order to save costs).

When it comes to creating a learning culture in organisations, where will this emanate from? Who will be the custodian of knowledge management (including knowledge creation and share)?

With regard to HRD showing added value, there is some similarity of arguments presented from HR material earlier. In a study of Indian companies, Rao and Varghese (2008, p33) found that:

- HRD managers need to recognise stakeholder expectations and understand the overall business and strategic context of their function.
- The HRD function should focus on intellectual capital generation activities and ensure good return on investment on training and other interventions.

- HRD practitioners need to equip themselves with capacity and competencies needed to build the HRD function, and become proactive strategic partners.
- HRD practitioners need to strengthen their partnership and credibility among stakeholders through involvement with policy-making.

Ulrich and Smallwood (2004) argue that HRD can create value through building organisational capabilities such as talent, speed of change, shared mindset, accountability, collaboration, learning and leadership.

More recently, the 2010 CIPD Learning and Talent Development report indicated that future skills requirements over the next two years would include: leadership skills (65 per cent), front-line people management skills (55 per cent), business acumen and awareness (51 per cent) and project/programme management skills (33 per cent). This report argued that the biggest change that is likely to occur over the next five years is a greater integration between coaching, organisational development and performance management to drive organisational change (46 per cent), and greater responsibility devolved to line managers (37 per cent).

REFLECTIVE ACTIVITY 2.5

The debate about how much added value HR can contribute to organisations carries on. Emphasis upon measurement and the use of metrics within HR, particularly in pinpointing 'outputs', may detract from appreciating the more qualitative aspects that add significant value to organisations.

Questions

1   What tensions arise for the HR function when trying to balance the needs of the external context (sustaining organisational performance in a competitive market), and the internal aspects of the organisation, such as engagement, capability and talent, culture and performance management?

2   Consider how HR can manage these tensions during times of both economic hardship and economic prosperity.

CASE STUDY 2.5

INNOVATIVE WAYS OF WORKING AND HR PRACTICES IN NEW FORMS OF ORGANISATION

Although many of us still work for a single employer, we increasingly experience work in a much more networked way than in the past (Marchington *et al* 2009, Swart *et al* 2007, Kinnie *et al* 2006). Think about the last project team in which you were involved: the chances are the members were drawn from both inside and outside your organisation. Despite this, we know very little about the management of human capital in a cross-boundary, or networked, context. Indeed, we might go further and say that much of current HR thinking, strategy, structure and practice is predicated on and reflects more traditional hierarchical structures. We therefore need to develop our understanding of these contemporary ways of working and how organisations use innovative forms of organising to manage human capital across boundaries.

A prominent way of working across organisational boundaries is to organise work in projects. Such arrangements are widespread, both within and between firms, in sectors such as pharmaceuticals, car manufacture, advertising, marketing and media and consulting. Complex, so-called 'mega-projects' or integrated project teams (IPTs) are the principal way in which large-scale major construction projects, such as Terminal 5 at London Heathrow Airport and the London Olympic Park, and IT integration projects, such as the change to online self-assessment tax returns for HMRC, are designed, developed and then operationalised. These changes reveal an interesting paradox: potentially fragmenting changes, which could mean that organisations may not be able to maximise the value from their human capital, are taking place at the same time as greater emphasis is placed on the central role of human capital in organisational success (Takeuchi *et al* 2011).

Increasingly, we are faced with the task of managing employees across organisational boundaries. In more traditional organisations we tend to equate employees with the people whom we directly manage; but more and more we are finding a disconnect between those whom we employ and manage. We may, for example, employ people but not manage them on a face-to-face basis because they may be providing outsourced services on a client's site, as in the recruitment process outsourcer Alexander Mann Solutions (AMS). Alternatively, the clients of AMS find they are interacting on a daily basis with staff who are not their employees but are central to their success. Indeed, Paul Fielden, Associate Partner in IBM, said in a recent interview for our research, 'I can draw on over 150 IBM people to staff projects for my clients, but I only directly manage three of them.'

These innovative forms of organising have multiple benefits because they allow firms to leverage the knowledge, skills and experience of staff they do not employ, but there are also various challenges. The financial services firm which outsources its call centre operations to India achieves both cost and expertise advantages, but it knows these call centre workers are perceived by their customers as the public voice of their organisation. These innovative ways of working in 'adhoctratic', project-centred, knowledge-intensive networks (see also Chapter 8) throw up challenges for achieving the traditional HR aims of integration, alignment and consistency (Marchington *et al* 2011). The consultant will have to display commitment not only to her employer, but also to her client, team and her own professional development. Indeed, many of these HR practices sit more comfortably in an environment where there is a single focus of commitment rather than the potentially multiple foci of commitment found in the networked way of working where employees are habitually working across organisational boundaries (Kinnie and Swart 2012).

We need to consider the consequences for HR if the source of competitive advantage shifts from the single firm to the complex network involving literally thousands of firms. This means that the classic HR practices for recruitment, talent development and retention are no longer solely the property of an individual firm.

Source: Kinnie *et al* (2012).

Questions

1 What are the potential benefits of these innovative, networked ways of working?

2 What are the potential conflicts and tensions in HR terms?

CONCLUSION

HR needs to operate effectively at strategic, tactical and operational levels. Rees and McBain (2004, p25) argue that in order for HR to maintain its importance, it needs to:

- participate in strategic decision-making, demonstrate added value, and act as a business partner
- move from assuming full responsibility for all HR managers and engage with line managers (and develop the capability of line managers)
- shift the focus from internal to external, including benchmarking against other organisations, and collecting data on competitors. This includes keeping in touch with business trends and how these impact upon people management practices within the organisation
- become more anchored in, and central to, the contribution to business, thereby building commitment from employees
- move away from reactive supporter to proactive strategic adviser, anticipating required changes.

This model echoes the principles of business partnership, but is less concerned with structural issues and focuses upon the role and contribution of HR more. This 'internality' argument on meeting customer needs is explored by Jenner and Taylor (2007, p8), where HR views employees (and potential employees) as internal customers, and 'anticipating, identifying and satisfying customer requirements'.

The IRS 2010 survey results contradict some of these aspirations, and bring HR back to its transactional role. The two most prominent measures assessing HR effectiveness are absence management and staff turnover data.

It appears that we have gone full circle, with the continuum ranging from notions of how HR can act as a strategic business partner, to a transactional cost-cutter. However, given the current economic climate and what 'has to be done', HR has an opportunity to further demonstrate its worth and contribution, and more importantly measure and communicate this effectively to major stakeholders. If it does not, it is unlikely that Cinderella will be attending the ball!

KEY LEARNING POINTS

- The HR department or function has changed considerably in the last 40 years, and currently tends to adopt a managerialist (corporate) position.
- HR needs to take time to evaluate and justify itself as a function or face attack or possibly outsourcing or replacement.
- Where HR sits within corporate planning is pivotal to its involvement with strategic and mainstream business activities.
- HRD and strategic HRD play an important function in the development of employees to adding to business success.
- The HR business partner model carries with it a series of potential benefits and limitations, and should therefore be adapted according to the organisation and context, and possibly face up to the fact that it simply won't work as a model.
- Despite the theory, there is a great deal of evidence to suggest that HR does receive the attention and support that it requires as a key function within organisations. The interplay between line management and HR is crucial in obtaining the right business outcomes.

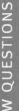

REVIEW QUESTIONS

1   To what extent can there be a 'perfect shape' to an HR function in an organisation? Consider the arguments both for and against this proposition.

2   Does the HR business partner role sit most comfortably within private, public or third sector organisations? Support your answer with practical benefits.

3   How can the HR/HRD function build relationships with line managers so as to put improved working practices into effect?

4   What is meant by 'strategic HRD'? Evaluate the major components of strategic HRD.

EXPLORE FURTHER

Aston Centre for Human Resources. (2008) *Strategic Human Resource Management: Building research-based practice*. London: CIPD.

Boxall, P. and Purcell, J. (2008) *Strategic and Human Resource Management*. 2nd edition. Basingstoke: Palgrave Macmillan. This textbook is strong on theory surrounding strategic HR.

Caldwell, R. (2008) HR business partner competency models: recontextualising effectiveness. *Human Resource Management Journal*, Vol. 18, No. 3, pp275–294. This article provides useful arguments around the business partner model.

Rees, G. and Smith, P. (2014) (eds). *Strategic Human Resource Management: an international perspective*. London: Sage Publications.

CHAPTER 3

HRM Contributions in Different Settings

Charlotte Rayner and Liza Howe-Walsh

LEARNING OUTCOMES

After reading this chapter, you should be able to:

- appreciate how HR practices may differ across sector types: private, public and third sector

- recognise that delivering HR services in smaller organisations differs from those in larger organisations

- consider the ways in which the HR function may change as an organisation grows in size

- understand the concept of global HRM and its implications for practice in terms of policy and practice for localisation and control from head office

- explore the notion of strategic international HRM; variegations in practice for staffing overseas.

OVERVIEW

This chapter takes theory from Chapter 2 and applies it to the working lives of HR practitioners (HRPs). In particular we will look at how, while the function of managing HR is similar in most organisations, the work of the HRPs themselves varies between different organisational contexts; this is partly dependent on size, and also whether the organisation is profit or not-for-profit. Without doubt the needs of an organisation change as it grows, and although all have to be compliant with the law, often small businesses only seek involvement by HR to ensure such compliance, commonly using external consultants. Following growth, generalist internal HR managers are typically appointed and, with further success and growth, specialists, policy designers and strategists broaden the input from HR. Their continued tenure means they are perceived as adding value to the organisation – although naturally the nature of value-added varies between roles.

Public sector and third sector (not-for-profit) HR practitioners can sometimes feel undervalued in academic research, which typically focuses on those organisations seeking profit. In this chapter we argue that all HR managers 'add value', and we will explore this notion in depth with examples.

Taking the concept of context further, we explore international and global HRM, presenting the practical issues of locus of control (how far the organisation controls from head office or allows localisation), and the movement of staff overseas by the use of expatriates and other forms of staffing (Judge *et al* 2009). Some expensive techniques are used by organisations for staffing overseas, often with little understanding of the benefits accruing to the organisation. Throughout this chapter, the relationship of HR practice and the interface between line managers and specialist HRPs is discussed, as we regard this link as a highly salient issue for the management and leadership of people in all types of organisation.

INTRODUCTION

Chapters 1 and 2 outlined the main influences on HRM and HRD with regard to managing and leading people. In this chapter we will seek to change the focus in several ways. First we will concentrate on how HR adds value, initially examining what it is to add value. Quite often it is perceived that value is only added by the introduction of high-quality products and services. Although value can be added in this way, it can be added in many other ways too. In the chapter we examine the original concept of 'value-added', which demonstrates that cost-cutting, efficiencies and simply resolving value-losing conflicts can add to the offering of the organisation. HRPs may not have headline visibility in these achievements very often, but are usually important players in the success of initiatives as part of their daily work (Paauwe and Boselie 2005). Hence we will explore the notion of adding value through a narrowing of focus to specific types of organisation and also using examples, and illustrate how the nature of the challenge within HR can vary enormously dependent upon the context one is working in.

In the second section of the chapter we will broaden our scope to an international focus in order to examine the management and leadership of people in multi-country organisations (Stahl *et al* 2012). It is not only when operating from sites in other countries that international understanding is needed. When one is sending employees abroad to work on assignments, or using staff employed by organisations based in countries offshore, there is a need to understand the HR implications of increasing geographic scope. With the success of Internet-based selling and recruitment, the need for international HRM is now not just the province of large multinationals, but a real possibility for many smaller organisations and the third sector. Hence practitioners' competence in international and global HR becomes more prevalent than unusual.

HR IN DIFFERENT CONTEXTS

It is essential that all staff contribute to the organisational effort. The work output of some staff such as those in sales is highly tangible and their contribution to the organisation's goals obvious. But what of HR practitioners? As a service function, one needs to be explicit in order to identify the organisational benefit from their work (Wright and McMahan 1992). HRM as a profession is connected to employees and their outputs regarding the organisation (Huselid 1995). Our understanding of how employees contribute is largely driven by the 'Resource Based View' (see Boxall and Purcell 2011 for a full description) where the value of the organisation is created from resources, of which one is employees, and HR practitioners are intricately involved in delivering such value (Glover and Butler 2012). Glover and Butler undertook a four-year study to gain a deeper understanding of HRPs' role within the organisation. Alongside HR's role at a strategic level, contributing to the business, the study highlights the contribution of HR behind the scenes. Such work includes amendments to policy and practices and negotiating with line managers. As this work is not immediately visible there is a danger that the HR function is not credited with any resulting benefit, putting into question how it adds value (Glover and Butler 2012, p212).

The notion of 'value' in contemporary strategic thinking was developed by the strategist Michael Porter, who saw those in the organisation adding value in a cumulative 'value chain' (1985). As an economist he saw 'value' being related to profits. This view is reflected in a CIPD Employee Outlook survey (CIPD 2012b). The survey for 2012/13 indicates that regardless of whether the organisation is private or public, the importance of managing performance is of paramount focus to the HR function, a purpose linked directly to enhancing profits. Porter would suggest that value is added in two ways: either by reducing costs (hence leading to higher profit margin); or by adding features and benefits which clients and customers value and are willing to pay for and, although they cost more to deliver, can be charged for at a premium, hence adding to the profit margin. Applying Porter's guidance to the HR context of managing and leading people reveals a multitude of ways in which added-value can be achieved.

Although public sector and third sector organisations do not usually seek to make profits, they are immensely budget conscious and hence we need to pay some attention to how they can use Porter's fundamentals of adding value. Being publicly funded, such organisations have to take care with all expenditure. Given that many public sector institutions carry a staff cost of at least 50 per cent of their overall budget as they are usually in a service capacity, the role of HR should be fundamental (Gould-Williams 2003). Value can be added by a reduction in overall expenditure after savings are made in an area or doing more with the same staff, or by developing staff so that the service they provide outweighs the cost of the development.

Let us consider the public sector. Given that wages are such a major cost, HR can influence added-value by contributing to projects which reduce staff costs. This might be through helping line managers reorganise work or job roles so that the same can be done with less. For example, local councils conduct much business using IT contact with their residents, meaning initial investment in website design, equipment and training existing staff, but eventual savings as automation takes effect. Paying parking tickets online rather than sending in a cheque (to be processed by staff and incurring bank charges) or visiting council offices (with the accompanying costs of being met and dealt with in-person) are two examples. The Ordinance Survey office has recently moved to a much smaller building after recruiting and training staff (over a long period) competent in technologically based mapping so that they simply didn't need their paper-based library of maps and bulky equipment. The long-term savings from the smaller new building should be significant. The new generation of staff can do more with less space. Value has been added through a very tangible change of operations stemming from the blend of HR-enabling new technology.

Truss and Gill (2009) investigated the process that HR delivered in the UK public sector, exploring the issues of social capital, perceived added value and HR process through in-depth interviews at two NHS hospitals and two local councils. Their study found both value-adding and value-reducing examples. Perceptions of value reduction included poor union–employer relationships which led to stagnation and blocks to change. Poor time boundaries within recruitment were an example where line managers saw HR as reducing value through the loss of good candidates (p679), and inconsistency in HR personnel in providing their internal services was always seen negatively (p680). One can see how this would add to costs as line managers and senior staff sought to use the HR department members they trusted and who had a reputation for delivering processes, whilst avoiding those less reliable. Timely responding by the HR department in the delivery of processes was perceived as value-adding by non-HR managers in all areas. It appeared that a visible and proactive HR leader was highly influential on how HR was perceived. In most cases the HR strategic contributions were acknowledged as solid; it was in the detail of more day-to-day process where value was not positive, and also through inconsistency of personnel. Their study included HRPs where they correlated stronger performances with a strong sense of identity and purpose such that even if HRPs were working at a level of isolation, they knew the HR strategy and understood their contribution. HR departments which were led less well and had a poor sense of identity and cohesion amongst members were perceived less well. These lessons are likely to be useful in non-public sector contexts too.

The CIPD carried out a study on high-performing HR departments in large organisations that includes the public sector (Sears 2010). They sought to discover how HR might function in the future. The report suggested that to provide sustainable value needed a mind-shift away from tactical short-termism. This provides a genuine challenge for the public sector, where government departments may change leadership with elections, meaning longer-term visions are avoided. Service providers such as health, education and welfare frequently have funding changes, meaning a context where risk-taking on larger projects might be shunned. Arguably, the imposition of austerity measures by governments after the 2008 financial crisis to reduce overall borrowing imposes a short-term focus in public, third and private sectors alike. However, all organisations need to keep longer-term strategies and scenarios active in the minds of their staff, even in such times of limited opportunity.

What comes across in the 2010 CIPD research is the embeddedness of high-achieving HR departments in the 'business' of their organisations. As such, 'HR initiatives' were rarely undertaken; instead the organisation (or a segment) has a new thrust which involves HR as organisational development consultants or involved in delivering changes connected to the new direction. Hence the notion of HR being strategic had become so much enacted that they were a natural and obvious player in any change. The study demonstrated how Surrey Police undertook a strategy allowing local managers more discretion, reaching into all parts of the operation. HR policies were reviewed, reduced and rewritten 'with broad principles rather than detailed dictat' (Sears 2010, p9). Hence sometimes financial constraints can lead to invoking better HR-related practice.

REFLECTIVE ACTIVITY 3.1

Consider the example of Surrey Police provided above.

Questions

1   In what ways do you think the relationship between line managers and HR may have changed as a result of the new approach?

2   How would staff in your HR department react to enabling more managerial discretion?

3   Discuss the strengths and weaknesses of devolving power to the line manager in the public sector.

Turning now to the private sector, costs are clearly important, and are more likely to be tracked stringently, although rhetoric does not always match reality (Woodall *et al* 2009). There are several large studies which have examined the link between HR strategy and business strategy (eg Wang and Shyu 2008) and these are based on private sector organisations, often taking 'top performing' organisations in a financial sense and then asking about HR practices. It is becoming clear that although researchers do find positive relationships between HR alignment with business strategy and performance, the causal direction is less clear (eg Biron *et al* 2011). Are the better financial performers just more organised and integrated, or is there something special about the alignment of HR?

An aspect which emerged for the private sector in particular in the recent CIPD research (Sears 2010) was the need for HR to challenge all types of managers. Naturally one has to already have a culture where challenging the status quo (and also those with status) does not carry a penalty. However, HR is uniquely positioned to add value as it reaches into all corners of the organisation. The ongoing debate regarding bankers' bonuses is a good example. Investment decisions are made in banks by individuals using skills (bringing together market knowledge from a range of sources), experience and professional judgement, contributing a key set of competencies that are central to the organisation's strategic success. A highly complex set of (often incomplete) data means the skill of bankers is at a premium. For a bank struggling with debt, there is an argument to pay more for skilled people who will create wealth (value) far beyond the cost of bonuses. This balance has to be weighed carefully and is one in which HR plays a role, bringing its own skills in knowledge and understanding of the implications on all parts of the business of 'perceived excess' in one area.

HRD can be the lynchpin for the achievement of strategies where redeployment of tasks is an aspect of implemented business strategies. Couriers now drop off and pick up parcels, entering parcel movements into the computer directly through mobile terminals; multi-tasking and upgrading their responsibility in a fundamental way to add value through cost-efficiency and using high-performance working practices (Katou and Budhwar 2009). Such changes are strategic in nature and designed to contribute to profit involving complex processes that result in redeployed staff undertaking altered roles, having been retrained and probably under new terms and conditions of service. HR is involved in achieving strategic change, and although it may never serve a customer directly, adds value (Ulrich *et al* 2008) through implementing business strategy.

The differences between the public and private sectors may not be great in many instances. Getting nurses to upgrade their skills to take over responsibilities previously the domain of qualified doctors is an increasing trend throughout the NHS. How far this is different in principle from the job redesign of the courier in the private sector is questionable. Both are about empowerment, learning and training so that responsibilities can be flattened in the hierarchy with cost savings. The value added might be spent in different ways; the hospital may do more with the same number of staff, the courier firm might expand using the savings from their strategy or pay higher dividends to shareholders. But the strategy was the same, and HR has played a key role, even though the spending of the value added might be very different.

The final sector we consider is the third sector (charitable and voluntary organisations), which often operate in fragile environments, vulnerable to changes in funder behaviour. The National Society for the Prevention of Cruelty to Children (NSPCC) has seen great changes in its activities over the years and although they have always provided care and protection for young people, they have extended their operations into training and advising local authorities, and now supervise the activities of ChildLine, one of the largest telephone helplines in the UK which employs highly skilled staff to deal with children who may be in extremely difficult circumstances. The need to turn their activities towards different streams of funding has meant they have had to be as nimble as any commercial organisation, but are constrained in ways not experienced by for-profit companies.

The sector has expanded as government has retracted from providing direct services, such as in elderly care where there are now far fewer council-run sites, with provision being delivered by private and third sector organisations (Wainwright *et al* 2006). There is a blurring between public, private and third sector (eg Rodwell *et al* 2008) with far more private sector organisations working within third sector constraints. We now turn to the challenges for HR to add value in the third sector context.

Without doubt, issues to do with recruitment can be especially tough in this sector. The handling of volunteers is a specialism many charities have to manage, and input from HR into the parameters one needs to provide for such unpaid workers to engage in a way traditionally associated with that where an employment contract exists can be tricky. It is usually the case that third sector pay at all levels, being open to scrutiny by funders and the public alike, is low (Cunningham 2008). How does one attract and retain talent in such contexts? How does one fund training and other learning opportunities in order to develop staff when budgets are commonly connected in discrete ways to deliverable projects? How far can 'rewarding work' be used or abused? The sector is poorly researched from an HR perspective, and one must question how far such organisations are able to voice concerns for fear of upsetting funders and users alike.

Central to issues around funding and reward of employees is the relationship between the third sector group and other agencies with which it partners. In elderly care the partner might be a local council; in education, a government department; in research it may be the NHS or specific benefactors. It is common that funders impose terms and conditions on those agencies which deliver services (Marchington *et al* 2005), thus leaving the third sector provider little room for movement. In addition, competitive tendering for third sector contracts may mean those involved with negotiating contracts have to be very lean with their highest cost factor, ie employees (Cunningham 2008). As funding is based on contracts typically lasting one to two years, substantial long-term investment or investment in potential new areas of work through HRD can be difficult to resource. Cunningham's study in the Scottish voluntary sector identified three types of agencies: those who aligned with local authority terms and conditions and developed reputation and quality consistency, serving many clients (hence dependent on few); those who compromised on some terms and conditions and were quite hand-to-mouth on contracts; and finally those who were 'struggling to care' (p1041) for employees being dependent on few large contracts and in poor bargaining positions.

To add to the pressure, third sector organisations have to protect their reputation with great care. The notion of employer branding has been used very well by those in the sector to bolster the non-financial rewards of employment and also provide an enhanced image for funders. It is essential to deliver on any promises made in branding in this sector, as so much funding is local and bad news can travel fast.

REFLECTIVE ACTIVITY 3.2

Funding HRD activities in the third sector can be problematic, especially providing learning events for the many staff who are on low wages. The Children's Society takes advantage of a strong link with the trade union UNITE. In several instances, the charity enabled a few employees (who are often workplace trade union representatives) to attend UNITE training, who then cascaded the knowledge and skills through the Society at far lower cost than external providers, but to exacting standards.

The Children's Society is quite a large charity. How might a small charity enable learning and development to be funded or delivered at low cost?

Some areas of HR add value directly in any organisation; for example, in the provision or overseeing of administrative tasks connected to people, eg wage systems, pensions, employment records, benefits and rewards systems. These are fundamental to the functioning of all organisations. However, they are often seen as 'hygiene factors' and so not necessarily valued when everything goes well, but heavily criticised when they fail to perform. Few employees are grateful for being paid on time, but most would be unhappy if wages arrived late! Their effectiveness provides value and ineffectiveness causes cost, thus reducing value.

Without doubt HR adds value through some of the roles described by Ulrich and Brockbank (2005). It is always valued for its contribution in keeping the organisation in compliance with legal requirements (the HR expert), and HR specialists have developed into providing policy advice and implementation at a strategic level (HR strategists).

The data for the performance value (financial and otherwise) created by HR professionals is difficult to study with certainty (Paauwe 2009) as if one uses broad-brush measures (such as return on capital employed) many non-employee components are involved, thus making a 'straight line' between HR involvement and organisation-level performance measures to be impossible to measure with certainty or at least to be treated with extreme caution (Wright and Haggerty 2005). Many HR initiatives concern longer-term development where an outcome (such as learning) might take many years to impact directly (Anderson 2007) and hence shorter-term value might be perceived in more fluid terms as a function of 'return on expectations' by senior and line managers (ibid). On the other hand, HR-based initiatives which are well communicated as aligned with strategy (eg Nijssen and Paauwe 2012) can make the case through clear articulation alone.

REFLECTIVE ACTIVITY 3.3

Consider a recent major change in your organisation.

Questions

1   Could this have been undertaken without HR input?

2   What was the nature of that input (with regard to that specific type of organisation) and did it add value through reducing costs further or achieving the change more efficiently or effectively?

HR ROLES AS THE ORGANISATION GROWS: SMES

The function of HR is needed in all organisations beyond the simple formation of a partnership between two or more individuals. Many small organisations do not see the need to employ an HR specialist and, forever cost-conscious, tend not to directly employ HR assistance until it is really needed – perhaps as a result of hygiene factors not being met. Instead, HR might be outsourced to an HR consultant retained for policy and administrative tasks with their legal expertise enabling the small organisation to adhere to regulations. The small business is highly reliant on the skills and knowledge of such consultants, and is dependent on the provider being effective. Many HR consultants do excellent work with small businesses, often beginning with a limited and legalistically geared brief and patiently expanding their role into OD, HRD and other facets of delivery as the organisation is successful. Indeed, contact with HR consultants is sometimes the only space when owner-managers of small businesses take time away from their operational focus to consider their staff in a systematic and future-oriented manner.

The next evolutionary step is to hire an HR generalist to service the small firm, and logically occurs when it is cost-effective to do so. A small business generalist needs by default to be a jack-of-all-trades (perhaps with the exception of legal support) and undertake (or at least co-ordinate) all HR roles. HR generalists may not be providing very sophisticated services, but it is likely they will be closely aligned with the 'business' as their day-to-day activities are immersed with those connected to clients, suppliers and the product/service to be delivered. Short lines of communication and close contact with seniors should mean fast delivery of change. Naturally the agenda will be limited in scope and subject to tight funding, but the capacity to add value focused on the business is very high.

Greiner (1972) suggests that as organisations grow they pass through a series of crises. Almost like a squeeze-box movement, the locus of control is central. Most small business owners like to have control, but this can become more difficult as the organisation grows, failing to deliver optimal effectiveness as the owner-manager becomes a bottle-neck of decisions and checking employees' work. In some senses many small businesses reflect the 'hard HR' model (see Boselie *et al* (2009) for a review of the Michigan Approach). A resolution of this early Greiner crisis for small business sees a middle line of managers having more autonomy to enable growth.

It is possible at this time to move into more staff development as typified by the 'soft HR' Harvard school (ibid), although hard HR may predominate. But greater autonomy risks fragmentation as the organisation may grow in different ways under the direction of a team of sub-unit leaders, leading to a crisis of control. Greiner's next crisis is therefore a need to pull things back into a more coherent whole again. Even at this stage, as often SMEs do not devolve much decision-making, the HR generalist has only a few key managers to deal with. Unitarism is assumed, and the atmosphere is often still patriarchal (Legge 2005), especially if the owner-manager is still in charge. If a full-time HR professional has not been hired before now, it is likely this crisis sets the scene to do so.

In what way can the generalist HR practitioner provide value for the SME? Becker and Huselid (2006) are clear that beyond the standard HR administration, the focus of any HR activity, if it is to be aligned into the organisation strategy, needs to focus on areas rich in human capital. Hence HR can provide insight on focusing effort to those who create the value which is essential for strategic success. Thus an importer geared to growth through extending market share can focus on rewards connected to performance targets with appraisal and feedback to those sourcing and selling products as the nexus of HRM strategy. A professional firm of knowledge workers may have a different focus such as that of HRD opportunities and an emphasis on work–life balance as a means to recruit, retain and foster performance in the professionals key to delivering the organisational offering. In the medium-sized organisation HR professionals thinking through these 'bundles' (Gould-Williams 2003) for the organisation can add great value. It should be noticed that Becker and Huselid concur with others that not all employees add strategic value to the organisation and they argue the strategic HRM architecture needs to be built around the human capital which adds the crucial value for the organisation's strategy. Their evidence concerns operational delivery of HR, holding interest to generalists especially, and they suggest 'workforce strategy' is a good term to use as everyone can grasp its significance, including line managers, who can partner in its formation.

As the firm grows, it is likely that so too will the number of HR professionals, with evolution into the better defined roles (as described by Ulrich). However as the medium-sized organisation works its way through the growth cycles, the final stage Greiner suggests is a 'crisis of red tape' as bureaucracy has been used to co-ordinate the organisation – a complaint which will not surprise any seasoned HR practitioner, and resonates with Reflective Activity 3.1 on Surrey Police.

QUICKSILVER'S HR CHALLENGES

Quicksilver has 200 employees and is a worldwide leader in yacht insurance worldwide, based in Cowes on the Isle of Wight. Careful stewardship through the early years, and the retraction of mainstream insurers from the niche, has allowed steady growth. Internet and magazine advertising links customers to the call centre (100 staff), which also deals with initial claims. Each staff area has a board director. There is an underwriting and claims group (40 staff), the marketing department works with IT (15 staff), and the finance department (18 staff) is under the direct control of the CEO, who is a qualified accountant. Quicksilver has a differentiated strategy, not the cheapest in the market, but reliable for reasonable claims.

The firm employs three HR practitioners who also oversee the building and non-IT facilities. One looks after recruitment – with call centre staff being a main headache – one deals with HR administration and facility issues, and the third, Sylvia Norris, is the HR director dealing with policy and strategic issues, and also helps out her line-reports. Call centre staff are trained by an external provider.

The financial crisis has not affected the company's financial standing, and retention of established customers has been excellent, although there has been a 20 per cent drop through customers giving up their expensive hobby. But new customers are looking for cheaper deals and 'dodgy claims' are increasing from this cadre. These dynamics have led to stagnation in sales, and internal tensions are rising in the firm as non-payment of claims affected the company's reputation in the close-knit boating community.

Sylvia has been challenged that the once positively regarded 'professional' practices in HR (clear job descriptions, target-setting and performance appraisal systems for example) are tying everyone down far too much as 'belts need to be tightened'.

Questions

1 How can Sylvia respond to these pressures?

2 In what other ways can she and her team add value at this time of stagnation?

The larger organisation holds different challenges for HR. Diversification may mean different strategies in different sub-units and human capital investment may vary across the organisation (Boxall and Purcell 2011). The drive for efficiencies through standardisation of processes and policies may mean over-bureaucratisation in some cases and insufficient support in others (*ibid*); in larger organisations there are many decision-makers and co-ordination within the HR department may become paramount to gather issues and focus effort (Sears 2010, De Vos and Meganck 2009, Morris *et al* 2009). As the distance between key areas for attention and HR increases, so gaps may appear. It is perhaps not surprising that the seam of 'critical HR' research (which includes examination of dysfunction between HR effort and what is valued) is undertaken almost always in large organisations (eg Truss and Gill 2009, De Vos and Meganck 2009). One might see that co-ordination activities within HR costs salaries, but the effect a synergistic team can provide can make a real difference (Becker and Huselid 2006, p907).

There has been a trend over the last decade away from vertical integration (where one owns all aspects of the organisation) towards outsourcing and supply-chain management. A common technique in large organisations, but how far can HR be outsourced? The strategy literature suggests that when outsourcing, it is only those aspects of the organisation that do not contribute to strategic success which should be considered – otherwise one has competitive competency owned by others. Many CIPD surveys show that payroll administration is commonly outsourced by organisations of all sizes – a specialist firm can often provide payroll cheaper than in-house. Other aspects of HR are far more contentious. How far should training and other learning events be outsourced? If knowledge is central to the product or service being offered, surely HRD must be provided in-house? Opinions differ, and there are bold examples of outsourcing, such as at Hampshire County Council, where the whole HR department was outsourced.

REFLECTIVE ACTIVITY 3.4

Visit the CIPD website at www.cipd.co.uk. Look through the collection of surveys and related articles on outsourcing there. Pick one function of HR that is contentious in terms of being outsourced and show how it is controversial. At this point you may wish to look at Chapter 4 and the discussion there on professionalism and ethics in HR.

1   Are the factors to be considered the same for private, public and third sector organisations?

2   Can HR ever be entirely outsourced and, if not, which aspects of HR should always remain in-house?

Give reasons for your conclusions.

Outsourcing in HR is a debate that will no doubt continue. An interesting set of data is shown by Wahrenburg *et al* (2006, p1747), displaying variation across the portfolio of HR activities. As one would expect, clerical functions are far more likely to be outsourced than top management advice. They found variation between industries with some commonality within industry (they examined finance in particular). We would argue that if the whole of HR is outsourced it is seen as a commodity, adding no strategic value, then in some senses the profession has failed (Priem and Butler 2001). One must recognise that some strategic advice will come from consultants who have broadened activities from being auditors and advising on finance to helping with cost and value-added. If HR is entirely outsourced, clearly the message from the architects of the organisation is that HR as a function is not seen as central to the management and leadership of people in providing competitive advantage (Woodall *et al* 2009). Clearly this argument has many decades to run.

The shift into and out of outsourcing has provided a highly variegated situation for HR practitioners and those seeking a career in HR. Opportunities for roles exist within all sectors, either fully employed by an organisation or acting as a consultant independently or as part of an outsourced agency. In the end the HR function is delivered. But how the value is created and by whom varies as to the context one is examining and the choices the organisation has made (Boselie *et al* 2009).

REFLECTIVE ACTIVITY 3.5

A small law firm is having difficulty attracting and retaining lawyers in a provincial office

overseas. It currently has no in-house HR function. The partner in charge has decided to introduce flexible benefits in line with the larger competitors.

Questions

1   Brief the management team on how the benefits could be introduced and managed.

2   How could they utilise HR input to assist with their goal?

EXPANDING OUR BORDERS: THE GROWTH OF INTERNATIONALISATION

This millennium is seeing the world connected internationally through the use of the Internet, changing the scope for recruitment, working and operations at a fundamental level. Such advances mean that national borders are being crossed by even small organisations who now find foreign markets offer the staff they need, or customers who might want their organisations' products and services. Thus the portfolio of skills needed in managing and leading people is becoming an international arena, and one for which the HR professional needs to be prepared. It is to the international context that our attention now turns.

Why do we need to explore global strategy in HRM? HR as part of the strategic component delivering organisational strategy is increasingly breaking national borders (Evans *et al* 2012). With wider globalisation, HR is under pressure to deliver policies and practices that will support the business objectives of the organisation and demonstrate results in an increasingly competitive economic environment. Working alongside the other business functions such as finance, operations and corporate departments, HR have to understand how they can help to deliver the vision to the business in an international context.

Changes to demographics, such as an ageing workforce and the emergence of developing countries, mean that looking towards future staffing may require an international approach. We see more organisations requiring staff to be internationally mobile. Organisations compete for talent across the globe as individuals broaden their search for the best employment opportunities, globalising recruitment markets. Those organisations with sites overseas require an understanding of the complexities involved with managing staff internationally and the impact this has upon the global HR strategy.

Global staffing can play a key role in shaping the competitive position of multinational enterprises (MNEs), via individuals' transfer of knowledge across the organisation, which is often cited as one of the main reasons to undertake an international assignment. Additionally, the widely accepted reasons for transferring staff from one country to another include developing the individuals' management or leadership skills, knowledge of markets or products or to strengthen the organisation's international competencies (Strack *et al* 2007).

Much of the research in IHRM focuses upon the management of staff within MNEs and involves the study of expatriates, but can also apply to small and medium-sized enterprises (SMEs) and a broader definition of international staff.

STRATEGIC INTERNATIONAL HRM

The trend over the last few years has been to attempt to link international HRM (IHRM) to the strategy of the organisation in line with fulfilling the company's global strategy (SIHRM) (Stahl *et al* 2012).

REFLECTIVE ACTIVITY 3.6

HSBC defines itself as 'The World's Local Bank' in its marketing. Visit its websites and examine their corporate messages.

Questions

1   What effect does this international branding have on HR in the UK?

2   Given its messages, how would you approach someone in a London office of the firm to undertake an overseas assignment in a subsidiary in Detroit for two years?

DEFINING STRATEGIC INTERNATIONAL HRM

In order to highlight the context of SIHRM, a definition is needed. Schuler *et al* define SIHRM as:

> human resource management issues, functions, and policies and practices that result from the strategic activities of multinational enterprises and that impact the international concerns and goals of those enterprises. (1993, p422)

The definition brings together a number of factors that includes literature from international business and management, as well as IHRM. 'In essence, MNEs are firms that need to be global and local (multi-domestic) at the same time' (Schuler *et al* 1993, p421).

Schuler *et al* (1993) explore this notion through the development of an integrative framework to further our understanding of SIHRM. The development of a framework leads to including three major components: issues; functions; and policies and practices, which in turn are influenced by MNEs' strategic activities. These are discussed below.

SIHRM issues

The organisation needs to decide how much control it allows the local business whilst considering that this may vary depending on the local environment. Cultural differences play a part in the decision as to which approach the organisation will pursue. HRM plays an important role within the organisation in terms of integrated or differentiating practices.

SIHRM functions

The function relates to human resource orientation; the time, energy and financial resources operating the human resource organisation; and the locations of the resources. There are several ways that the company may choose to manage its human resources. For example, all HR policy and practice activities are handed down from the headquarters of the MNE. In contrast, local divisions are able to tailor HR practices that are more locally accepted, such as promotion criteria.

SIHRM policies and practices

Policies and practices involve developing general guidelines on how individuals will be managed and developed within the organisation. For example, the HR policy may outline the reward structure and instruct all sites to pay the local median for certain grades of employees. However, it may be part of the company's overall strategy to take into consideration the nuances within a particular environment. For example, providing specific practices that are appropriate to the local market such as incentivised pay schemes for specific talent sectors. Indeed, there may be particular local requirements that will impact upon HR policy and practices in terms of legislation such as a minimum wage, etc. Therefore a single policy acts as a guide whilst consideration is provided as to local terms and culture.

It can be seen that one thread throughout the issues, functions and policies described above is that of the degree of localisation allowed by the parent office. Organisations vary enormously as to how far this is granted, and it may not be standard across the whole organisation (Farndale *et al* 2010).

But how does international or global HRM differ from domestic HRM? Evolution to IHRM complicates HRM practices (Kiessling and Harvey 2005). There are different types of employees to consider, such as host-country national (HCNs), parent-country nationals (PCNS) and third-country nationals (TCNs).

Let us use the illustration of IBM, where the parent organisation is based in the USA. It has offices in the UK, where British employees would be seen as HCNs. It might also have staff from the USA (PCNs), and employ specialist staff from anywhere in the world who are neither British nor American nationals (TCNs). The international context introduces different ways in which these employees are employed, such as: expatriates (the USA manager takes a two-year job in the UK, but is still employed by the parent office); inpatriates (coming from a subsidiary into headquarters – in our example a UK manager taking a two-year contract to work in IBM in the USA but still employed through the British office); hybrid arrangements or on local conditions, where a foreign national decides to be employed directly by the local organisation.

REFLECTIVE ACTIVITY 3.7

Your organisation, a UK-based telecoms company employing 100 people, wants to expand its market share in South Africa, and opens a dedicated office in Johannesburg as part of its long-term strategy. The office will provide the hub for future training of local employees. Advise the organisation on which strategy would achieve its aims to introduce the headquarters culture and ethos in terms of work practices to the new office. The current HR function is served by one consultant with part-time administration support. Which of the following approaches would you advise and why?

- Use a two-year long-term assignment, traditional expatriate package.
- Use a short-term assignment.
- Hire someone locally and provide them with some headquarters training.
- Employ someone from the headquarters on local terms and conditions.

It is useful at this point to highlight the various staffing strategies that global organisations utilise. Influences towards staffing strategies were first addressed by Perlmutter (1969) and later extended to provide the following approaches to global staffing (Heenan and Perlmutter 1979):

- *Ethnocentric* – strategic decisions are made by the headquarters by PCN expatriates. Therefore it is accepted that all policies and practices emanate from the headquarters. Arguably, the advantage is that qualified managers are available from the home country (precluding any local labour shortage). However, this approach does limit the opportunity to promote HCNs to senior managerial positions, thus risking the loss of staff with this potentially short-term view.
- *Polycentric* – generally the operations would be managed by HCNs with the intention that they remain in the host country, precluding the use of expensive expatriates from

the parent company. There are disadvantages to this approach in the limiting of assignments by home or host, reducing knowledge transfer and management.

- *Geocentric* – this approach seeks to resource the best person for the position regardless of their nationality.
- *Regiocentric* – some autonomy is reflected in this approach towards decision-making. This approach is likely to facilitate more local responsiveness towards operation and form regional boundaries according to geographic location, such as Eastern Europe, the Mediterranean, Northern USA, etc.

Both polycentric and regiocentric approaches allow for more local responsiveness, with less corporate integration. However, the danger is that there is knowledge being built in subsidiaries by HCNs which the parent does not benefit from, at a risk of losing competitive edge.

Many of these strategies ask people to work overseas. The term 'expatriate' refers to someone who is temporarily assigned to an overseas location from their home organisation. Some organisations refer to such individuals as 'international assignees'. Traditionally, expatriate assignments are considered to fall into either long-term assignments over 12 months to a maximum of four years; short-term assignments lasting three to 12 months; or business trips typically lasting no longer than three months.

Long-term assignments are considered to be over 12 months in duration and offer a full compensation package whereby the expatriate is provided host housing, living allowances, removal services, etc. Often in long-term assignments a partner and children will be included in arrangements. In terms of cost it is generally accepted that an assignment will cost the organisation three to four times the expatriate's salary. PricewaterhouseCoopers (2012) predict that there will be a further 50 per cent growth in international assignments by 2012. Their research highlights that the use of on average 18-month assignments has become the norm, rather than the expensive traditional long-term assignments.

REFLECTIVE ACTIVITY 3.8

If the costs for the use of expatriates are so high, what arguments are there for such assignments to be used by organisations?

The rationale for an overseas assignment should always be considered. MNEs often favour a long-term assignment when the objective is to commence business operation in an overseas location. However, a smaller organisation may not have the resources to utilise a long-term assignment as that individual is intrinsic to the home company. Therefore the strategy of staffing may well differ depending on the size of the organisation.

AGILENT TECHNOLOGIES

CASE STUDY 3.2

The move to reduce costs has seen a decline in the number of long-term assignments, with organisations utilising short-term assignments instead. Agilent Technologies has seen an overall reduction in headcount in line with many MNEs over the last few years in order to reduce costs. This led to reducing its multi-million-dollar expatriate programme (Workforce Management 2004).

In order to understand the cost involved in its expatriate programme, Agilent outsourced the administration of its expatriates. In 2000 Agilent had approximately 1,000 expatriates, costing $72 million. Over the next three years, the company reduced the number of expatriates to around 300 expatriates. In order to achieve this large reduction in headcount Agilent looked at alternative ways of resourcing positions, favouring the local market. In addition, a review of its policy and expatriate package has seen large-scale reduction in benefits offered, to reduce costs by 70 per cent to $23 million.

Agilent's example raises some interesting points. Until the company decided to outsource its expatriate programme it had not considered the actual costs; it knew expatriates were expensive but did not realise the extent. The challenge of tracking expatriates is echoed by many MNEs (Workforce Management 2004).

Questions

1   How would you recommend Agilent assess the success of its programme, other than the reduction of cost for its expatriate programme?

2   What do you think the effect of reducing the number of expatriate opportunities could have been at Agilent head office?

3   How would you be able to track such effects?

4   What effect might you want to look for in the various subsidiaries?

5   How might you measure the impact?

SHORT-TERM ASSIGNMENTS

The move towards cost reduction has contributed towards the increase in short-term assignments. Instead of providing an expatriate package that allows the employee to take their immediate family on assignment, the organisation supports only the assignee. Costs are saved by precluding education costs as well as reduced housing costs (as the expatriate is not accompanied by their family) and further allowances associated with a long-term assignment such as family healthcare insurance. Thus the employee is sent overseas with minimal support and cost.

 REFLECTIVE ACTIVITY 3.9

Consider this description:

Avaya Inc, a provider of communication systems, has started sending more employees on short-term assignments. Typically assignments last for six months and are managed as a business trip. The employee stays in a hotel or company apartment and is reimbursed for meals and trips home every other month, eliminating the need to pay costly housing allowances and costs related to moving the employee's family (Workforce Management 2004).

Assume the previous system was one of two-year assignments accompanied by a family.

Questions

1   What effect would this change have had on the type of applicants for the job?

2   What effect would the change have had on recipients of the services of these assignees in the host country?

3   Would any of these changes worry you from an HR perspective?

4   How would you advise Avaya to proceed?

THIRD-COUNTRY NATIONALS

A TCN is an individual who works for an international organisation and whose nationality is different from that of the company, and of the country, in which the organisation operates. For example, a UK manager working for a Spanish subsidiary of an American company. The advantages of TCNs from the company's point of view are that they need to provide very limited additional assistance, such as housing, and education tax, for a restricted period. There is an increased trend towards this type of employee and companies such as Avaya have increased TCNS by over 50 per cent during the last decade (Workforce Management 2004).

LOCALISATION

Another alternative to an expatriate assignment is the use of localisation. This is where expatriates move permanently to local terms and conditions, and it has seen an increase over the last decade (Harry and Collings 2012). This could be at the end of a long- or short-term assignment at the choice of the individual, or that an individual was sent on assignment with the expectation that they would localise with minimal support from the company. The move towards recruiting expatriates on the basis that they will localise from the beginning is not new, especially within the 20-year-old-plus market. However, what has changed is the push to hire employees locally and not use expatriates at all – here the local employer might take on someone who lives only miles from the parent company but who is never employed by the parent. The benefit to the organisation is the significant saving in expatriate terms and conditions, especially education and housing costs. An emerging trend of hybrid packages allows expatriates access to some of the expatriate 'package' initially to set them up in the new country and then gradually remove the benefits during the year, such as help with rented accommodation.

SELF-INITIATED EXPATRIATES

A relatively underexplored area is the increase in self-initiated expatriates (Howe-Walsh and Schyns 2010). A self-initiated expatriate independently moves to another country for employment. As such, a self-initiated expatriate does not receive any additional support from their home country employer. However, there are opportunities to manage this growing pool of resources more effectively. Research has shown that self-initiated expatriates themselves note several combined reasons for pursuing an overseas appointment: career development; location of vacancy; no family ties; dissatisfaction with current lifestyle; timing (Fitzgerald and Howe-Walsh 2008).

Who manages these types of staffing arrangements can often become blurred. Whilst the self-initiated expatriate will be treated as an ordinary new joiner, other support mechanisms can be put in place to support their initial move. There are additional considerations to explore regarding the level of support the HR function can offer during the recruitment phase. In a traditional expatriate assignment services such as cultural training would be offered prior to the assignment.

Howe-Walsh and Schyns (2010) show how different types of adjustment require the use of differing HR practices. In order to make the most of self-initiated expatriates, consideration of how the organisation can aid their initial adjustment can provide a strategic advantage over companies that do not provide support by attracting good candidates. The points below are highlighted as areas to explore in order to improve the process of recruitment and retaining self-initiated expatriates:

Recruitment strategy

Developing the reputation of the organisation as an employer of choice attracts candidates, thus assisting with recruitment of talent (Glen 2006). Selecting the right candidates poses challenges for any organisation. Self-initiated expatriates offer additional benefits to the organisation during the early stages of their employment as they are already receptive to working in an overseas location, so the likelihood of problems to adjust to the local culture are reduced (Tharenou 2008). In addition, they have chosen the organisation and the position offered, rather than 'being sent' on an assignment.

Training and mentoring

Whilst new joiners are often provided with some sort of induction training it is unlikely that a self-initiated expatriate will be offered any cultural training for reasons outlined above. However, the benefits of mentoring should be considered. One area in which a mentor can provide assistance is in helping the self-initiated expatriate to gain a greater working knowledge of the organisation, again akin to the services offered to any new joiner.

Non-work support

The types of activities that HR would traditionally support for an expatriate should also be considered in terms of self-initiated expatriates. Finding accommodation can be one of the most stressful parts of relocation. HR can provide support in terms of facilitating the search for properties as well as assistance with tenancy agreements. Other forms of support include: opening bank accounts; social security and residence registration; communication connections; and expatriate social groups. When facilitated, these types of support enable the self-initiated expatriate (SIE) to start work faster and add value to the organisation.

GLOBAL/INTERNATIONAL HR AND THE SME

The discussion so far has revolved around MNEs. Arguably, however, much business conducted today is undertaken by SMEs, many of whom have a global dimension, often levered through the Internet, but with implications for the HR function (Engle *et al* 2008). As IHRM literature is mainly focused upon MNEs, there is an argument that transferability of HRM practices from MNEs to SMEs is limited (Festing 2007).

Drawing upon the research of MNE organisations, SMEs pose different challenges (Anderson and Skinner 1999). SMEs are more dependent upon environmental situations in different countries. Anderson and Boocock (2002) suggest that this includes:

● The importance of the founder/owner. Within any organisation there are links to how the organisation is perceived and their leader (Festing 2007). Within an SME the owners' entrepreneurial style and the way they conduct business can be part of the attraction of working for the organisation.

- Recruitment, selection and retention within an SME is likely to be managed without the assistance of an HR function as much more informal processes are utilised.

The most striking difference between MNEs and SMEs is that the SMEs do not have the same HRD infrastructure capability, as mentioned above. Therefore, sending managers overseas to open or start new business ventures is not supported by an HR function locally or any specialists at the parent organisation. Being able to construct value-adding arguments for managing a limited number of staff overseas becomes more difficult in such circumstances (Bowen and Ostroff 2004).

WHO IS RESONSIBLE FOR INTERNATIONAL HR POLICY?

Traditionally within MNEs, IHR policy and practice is undertaken by specialists, either as part of the HR team or partially or fully outsourced, as outlined in Case Study 3.2. The decision of what policies the company chooses to adopt towards its international workforce ultimately rests with the organisation's overall strategy. Nearly two-thirds of companies (64 per cent) have no specific procedures in place to measure the success of their expatriate benefit programmes (Mercer 2008/09). Thus from the outset there are issues with retention and monitoring the expatriate's career path.

DEVOLUTION TO LINE MANAGERS

With increased devolution to line managers it is important to consider the perceptions of more than one stakeholder. We have already noted that HR delivery of international services may be internal to the HR function, a separate specialised function or outsourced. It is increasingly becoming the norm with MNEs that HR policy and practice delivery is undertaken by the line manager (Perry and Kulik 2008). In an international context, the likelihood within an MNE is that there will be a duplication of stakeholders within the home country and host country. The multiple stakeholders involved in managing individuals across more than one country add another dimension to managing people. A greater understanding of the stakeholders highlights the necessity for clear and transparent strategy supported by HR policy and practice.

CONCLUSION

In concluding this chapter, one can see that approaches for delivering support for managing and leading people becoming more complex as the organisation expands in terms of the number of employees, the scope of the organisation, and its geographical reach. We have examined how the emphasis on what an HR practitioner actually does varies with the size, stage in development and sector of the organisation being served. Adding value from HR is possible in all circumstances. Although much is made of HR aligning with the strategy of the organisation (eg Wang and Shyu 2008), this becomes more difficult as the organisation grows and the physical and psychological distance between HR and decision-makers increases. No doubt an area for development in research is the political skills HR practitioners need to develop in order to influence and ensure that their value-adding ideas are tried by the organisation (Dany *et al* 2008), and that their work receives sufficient profile to make sure it is perceived as value-adding (Sears 2010).

We have seen that cutting costs through outsourcing is a common trend, and likely to continue as vertical integration is lessened. HR is not immune from these trends, but if it is to remain a strategic component of success, aspects of HR need to be kept in-house (Woodall *et al* 2009). The level of outsourcing provides many varied career opportunities for HR practitioners working in providers of services. There is a danger, though, that career paths in these directions may be limited to 'being efficient' only in cost-effective terms rather than adding value in more subtle ways.

Less and less are international issues the prerogative of large multinationals. Globalised job markets, as well as the opportunities that the Internet provides for selling products and services abroad, means that complexity can arrive sooner rather than later for many in the HR function.

KEY LEARNING POINTS

- The HR function adds value to the organisation in a number of ways through delivering business strategy.
- The HR function adds value, but how it does so, and who is perceived as adding value, is complex and sometimes a function of internal politics and the perceptions of line managers.
- The way in which HR adds value changes as the organisation grows, and also between sectors.
- Outsourcing aspects of HR is common, but needs to be done carefully to ensure the organisation does not lose competitive edge.
- Internationalisation is a current issue for those who recruit, and for those involved in mobilising staff between countries.
- The degree of control from the parent company in the area of international HR presents a challenge which needs to be balanced depending on the context.

CASE STUDY 3.3

INTERCONTINENTAL HOTELS GROUP

Asia is a rapidly developing continent and the ubiquitous 'war for talent' is accentuated for Intercontinental Hotels Group (IHG), with rival hotels from China constantly approaching staff with job offers. HR's biggest challenge, according to Ricky Wong, HR director, IHG Hong Kong, is finding and keeping the right people in such an aggressive labour market.

'I'm really concerned that our staff will be poached by competitors,' Wong says. 'Managers from hotels in Macau come to our hotel and sit in the lobby to check out the staff they want to poach. The particular hotel I'm talking about has 3,000 rooms and they need experienced managers.'

So where will they find them? 'They'll find them at the five-star hotels in Hong Kong – hotels like ours,' says Wong. As

a result of such measures, he takes career development very seriously. Many of IHG Hong Kong's employees have been at the company for several years, and while he cannot promise promotions, on-the-job learning with greater participation in management decisions is a must to keep staff engaged.

'Many employees are looking for personal development. They can suggest how to do the job better, and we encourage that. They can disagree with managers – and that's not easy in the traditionally hierarchical culture of Asia. We "allow" them to disagree and to have a sense of involvement,' says Wong. This mature approach to managing employees seems to be working. IHG's staff turnover is at 12 per cent, a hefty 8 per cent lower than that of its main Hong Kong competitor (another five-star hotel), according to Wong.

Source: XpertHR (2008)

Questions

1   Identify and appraise the attitudes and approaches adopted in this excerpt.

2   What other tactics might be employed to further enhance the achievement at IHG?

3   In what ways is the HR strategy adding value to the organisation?

REVIEW QUESTIONS

1   Do you think HR professionals at all levels can demonstrate value-added, or is this an issue only for people at the top?

2   What would you see as the challenges of someone changing job from being an HR business partner in the private sector to one in the public sector? How would you suggest such an individual prepares for their new role?

3   Assuming there are financial gains for providing an outsourced HR service, what other parameters would you consider when evaluating this issue?

4   Why is adding an international dimension to one's operation so challenging for HR? Use the example of a UK organisation setting up a sales office in Canada to illustrate your ideas. In this operation some local Canadian staff would be employed, but need head office assistance during the set-up period.

EXPLORE FURTHER

Becker, B. and Huselid, M.A. (2006) Strategic human resource management: where do we go from here? *Journal of Management*. Vol. 32, No. 6, pp898–925. This article is a very effective overview of the strategic issues within HR. Their application of business strategy into the undertaking of HR roles is both thought-provoking and holds a list of key texts, should readers wish to pursue the forms of HR delivery within organisations.

Boselie, P., Brewster, C. and Paauwe, J. (2009) In search of balance-managing the dualities of HRM. *Personnel Review*. Vol. 38, No. 5, pp461–471. This paper provides an excellent overview of strategic HR issues and constructs in contemporary thinking with an excellent reading base for further exploration. This can be compared to the CIPD-sponsored research (Sears 2010), which is drawn from large organisations where the notion that practice outstrips thinking and academic work is put forward.

Howe-Walsh, L.J. and Schyns, B. (2010) Self-Initiated Expatriates: Implications for HRM. *International Journal of Human Resource Management*. Vol. 21, No. 2, pp260–273. This contribution gives useful insights into the developing area of self-initiated expatriates – a field which is likely to become more important for recruiters in all organisations and one which is not often studied.

Sparrow, P.R. (2012) Globalising the international mobility function: the role of emerging markets, flexibility and strategic delivery models. *International Journal of Human Resource Management.* Vol. 23, No 12, pp2404–2427. This paper reports on the international HR function and how IHR supports globalisation.

Tharenou, P. (2008) 'Self-Initiated Careers'. In Baugh, G. and Sullivan, S.E. (2008) *Maintaining focus energy and options over the career.* Charlotte, NC: Information Age Publishing, pp197–224.

Woodall, J., Scott-Jackson, W., Newham, T. and Gurney, M. (2009) Managing the decision to outsource human resources. *Personnel Review.* Vol. 38, No. 3, pp236–252. This article provides a very good literature review of outsourcing HR and a fascinating study of practice in contemporary UK-based organisations. Tracking through their references, readers will find key evidence regarding the need for HR to not only undertake an effective role, but also to be seen to do so.

CHAPTER 4

Professionalism and Ethics in Managing People

Charlotte Rayner and Richard Christy

LEARNING OUTCOMES

After reading this chapter, you should be able to:

- understand the concept of business ethics

- explain the difference between the duties, consequences and virtues approaches to ethics

- comprehend what may be meant by an 'ethical dimension' to the management and leadership of HR

- identify the link between ethics, equal opportunities and diversity management

- appreciate the role of ethical codes of conduct

- understand the role of professional associations

- consider the implications for professional leadership in HRM.

OVERVIEW

Professionalism is not just what you do; it is also the principles behind what you do. People in organisations detect signs of what is acceptable and the tenets by which the organisation works from their line manager, as well as their basic upbringing (Wiley 2000). HR practitioners play a key role in standard-setting. Naturally they get involved when situations go wrong, but their key work is in preventing misbehaviour through their own role modelling, the advice they give to line managers, and the type of attention they pay to policies.

In this chapter we will examine ethics in general terms and the professional leadership that HR practitioners can bring. We will suggest that being ethical is part of a professional identity. We begin this chapter by considering ethics in a general sense and applying ethical decision-making to the workplace. We use a variety of examples including an illustration of equal opportunities and the potential for positive discrimination – no doubt a debate set to run for some time. Finally we focus on the role of the HR practitioner as a professional, examining the key elements of professionalism (including the role of the CIPD) and discussing some contemporary ideas about the HR profession.

INTRODUCTION

One way to think about business strategy is to see it as the way in which an organisation deploys its resources in order to achieve its goals. To be successful in a changing environment, an organisation needs to keep all of its resources aligned to the chosen strategy, which may involve acquiring new resources, developing existing resources and disposing of resources that are no longer of value to the organisation and its strategy (Caligiuri *et al* 2010). These days, the phrase 'human resources' is in general use, so we might pose the question: is it acceptable for an organisation to treat its human resources in the same way as other non-human resources? If not, why not, and what rules should apply?

Thinking about these issues is important because the ethics of managing human resources will depend to some extent on the nature of the relationship between an employer and its employees. A firm's delivery van, for example, could be defined as part of its 'transportation resources'. This van is exclusively available to the firm, can be used (within the law) as the firm sees fit, can be rented out or sold when no longer needed or scrapped when no longer useful to the firm. Is the same true of the firm's human resources? Of course not – but why not?

The first point to make is that employers do not actually own their human resources, otherwise the word would be 'slavery' rather than 'employment'. The actual arrangement is a contractual one between two parties, who choose to take on certain rights and duties towards each other (see also Chapter 11). It is quite true, of course, that human resources (employees) can be motivated and otherwise persuaded to act in the interest of the employer, sometimes to an astonishing degree, but they remain individuals who choose to act in that way. This aspect of the relationship, however obvious, is central to effective HRM.

It is also usually true that the employment relationship is a continuing one. A continuing relationship brings benefits for employers, in terms of reduced transaction costs, such as recruitment and training. It also brings benefits for employees, for example by providing a more stable income stream. Furthermore, from an ethical point of view, the employment relationship needs to be seen as different from other buyer–seller relationships because of the great asymmetry of power between most employing organisations and individuals. Employers are usually economically more powerful than individual employees and have ready access to far more specialised resources: it is perhaps not surprising that laws and other controls have emerged to provide special protection for the 'sellers' in employment transactions (Gilmore and Williams 2012).

Above and beyond these practical points about people as employees, there is a strong sense that humans are special: that they have rights that other inanimate resources do not have, purely by virtue of being human (we will side-step the question of animal rights in this chapter). Humans are individuals and citizens as well as employees, meaning that they can reasonably demand to be treated in certain ways by employers, whether or not those rights are reinforced by law.

Thinking about the nature and purpose of the employer–employee relationship helps to illuminate how that relationship should be conducted ethically (by both parties). Before examining how ethics can be applied to the main aspects of HRM, we review briefly the fundamental perspectives on ethics.

APPROACHES TO ETHICS

The study of ethics seeks a systematic and defensible understanding of good and bad. In Western philosophy, this is usually considered to have resulted in three main perspectives on ethics:

- *Ethics seen as duties*: things that should be done or refrained from, because they are good or bad in their own right.
- *Ethics seen as consequences*: good acts are those that lead to good results, and bad acts are those that lead to bad results.
- *Ethics as virtues*: the desirable qualities or character traits that are possessed by good people.

For a long time, strong arguments have been made to support each of these main outlooks and most readers will recognise the role that each plays in day-to-day ethical reasoning. However, the question of what is good and bad in human behaviour remains complex and difficult, with the possibility of contradictory answers from the different perspectives (Crane and Matten 2010).

Duty-based views of ethics (known as 'deontological' ethics) see goodness or badness as inherent in the act itself, rather than in the consequences. If lying is bad, for example, it is because the act of deliberately saying something that the speaker knows to be false is bad in itself, plain and simple. Deontological ethical frameworks offer a set of duties or principles which must be respected, irrespective of the consequences. The German philosopher Kant (1724–1804) has been one of the leading voices in duty-based ethics: in his view, ethics are based on the duties that we owe each other as fellow members of a rational species. We should, for example, only act in ways that could reasonably be adopted by anyone in similar circumstances (which is close in meaning to the golden rule: 'do as you would be done by'). Keeping promises, for example, is required, because not to do so would render the idea of a promise absurd. Also, people should always be treated as being of value in themselves, rather than simply used as a means to achieving someone else's goals. In other words, people should be treated with respect for their equal status as moral beings and not subjected to degrading or humiliating treatment, coercion or abuse.

The general problems with an exclusively duties-based view of ethics involve:

- excessive rigidity, which can result from taking no account of possible consequences of following a principle or duty
- complexity: if principles are made more detailed in an attempt to deal with the wide range of real-life situations, then the resultant algorithms can become very unwieldy
- priority: which principles should take precedence over which others (and what is the new principle that governs this precedence)?

Those who see ethics only in terms of consequences look for good or bad in the results of the act, rather than in the act itself. A deliberate untruth, for example, is neither good nor bad in itself – it depends on the consequences. From this point of view, the ethics of stealing, or even killing, can only be judged by asking what happens as a result of the particular act. One familiar form of consequentialism is utilitarianism, which looks for the greatest good for the greatest number. In its original form, utilitarianism tries to assess the change in happiness for everyone affected by a proposed act (later forms sought to consider the consequences for those affected if the proposed action were to become commonplace). There are two main types of difficulty in an exclusively utilitarian view of ethics:

- Methodology: while measuring changes to happiness may sound like a good idea, it is extraordinarily difficult to do so with any precision or consistency, as a moment's thought will confirm.
- Justice: as Mackie (1977) points out, the problem with this approach is that it can allow undeserved bad consequences for one group to be offset by good consequences for another group, as long as the net change in happiness is positive. This can be potentially very bad news for minorities, in particular.

The contrasting views of duty-based and consequences-based ethics are reflected in the quote ascribed to Machiavelli: 'The end justifies the means.' 'Ends' are results and 'means' are principles or methods, and the argument between the two views has been running for centuries.

REFLECTIVE ACTIVITY 4.1

You are running late for a meeting in which job redundancies are being discussed, and you wish to protect your own department from this threat. The only parking space available near the meeting location is restricted for disabled access (you do not have a disabled sticker).

Confronted with this dilemma, explain your thought processes and actions with reference to both the duty-based and consequential approaches to ethics.

Virtue ethics is a separate way of thinking about good and bad. Virtues are desirable character traits, exhibited by good people. For Aristotle (384–322 BC), human virtues are those qualities that allow us to fulfil our highest purpose as humans: these qualities lie between undesirable extremes (as 'courage' lies between 'cowardice' and 'foolhardiness') and wisdom is required to recognise the virtuous approach.

REFLECTIVE ACTIVITY 4.2

In recent years, a number of 'ethical' investment products have been marketed, which explicitly avoid any contact with businesses in a potentially wide range of categories (for example, tobacco, armaments and gambling). To what extent should the purpose of an organisation be taken into account in judging the ethics of those who work in that organisation? For example, is it still virtuous to display loyalty towards an organisation whose outputs are seen by some as bad? Give examples to illustrate the points you make.

The virtues approach is about how people should live their lives, in order to realise their highest potential. This takes time and experience: rather than proposing a series of rules or principles, the main way of becoming virtuous is to study the lives of good people and learn to imitate them.

REFLECTIVE ACTIVITY 4.3

Special people, special treatment?

When Apple co-founder Steve Jobs died in 2011 at the age of 56, the commentaries discussed his charisma, dynamism and enormous achievements, many of which can genuinely be said to have changed the way we live. Jobs dominated the company, leading and driving its product strategy and providing it with a very charismatic public face: Apple product launches were compared to rock concerts. Amongst the millions of words about him on the Internet, however, adjectives like 'abrasive' and 'demanding' are more likely to feature than 'easy-going' or 'tolerant'. Jobs' many admirers point out that he set himself very high standards of perfection and was strongly intolerant of those who did not, or could not rise to the same level. When he was disappointed, those who had fallen short of his expectations were left in no doubt: the frustration and anger were plain to all present.

In some other organisations, behaviour like this by the boss would be viewed with concern and disapproval, but some might argue that Apple's extraordinary commercial and innovative success was inextricably linked to Jobs' personality.

Questions

1   To what extent do you think that this situation is unusual?

2   In this case, what are the ethical factors that need to be considered?

3   What should HR do in such circumstances?

ETHICS IN THE WORKPLACE

How useful are these ethical perspectives in thinking about the ethics of managing people at work? Plainly, all three approaches have some relevance:

- Most would agree that there are some ways of treating employees that are just plain wrong, whether or not they are also illegal. Bullying and intimidation, for example, are plainly unacceptable. Duties-based thinking also underlies the establishment of employees' rights (and corresponding duties on employers).
- Similarly, an organisation can hardly avoid considering the consequences of proposed actions, for the organisation, for its employees and for third parties.
- Discussions of leadership often consider what are, in effect, virtues. Yukl (2009) describes the 'qualities' or 'traits' approach to understanding leadership and lists characteristics such as self-confidence, initiative and self-belief. These qualities are very like the idea of virtues – each could be seen as a desirable point between undesirable extremes, for example.

However, if we define business ethics as the study of good and bad in business conduct (an approach that can be extended to non-business organisations as well), then the ethical approaches that have been developed for personal ethics may not be adequate to apply at the 'business' level, because organisations are not people. Organisations are different from completely inanimate objects for two reasons:

- they do behave with intent, in pursuing their objectives through strategies
- they are, from one point of view, groups of individual people, who singly or jointly make the organisation's decisions and who do so as human beings, with the ability to reason ethically. Employees generally do not leave their own values at the door when they go to work and they retain a capacity to imagine the effects on other people of the choices they make at work.

REFLECTIVE ACTIVITY 4.4

Utilitarian thinking

In recent years, there have been many reports of financial services and other companies 'outsourcing' call-centre or back-office work from the UK to lower-cost Anglophone locations such as India or Sri Lanka. This has led to controversy, since the outsourcing initiatives are often accompanied by redundancies in the UK.

This phenomenon provides an opportunity to explore the utilitarian approach to ethics. Imagine a hypothetical case of a large UK-based insurance company that is proposing to outsource its customer service call centre from a medium-sized town in the north of England to Bangalore. The UK centre is to be closed and there will be several hundred redundancies.

Make a list of the groups of people who will be affected by this initiative and then:

- describe the likely nature of the effects for each group; and
- take a guess at the likely size of each group.

Questions

1   How useful is this approach in illuminating the ethical implications of the proposal?

2   Is it possible to judge the 'greatest good for the greatest number'?

3   What difficulties would arise in trying to make this analysis more detailed and precise?

4   Putting these methodological difficulties to one side, how satisfactory does the utilitarian approach seem to be as a way of assessing good and bad in this case? If it seems to be unsatisfactory or incomplete, what is missing?

THE PURPOSE OF AN EMPLOYING ORGANISATION

An important additional factor to consider, when thinking about the ethics of HRM, is that of the aims and purpose of the employing organisation (Ellesworth 2002). Organisational purpose relates directly to ethics in HRM because organisations can be taken to employ people primarily in order to pursue that purpose. The idea of organisational purpose is an important one in trying to understand the ethics of actions taken by an organisation: an investment bank, for example, has a very different purpose (or set of purposes) from a university. Some types of organisation have multiple purposes: local governments, for example, have many different demands to satisfy, while others, such as small businesses, are in principle simpler.

Business organisations generally might be thought to have a simpler purpose, but this is a subject of some controversy. One school of thought defines the business purpose as that of maximising owner (shareholder) wealth, on the basis that this is the aim of shareholders in investing their money. There is therefore a duty on the directors of the company to pursue this aim in their running of the company, and coincidentally a 2009 CIPD Employee Outlook report found that 49 per cent of participants saw their purpose as 'making the most profits for investors and owners' (CIPD 2009a).

Friedman (1970) provides a succinct and often-cited summary of the view that the social responsibility of business is to make as much money as possible for the owners, within the law and the rules of competition. If this definition of purpose is accepted, then for a company to spend shareholder funds in ways that cannot be shown to be consistent with maximising owner wealth is unethical. This amounts to an ethical objection to some of what companies do under the heading of corporate social responsibility (CSR), unless, of course, the CSR programme has the aim or effect of increasing or safeguarding the company's profit (see below).

Sternberg (2000) proposes a three-way test of business ethics, in which an action proposed by a business has to be:

- consistent with the business purpose (which is defined in a similar way to Friedman)
- consistent with the requirement of ordinary decency (eg not cheating, stealing, coercing and so on)
- consistent with the requirement for distributive justice (that rewards should be proportional to contribution, in order to reflect fairness).

However, many define the business purpose much more broadly, suggesting that a business has a wider responsibility to the society in which it operates and that the task of a manager must recognise additional duties associated with the needs and claims of various stakeholder groups (eg Springett 2004). In the original sense, stakeholders were disinterested individuals who safeguarded the stake in a bet, but the word has now become used to denote any groups with an interest in an organisation – those that may affect or be affected by the actions of the business. In business organisations, shareholders are one such group, but so are employees, customers, the local community, suppliers and so on. Effective public sector organisations usually have a keen sense of their stakeholders. The task of a manager, from this point of view, is to 'balance' stakeholder needs, which provides a very different ethical yardstick for a business from Friedman's view (and some practical difficulty in knowing when that balance has been achieved) and enables similarities to be drawn between profit-making and non-profit-making concerns.

Donaldson and Preston (1995) discuss the various ways in which businesses can respond to stakeholder groups, pointing out that a company may decide to engage with stakeholder groups because it is a more effective way of making money for shareholders. Alternatively, a 'normative' approach to stakeholder theory recognises duties towards stakeholders that must be discharged even if those actions are not clearly consistent with maximising owner wealth. One example of the latter might be a company's involvement in local community projects, in which the expenditure cannot be shown to be maximising owner wealth. This is not say that there will be no commercial benefits from this type of expenditure – customers may approve of the venture, for example, and so switch more of their purchases to the sponsoring company – but it may be very difficult to convert those benefits into forecast cashflows. In a normative view of stakeholder theory, an organisation will acknowledge duties to get involved in this way, even if the commercial benefits are partly unclear.

Since employees are one stakeholder group, the potential importance of the distinction between a shareholder and stakeholder approach should be clear. In the shareholder view, employees are one of the resources deployed by the organisation in its efforts to maximise owner wealth, usually in competition with other organisations trying to appeal to the same market. In the stakeholder view, the employee stakeholder group is one of many whose interests and needs are part of the organisation's agenda, to be balanced in some way with the needs of other groups. At first glance, the shareholder approach to HRM may seem to require the lowest possible salaries, barely legal working conditions and a generally oppressive and exploitative approach to the management of employees. However, the first impression may be misleading: the shareholder-focused company can only make money for its owners by successfully developing and marketing products and services in competition with other suppliers. It will therefore have to find ways of attracting, retaining and motivating good staff, in order to stay competitive. A stakeholder approach to HRM might make different claims about its motives, but on any given day might also look remarkably similar to the HRM practised by a shareholder-focused company.

As a special survey in *The Economist* (Crook 2005) pointed out, corporate social responsibility (CSR) has become an accepted part of the corporate dialogue with the rest of the world although the debate on the scope of activities continues (eg Porter and Kramer 2006). As Crook comments:

> It would be a challenge to find a recent annual report of any big international company that justifies the firm's existence merely in terms of profit, rather than 'service to the community'. Such reports often talk proudly of efforts to improve society and safeguard the environment – by restricting emissions of greenhouse gases from the staff kitchen, say, or recycling office stationery – before turning hesitantly to less important matters, such as profits. Big firms nowadays are called upon to be good corporate citizens, and they all want to show that they are. (2005, p3)

Readers would be correct to infer from the sardonic tone of this quote that *The Economist* special survey raised some concerns about the way in which the notion of CSR is developing. As the report suggests, a prominent CSR programme is no guarantee of a well-managed and robust company, something that might be observed in the fallout from the 2007/08 global financial crisis. Companies are now called upon to report according to a 'triple bottom line', in which economic results (profits) are joined by effects on the natural environment and on social well-being. This raises methodological difficulties: while there are clear conventions for measuring profitability, it is much more difficult to find generally accepted yardsticks for environmental protection or social justice (Vilanova *et al* 2009).

However, assuming that these methodological difficulties can be overcome in due course, concerns are also expressed about the principle of this type of CSR. Friedman (1970) expressed doubts that companies have the expertise to undertake non-business projects and opined that social projects should be the domain of elected governments, rather than unelected boards of directors. This perspective echoes Adam Smith's concept of the 'invisible hand', through which individuals pursuing their own interest are guided to benefit society, even though they had no such intention. However, CSR in its broader sense is now the accepted orthodoxy: for as long as customers expect the firms they buy from to give an account of their effects on society and the environment, then prudent companies will be likely to comply (Porter and Kramer 2006). Many companies are genuinely seeking to do much more than toe the line in their CSR programmes, of course, with clear positive effects for many communities.

EQUAL OPPORTUNITIES AND ETHICS

To discriminate originally meant to distinguish between one thing and another. Strictly speaking, therefore, the word 'discrimination' is ethically neutral – indeed, HRM activities such as recruitment or promotion must entail discrimination (between the one that is to be appointed and the others, for example); see also Chapter 9. However, discrimination has recently acquired a pejorative sense, alluding to the exercise of prejudice, which is clearly unethical, and often illegal. In this sense of the word, it is 'unfair' or 'irrelevant' discrimination that is objectionable: the introduction into the process of factors that have no connection with the work to be done. Discriminating against lazy or dishonest people is thus acceptable (and perhaps even advisable), but discriminating on the basis of gender, ethnic origin or age is unethical.

The principle of equal opportunity (EO) requires that people should be recruited on the basis of their ability to do the job, with no other factors intruding into the decision (Noon in Beardwell and Claydon 2010). In what ways can this be said to be ethically desirable (ie whether or not it is also legally obligatory)? In this case, both duty-based and consequentialist ethical arguments can be made to support the equal opportunities principle. The duty-based ethics point is clear: to treat employees on some basis other than EO (for example, to allow ageist or homophobic sentiments to enter into decisions about them) is to fail to show respect for their equal status as fellow members of the moral community. As discussed by Boatright (2000), prejudice also treats people only as members of groups, rather than affording them the individual treatment that they should reasonably expect. Making recruitment, promotion or redundancy decisions on the basis of prejudice is therefore manifestly unjust to those who are disadvantaged.

From the employer's point of view, a strong consequences-based case in favour of EO can also be made. Organisations that rule out candidates from a whole group on the basis of prejudice are depriving themselves of a significant pool of talent in the labour market, and this failure to engage with diverse groups is likely to lead to non-optimal performance (Von Bergen *et al* 2005, Hunt 2007). Organisations may therefore be damaged by the exercise of prejudice, irrespective of any legal penalties to which they may be exposed. However, anti-discrimination legislation is commonplace in modern economies, which suggests that the market-driven response to prejudice has been found to be inadequate. This may be because in real life, some employers might perceive enough scope to exercise their prejudices without significant disadvantage, unless legal penalties were also in prospect. Also, not all employing organisations are subject to competition and thus, in the absence of prohibitive legislation, would suffer little or no penalty for unfair discrimination. Alternatively, a government may find that the theoretically purgative effect of competition is taking too long to eliminate unfair discrimination and decide that legislation is desirable for utilitarian reasons.

It would be wrong, however, to infer from these arguments that equal opportunities is the sole – or even the pre-eminent – ethical principle at play in contemporary HRM. In large numbers of businesses around the world, the owners or managers may regard it as perfectly normal and desirable to prefer to recruit or promote an acceptably competent member of the same family over a better-qualified stranger. This is not the place to debate the relative merits of the two principles, but rather to suggest that EO is often not the sole governing principle in HRM, however strong the deontological and consequence-based arguments in its favour.

Even in Western employing organisations, the EO principle is made more complex by the growing interest in two other ideas – diversity management and so-called 'positive' discrimination, in which measures are taken to improve the chances of a particular group that is seen as being disadvantaged. A moment's thought will show that these two ideas could each have the practical effect of diluting or directly contradicting the EO principle in some cases. This should not be surprising – EO is a proposition about justice in the process of things like deciding on job offers or promotions. However, both diversity management and positive discrimination make separate arguments about justice that start from the observed end result of the process.

Arguments about positive discrimination have been going on for several decades. We review them briefly here because they provide an example of the complexity of ethical arguments in practice, and also because their practice seems to be becoming more prominent in some European countries, having been much more familiar in the United States up to now. For example, the Norwegian government introduced legislation to make it a requirement from 1 January 2008 that 40 per cent of main board seats in public companies should be held by women. This rule, first announced in 2003, was virtually completely achieved by the deadline. In contrast, in 2013 men dominated FTSE 100 boards, although non-executive members fared better. Davies (2013) reported that there were 18 female (compared to 292 male) executive directors in the FTSE 100, and 32 female executive directors in the FTSE 250 (558 males), which he used to illustrate the talent pipeline being constrained, and providing stark comparison to the Norwegian situation.

REFLECTIVE ACTIVITY 4.5

Some see pay gaps between men and women – as well as different levels of board representation – as evidence that EO policies are not working. Others, however, interpret the same evidence differently. For example, Hakim (2011) finds that EO policies have been successful in respect of women's access to the UK labour market: differences between the jobs held by men and women (and consequently the average levels of pay of each group) result from different career aspirations and priorities. HR professionals should perhaps not be dismayed that rigorously applied EO policies do not result in equal outcomes for men and women.

Read Hakim's 2011 work and indicate the extent to which you agree with her that the EO debate

is infused with 'feminist myths'. Give reasons for your conclusions.

In the UK, the Equality Act (2010) includes 'positive action' in certain circumstances in the interests of increased equality (see Jarrett 2011 for explication and discussion) providing measures in which some groups will be given preferential treatment of some sort, in order to address end distributions that are seen as lastingly unfair: in effect, EO in the process of appointment has to be modified or even suspended in some cases, in order to have an end result that is more satisfactorily equal.

Respectable ethical arguments can be made to justify this type of discrimination. Boatright (2000) reviews three main types of argument in favour:

- *Compensation*: some groups have been unjustly discriminated against for a long time and this injustice calls for the compensation that positive discrimination can offer.
- *Equality*: where distributive injustice has been entrenched for a long time, the gap between the majority and the disadvantaged minority may require to be closed through legislative action, in order to allow EO policies to operate fairly.
- *Utilitarian*: positive discrimination in some circumstances can be justified as a means of addressing urgent social problems.

However, the arguments against positive discrimination are also considerable: at the individual level, it can amount to unfair discrimination and each of the arguments about EO discussed above must apply. Those who are (rightly or wrongly) perceived to be 'filling quotas' in recruitment or appointment may also face the problem of unkind (if unspoken) assumptions about their individual abilities and there may also be a risk of being seen to patronise the disadvantaged group as a whole.

Perhaps the vexed question of which type of ethical argument should be given primacy over the others is one that is best left to the interplay of democratic forces in society.

 REFLECTIVE ACTIVITY 4.6

Think of an example where there would be very strong arguments for and against using positive action for recruiting and selecting job applicants.

By contrast, diversity management (DM) as an idea is not centrally concerned with the arguments for and against positive discrimination. The idea of DM is mainly about organisational performance. As one definition explains:

> … we will use the term 'diversity' to refer to differences among people that are likely to affect their acceptance, work performance, satisfaction, or progress in an organisation. When we speak of 'managing diversity', we mean the purposeful use of processes and strategies that make these differences among people into an asset, rather than a liability, for the organisation. (Hays-Thomas 2004, p12)

As the same author later observes, a policy context of affirmative action (such as has applied in the USA since 1965) is relevant to DM, since it will have the effect of increasing the diversity to be managed. However, the idea of DM is that diversity is to be desired by an organisation in its own right, irrespective of any legislative context. The DM proposition is essentially instrumental – learn to promote and manage diversity effectively and your organisation will perform better. The reason for this is that a diverse set of human resources will far better equip an organisation to sense, understand and respond to changes in its business environment, with benefits in terms of successful innovation, better risk management and in greater resilience to environmental turbulence. As such, the proposition seems to be irresistible to a business – who would not want the bottom-line benefits that are seen as the reward for effective DM? Some caution needs to be exercised with this simple equation, however: for example, effective DM is likely to require far more than just lip service and to take time to achieve. This may be one reason why the evidence of bottom line benefits is sometimes mixed, as suggested by Von Bergen *et al* (2005). We should perhaps not be surprised to find that the DM task is complex and that success is unlikely to be instantaneous. In terms of ethical human resource management, DM is a proposition that is mainly justified in terms of its beneficial consequences, although the more respectful treatment of individual employees that can result from effective DM is also desirable from a deontological point of view.

CASE STUDY 4.1

 DIVERSITY AND TALENT AT TESCO

An organisation that does pay attention to diversity issues may be seen, and indeed brand-marketed, as ethically aware. Tesco's chairman and chief executive responded directly to the issue raised by Mervyn Davies' original report about women on boards (see above for a 2013 update) with evidence for them acting to develop a strong pipeline of talent:

'At Tesco, we are proud to be a diverse business and we have always valued the benefits which diversity brings …We aim to continue to increase the proportion of women on our board … and will work towards an aspiration of 25% on our PLC Board by 2015, subject to the availability of candidates with the right skills and experience.'

Source: Chairman's statement on diversity (26 September 2011): www.tescoplc.com/index.asp?pageid=14

Questions

1   What are the potential advantages of an organisation like Tesco actively promoting these aspects of diversity management achievement?

2   What could be the potential problems to such an approach?

3   How could these be constructively addressed?

ETHICS IN BUSINESS – THE ROLE OF HR

The view that 'good ethics means good business' is one that would probably be shared by both shareholder- and stakeholder-focused enthusiasts, although they might well differ on the precise meaning of 'good ethics', as discussed above. If this is so, then all organisations have strong prudential reasons for promoting ethical conduct by their employees. Given the importance of ethical conduct in business, what contribution can or should a human resource professional (HRP) make to an organisation's ethical policy?

There is no doubt that much of the work of HR professionals involves ethical issues. The 'expert' role outlined by Ulrich (1997) has implications for the discussions of legal compliance in this chapter: HR can be valued as keeping those who are directly managing people on track regarding employment law. We have suggested that the law is a minimum requirement and that those organisations which desire to be competitive (in any sense) for people, customers, league tables or funding may be well advised to do more than the law requires and take ethical issues seriously. All HRP roles provide opportunities for extensive impact regarding ethics. Through creating and embedding policies for practice, in areas of recruitment, selection, job evaluation linked to pay, and performance management for example, HRPs have been highly influential in achieving equality for staff in hiring, reward and censure. HR business partners working with line managers are ideally placed at the front line to highlight areas of practice for attention and give informed advice and guidelines to operational staff and managers. As such they can achieve an 'ethical guardian' role for the organisation (Lowry 2006). In many ways one might see ethics as good professional practice as much as 'good business'.

In pursuance of good ethical standards, the CIPD, as the professional association for the UK HR profession, has a Code of Professional Conduct (2012c), to which all members must conform. In this way the CIPD is fulfilling its role as a professional institution. Before we return to the code, it is important to have an idea of the importance of ethical and practice codes in professions.

Perkin's review of professional associations (1989) shows the development of some occupations included a system of quality control whereby users of that occupation could know the practitioner met certain standards. For example, one cannot practise as a medical consultant in most countries without certain qualifications and experience, and neither can one claim to be a 'lawyer' without certain credentials. Professional associations continue to perform the role of providing credibility to their members through the control of membership (Farndale and Brewster 2005) although our understanding of 'professions' is broadening (Hanlon 1998).

The CIPD, like many professional associations (Gilmore and Williams 2007), seeks to raise standards of practice. Embedded in the qualification process are ethical issues and standards of practice which promote 'professionalism' and include the development of ethical understanding. If the HR practitioner can advise and model ethical behaviour, then they can contribute to raising the standards of practice in all managers. This approach does not come without caveats. Given the recent push towards enabling line managers to undertake some functions, one might argue that the HR profession has diluted its exclusive claim for achievements, and in addition many of those practising at board and other senior levels do not have CIPD qualifications or indeed membership (Caldwell 2008, Wright 2008).

In the United States a survey found that although most managers suggested they learned ethical decision-making at home (from their family or church), professional organisations showed a high influence (55 per cent) as did business colleagues (60 per cent) (Wiley 2000). Being a member of the CIPD and 'acting as a professional' entails far more than passing exams, as indicated in the CIPD code (2012c). It includes continuing to update professional knowledge, uphold legal thresholds and behaving with integrity at all times. In addition, CIPD members are required to 'challenge others if they suspect unlawful or unethical conduct or behaviour' (p2). It is clear the CIPD accepts no exceptions to positive professional behaviour in all aspects of working life. Those embracing such standards may use it as a frame for 'professional identity', where the standards become part of their working self (Alvesson and Willmott 2000).

A code of conduct can allow an organisation to signal to its employees or members the standards of behaviour required, sending a clear signal to the outside world: 'these are the standards by which we are happy to be judged'. From the point of view of ethical theories, codes of conduct are certainly partly deontological in nature, since they will usually include principles or duties to be respected by those covered by the code. However, it is usually true that the principles in the code have been developed by senior members of the industry, profession or organisation, based on their extensive experience of the outcomes of different courses of action, which is an example of consequentialist thinking. One reason why a well-written code of conduct can be so valuable to employees is that, at any given time, it may be very difficult to forecast exactly which course of action is going to be in the best interests of the stakeholders, even for individuals who are strongly committed to acting in an ethical way (Foote 2001).

REFLECTIVE ACTIVITY 4.7

A professional code

Locate the CIPD's Code of Professional Conduct (for example, on the CIPD website at www.cipd.co.uk).

Consider the standards of professional conduct. In what ways do these standards seem to reflect the influences of deontological (duty-based), consequentialist and virtues approaches to ethics?

As with any professional code of conduct, the CIPD code has to cover a potentially very diverse range of real-life situations. Read through the code and discuss the role these standards and requirements would be likely to play in helping CIPD members to identify ethical courses of action in their work.

Even the best codes of conduct, however, cannot possibly cover every possible situation that will arise, particularly when organisational environments are changing so quickly. Role modelling and a clear commitment to ethical behaviour from the top of the organisation is essential (Wiley 2000). This clear commitment is not simply a matter of communicating in words and actions to employees – feedback channels are also important. As Sternberg (2000) points out, good corporate governance should include the provision of effective communication channels, through which possible whistleblowers can make potential problems known to those at the top of the organisation (ie those who are in a position to do something about the issue). What bothers a whistleblower should also be of direct concern to the management of the organisation, not least because of the potential damage to the organisation's reputation.

REFLECTIVE ACTIVITY 4.8

Choose one example from the last three years of cases of unethical conduct in business or the public sector: these may be connected with health and safety, customers, suppliers or financial mismanagement or misbehaviour. Collect information about what happened from published sources such as news organisation websites (the BBC site, for example, at www.bbc.co.uk is particularly useful in this respect).

1   How far was this 'led from the top'?

2   Identify the key turning points of what was done. What should (not) have been done, and which professionals should have acted differently?

3   Discuss the role of the HR department and the role of HR-designed policies and practices.

As suggested above, there is much that HR professionals can do to brief, train and communicate in the area of ethical conduct, but there are a number of reasons why an organisation's ethical policy will work best if it is accepted as the responsibility and part of the identity of every employee. If corporate ethics is allowed to become the concern of a few specialists, rather than the responsibility of all, then the risk of major problems will remain high. This point applies even more to smaller businesses, which may lack extensive HR resources. Should governments over the next few years succeed in reducing the burden of some regulations on smaller businesses, in order to promote economic and employment growth, then managers in those businesses will find that some decisions become a matter of moral choice, rather than compliance with regulation.

So far in this chapter we have provided an agenda for HR in the field of ethics that will not be very different from that of other professions. How well is HR doing? Since the 2008 financial crisis there has been a growing set of studies analysing the delivery of ethical practice in organisations. The HR role services many stakeholders and we have always known this can present challenges (eg Legge 2000) and the possibility of split allegiances for HRPs (Guest and Woodrow 2012). Is there necessarily a tension between the roles of HRPs in serving strategic organisational needs, working with line managers and ensuring that employees are treated properly? Some recent publications have examined the practice of HRPs and looked at the ethical implications of their work.

Van Buren *et al* (2011) studied Australian HR professionals and their involvement in ethically related decisions. As in any other managerial role, tasks had to be prioritised, and the study suggested that strategic and managerial issues were often accorded a higher priority than those of staff coming to them for assistance. Given the nature of the HR remit, many will not be surprised by this, but if an HR department positions itself as the ethical guardian of employees, then there is clearly some scope for scepticism on the part of the workforce (Searle and Skinner 2011).

Working from employee reports of very poor attention from HR when handling complaints about bullying, Harrington *et al* (2012) sought the views of HRPs on the issue. Qualitative data from a British sample found that HRPs knew that staff were not always properly supported, but the reasons for this were complex. It appeared that HRPs' dependence on line managers for their power could influence their judgement, almost always meaning that the HRP denied a situation was bullying, in order to avoid challenging line managers. Several HRPs reported that even raising the accusation of bullying with line managers would be destructive to that relationship, a relationship central to their day-to-day work. The researchers concluded that while the HRPs' actions were entirely understandable, it left employees unsupported. Their findings helped to explain the cynicism of those who felt bullied, and their anger towards HR and its claim to be the guardian of the anti-bullying policy.

Another study in Australia (De Gama *et al* 2012) examined the competing priorities for HRPs in a time of economic difficulty and downward pressure on employment. Drawing on a Canadian sample, this study found that HR managers' tendency to depersonalise staff and think of them as 'resources' resulted in an attitude which the authors argued was dehumanising.

How do these concerns relate to the ethical ideas discussed earlier in the chapter? Given the competing claims about how HRPs should behave – as well as the extra pressure that results from a recessionary business environment – it is important to focus on what the HR responsibilities actually are. An HR department is set up and funded by the organisation in order to provide specialised professional support to its aims. Arising from this, HRPs have a clear duty to the employing organisation to act in ways that support its interests. As Sternberg (2000) points out, however, that duty is to the organisation (and in the case of a business, to its owners) and not necessarily to any particular manager whose behaviour is not consistent with the organisation's best interests. As regards employees (whether or not they are also managers), the HRP's ethical duty is equally clear: it is to treat them always with common decency and to observe distributive justice (Sternberg 2000). There is no ethical duty to act in ways that will guarantee the happiness of employees: furthermore, it would be a mistake to make employee happiness a direct indicator of effective HRM. There is also no necessary conflict for HR between supporting the organisation's aims and helping individual staff. An economically successful organisation can be a very pleasant and invigorating place to work, just as an organisation in trouble may well bring anxiety and stress for staff. In the case of workplace bullying, the ethical position can be justified in terms of both duties and consequences. Acts of bullying are an obvious violation of the general duty to treat others as ends in themselves, rather than as a means to someone else's goals, and HRPs following the principle of common decency must oppose any such behaviour. Bullying is also potentially damaging to the organisation in which it takes place, not only in terms of possible legal penalties, but also in areas such as high staff turnover, low productivity and employee disengagement. Again, HRPs wishing to serve the organisation effectively must work to eliminate workplace bullying, with no necessary conflict between the needs of staff and the needs of the employing organisation.

 THIS DOESN'T FEEL RIGHT...

CASE STUDY 4.2

David Hutchinson enjoyed his job as a junior HR manager with Accuset Engineering, a widely admired UK company that had grown rapidly since its foundation 20 years ago. Its distinctive capabilities in high value-added engineering and customer service had enabled it to build up an impressive list of major industrial clients in a range of sectors, both in the UK and internationally. David had joined the company 15 months ago, as part of an expansion of the HR department: Accuset had realised that its growth had necessitated a greater investment in professional HR support.

The company's HR director had arranged for members of the HR team to be designated as business partners to specified operating divisions in order to build up closer working relationships. David had recently been appointed as business partner to the company's Europe, Middle-East and Asia division, which focused on sales and business development in these regions. Accuset's business had initially been built up in the UK and then North America and the board was determined to develop its presence in the newer, high-growth markets in the East. His new colleagues in the division

had seemed very welcoming and David had already been able to provide useful guidance on the various approaches to international recruitment.

A couple of months earlier, the divisional manager had suggested that David should attend the autumn Business Forum, an annual event to which the division would invite its major clients. Keynote speakers would give presentations on strategic issues for the world economy and the occasion provided a valuable opportunity to deepen relationships with key clients. This year, the Business Forum was taking place in a very prestigious hotel complex in the Alps, which the company had hired for four days. David had heard of the venue, of course, and was looking forward to his first experience of this kind of world.

At the Forum, the keynote speeches had been fascinating and David was pleased to see the level of interest generated among the client guests. The venue was every bit as splendid as its reputation would suggest and both the hotel and the restaurants of the neighbouring town provided a range of agreeable environments for continuing discussions into the evening. On the second evening, David had been present at one large table for dinner, where a group of guests from one major international client were consuming copious amounts of alcohol and appeared to be getting 'a little the worse for wear'. After a while, it was impossible not to overhear the conversation, which seemed to centre on playful but insistent demands for further supplies from the expensive end of the wine list, as a prelude to 'seeing what further delights the town could offer'. The group then departed, accompanied by the company's divisional sales manager and his deputy, none of whom were to be seen at breakfast the next morning. David found himself troubled by this episode and spoke about it informally with the Forum organiser, who laughed and told him not to worry: clients were clients, after all, and this was how business was done. David did not find this at all reassuring and was further concerned about the stories he later heard about business entertainment practices in the Division.

On his return to the office, he spoke to colleagues about his concerns and then arranged to see the HR director. She had listened carefully, thanked him for raising the matter and then asked him to 'Leave it with me'.

That was four weeks ago and David had since heard nothing. He is worried and unsure what he should do next.

Questions

1   David's concerns arise from his experience at the Business Forum. In your view, what was disturbing about the behaviour he observed? If some individuals seem to have been behaving badly, what makes that behaviour bad? Are there any counter-arguments that could be used to partly justify the behaviour?

2   What seem to be David's choices now? Evaluate these choices and explain which course of action you would be likely to take.

3   What actions can an employer take in order to minimise the risk that employees will find themselves in apparently compromising situations in the course of their work?

CONCLUSION

Professionalism and ethics are topical in this period of global financial crisis and, hopefully, recovery. Demonstrating good ethical practice means thinking decisions through in a careful manner and developing one's own moral compass.

One common problem is that managers fail to perceive the ethical implications of a decision or action at the start. In this area HRPs can contribute uniquely across the organisation. By setting ethically screened policies, they can attempt to provide a framework within which managers can operate that precludes some unethical choices. By working with partner line managers, they can bring an independent view to bear on decisions where the manager might not have considered the ethical implications fully. Embedding ethical principles in training and learning events, the HRD specialist can prompt all employees to be more aware of the nature of their professionalism and the role of ethics within it.

There are codes of conduct provided by professional and industry bodies with which professionals affiliated to them need to comply. These codes are a welcome addition to guide practice. However, codes, by their very nature, operate with a broad brush. There is a need for all professionals, and especially those in HR, to pay close attention to both micro and macro decisions such that high standards are set in professional ethical practice for others to follow.

Evidence is beginning to be gathered on ethical behaviour, and HR is among the professions to be studied. The dynamics are complex, and remain to be fully understood, but in the process we may see further developments in ethical approaches within the profession.

KEY LEARNING POINTS

- In this chapter we have outlined areas that are becoming increasingly urgent in the HR field and which relate to ethical practice generally and professionalism specifically. These are not easy topics, and possibly require all staff to reflect at a deeper level than previously.
- There are a variety of approaches to analysing situations from an ethical point of view. Sometimes these can lead to very different logic and actions.
- Often employees do not analyse the ethical principles they employ.
- There is a strong case that good ethics makes sustainable business sense.
- Some issues (such as equal opportunities) are enshrined in law and regardless of one's personal feelings, one must facilitate the adherence to these rights, promoting them and leading the organisation through changing policies and practice.
- HR and line managers have an important role to play in influencing the level and type of integrity observed beyond the law and thence adopted by others.
- The CIPD plays an important role in the HR profession. Regardless of one's specialism, membership of the CIPD involves needing to abide by its Code of Professional Conduct.

REVIEW QUESTIONS

1   Think about an organisation with which you are familiar. Provide practical examples of ways in which it is operating ethically. Can you relate these examples to the duty, consequences or virtue perspectives on ethics?

2   Discuss the view that an organisation that is providing good value products or services to its customers, paying its bills and treating its staff decently over a long period of time is acting as ethically as anyone can reasonably expect.

3   How do HR decisions become conflicted in an ethical sense? Consider situations where you have felt professionally 'torn' between courses of action, and analyse your response using ethical frameworks.

4   Given that HR gains much of its power from line managers, how far might this influence the profession's 'honest broker' position? Does this matter?

5   Can one be an 'HR professional' without being a member of the CIPD?

EXPLORE FURTHER

Crane, A. and Matten, D. (2010) *Business Ethics*. 3rd edition. Oxford: Oxford University Press. One of a number of well-written texts on business ethics. Crane and Matten provide a balanced and accessible discussion of the various viewpoints.

Sternberg, E. (2000) *Just Business*. 2nd edition. Oxford: Oxford University Press. This book is recommended as a strongly argued account of the importance of a purpose-based view of business ethics.

The conflicts that confront HR professionals are explored in the articles by Wright and Caldwell in the References section. Read any one of these along with the CIPD code and consider how you might be impacted as a professional.

LEADING, MANAGING AND DEVELOPING PEOPLE: MAJOR CONTEMPORARY THEMES

CHAPTER 5

Leadership

Gill Christy

LEARNING OUTCOMES

After reading this chapter, you should be able to:

- explain the difference between the terms 'management' and 'leadership'
- identify the significance of leadership for a variety of organisation types
- understand the key theoretical approaches to the study of leadership
- apply knowledge of these approaches to the work of the HR professional
- suggest development activities to support the changing nature of organisational leadership.

OVERVIEW

In Part 3 of this book, we turn to examine key themes within the area of leading, managing and developing people. Central in this regard is the concept of leadership. The purpose of this chapter is to introduce the main theoretical approaches to the study of organisational leadership, and to provide an awareness of the strengths and shortcomings of these approaches. Current areas of academic research are briefly outlined to indicate the dynamic nature of the research agenda and possible future developments.

The chapter begins with a discussion of the terms 'management' and 'leadership' and relates both to the strategic purpose and direction of an organisation. Seven influential approaches to the study of leadership are presented and discussed, with the aim of providing a critical awareness of their implications. Important links are made between organisational leadership in general and the role of the HR professional in particular. Finally, some of the newer approaches to the study of leadership are briefly outlined, again with reference to the role which might emerge for both the specialist HRP and everyone who is involved in working with people in the more general sense.

INTRODUCTION

This chapter focuses on leaders in a business or organisational context, and views leaders as key players in both devising and implementing organisational strategy. It considers how existing theories and frameworks help to address the question of what exactly makes a leader effective in a business or a working environment. Some concepts and models clearly derive from, and apply to, other areas of human activity such as politics, sport and warfare. The notion of leadership provides an enduring fascination; not only to academics such as psychologists and political or social scientists, but also to journalists, biographers, authors, dramatists and film-makers, for whom it provides a rich source of material both factual and fictional. As we shall also see, many terms and metaphors associated with the study of leadership derive from sporting and military contexts. However, when we enter the more usual organisational arenas – businesses, public sector and governmental organisations, non-profit-making organisations such as charities – we tend to encounter the term 'manager' more frequently than 'leader' as the term to describe such key players. It is, therefore, important to start by considering how far these two related concepts, leadership and management, overlap.

REFLECTIVE ACTIVITY 5.1

Before we delve into the academic literature on leadership, it may be helpful to review your own views on the topic through consideration of some prominent business leaders, for instance, Deborah Meaden (of TV's Dragons' Den), Michael O'Leary, Ingvar Kamprad or Lakshmi Mittall. Conduct brief research into your chosen leader's business career.

Questions

1   Can you identify common traits among these leaders? What style of leadership do you associate with these people?

2   Have they always been successful?

MANAGEMENT OR LEADERSHIP?

There has been a revival of interest in the concept and application of leadership in recent years. Two decades ago, ambitious candidates for top-flight jobs in the world of business and public affairs might have enrolled on programmes to become Masters of Business Administration or to take diplomas in management studies. Today there is a burgeoning market in postgraduate degrees such as leadership studies, or business development and leadership. The Management Standards Centre (MSC) included the term in its revised National Occupational Standards for Management and Leadership; and in 2003 Investors in People UK launched its supplementary Leadership and Management model, discussed further below. Similar thinking has also led to the development of the CIPD's own Leadership and Management Standards, now integral to the professional development and qualification programme. So an initial question to consider is why there is such renewed interest in the concept of leadership, and how this fits with traditional ideas about organisational management. Perhaps part of the answer is to do with changing patterns of organisational life and similar changes in social expectations within the working environment.

Traditional organisations with strongly hierarchical structures are becoming rarer, and newer forms of both commercial and public sector organisation tend to be more flexible and task- or client-focused. What Handy (1976) described as 'matrix' organisations are generally considered to be more effective in a highly fluid commercial or operating environment; and the 'shamrock' style of organisation (Handy 1989) charts the move towards further operational flexibility. This type of organisational flexibility was also described by Atkinson (1984) in his model of the flexible firm, which disaggregates different organisational requirements and builds in a further form of organisational flexibility by outsourcing or subcontracting a number of its activities. This kind of articulated organisational structure works against the maintenance of strong hierarchies based around position (or legitimate) power (Mullins 2013), and often requires individual managers to exercise a different form of authority from that conferred simply by virtue of status or rank. Similarly, wider social attitudes towards authority have changed and, as in other walks of life, people generally expect to be consulted and involved in their work rather than simply instructed. In some circumstances these expectations are now supported by the law, for instance through the Information and Consultation of Employees (ICE) Regulations of 2005, which now apply to all businesses with more than 50 employees. Together, these trends may have renewed the interest in leadership as an important skill for those attempting to 'get things done through other people'.

Mullins (2013) suggests that there is a close relationship between the concepts of management and leadership, and recognises that at least some authors and commentators dislike attempts to separate the two. Other writers, such as Hollingsworth – someone with both military and commercial experience – and Kotter (Bloisi *et al* 2007, Huczynski and Buchanan 2013), make a very clear distinction. Kotter describes leaders as those who set a direction, align people to the vision and motivate them; whereas managers plan, organise, control and resolve problems. In Hollingsworth's model, leadership involves innovation, development, a focus on people, inspiring trust, having an eye on the horizon and 'doing the right things'. By contrast, management is associated with administration, maintenance, systems/structure, control, paying attention to the bottom line and 'doing things right'. This distinction is also reflected in the National Occupational Standards for Management and Leadership, which appear to show a transition between operational and/or supervisory levels of management at levels 2 and 3, and a more strategic approach at levels 4 and 5 (Management Standards Centre). It is, therefore, a useful means of organising further discussion of the subject in terms of organisational people management practice.

For the purposes of this chapter, strategic leadership is taken to mean the activities involved in the initial creation of an overall business or organisational strategy, then directing and energising organisational resources towards the achievement of that strategy. Insofar as it then relies on others to carry out the strategy it may involve some management, but it is primarily about business vision and mission and engaging the energies of the workforce in pursuit of that vision. This means 'doing the right thing', creating the differentiators which, in people terms, involve becoming an employer of choice, an organisation which is able to encourage outstanding performance from its workforce and thus achieve superior results. On the other hand, managerial leadership is taken to mean activities surrounding the creation, maintenance and development of an appropriate infrastructure for business operations, including that which involves organising the work of other people. It means creating a working environment that can help a business or other organisation to achieve its objectives. In this sense management includes leadership to some degree: it is about 'doing things right'.

STRATEGY AND LEADERSHIP

As we saw in Chapter 2, the term 'strategy' is conceived as a means of identifying the ways in which an organisation seeks to pursue its purpose, or achieve its objectives. A prominent view of business strategy is 'resource-based', that is to say, mainly to do with identifying the key resources that give the organisation a distinctive capability and finding ways of applying those capabilities to parts of the market that offer the best prospects (Johnson *et al* 2011, Legge 2005, Boxall and Purcell 2011). Following from this, the key tasks in the strategic planning process could be said to be:

- analysing the organisation's environment and the changes that are expected over the plan period

- identifying and evaluating the organisation's key resources: those that are distinctive (by comparison to competitors) and those that are also important to delivering value to customers, taxpayers or client groups
- considering strategic options: ways of matching organisational resources to particular parts (segments) of the market, looking for the approach that is forecast to create maximum added value for shareholders, or to achieve the most effective use of public or donor money
- choosing the preferred strategic option
- realigning the organisation's resources (human and others) behind the chosen strategy: acquiring new resources, modifying existing resources and getting rid of those that cannot be economically reconfigured (which, of course, opens up questions about the ethical treatment of human resources)
- directing and energising those resources towards implementing the strategy
- responding to unexpected events during implementation.

Most of these activities are focused at the higher levels of a business or organisation, and are often the province of a single individual (for instance in a small business or owner-managed enterprise) or a small group such as a company chief executive and board of directors. In the public sector, strategic management will be in the hands of those who exercise political power and the professional experts who advise them and find appropriate means of executing political decisions. They are activities which are primarily about making informed strategic choices, in other words responding to the question 'What is the right thing to do?' They are also about convincing and energising others to put their effort behind the chosen strategy, and in this sense involve many leadership skills. In terms of people management, this level of leadership is about defining approaches to ensure that appropriate talent is recruited and motivated to achieve superior results.

REFLECTIVE ACTIVITY 5.2

List five personal qualities or attributes which you associate with successful leadership and place them in order of importance. Ask others (in your family, friendship group or class) to do the same then compare the lists. How many attributes are common to all lists? Do you agree on the relative importance of these attributes? Do you think they are culturally specific, or relevant in all cultural contexts?

MANAGEMENT AND LEADERSHIP

As mentioned above, in 2003 Investors in People UK launched its supplementary Leadership and Management model, which seeks to help organisations create and maintain effective leadership skills amongst managers (Investors in People website: www.investorsinpeople.co.uk). This emphasises the important links between the two functions as well as indicating the increased significance of developing leadership within UK organisations. Leadership ability is defined as one of the attributes of the successful manager, along with the intellectual skills required for the assimilation of information, analysis and planning, technical and professional knowledge of the business area or sector, and a clear understanding of the specific organisation and its capacities.

Similarly, the Management Charter Initiative (MCI), which developed as a result of the recommendations in the Handy and Constable and McCormick reports of the late 1980s, undertook a major analysis of the nature of management for the purposes of establishing a clear framework for managerial qualifications. Its work resulted in the adoption of a competency-based approach which quickly became highly influential in the field of management development in Britain (Frank 1991). The 1997 edition of the occupational standard was based around four major components: managing operations, managing finance, managing information and managing people, only the last of which could be clearly seen as requiring leadership skills. Ten years later, the MSC researched and developed a new set of standards, which also provide a functional map and set of units of competence that encompass the important knowledge and skill components of effective management. The significance of leadership is more clearly emphasised in the title of the new standards themselves: the National Occupational Standards for Management and Leadership. The six basic elements of the new standards, which can be viewed at the MSC website (www.management-standards.org), are:

1   managing self and personal skills (depicted as a central aspect of the remaining five standards)

2   providing direction

3   facilitating change

4   working with people

5   using resources

6   achieving results.

Leadership ability can be firmly associated with the second, third and fourth of these elements; and indeed the term 'working with people' has replaced 'managing people' in a way which might indicate the reducing of emphasis on formal control and the increased need for collaboration in present-day work environments noted above.

The CIPD Professional Standards recognise that soft skills are just as important as technical ones, and so these are better represented and thus reflect more fully aspects of leadership which are essential to good management practice. Nevertheless, these functions are qualitatively different from those required of strategic leadership which, as we have noted, appear at the higher levels of organisations. The majority of the Standards are much more concerned with 'doing things right' in the sense of providing an effective structure within which people can achieve high levels of performance for their organisation.

It is now possible to turn to some of the concepts and theories about leadership, and to identify how well they might support the development of effective people management, either at a strategic or at a more operational level.

LEADERSHIP: THEORETICAL FRAMEWORKS

It is useful at this point to remind ourselves of some of the key frameworks which have developed for the analysis and study of leadership. A summary of differing academic approaches to the subject is offered by several writers, including Mullins (2013), Bloisi *et al* (2007), Hersey *et al* (2001), Huczynski and Buchanan (2013), Kreitner *et al* (2002) and Yukl (2006). Most offer a framework for leadership studies which identifies the following main schools of thought (Mullins 2013):

● the qualities or traits approach
● the functional or group approach
● the approach which sees leadership as a behavioural category
● the leadership styles approach
● the situational approach and contingency models
● transformational leadership

● inspirational leadership.

Taking each of these approaches in turn, we can examine the general principles and models involved, and comment on their suitability in relation to either strategic leadership or managerial (operational) leadership. Some comments about the implications of each model for the development of effective organisational leaders are also included.

QUALITIES OR TRAITS APPROACHES

This approach is essentially the 'great person' theory of leadership, and takes an approach which tries to identify the significant features of acknowledged leaders. Early approaches to the study of leadership (mostly undertaken before and shortly after the Second World War) dwelt on the personal qualities and characteristics of successful leaders in an attempt to isolate the 'magic ingredients'. They have not generally agreed on a common set of characteristics, although one or two, such as self-confidence and intelligence, did figure in a number of models (eg Kreitner *et al* 2002). Indeed, it is possible that the very act of selecting successful leaders for study introduces a form of bias which prejudices the results of any subsequent analysis. For instance, the absence of women from many research samples may well reflect the social constraints of the time rather than indicating that women lack innate leadership qualities. Indeed, it has been argued (Alimo-Metcalfe 1995) that studies of women leaders actually identify a different range of effective leadership qualities compared with studies of men; and that it is important to: 'challenge the dangerous implicit assumption that identifying the criteria for leadership positions from groups of senior managers, all or most of whom (chances are) are male, may well lead to gender-biased criteria for the subsequent assessment process' (pp7–8).

Her research also has relevance when considering the contrast between so-called 'transactional' and 'transformational' styles of leadership and is discussed further below.

Similarly, it is also important to note that the characteristics that have been proposed as significant may not be universally applicable. Cultural factors, for instance, may result in very different values being placed on a specific personal quality (such as willingness to take risks, to break the rules in pursuit of an objective, or to act openly in pursuit of personal ambition) in different societies. Hofstede's model (1991) identified dimensions of cultural difference which he termed 'uncertainty avoidance', 'power distance', 'masculinity/femininity' and 'individualism/collectivism', and he described how combinations of these formed the characteristics of particular cultural environments. Clearly some cultures might accept and applaud qualities such as personal ambition and risk-taking where others would be more likely to value behaviours which support collective achievement or stability and a sense of social inclusion. The importance of cultural difference in relation to appropriate leadership styles and behaviours is developed more fully under the heading of situational or contingency theories of leadership.

As a result, we might consider that trait theories offer few pointers which can help aspiring managers assess their potential other than by trying to decide if they possess the appropriate qualities, or can develop (or even simulate) them. Trait theories offer little help in terms of suggesting how managerial leaders can prepare and adapt themselves to the reality of work to be performed.

Furthermore, little connection is made with the variety of organisational circumstances where leadership needs to be exercised, including those circumstances where leadership shifts from the operational to the strategic levels of activity. The high public profile of both political and business leaders who operate at a strategic level may well tempt us to analyse their qualities, but our information is imperfect (even about high-profile individuals) and of course the same individual can be both successful and unsuccessful during his or her career.

Adoption of the 'traits' approach also has implications for the role of people management in an organisation. If the development of successful organisational leaders is largely a matter of identifying those individuals who possess the desired characteristics and then offering the selected potential managers opportunities to develop and exercise these abilities, then the focus of people management will probably be on devising appropriate tests (such as psychometric or aptitude tests) which will help identify the 'right stuff', and devising systems of training and promotion which will support their development.

THE FUNCTIONAL APPROACH

The functional approach to leadership studies generally considers what leaders do to be effective, rather than examining what they are. One of the main exponents of a functional approach in the UK is John Adair, an author with a military background, and the influence of his theory of action-centred leadership (Adair 1983) derives from its adoption by the Industrial Society (renamed the Work Foundation in 2002) as a central plank of their management and leadership training programmes in the 1980s. He suggested that there are three main areas of managerial leadership activity: those concerned with building the team; those concerned with developing the individual within the team; and those which are directed at the achievement of the task. This type of approach has an important appeal in that it suggests that leadership skills can be acquired, and that pre-existing characteristics are less significant than the ability to learn how to act in such a way as to balance the three key areas of activity. From the people management perspective, it places less emphasis on selection and more emphasis on training than trait theory would imply. It gives individuals a better framework for self-selection into managerial roles, and a clear set of development tasks to help them to create a successful infrastructure as managers. Adair's approach has proved highly successful as the basis for a robust and accessible system of training for supervisors and middle managers. However, it has little to say about the type of leadership that is involved in actually creating and driving organisational strategy. This is not to suggest that Adair himself has nothing to say about strategic leadership in other contexts (see, for instance, Adair 2003).

The approach taken firstly by the MCI and now the MSC in their review of management standards is that of functional analysis, and the resulting functional map forms the basis for the 74 units which comprise the current standards. It is similar to action-centred leadership in the sense that it provides a general prescription, and one which has been thoroughly researched in a variety of sectors, for managerial competence. In terms of people management, yardsticks such as these have significant value in terms of setting required performance standards for supervisors and managers, identifying both individual and job-related managerial training needs, developing career structures, and of course can be used for selection purposes. What all functional approaches might fail to recognise sufficiently well, however, is the significance of such elements as tacit knowledge regarding effective performance: the sort of knowledge of and 'feel' for organisational context which generally only results from experience (Pilbeam and Corbridge 2010). It is possible that leadership and management are a more integrated set of activities than competency-based or unitised approaches might lead us to believe. Leadership, and strategic leadership in particular, may be more than the sum of its parts.

REFLECTIVE ACTIVITY 5.3

| In a press release of December 2012 announcing the results of its Research Report | 'Managing for Sustainable Employee Engagement', CIPD head of public policy, Ben |

Willmott, commented that, 'managers who don't find time to talk individually to their employees, who pass on stress, who panic about deadlines and fail to consult and provide advice, erode motivation and undermine employee health and well-being.'

Review the results and conclusions of this report and consider occasions when you may have experienced either negative or positive behaviours. What effect, if any, did they have on your feelings of engagement at work?

THE BEHAVIOUR OF LEADERS

Behavioural theories extend the basis of study beyond the leader him or herself, and have as their basis a consideration of the effects which leaders have on the actual performance of groups by examining leader behaviours and relating them to outcomes. The Ohio State studies and those of the Michigan Institute for Social Research in the 1960s and 1970s pioneered this approach and produced remarkably similar results. Mullins (2013) summarises these as being leader behaviours concerned with task functions (the 'structure' dimension in the Ohio State studies and 'production-centred' supervisory behaviour in the Michigan one) and leader behaviour concerned with maintenance functions ('consideration' in the Ohio State term and 'employee-centred' behaviour in the Michigan one). He further relates them to McGregor's 'Theory X and Theory Y' managerial assumptions and the dimensions of concern for production and concern for people first proposed in Blake and Mouton's (1964) managerial grid and now revised and renamed the leadership grid (Blake and McCanse 1991).

Behavioural studies have the advantage of offering would-be managers some options regarding behaviours which can be effective, rather than a single prescription for success. Whilst the studies concluded that there was no universally superior style, and that the circumstances of leadership might have an important influence on the effectiveness of one style over another, they did conclude that a balance between these two dimensions of behaviour seemed to be important in achieving success. In this respect they have much in common with situational or contingency theories, which have more to say about the way in which behaviours can be matched to circumstances. Once more, this type of approach offers a wider range of options for the use of training and development techniques as a means of encouraging managerial leadership capacity. In relation to strategic leadership, 'consideration' and 'structure' are both relevant to strategic tasks, but in general behavioural theories have little to say explicitly about leadership at this level of organisational life.

LEADERSHIP STYLES

Approaches to the study of leadership that analyse the differences between leadership styles are generally focused upon the leader's attitude towards people and the resulting behaviours which they exhibit in their day-to-day dealings with members of the team. This generates a range of possibilities, and the resulting classifications usually identify a range of styles, perhaps most succinctly described by Tannenbaum and Schmidt (1973). They focused on the relative strength and power of managers and non-managers (ie subordinates) in terms of decision-making. At one end of the resulting continuum is 'boss-centred' (autocratic) decision-making where a manager largely decides what is to be done in a specific circumstance, and others accept and follow the decision. At the other end is joint (or democratic) decision-making, where a manager will define a problem or situation and then participate in the decision-making simply as a member of the team. This model recognises the need for an understanding of the relationship between specific managers and their teams from a basis of both leader and follower characteristics (such as personality, relevant knowledge and experience, sense of security, etc) and permits the inclusion of circumstantial considerations (organisational and societal factors, etc) in the equation. In this respect it bears considerable similarity to the contingency models discussed in the next section. Insofar as it examines the skills and requirements for leading a team, the approach is not prescriptive, and is an appropriate tool for analysing and identifying the range of successful managerial leadership styles. It also offers some important messages about the importance of flexibility in terms of managerial style. Like the behavioural theories discussed earlier, these approaches have significant value in terms of management development; but also have similar shortcomings when it comes to the consideration of strategic leadership.

SITUATIONAL AND CONTINGENCY MODELS OF LEADERSHIP

While traits-based and functional models of leadership concentrate on the leaders, and behavioural models examine the effect on the led, situational perspectives add a third dimension: that of the circumstances, both organisational and environmental, in which the leadership activity occurs. This allows the development of what is generally termed the contingency approach to leadership; in other words an approach which might answer the question 'What type of leadership actions and behaviours are appropriate?' with the phrase 'It depends on the circumstances'. Contingency approaches thus suggest a wide range of different but equally valid ways of leading and managing people. Some, such as Hersey and Blanchard's model of situational leadership (see Hersey *et al* 2001), focus on the appropriate leadership styles for groups or individual followers who are at different stages of 'readiness' or 'maturity' to achieve a task; readiness being defined as a combination of both ability, willingness or confidence to carry out the task in question. As these vary over time, so the leader needs to choose and use the most appropriate style to fit the circumstances. The four styles suggested in the situational leadership model are summarised from Hersey *et al* (2001, pp182–87) as follows:

- *S1 – telling*: this provides high amounts of guidance and direction but little supportive behaviour. This style is most appropriate for low follower readiness, including situations where followers are unable and/or unwilling. The leader structures the task and concentrates on step-by-step help and instruction.
- *S2 – selling*: this requires high amounts of both directive (task) and relationship behaviours. This style is most appropriate for low to moderate follower readiness; particularly when followers are willing but still not fully capable of performing. The leader encourages more dialogue to achieve 'buy-in' amongst the followers.
- *S3 – participating*: this shows high levels of two-way communication and supportive (relationship) behaviour but low amounts of guidance (task behaviour). This style is most appropriate for moderate to high follower readiness: in other words situations where followers are competent but inexperienced, or competent but demotivated. The leader should focus on discussion, encouragement and facilitation rather than instruction.
- *S4 – delegating*: this involves little direction or support; in other words, low levels of both task and relationship behaviours. This style is most appropriate for high follower readiness, in other words situations where managerial intervention is largely unnecessary (unless there are significant problems), and can focus on monitoring.

For instance, a human resources assistant who is highly capable and confident about carrying out selection interviews would respond well to a delegating style of management in relation to this work. However, if they then find themselves in changed business circumstances and need to carry out redundancy interviews without having had much relevant experience, then a 'selling' style of managerial leadership might be more suitable, or possibly a 'telling' style if the individual was particularly resistant to carrying out the new task. There is also evidence that contingency approaches to leadership have particular relevance when considering inter-cultural situations. Kreitner, for instance, suggests that national culture is an important contingency and that cultural analyses such as those of Hofstede can be helpful in identifying appropriate styles for the needs of different cultural groups (Hofstede 1991, Kreitner 2001, Kakabadse *et al* 1997).

There seems, from Kreitner's research, to be some indication that the most widely applicable style is the participative one. It is well suited to many national cultures but particularly those such as that of the US and Sweden where there is limited 'natural' respect for hierarchy and seniority: what Hofstede would term a 'low power distance' culture. Nevertheless, it can be successful in a wider range of cultures than the directive style. The latter is more specifically suited to 'high' power distance cultures where status automatically commands respect (Kreitner suggests French and Indian cultures), and where subordinates will generally expect their managers to have the answers by virtue of the expertise which has enabled them to achieve their status. The directive style translates poorly into 'low power distance' cultures or those where joint regulation or co-determination is the norm (for instance the German one). He explains, however, that:

> Participative leadership is not necessarily the best style; it simply is culturally acceptable in many different countries ... directive leadership turned out to be the least appropriate leadership style. (Kreitner 2001, p613)

Moving more directly into the area of strategic leadership in a business context, Clarke and Pratt (1985) and Rodrigues (1988) both consider the importance of the stage of growth which a business has reached and suggest that this too can be an important contingent factor with relation to the choice of strategic leadership style. Taking a basic model of the business growth cycle such as the 'Boston box', which identifies four developmental stages of an enterprise – start-up, growth, maturity and decline – these authors suggest that there are matching styles of strategic leadership: champion, tank commander, housekeeper and lemon-squeezer. The start-up organisation or venture needs a 'champion' style: a leadership style which is prepared to fight for the enterprise on a variety of fronts, thus suggesting the need for an energetic individual with a wide variety of technical management skills. An example of a champion might be the founder of easyJet, Sir Stelios Haji-Ioannou. At the end of 2002, having developed this very successful low-cost airline, he stepped down as chairman in order to use his talents in what he considered to be the most effective manner, involving himself in new ventures, entrepreneurial innovation and similar 'no frills' developments in other markets. His easyGroup (see www.easy.com) has initiated a wide variety of new ventures including mobile phones, low-cost cinemas, car rental and, more recently, Internet cafés and gyms.

The skills of the champion relate closely to those of the tank commander, whose strategic role is to develop strong teams that can drive the business forward once it has entered a growth phase. The housekeeper needs fewer entrepreneurial skills but must be able to achieve more in the way of planning, cost control and the formalisation of processes and organisational structures such as reward and training systems. The lemon-squeezer, who is trying to extract the best from a declining business and if possible turn it around, needs a range of skills which are more to do with taking tough and difficult measures as effectively as possible than fostering and encouraging growth. Possible examples of this type of leadership might include Sir Stuart Rose at Marks & Spencer between 2004 and 2006, and Justin King at Sainsbury's in late 2004–05. Such circumstances are common in business life; examples which came to prominence at the start of 2008 include the challenges faced by the new management of Northern Rock, and for Tata following its purchase of the Jaguar and Land Rover brands from Ford. Clarke and Pratt consider that most managers have one primary style and are not necessarily suited to all stages of business development.

The contingency approach to leadership emphasises contextual factors as an important influence on leader success. Professor Joseph Nye, in a BBC interview ahead of the UK publication of his book *The Powers to Lead: Soft, Hard, and Smart* in May 2008, stressed the relationship between contextual knowledge and leadership power, explaining that contextual knowledge helps leaders to determine what balance they should strike between the use of what he terms 'hard' power (issuing commands) and 'soft' power (the ability to attract and retain followers). Contingency approaches remain highly relevant for the exercise of leadership in modern organisations, having perhaps two main implications for organisational leadership and its development. First of all, training for management and leadership skills needs to include the use of tools and techniques which can enable those in managerial and leadership positions both to identify salient circumstantial features, and then choose the right method to match those circumstances. It might also suggest that leadership can, and perhaps should, change hands in response to changed circumstances if one person's skills are more appropriate than another's, which clearly has implications for management structures and individual careers. It also has particular relevance for strategic leadership. Radical change in organisational circumstances might necessitate such a significant change in strategic direction that a leader who is firmly associated with the former strategy may be far less able to lead in the new direction (Rajan 2002). High-profile examples of this phenomenon would be the changes in leadership of all three of the main political parties in the UK since 1980.

CASE STUDY 5.1

A CRISIS OF LEADERSHIP AT THE BBC (PART ONE)

For 85 years the BBC has pursued its mission to 'inform, educate and entertain', not only in the UK but worldwide. It is funded by British licence fee-payers through a sort of 'television tax' and governed under Royal Charter by the BBC Trust. This arrangement makes it vulnerable on several fronts. Other commercial broadcasting and news media companies may consider that it has an unfair advantage in the market; it doesn't (indeed, is not permitted to) compete for advertising revenue in the UK. Licence fee-payers may demand particularly high standards and responsiveness to a wide variety of diverse programming requirements; and its links with the government make it open to charges of political bias. Leadership of this much loved, quintessentially British but sometimes reviled and criticised organisation is thus a difficult, but immensely important, job. In the words of veteran broadcaster David Dimbleby, 'The

Director General [DG] has to fight like a tiger to defend the BBC.'

In September 2012 George Entwistle took up the post after a competitive process managed by executive recruitment agency Egon Zehnder. He had been selected from a senior BBC role in July to succeed the outgoing DG Mark Thompson; but whilst both Thompson and Lord Patten (chairman of the BBC Trust) praised Entwistle as an outstanding and creative leader, some media commentators were surprised at his appointment. He was clearly an insider, having joined the BBC in 1989 as a trainee journalist and risen from reporting to editing news and factual broadcasts, including the flagship weekday *Newsnight* programme between 2001 and 2004. But despite this long and successful service he was thought too 'quiet' for the role of BBC tiger – shy and uncomfortable in the public gaze, uncommunicative and an unimpressive public speaker (Brown 2012, Sabbagh 2012).

In October 2012, a storm of unprecedented ferocity hit the BBC squarely in Entwistle's area of expertise. Revelations on ITV about the late Jimmy Savile's sexual offences led to serious embarrassment for the corporation, which had withdrawn a *Newsnight* programme on that very subject as early as December 2011; to some, the BBC appeared to be attempting to cover up criminal behaviour which had taken place in its own back yard. Then, on 2 November, as further evidence of abusive behaviour came to light in the press, *Newsnight* broadcast what turned out to be an unfounded allegation of paedophilia against 'a very senior political figure' of the Thatcher era. Whilst not naming the individual during the programme, the journalists concerned allowed a trail to appear on the Internet amid the following frenzy of speculation, prompting a public denial and legal action from the accused. The sole witness and accuser interviewed for the *Newsnight* report subsequently made a statement of apology, explaining that he had mistakenly identified his abuser from a photograph shown to him in the early 1990s.

The *Newsnight* team had failed spectacularly to follow the basic rules of journalism which are included in the BBC's own editorial guidelines. Checks had not been carried out by either the programme or station editors; nor had this controversial story been cleared by the DG. But the true test of Entwistle's leadership came during the aftermath. After a week of turmoil, *Newsnight* finally had to broadcast a humiliating climbdown and Entwistle suspended all journalistic investigations by the programme team. He appeared complacent, claimed that the matter 'had not been brought to his attention' and seemingly adopted an overly bureaucratic and poorly informed, even uninterested, attitude to the management of the affair. This attitude was revealed during a radio interview on 10 November when his approach was publicly dismantled by interviewer John Humphrys, making his continued tenure as DG impossible. He resigned later that day.

Questions

1   Would you describe George Entwistle as a leader or a manager? Explain your reasons.

2   What might the situational leadership model have to tell us about the type of leadership required during organisational crises?

3   What benefits might an organisation gain from using external recruitment agencies to fill high-profile leadership roles such as this? What are the associated risks?

TRANSFORMATIONAL LEADERSHIP

Recent literature on leadership has noted the difference between 'transactional' forms of leadership and 'transformational' ones. This contrast relates back to ideas about the nature of leadership in a society which no longer accepts authority as the basis for command. If authority and 'position power' (French and Raven 1968) no longer works, what are the alternatives? One approach is to bargain: in other words to appeal to the self-interest of the followers. So-called transactional forms of leadership rely on the leader's capacity to negotiate appropriate follower behaviours based on legitimate rewards or punishments – although there is, of course, an inherent assumption that the leader has the appropriate authority to offer such rewards or administer punishments. Alimo-Metcalfe (1995) notes the findings of Rosener (1990) that the men she studied were more likely than the women to adopt transactional styles, and suggests why women have tended to be more participatory:

> The fact that most women have lacked formal authority over others … means that by default they have had to find other ways to accomplish their work. (Rosener 1990, p124)

This is contrasted with transformational leadership, which is a process by which leaders create high levels of motivation and commitment by generating and communicating a clear vision and, often, appealing to higher ideas and values amongst followers. Rosener (1990, p120) defines it as motivating others by 'transforming their individual self-interest into the goals of the group' and by trying to make people feel part of the organisation. Whilst recognising this apparent gender difference, Alimo-Metcalfe (1995) warns against too close an association between female management styles and transformational leadership, suggesting that even here there are gender differences in the use of transformational techniques (such as empowerment). In her view, the 'female' version of transformational leadership is mainly focused on the creation of a sense of belonging, inclusiveness and connectedness with others in the organisation as well as its goals, whereas the same technique used by men is more focused on separateness and autonomy in pursuing organisational aims. Thus she suggests that a more general move within organisations to adopt such transformational approaches is not necessarily a means by which women can expect to achieve status and leadership positions more readily, despite an initial expectation that it might.

Legge (2005) explains how this focus on a shared vision and personal commitment was, in the 1980s, part of a transformational leadership style which was characteristic of successful Japanese companies. It was reintegrated into American management culture (which was more focused on transactional leadership) via the work of the excellence gurus like Peters and Waterman, or Ouchi. She charts the appeal of this style of leadership, and in particular its association with the American dream and thus some of the 'soft' HRM practices which facilitate the growth of an enterprise culture. She also offers a critique of this essentially paternalist and unitary approach to the management of people, which (when push comes to shove) will always prioritise business needs over individual or workforce needs, thus perhaps laying managers open to charges of hypocrisy when individual and corporate interests come into conflict.

These concepts are clearly relevant to many strategic situations: for example, can an organisation that develops its own leaders respond effectively to discontinuous external change? Also, this set of ideas helps to illuminate the process of realigning the organisation's resources described above, as well as bringing new insight to the strategic analysis of the organisation's external and internal environments.

INSPIRATIONAL LEADERSHIP AND AUTHENTIC LEADERSHIP

Finally, it is impossible to discuss questions of leadership without considering the concept of inspirational leadership, which has regained some currency in recent years. In some ways this brings us back to concepts associated with trait theories, and in particular the characteristic usually described as charisma. Inspirational leadership, we are told by Adair (2003) and others, is about creating and communicating vision, having a passion and a dynamism that drives the leader and engages the enthusiasm and efforts of the led; even exhibiting unconventional behaviour and performing heroic deeds (Conger 1999). It includes the ability to take a long-term view, to inspire trust and confidence, which unlocks talent and enables the organisation to achieve exceptional performance. A recent trend in the world of management training and development that reflects this renewed attention to the highly personal nature of leadership, and in particular strategic leadership, is found in the growing interest in emotional intelligence as a relevant and learnable management skill.

Mullins (2013) and Legge (2005) both sound notes of caution in their consideration of inspirational leadership and draw attention to some of its drawbacks. Certainly it is difficult to see how charismatic leadership can be developed effectively. This is not to deny that many business founders have been charismatic and inspiring individuals, but their skills have often been better described as those of the champion which, as we have seen, relies on a wide range of business skills as well as the ability to protect and nurture a project. It is also less than wholly evident that inspirational leadership in itself results in significant benefits for organisational performance; in some cases it may be that the loss of the visionary results in the dissolution of the organisation. A specific attack on the cult of the inspirational leader was made by Beverly Alimo-Metcalfe at the HRD 2008 event, where she was reported as saying that:

> Organisations shouldn't be choosing leaders who were 'charismatic and inspirational' because these qualities in the hands of some people can be lethal. People at the top who are charismatic get there through the demise of others – they emasculate everybody else along the way. This kind of leadership can be toxic. (Evans 2008)

Adrian Furnham has also written about arrogance and egotistical leadership behaviour using the legend of Daedalus and Icarus (Furnham 2005). Inspirational leadership relies on a certain degree of emotional manipulation, and so its ethical status as a general management strategy might be open to challenge. It may also inspire less desirable characteristics in the followers, such as a high level of individual dependence on the approval and support of the leader; a fear of 'going against the grain' or groupthink; and a degree of enthusiasm for the vision which could encourage people to act in ways which stray beyond the boundaries of what might be considered ethical, or even legal (Conger 2002). Inspirational leaders can be bullies as well as visionaries; and the more powerfully they communicate their values, the less space there is for reasoned doubt or even opposition.

It is sometimes difficult to separate the concept of charismatic or egotistical leadership (with all its potential failings) from another idea which seems to have a more positive image – that of 'authentic' leadership. Authentic leadership is sometimes described as 'an expression of the leader's true self' – although of course the perception of authenticity might simply result from good acting (Ladkin and Taylor 2009). Techniques from the world of performance art are often discussed in this context; for instance the Stanislavski method (ibid) and classically rooted concepts such as mastery and congruence (Ladkin 2008). All this might suggest that followers can never really know if the leader's display of their 'true self' is anything more than an illusion. However, illusions can be powerful things, and some researchers have noted that the outcomes of authentic leadership on followers' attitudes and behaviours can have significant predictive validity in terms of enhanced trust, job satisfaction and job performance (Walumbwa *et al* 2008).

LEADERSHIP: THE RESEARCH AGENDA

Writing in the February 2008 issue of *Impact*, Linda Holbeche, the CIPD Director of Research and Policy, noted the evolving nature of management and leadership, and suggested that some important new themes are emerging from current research. Amongst these are the challenges created by the need to lead in situations of increasing complexity, ambiguity and uncertainty; the idea of building 'communities of leaders'; and the influence of leader values in shaping the behaviour of those around them. These ideas have clear implications for HR practitioners, who are often charged with the responsibility for developing organisational leaders.

It is also evident that the question of leadership remains an important area for academic research. The growth of 'virtual' organisations and teams has led to an interest in the practice of 'e-leadership', and this is likely to be of growing significance as technology offers more and better opportunities for work to be organised using geographically dispersed expertise (Avolio *et al* 2000). Ilze Zigurs has developed some ideas about the transfer of traditional team roles into a virtual environment, including that of leadership. If physical presence is an important means of signalling and reinforcing leadership in traditional teams, what happens when there is no such presence? The concept of 'telepresence' becomes relevant here; but as she explains:

> … being telepresent is more than just keeping up a steady stream of email messages to team members. Leaders need to learn how to use the vividness and interactivity of media to make their presence felt in a positive way. (Zigurs 2003, p344)

She goes on to suggest ways in which aspects of leadership, such as communicating vision, motivating, mentoring and building trust, can be transferred from face-to-face to virtual environments, and makes specific recommendations for leadership in virtual teams.

There is also significant focus on cross-cultural leadership, most notably in the continuing work of Project GLOBE (Global Leadership and Organizational Behavioral Effectiveness), which involves over 160 researchers working in 62 societies (see French 2010). An in-depth study of some of the project's findings has examined culture and leadership styles in 25 of the countries under review, and uses Hofstede's model as the basis for comparative analysis (Chhokar *et al* 2007). From other perspectives, the relationship between leaders and followers continues to generate new ideas and approaches, including developments based on the theory of leader-member exchange (LMX). This examines the two-way or dyadic relationships between a leader and a follower (rather than a leader and the group as a whole):

> LMX theory of leadership focuses on the degree of emotional support and exchange of valued resources between the leader and members. Thus, LMX leadership theory's main focus is to diagnose this relationship so a higher quality can be developed in this relationship, enabling improved performance. (Kang and Stewart 2007, p532)

Kang and Stewart detail the significance of trust and empowerment in high-quality leader–member exchange, and suggest that LMX might have important implications for the practice of human resource development. It also provides the basis for a renewed interest in another conceptualisation of leadership which had its origins in the 1970s, that of 'servant leadership'.

Servant leadership as a term was initially used by Robert Greenleaf (1977) and has come to the forefront of research as the focus of leadership studies continues to move from the leader to the followers. The concept positions the leader as a steward rather than as a commander, and places him or her in a role which is defined by commitment to serve the organisation's needs rather than personal ambition; and to support the autonomy, growth and well-being of others. Key attributes therefore include humility, authenticity, empathy and a willingness to put the needs of others (the followers, the institution and society) above those of the self when providing direction. It also requires a recognition of the implications of organisational activity for the society (or, in an increasingly globalised world, the societies) affected by its operations. In this respect it has significance not only for the nature of the leader/follower relationship, but also for the ethical integrity of the organisation as a whole (Van Dierendonck 2010).

Whilst apparently somewhat idealistic, the notion of servant leadership is perhaps becoming attractive as an antidote to many of the widely reported failures of leadership, particularly in financial services organisations which, in 2007, sparked major disruption to the global economy, the repercussions of which are likely to last for a decade or more. Concern with the psychological flaws of chief executives has led to a line of research based on ideas of hubris, overconfidence and narcissism – the very opposite of servant leadership. This is well summarised by Bollaert and Petit (2010), whose exploration of the work seeks to move beyond an examination of this 'dark side' of executive psychology and appeals for a better understanding of (amongst other things) its causes:

> We believe that it is important to understand the contextual factors which may cause or aggravate hubristic tendencies, including the possible 'hubrisizing' effect of the executive function, as preventive measures could then be discussed in the context of corporate governance reform. (Bollaert and Petit 2010, p12)

HR professionals might be well placed to contribute to processes that attempt to identify the antecedents of hubristic behaviour and contribute to the necessary elements in corporate governance systems that would help to control their growth and impact.

Whether we are concerned with traditional, virtual, inter-cultural, good or bad leadership, the academic field can offer the practitioner insights into useful approaches, as well as extending the range of knowledge and understanding about effective leadership in new contexts and situations.

 A CRISIS OF LEADERSHIP AT THE BBC (PART TWO)

CASE STUDY 5.2

Following the resignation of George Entwistle the BBC appointed Tony Hall (Lord Hall of Birkenhead) as its new DG with a start date of April 2013 when the interim DG, Tim Davie, stood down. Like Entwistle, Hall had joined the BBC as a news trainee in 1973 and worked there for 28 years before leaving to become chief executive of the Royal Opera House in 2001. This appointment was made without competition and as the result of a direct approach by the BBC Trust. One of his major challenges will be to restore the confidence and morale of staff at the corporation, particularly those involved with news and current affairs programming.

Questions

1   What can recent research into the nature of leadership contribute to our understanding of how leaders can re-engage a demotivated workforce?

2   Is it ethically justifiable to award a publicly funded post like this without competition? Outline the arguments both for and against the decision not to use an open recruitment process in this case.

CONCLUSION

It is clear that there is a renewed sense of the importance of good leadership amongst those most concerned with setting standards for today's managers, be they in business, the public services, or elsewhere. This comes from both social and political changes, which have encouraged more individualism and less obedience to traditional forms of authority. It also stems from the need, as Handy predicted in 1989, for organisations to become more federal than monolithic, and for new styles of management and leadership to emerge to suit the changed environment, including the virtual one. It reflects a growing public interest in the standards of behaviour of those who run businesses and direct our lives through political decisions, and their competence to carry out the tasks entrusted to them. In this respect it links firmly with discussion about ethical standards and organisational practices considered elsewhere in this book.

Personnel and HR professionals will be concerned to ensure good people management and leadership in their organisations, to improve both the performance of the organisation itself and to enable it to attract and keep good staff. This means choosing appropriate frameworks for the selection of potential leaders, their initial training, managing the performance expected of them once in the job, appraising, developing, and rewarding them, facilitating their careers and, sometimes, removing them. A coherent, fair and equitable approach to these tasks is thus essential.

In terms of their applicability to managerial leadership, functional approaches, such as those developed by the MSC, have a lot to offer in terms of managerial leadership and professionalism. They are accessible to all, and can be used for a variety of organisational people management purposes. They offer a valuable way of ensuring that we 'do things right'. In terms of strategic leadership, and particularly when considering international and cross-cultural ventures, contingency theories seem to have more currency, offering a means by which those in charge of organisational strategy can ensure that they make the sort of choices which connect successfully to their business environments: 'doing the right thing in the circumstances'.

REFLECTIVE ACTIVITY 5.4

Much of the literature on leadership focuses on qualities and behaviours which create vision, loyalty and a sense of purpose. The image of someone who is racked by guilt does not immediately seem consistent with leadership potential. Yet recent research at Stanford University (Kremer 2012, Schaumberg and Flynn 2012) may indicate that it is. Data assessing people's susceptibility to feelings of guilt was measured using scenarios and plotted on a 'GASP' (guilt and shame proneness) scale (Cohen *et al* 2012). Study participants then took part in an experiment during which they were required, as a group, to complete a task. No leader was appointed, and there was no incentive to take charge of the group and ensure completion. The experiments showed that group members with high guilt scores generally took the lead. Schaumberg's research therefore suggests that a sense of guilt can be an effective spur to action, and encourage leadership behaviour. But is this type of leadership effective? Schaumberg believes that it might be; particularly since a review of people in real management jobs seemed to show that those who scored higher on the guilt scale also received positive judgements about their leadership from those who reported to them.

Question

1 To what extent do you find Schaumberg's findings to be plausible or counter-intuitive? Explain your reasoning.

CASE STUDY 5.3

LEARNING TO LEAD IN SOUTHSHIRE SCHOOLS

Anil Gupta and Sandra Carter have recently been promoted to the headships of two primary schools in Southshire.

Leadership in modern schools is especially challenging as it requires high-level technical skills combined with well-developed relationship skills. As part of the trend to free schools from local authority control and grant them more autonomy, head teachers have had to learn a range of new technical skills including project management, human resource management, financial and budgetary management, public relations skills and political sensitivity. They need to be respected leaders of staff and pupils alike, and whilst they have scope to shape the strategic direction of their school, the increased autonomy has been accompanied by increased scrutiny and accountability. Schools are a vital part of their local communities and their reputation among parents is a constant source of discussion and concern. Tricky issues abound: beyond a school's gates head teachers are expected to collaborate with other schools (some of which may be competitors for funding or pupils)

and a host of agencies with responsibility for children's welfare.

Anil's background is in physics, and he has been teaching for 12 years, six of them in Southshire schools. He was made deputy head of the John Pounds Primary School (a city-centre school with a diverse ethnic mix, which takes approximately 350 8–11-year-olds) two years ago and has now been promoted to the headship of the school, which will become vacant at the end of the school year when the current Head, Jim Graham, retires. Jim has been head for 17 years, and whilst well known and respected in the community, is somewhat traditional in his approach – a strong disciplinarian with considerable personal charisma. At the same time, Sandra (a modern linguist) is due to take up her first appointment as head of Teapot Row School on the outskirts of the city, which is of a similar size to John Pounds but with less of an ethnic mix. She has been promoted from a deputy headship of another school in rural Southshire. She has met the staff at Teapot Row, and whilst she finds them all to be friendly and devoted teachers, she thinks that the school has tended to rely on its reputation to attract pupils and may need to become more competitive and outward-looking in the future.

Schools in Southshire are able to draw on the resources of the Southshire Teaching and Leadership College (STLC). STLC offers a distinctive approach to leadership development: no two schools, or leaders, are alike and so STLC has adopted a highly personalised approach to leadership development. STLC has been asked to provide a suitable development programme for Anil and Sandra to facilitate their entry into their new leadership roles. Think about the design of such a programme, and consider the following questions.

Questions

1   How might leadership theories inform the content of the programme?

2   Which theories would you choose as the basis for this leadership development programme, and why? Are there any which you think are particularly unsuitable for the context?

3   How would you address the need to develop both the strategic leadership capability as well as the managerial leadership ability which Anil and Sandra need to have as heads?

4   What possible learning and development techniques could be employed? Which would you consider most suitable?

5   How do you think the programme could be evaluated?

You may wish to refer to Chapter 10 to help with your answers.

REVIEW QUESTIONS

1   What do you see as the significant differences between leadership and management? Must all good managers be good leaders? Do all business leaders have to be good managers?

2   Imagine you are in charge of devising a management development programme for a large commercial organisation. What would you include on the subject of leadership and how you would teach this topic? How would you do things differently if you were designing a management development programme for a local authority? You might like to consider the leadership training programme for JT (formerly Jersey Telecom) described by Nicola Reeves (2012).

3   Think about someone you know who you would describe as a good leader, preferably in an organisational context. What makes them good in your view? Would the skills and attributes you identified earlier be suitable in all contexts?

4   Are you a member or leader of a virtual team? If so, try to analyse what sorts of leadership behaviour appear to be effective in this environment. If not, what challenges might exist for leaders of such teams, and how could an HR specialist help to identify them? You might like to consider if any lessons can be learned from the way in which virtual communities such as Facebook or Second Life operate.

EXPLORE FURTHER

Mullins, L. (2013) *Management and Organisational Behaviour*. 10th edition. Harlow: FT/Prentice Hall. This text offers comprehensive descriptions and discussion of all major conceptualisations of both management and leadership, including those relating to gender, as well as relevant case studies.

Yukl, G. (2006) *Leadership in Organisations*. 6th edition. London: Prentice Hall. Another comprehensive review of the nature of leadership in an organisational setting.

Nye, J. (2008) *The Powers to Lead*. Oxford: Oxford University Press. Harvard professor of international relations Joseph Nye considers leadership styles and skills, and also discusses the transferability of leadership between different arenas such as the military, politics and business.

Avolio, B., Walumbwa, F. and Weber, T. (2009) Leadership: current theories, research and future directions. *Annual Review of Psychology*. Vol. 60, No. 4, pp421–49. This offers a summary of recent directions in academic leadership research.

Van Dierendonck, D. (2010) Servant Leadership, a Review and Synthesis. *Journal of Management*. Vol 37, No. 4, pp1228–1261. This provides an overview of the antecedents, behaviours, mediating processes and outcomes associated with the concept of servant leadership.

French, R. (2010) *Cross-Cultural Management in Work Organisations*. 2nd edition. This includes a chapter on the implications of national culture for organisational leadership as well as some information about key authors on cultural difference, and the relevant findings of Project GLOBE.

Information about Project GLOBE (Global Leadership and Organizational Behavior Effectiveness) can be found at the project's website, now hosted by New Mexico State University, at business.nmsu.edu/programs-centers/globe

Information and press releases about the 2012 crisis at the BBC can be found on the BBC Trust's website (www.bbc.co.uk/bbctrust) as well as those of most reputable newspapers.

CHAPTER 6

Managing Change

Gary Rees and David Hall

LEARNING OUTCOMES

After reading this chapter, you should be able to:

- explore the nature and types of change
- examine the context, process and content of change
- explore and examine change interventions
- examine change leadership and change capability
- examine the role of HR and change.

OVERVIEW

Change continues to take a front-of-stage role in both academic research and industrial practice. Whilst it is difficult to gain a universally accepted definition of change, we are reminded that change management is not a distinct discipline with rigorous and defined boundaries, but more that the theory and practice of change management draws upon a number of social science disciplines and traditions (Burnes 2004). This chapter encapsulates the major theories in the field of change, adopting a strategic perspective, and considers how HR can impact upon change in organisations.

The appropriateness of change planning and intervention is dependent to some extent on how we fit theory into practice, and vice versa. Grint (1997, p1) sums up the argument particularly well:

Theory is where you know everything and nothing works;

Practice is where everything works,

But nobody knows why;

Here we combine theory and practice:

Nothing works and nobody knows why.

Whilst it is unlikely that any one change model fits perfectly, there is scope to consider a more hybrid approach to change. There needs to be a move away from 'static' models of change, which stress the content and substance of change (Nelson 2003), to the dynamics of change, with the expectation that change occurs within a less certain environment, where flexibility is required to maintain or enable competitive advantage. These issues are explored throughout this chapter.

INTRODUCTION

DEFINING CHANGE AND CHANGE MANAGEMENT

Small-scale and relatively simple change, typically categorised as 'hard' problems, are usually managed within the day-to-day operational management activity. This type of change is not usually referred to as 'change' by managers, and the process of managing it is not described as 'managing change' or 'change management' within organisations.

Managers have to consider the many factors involved in a complex and dynamic situation before making decisions that implement actions that will influence the effectiveness, efficiency and ultimately the sustainability of their organisations.

Brech (1975, p19) defines management as:

A social process entailing responsibility for the effective and economic planning and regulation of the operations of an enterprise, in fulfilment of given purposes or tasks, such responsibility involving:

(a) Judgement and decision in determining plans and in using data to control performance and progress against plans;

(b) The guidance, integration, motivation and supervision of the personnel composing the enterprise and carrying out its operations.

Brech describes the four main elements of management as being planning, control, co-ordination and motivation. Fayol (1949) describes the function of management in similar terms, proposing five elements of management: planning, organising, commanding, co-ordinating and controlling.

Management can be described as, essentially, an intervention for controlling operational performance outcomes in line with an organisation's purpose and objectives.

In carrying out their responsibilities, managers deal with change on a day-to-day basis, which raises an interesting question: when does management become 'change management'? Is this purely an academic question (it will be for many managers), or is it helpful from a management and organisational perspective to understand what, if anything, differentiates the two?

Change may be defined simplistically as making things different, but needs to make explicit mention of actual and perceived change(s). Fincham and Rhodes (2005, p525) define change management as 'the leadership and direction of the process of organisational transformation – especially with regard to human aspects and overcoming resistance to change'.

The Society for Human Resource Management defines change management as:

The systematic approach and application of knowledge, tools and resources to deal with change. Change management means defining and adopting corporate strategies, structures, procedures and technologies to deal with changes in external conditions and the business environment. (www.shrm.org/templatestools/glossaries/hrterms/pages/c.aspx [accessed 30 May 2013])

Therefore, managing change or 'change management' is a form of management control through the application of systematic management interventions that involve people to achieve a desired future state with defined performance outcomes in line with the organisational strategy.

From this definition, it is clear that there is a strong and inextricable link between organisational change, performance and strategy.

TYPES OF CHANGE

Dependent upon the perspective that has been adopted, a variety of models and concepts can be utilised in order to consider the types of organisational change. This chapter will consider the level of change, the size and scope of change, the nature of change and the momentum of change.

THE LEVEL OF ORGANISATIONAL CHANGE

Carnall (2003) suggests that there are three levels of strategic change. Firstly, organisation-specific changes, such as a new information system. Secondly, generic organisation-wide change programmes, such as business process engineering (BPR) and thirdly, generic multi-organisational change programmes, for example, mergers and acquisitions.

THE SIZE AND SCOPE OF CHANGE

Child (2005) provides a useful model on how to differentiate between the scope of change and type of change – see Figure 6.1.

Figure 6.1 Child's approaches to organisational change

Approaches to organisational change

	Planned	Emergent	
Radical	BPR	Organic development (eg start-up company)	whole org.
	Merger of departments	Changes to selection of new members made by teams	part org.
Incremental	Annual targeted improvements	Organisational learning	whole org.
	Changes agreed in staff performance plans	Continuous improvement through project teams	part org.

It must be borne in mind that whilst radical and incremental change may be defined and measured, that often it is the perceived scale of change that may be more important than the 'actual' scale of change.

THE NATURE OF CHANGE – PLANNED OR UNPLANNED?

Whilst it may be assumed that all organisational change is both rational and planned, with control of nearly all processes and resources, there may be occasions when a less planned and logical method may be adopted. A parallel argument is one of adopting an organic approach to change (Burns and Stalker 1994) versus an expected mechanistic approach. If it is assumed that change can emerge, then one approach by management may be to throw a metaphorical hand grenade into the organisation, and then see what emerges.

For example, an organisation may deliberately set about rumour-mongering around restructuring and job cuts, then formally notify employees that all jobs have been red circled and that employees have to make applications for new posts. During this time, communication and consultation is deliberately kept to a minimum. Management then see what emerges after a period of time. A less contentious scenario could also be envisaged, where the management of an organisation simply let things run, without obvious intervention.

Change models tend to centre around planned change, which in itself will determine the various factors or characteristics that are then compared to, for example: strategic/tactical and operational change; radical, transformational and incremental change; the rate of change (change momentum); and hard versus soft change.

However, complex large-scale change, usually driven by external factors and having a significant 'soft' change element, are planned and co-ordinated. The terms 'managing change' or 'change management' can be used to describe the application of systematic interventions to implement a planned change within organisations to achieve a desired future state. In the following section, several key change management models are considered.

The nature of change – hard and soft change

The 'hard' elements of change are the tasks within change management, which are defined and measured. 'Soft' factors, such as culture and motivation, may be more difficult to assess. Emphasis may be placed upon managing task factors at the expense of soft factors during change interventions; however, Sirkin *et al* (2005) argue that four hard factors correlate to the outcome of change interventions, namely: duration (length of time); integrity (reliance on managers); commitment (of all involved in change); and effort (within the opportunity of time allowed).

When characterising change, we have considered the speed and magnitude of change, and related this to the problem of complexity. The problems that change present to an organisation can be perceived by managers as 'difficulties', which are 'bounded' in that they can be well defined (specified) and can be dealt with without involving or impacting on the wider organisation.

Another category of problems are those which cannot be well defined and are 'unbounded' in the sense that the wider organisation is implicated and needs to be involved in dealing with these types of problems.

The nature of change – top–down versus bottom–up

Top–down change can stem from a managerial prerogative for maintaining control throughout the change. Change can be driven through by management, and resistance controlled and eliminated. Here change can become more of a political issue (Gioia and Thomas 1996). Lupton (1991) argues that a bottom–up approach has its benefits in that employees at all levels have skills and expertise that are often lost in change processes. A third option is a combination of top–down and bottom–up approaches.

Change momentum: magnitude and speed

The momentum of change, ie the combination of speed and magnitude of change, is a useful concept to analyse and characterise different types of change. As we have seen, change momentum is not always easy to predict, but if it can be anticipated (which is often the case) interventions to manage change may be considered from the options available. In other words, if managers are able to characterise the type of change an organisation will experience, this can be helpful in considering appropriate interventions to manage change in an effective way. We will consider change management interventions later, but let us return to characterising change. Figure 6.2 below represents a model of change momentum based on the two key variables of speed and magnitude.

Figure 6.2 Model of change momentum

Magnitude of change

'Planned' Large change Slow change	*'Big Bang'* Large change Fast change
'Smooth' Small change Slow change	*'Bumpy'* Small change Fast change

Speed of change

'Smooth' and 'bumpy' change are both characterised by relatively small (and less complex) change, but differ in speed of implementation, with 'smooth' change happening over a longer period of time than the latter. Smooth change happens in small steps and is often described as being 'incremental', being barely noticeable in the day-to-day business of an organisation. Relatively minor changes to policies and procedures would be examples of this type of change. It is typically driven by internal factors.

'Bumpy' change is more noticeable, as the speed of change is fast and therefore requires a quicker response time by managers and employees in dealing with it. It is typically driven by external factors which require an organisation to move quickly to respond. Examples of this would include organisations responding to crisis, which require significant investment and/or changes in practice, eg health, safety and the environment, regulatory reform or legal proceedings. Companies involved in fast-moving markets often have to manage this type of change as consumer opinion and tastes quickly change.

Grundy (1993) describes three types of change related to speed of change. The first is 'smooth incremental change' as change that evolves slowly in a systematic and predictable way. He also describes 'bumpy incremental change' as periods of relative calm, ie little or no change that is punctuated by accelerated change. The third type of change described by Grundy is 'discontinuous' change, which he defines as 'change which is marked by rapid shifts in strategy, structure or culture, or in all three' (Grundy 1993, p26). This equates closely to 'Big Bang' change in terms of change momentum.

Grundy's 'discontinuous change' and 'Big Bang' change describes many of the characteristics of what has become known as 'transformational' change – a type of change that involves the values, attitudes and behaviours of people that contribute towards shaping the culture of an organisation. This form of complex change focuses on the motivation and commitment of employees and their contribution towards performance outcomes. Leadership which emphasises these employee attributes in managing change is described as 'transformational leadership' (Bass 1985), to which we shall return later.

In conclusion, a range of differing variables have been used to examine the different types of change. However, there may be other more relevant comparators than the ones presented. It is necessary to examine the context of change as well in order to assess whether the most appropriate comparators have been used.

ANALYSING THE CHANGE CONTEXT

The question as to why organisations change is often determined by a combination of push and pull factors. Organisations sometimes have choices as to whether they want to change, or are sometimes forced to change, because of legal or other reasons. The importance of why organisations change is linked to the timing of change.

Whilst there may be a range of comparators with which to analyse change dimensions, a potential metaphor is one which considers a combination of change interventions running concurrently – see Figure 6.3. The metaphor shows a range of change interventions, some of which start anew, some end, and all of which may impact upon each other.

Figure 6.3 Combination of concurrent change interventions

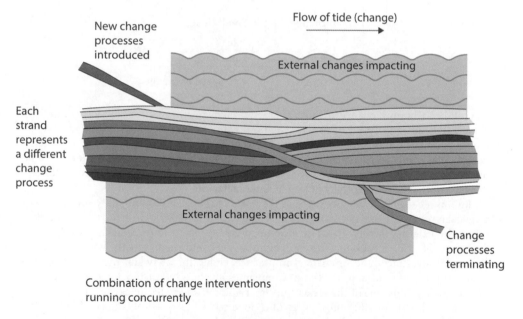

Whilst classic change models may posit a start, middle and end part of the change process, it is important to have to start at some point in terms of determining where the organisation is now and where it wants to arrive at in terms of change. Change models can either adopt a reactive approach ('this is why we need to change'), or adopt a proactive approach ('where do we want to get to as an organisation?').

Figure 6.4 demonstrates the iterative nature of change, and planning for change.

Figure 6.4 The iterative nature of change, and planning for change

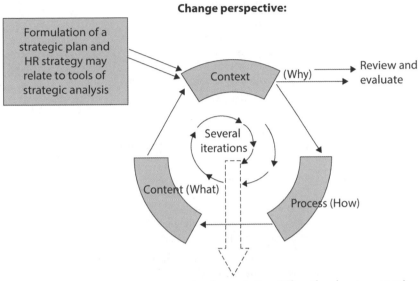

Change perspective:

With strategic change, we may start with a strategic plan, or possibly a vision or mission statement, which leads to a strategic plan. When analysing why organisations change, there is often a trigger for change. The following factors are proposed here as triggers for change – see also CIPD (2009b):

- challenges of growth, especially global markets
- challenges of economic downturns and tougher trading conditions
- changes in strategy
- technological changes
- competitive pressures, including mergers and acquisitions
- customer pressure, particularly shifting markets
- pressures to learn new organisation behaviour and skills
- government legislation/initiatives.

When it comes to analysing the strategic context, a range of models can be utilised. Both the internal and external context need to be analysed.

Caldwell (2013) argues that change should be understood from a 'changing organisation' perspective, which places multiple, simultaneous adaptive demands upon individuals (employees) from many forces within the organisation, which in themselves may be planned or possibly unplanned.

EXTERNAL DRIVERS OF CHANGE

A useful tool to examine the external drivers of change involves the PESTLE taxonomy. The earliest known reference to a framework for describing the external business environment is by Aguilar (1967) who presents 'ETPS' as a mnemonic to represent the four sectors: Economic, Technical, Political, and Social. Variations of this include 'PEST' and 'PESTLE', which adds the Legal and Environmental dimensions – see Table 6.1.

Table 6.1 PESTLE framework

Factor or driver	Typical considerations
Political	• Taxation and other policies • Current and future political support • Funding, grants and initiatives • Trade organisations • Internal and international relationships
Economic	• Economic situation • Consumer spending • Levels of government spending • Interest rates, inflation and unemployment • Exchange rates
Social	• Demographics and social mobility • Lifestyle patterns and changes • People's attitudes and actions • Media perception and influence • Ethnic and religious differences
Technological	• Research, technology and innovation funding • Consumer behaviour and processes • Intellectual property • Global communication technological advances • Social networks
Legal	• Legislation in employment, competition and health and safety, etc • Changes in legislation • Trading policies • Regulatory bodies • International protocols
Environmental	• Clean technologies and processes • Waste management and recycling • Attitudes of government, media and consumers • Environmental legislation • Global warming and emission protocols

The PESTLE taxonomy provides a useful external environment scanning framework and a methodology for identifying and analysing factors that shape the external business environment. When combined with a SWOT (Strengths, Weaknesses, Opportunities and Threats) analysis, this evidence-based approach provides valuable information for strategic decision-making.

The external environmental factors identified from a PESTLE are typically considered as opportunities or threats in a SWOT analysis. Strengths and weaknesses are usually regarded as internal organisational factors which can be considered against the external opportunities and threats. This 'looking out' and 'looking in' approach provides a basis for internal–external organisation analysis and is an important part of the strategic management process, if carried out in a purposeful and rigorous manner.

INTERNAL DRIVERS OF CHANGE

Not all organisational change can be attributed to managers responding to a business environment comprising external factors. Internal drivers of change can also play a major role in initiating change and these include:

- new leadership
- new strategy
- new structures
- new business model
- organisation growth
- redesign of jobs
- redesign of business processes
- outsourcing
- change of location
- installation of new technology and systems
- changes to employees' terms and conditions
- being acquired or merged with another organisation
- redundancies.

These changes can be and often are influenced by external factors but they can also be triggered by decisions which are not made as a response to changes in the business environment.

Pettigrew and Whipp (1993) argue that environmental assessment is only one of five factors that determine the success of managing change. The other four factors are leading change, linking strategic and operational change, considering human resources as both assets and liabilities, and a central factor in all of this – coherence – pulling together the other four factors.

REFLECTIVE ACTIVITY 6.1

Duty of care

Change has been equated to bereavement (Marris 1986). Constant change may not allow employees time to grieve. It could be argued that organisations have a duty of care to ensure that the welfare of their employees is paramount and thereby limit constant and dramatic change. If an organisation does not constantly seek employee feedback and make an assessment through an organisational stress thermometer, then how will it know how much employees can take? Acas (2010) recommends that employees' emotions are taken into account when managing change, by including the following within every change process:

- create a vision
- lead (the change)
- consult (with employees)
- engage (employees)
- reflect upon the change process (including employees' views).

Question

1   What are the implications for organisations when deciding upon the nature and type of change, and how change should take place?

It is important to differentiate between external and internal factors when considering change, with the key difference being that organisations and managers may have little, if any, control over the external factors. However, internal factors are typically management decisions which are designed to exert some form of control aimed at achieving certain performance outcomes.

. Organisations lobby governments on many issues in an attempt to influence politicians' decisions and the outcomes that define the external factors which ultimately shape the business environment in which they operate. Climate change and the environment are examples of contemporary issues that continue to attract the lobbyists in the early part of this century.

Control is the primary motivation for doing this because if organisations can be a factor in shaping their business environment, this enables them to predict more accurately what this environment will look like. This, in turn, puts these organisations in a stronger position to be able to make informed strategic decisions to control their future direction and performance.

The UK Government's 'modernisation programme' of public services described in a 1999 White Paper set out a 10-year change programme aimed at delivering more responsive and high-quality public services which can be measured by better results. The NHS is probably the most widely publicised example of this modernisation agenda, having been subjected to a plethora of change initiatives and performance targets.

A combination of external and internal factors typically drive this type of change in organisations.

CHOICE OF CHANGE INTERVENTION

After the context has been analysed, the choice of change intervention needs to be considered. Five different change management tools and techniques are discussed below in order to provide an understanding of how the organisation can manage change.

TROPICS test

The Open University (1985) describes two types of problems as 'difficulties' and 'messes'. Paton and McCalman (2000) use the terms 'hard' and 'soft' respectively to describe these same sets of problems, and devised the 'TROPICS' test as a guide to help determine the nature of change in terms of a continuum from hard to soft (see Table 6.2).

Table 6.2 The TROPICS test

Hard	Soft
Timescales clearly defined/short- to medium-term	Timescales ill-defined/medium- to long-term
Resources needed identified	Resources uncertain
Objectives specified and quantified	Objectives subjective and ambiguous
Perceptions of the problem shared by all	No consensus of problem
Interest in problem limited and defined	Interest in problem is widespread and ill defined
Control within managing group	Control is shared with people outside of managing group
Source of the problem lies within organisation	Source of the problem is from outside the organisation

This test provides a useful reference framework to help characterise and understand the parameters involved when facing change. It is important to recognise that this is a continuum, and many change programmes will combine elements of hard and soft change.

When managers have knowledge and understanding of the issues involved in a change scenario, they are in a better position to be able to assess the situation and decide on an appropriate course of action to help control and manage the change process.

Lewin's three-phase change model

One of the earliest known models applied to managing change is a three-phase model by Kurt Lewin (1951) which focuses on the psychological aspects of behaviour modification:

1   *Unfreezing* – lowering resistance to change by recognising and accepting the need for change.

2   *Movement* – developing new attitudes to encourage behaviours necessary for change to occur.

3   *Refreezing* – stabilising, supporting and reinforcing the new change conditions.

This model presents a systematic approach to change management, describing a sequence of well defined and interrelated processes. The premise for this model is that by identifying and understanding the key stages involved in the change process, the likelihood of effective change management is increased – by managers making better informed decisions about which interventions to use in managing change.

Lewin (1947) was also responsible for developing the Force-field analysis, a diagnostic technique which considered the forces or 'drivers' for and against change. At any time, there will be a number of forces in play that resist change and support the status quo, and forces that encourage change. These can be internal or external forces, or, as is usually the case, a combination of both.

When the sum of the forces 'for' and 'against' change are equal, they cancel each other out, resulting in equilibrium, i.e. a steady state. However, when the forces driving change are greater than the forces of resistance (either by the driving forces increasing or the restraining forces decreasing) then change will occur, and the organisation will inevitably change and move to a new state, as shown in Figure 6.5.

Figure 6.5 Lewin's Force-field analysis

Forces resisting change

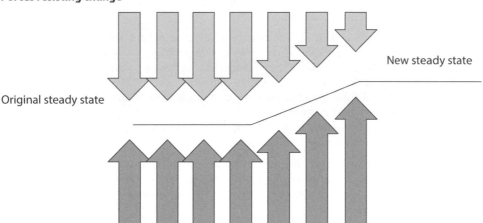

Forces driving change

Although Lewin's model is criticised for over-simplifying change by describing a sequential linear process, its three stages of change are reflected in other more contemporary change management models. French *et al* (1985) list eight components of a planned-change effort, which can be related to Lewin's model:

1. Initial problem identification ⎫
2. Obtaining data   ⎬ *Unfreezing*
3. Problem diagnosis   ⎭

4. Action planning   ⎫
5. Implementation   ⎬ *Movement*
6. Follow-up and stabilise   ⎭

7. Assessment of the consequences   ⎫
8. Learning from the process   ⎬ *Refreezing*

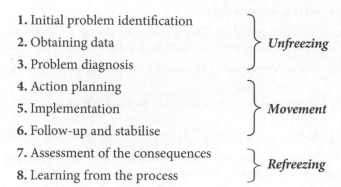

The other main criticism of Lewin's model and other linear change models is that they describe the process of change transforming from an initial state to a final stage. Today, change is widely recognised as being a constant and continuing phenomena for all organisations, albeit at a faster rate for some compared to others.

RESISTANCE TO CHANGE

A multitude of factors could contribute to resistance to change. Prahalad, quoted in Allio (2008), cites three primary reasons for resistance to change in organisations. First, the logic of management actions and behaviours is not always obvious. Secondly, if change occurs, the accumulated intellectual experience of the players becomes devalued and change is taken as a personal threat (so a safety net is needed). Thirdly, managers need to have their hand held while they are learning. Prahalad emphasises the need for managers to be constantly learning new skills.

French *et al* (2011) suggest that in order to minimise resistance in such cases, the change agent should make sure that the people affected by the change know specifically how it satisfies the following criteria:

- *Benefit.* The change should have a clear relative advantage for the individuals being asked to change; ie, it should be perceived as 'a better way'.
- *Compatibility.* The change should be as compatible as possible with the existing values and experiences of the people being asked to change.
- *Complexity.* The change should be no more complex than necessary. It must be as easy as possible to understand and use.
- *Triability.* The change should be something that people can try on a step-by-step basis and make adjustments throughout the process.

Frahm and Brown (2005) argue that one of the key aspects of creating strategic change is the receptivity of employees to organisational change. They argue that organisational communication can significantly help alleviate problems often associated with change fatigue and change resistance.

REFLECTIVE ACTIVITY 6.2

Your organisation (or an organisation of your choice) has decided to introduce job evaluation and performance management organisation-wide. It is also operating a recruitment ban and pay freeze. As the HR business partner, use Lewin's model to identify some of the potential forces acting for and against this change initiative.

Kotter's eight-stage change model

John Kotter (1996) described an eight-stage change process for managing change in large organisations following his research into US organisations who had failed to manage change effectively:

1   Establish a sense of urgency – *the need to change.*

2   Create a guiding coalition – *with authority and credibility.*

3   Develop a vision and strategy – *a clear aim and way forward.*

4   Communicate the change vision – *promote understanding and commitment.*

5   Empower broad-based action – *enable people to act and overcome barriers.*

6   Generate short-term wins – *to motivate and ensure further support.*

7   Consolidate gains and produce more change – *maintain change momentum.*

8   Anchor new approaches in the culture – *new values, attitudes and behaviours.*

This model appears to be a linear and sequential set of processes, and has been criticised for these reasons. However, in the final two steps, Kotter attempts to address the problem of the 'refreezing' stage in Lewin's model by encouraging organisations and their employees to develop attitudes and values which help to promote the behaviours required to encourage and support further change. Developing an organisational culture that is proactive to change helps to create a feedback mechanism which transforms a linear change model into a continuous process.

Many change management programmes applied in organisations are based on systematic change management models comprising sequential processes similar to the examples outlined above. However, a common modification to these models in practice is to introduce an additional process at the end, which provides a feedback step from the final to the initiating stage. With this modification, these models describe a cyclical and continuous change management system.

A significant feature of Kotter's model is the role of leadership, particularly in developing and communicating the vision for change, which is critical to effective transformational leadership, and management of change in large-scale organisations (Bass 1985).

This type of approach to change tends to be effective for change that is predominantly 'hard' by nature, ie as characterised in terms of the TROPICS test. Objectives, milestones and performance can be quantified and applied within the boundaries of a specific change programme, thereby offering a means to assess progress of the managed change programme.

Organisational development

There is another approach for intervening to improve organisational performance through managing change called organisational development (OD) that offers appropriate solutions to the 'softer' aspects of change. We must remember that hard and soft change is part of a continuum, and that the majority of change scenarios involve both aspects. When managing change, organisations will apply a range of interventions often using both approaches described in this chapter. These different approaches are not mutually exclusive.

There are many definitions of OD, but the following definition is particularly useful in helping to develop understanding of the context, content and processes involved in OD as a change and organisational performance intervention.

French and Bell (1999, pp25–26) define OD as:

a long-term effort, led and supported by top management to improve an organisation's visioning, empowerment, learning and problem-solving processes, through an ongoing, collaborative management of organisation culture – with a special emphasis on the culture of intact work-teams and other team configurations, using consultant-facilitator role and the theory and technology of applied behavioural science, including action research.

CIPD (2009b) offers the following succinct definition of OD: 'planned and systematic approach to enabling sustained organisational performance through the involvement of its people'.

OD emphasises the management of culture and employee behaviour as the central interventions for sustaining organisational capability to deal with long-term change and improve performance. An examination of several definitions of OD reveals a number of common features which highlight the distinguishing characteristics of the OD approach to change:

● It has top management support and involvement – it is participative.
● It deals with change over the medium- to long-term – it is strategic.
● It applies to an entire organisation and its component parts – it is systematic within institutionalising change.
● It draws on the theory and practice of behavioural science – such as leadership, group dynamics and work design.
● It emphasises the transfer of knowledge and skills through training and developing people – using action-research and organisational learning methods.
● It is concerned with planned change but is adaptable to new situations – rather than prescribing a rigid process which must be followed.
● It is uses data to inform decision-making and progress – it is 'evidence-based'.
● It often makes use of change agents or OD practitioners to facilitate the OD process.
● It is aimed at facilitating planned change and improving organisational performance over the longer term.

The roots of OD can be found in the motivation theories of the 1940s and 1950s, which gave rise to the human relations school of management and organisation. It became popular towards the end of the last century as an alternative approach to the hard systems approach shaped by the models which flourished in the 1980s and 1990s. These models struggled to deal with the complexities and often unknown factors that were common components of the 'unbounded' soft and messy problems organisations faced as their environments rapidly changed.

OD focuses on managing organisational culture by promoting values and attitudes associated with personal and professional development, problem-solving, openness, engagement and commitment. The premise of this approach is that if an organisation's employees share such common values, this will manifest in desirable and normative behaviour at all levels: individual, team and organisation.

An example of where the application of the OD approach would be particularly relevant is in developing a 'high performance culture' within an organisation. By establishing a shared set of values which employees, particularly managers, agree to adhere to in the work environment, this provides a guide for what is regarded as acceptable employee behaviour, which, over a period of time, becomes regarded as normal behaviour by most employees.

The set of values would typically include values related to learning and improvement, working with others, being honest and respectful, etc, which ultimately influence an individual and group behaviour to enable performance improvement. These values would typically be applied in performance management interventions, recruitment and selection, career development and progression, reward schemes and leadership development, to facilitate and embed an evasive organisational culture that encourages and supports high levels of commitment to performance.

This is a sophisticated and complex form of organisational control based on influencing normative behaviour which is acceptable to managers and employees. The principles of OD also facilitate management of the psychological contract, which is defined by Guest and Conway (2002) as 'the perceptions of the two parties, employee and employer, of what their mutual obligations are towards each other'.

Guest and Conway propose in their model of the psychological contract that the implicit nature of contract is moderated by the employees' and employer's sense of fairness and trust, and the belief that the employer will honour the unwritten arrangement between them. It is suggested that a healthy psychological contract will promote employee commitment and satisfaction and have a positive influence on performance.

How employees experience and perceive the workplace, and their relationship with managers and colleagues, will play a role in shaping their attitudes and consequent behaviour. OD, with its emphasis on values and attitudes as a means of managing culture and change, also presents an opportunity for employers and employees to develop positive psychological contracts to the benefit of both parties.

Although OD is an intervention for managing change and improving performance, because it focuses on the culture of an organisation influencing the attitudes and values (and ultimately behaviour), it pervades all areas and activities of an organisation. With an emphasis on learning and improvement, at individual, group and organisational levels, through techniques such as action learning, it develops and sustains the performance capability of an organisation through its people asset (human capital) and prepares an organisation for dealing with continuous change, ie it develops a state of enduring readiness for change.

In doing this, OD shapes the culture of an organisation to encourage managers and employees not to resist change but to be accepting and even embrace change, and approach it in that way. In other words, OD influences the ethos of an organisation and its people in dealing with change. It is an approach which addresses the soft and often intangible aspects of managing change which, because of the complexity involved, the rationality-based linear change models do not adequately accommodate.

Organisations that take the OD approach towards managing change tend to rely less on specific and explicit change programmes, but approach change as a normal part of everyday business. In the UK, the NHS has attempted to take this approach, having undergone radical change since inception of the modernisation programme (see above). The OD approach implies that normal business is about change and that dealing with change is implicit in what organisations and their people do – it is 'business as usual'.

This makes a lot of sense because if we accept that organisational change is a permanent phenomenon, employees will soon become exhausted and demotivated if they are presented with one change programme after another, and sometimes multiple change programmes at the same time.

That is not to say that organisations that adopt the OD approach cannot and do not roll out specific projects for introducing change. This would be a particularly appropriate approach for managing when hard changes which are specific and contained, and lend themselves to being managed as a project with clearly defined and measurable objectives.

CASE STUDY 6.1

IMPRESS: MEETING COMPANY GOALS THROUGH STRATEGIC ACQUISITIONS

Impress is a privately owned worldwide manufacturer of metal food cans, operating in 21 countries, with 8,000 employees, and turnover of 1.6 billion euros in 2006. Impress as a legal identity is based in the Netherlands, but has its head office in Paris, and operates primarily throughout Europe. Its strategy is to be the best metal-can manufacturer as opposed to the most profitable or biggest, and places great emphasis upon values surrounding operational excellence. The corporate culture centres around trust, transparency and teamwork.

Impress adopts an acquisition strategy in order to meet company objectives, and not as a purpose in itself. After Impress has considered acquiring another organisation and has evaluated if there will be a resultant strategic advantage, questions around the target company's readiness to change are considered. All relevant parties are brought to the table, and HR, finance, legal, production, management and technical teams are consulted in an unaggressive and unobtrusive way.

Impress managers seek to understand the culture and management model of the organisation and its capacity for change, as well as explore the leadership of the change process. The reputation of the company in the local area is considered, employee behaviours and skills are analysed and consideration given to company values and how they are communicated throughout the company.

During the post-acquisition process, welcome meetings are arranged, existing signs and logos are replaced by the Impress brand, plans for integration of the two company structures set out, synergies and benchmarking sought, and restructuring plans made. Information is communicated as clearly and widely as possible in order to keep all relevant parties informed. Management changes are made as quickly as possible and a vision developed for the acquired company.

Impress use a 'learning by doing' framework for acquisitions, which facilitates the integration process and creates enough flexibility to allow processes and values to be influenced by the cultures of the company that it acquires and the countries in which it operates.

Source: Huws and O'Keefe (2008)

Question

1   Consider the extent to which Impress adopts Kotter's approach when managing acquisitions and change.

Whilst the concept of a systems approach may on the face of it appear simplistic, systems models allow for a great deal of complexity and data to be analysed. Figure 6.6 demonstrates the key components of a process model of change.

Figure 6.6 A systems approach to change

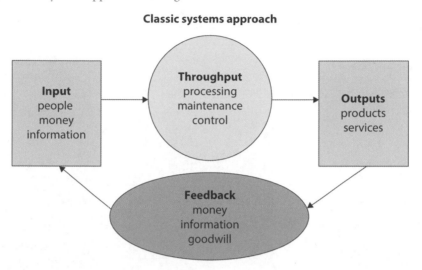

A systems approach to change

Whilst there is a range of systems models available to the change agent, Mayon-White (1993) highlights the example of systems intervention strategy (SIS) as a useful tool for undertaking change. The diagnosis phase asks 'Where are we now?'(the description), then 'Where do we want to be?', which evolves the identification of objectives and constraints. The question 'How will you know when you get there?' is addressed by the formulation of measures to achieve the objectives. In the design phase, we ask 'How can we get there?', in order to generate a range of options, then ask 'What will it be like?', where we can model options selectively. During the implementation phase, we consider whether we will like it, and then evaluate options against measures. Finally, we ask 'How can we carry it through?' then consider the design of implementation strategies and carry through the planned changes. Figure 6.7 demonstrates how the 'problem owners' fit within this model. Whilst McCalman and Paton (1992) argue that the problem owner may clearly define the nature of change, those affected by the change, the boundary and scope of the change and the relationships affected by the change, it could be contested that establishing who is affected by the change is not always apparent. 'Affected' could be considered in terms of job, role, task, function etc, but may not account for emotional or cultural ties, etc.

Figure 6.7 Systems intervention strategy

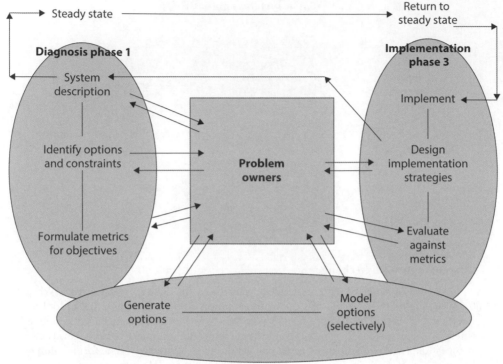

Mayon-White (1993, p136) provides a chart showing the types of action and tools and techniques that are used in systems intervention strategy (see Table 6.3).

Table 6.3 The key features and methods of SIS

The three phases of the strategy	The steps of the strategy phases	What kinds of actions are appropriate to each step?	What tools and techniques are available to help?
Diagnosis	0. Entry	Start by recognising that change is a complex process.	Make use of the concepts of 'mess' and 'difficulty'.
	1. Description	Structure and understanding the change in systems terms. Get other points of view on the change problem or opportunity.	Use diagrams. Set up meetings (NGT, Delphi, etc). Create a model of things as they are.

The three phases of the strategy	The steps of the strategy phases	What kinds of actions are appropriate to each step?	What tools and techniques are available to help?
	2. Identify objectives and constraints	Set up objectives for the systems that you are examining. Think of the objectives of the change itself.	Set up an 'objective tree'. Prioritise your objectives for change.
	3. Formulate measures for your objectives	Decide on ways of measuring if an objective is achieved.	Use '£s' or quantities where possible. Scaling or ranking methods elsewhere.
Design	4. Generate a range of options	Develop any ideas for change as full options. Look at a wide range of possibilities. Your objectives may suggest new options.	Brainstorming. Idea writing. Interviews and surveys. Comparisons with best practice in other organisations.
	5. Model options selectively	Describe the most promising options in some detail. Ask of each option: what is involved? Who is involved? How will it work?	Diagrams are simple models. Cost–benefit analysis. Cash flow models. Computer simulations.
Implementation	6. Evaluate options against measures	Test the performance of your options against an agreed set of criteria.	Set up a simple matrix to compare the performance of your options. Score each option against the metrics.
	7. Design implementation strategies	Select your preferred options and plan a way of putting the changes into place.	Look for reliable options. Check back to 'problem owners'. Plan time and allocate tasks.
	8. Carry through the planned changes	Bring together people and resources. Manage the process. Monitor progress.	Sort out who is involved. Allocate responsibility. Review and modify plans if necessary (CPA etc).

(Mayon-White, B. and Mabey, C. (1998) *Managing Change* 2nd ed. Open University Press)

A range of models have been presented, some of which show signs of overlap; for example, systems intervention strategy includes Lewin's Force-field analysis. The choice of model(s) is up to the change agent and key stakeholders. It is possible to combine aspects of different models, for example, having a combination of OD and SIS, but caution needs to be expressed so that there is no confusion as to what the process actually involves.

LEADING CHANGE

The choice of change agent is critical to the success of any change intervention. Whilst a universal definition of a change agent proves impossible to locate, characteristics, competences and skills can differentiate across change agents.

In simple terms, Rosenfeld and Wilson (1999, p294) define change as 'the individuals or groups of individuals whose task it is to effect change'.

What does a change agent look like?

Whilst the determination of choice of change agent will be determined by a range of factors, Lessem (1989) provides a range of change agent characteristics:

- *You are professional*, with an in-depth knowledge and experience in a particular field, and often with greater loyalty to your profession than to your organisation.
- *You learn from change*, by observing, conceptualising, experimenting and validating. Also, by accommodating through flexible communications.
- *You troubleshoot*, rapidly identifying opportunities for change, and coming up with alternative courses of action to exploit them.
- *You adapt to change*, by mapping out the internal and external environment, and by creating systems and procedures for dealing with change.
- *You experiment with change*, by continually forming temporary project groupings and solving ongoing problems in interdisciplinary teams.
- *You plan for change*, by constructing long-term plans with contingencies built in, monitoring changes and adapting plans accordingly.
- *You embody the spirit of change*, and are respected as a free thinker. You also embody the organisation's cause.

 REFLECTIVE ACTIVITY 6.3

To what extent can the HR function adopt Lessem's seven characteristics and demonstrate these during a change process?

Doz and Prahalad (1988) cite a range of tools that change agents can select from and use. Firstly, data management tools concern the manipulation of information, systems, resource allocation procedures, strategic planning and budgeting arrangements. These tools are used to guide decision-making. Secondly, management tools are a combination of hard and soft approaches. 'Hard' tools involve manipulation of key appointments, career planning and reward systems. 'Soft' tools include changes to management development and socialisation patterns. These tools dictate the rules of the game. Thirdly, conflict management tools involve relocation of decision responsibility, formation of business teams, task forces and co-ordination committees, the appointment of 'integrators', and establishment of procedures to resolve issues. These tools may be used more predominantly at different stages of a change intervention, where data management tools may prove most useful at the early stages of change, but conflict management tools may be used throughout some change interventions or perhaps during the 'movement' and 'refreezing' stages of a change process.

Buchanan and Boddy (1992) identified 15 competences that change agents adopt, clustered into five areas, namely: goals, roles, communication, negotiation and managing up. These competences sit within a framework which emphasises the political dimension. The importance of both front stage and back stage activity emphasises how the change agent has to manage their position continuously so as ensure their tenure and sustainability through the change intervention. Figure 6.10 displays the three critical agendas that may impact upon the determination of the change agent, where the content agenda relies upon technical competence (similar to Doz and Prahalad's data management tools), and the process agenda matches implementation skills, where communication, consultation, team-building, influencing and negotiation skills are key (similar to Doz and Pralahad's conflict management tools).

Figure 6.8 The expertise of the change agent

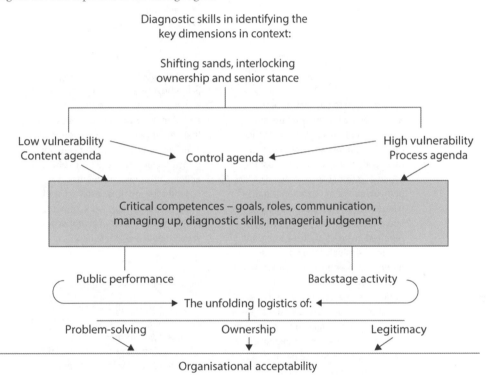

Source: Buchanan and Boddy (1992)

It could be argued that the more strategic the change, the more politically charged it will be and thereby draw upon more power bases. Balogun *et al*'s research (2005) supports Hardy's argument (1994, 1996) that change agents address and engage the 'power of the system', mobilising existing power to negotiate power interdependencies to enrol staff to their cause. This parallels with Kotter's (1999) notion of forming powerful coalitions so as to effect a change agenda. Kotter argues that managers typically form powerful coalitions through network building and setting both business and personal agendas.

When making an assessment as to whether change agents could be recruited internally within an organisation, it might be useful to conduct an evaluation of whether there is a critical mass of the various skills within this context. If not, perhaps the necessary skills can be bought in.

The choice of who leads the change is a critical one, and should not rely purely on technical expertise. Endemic to this change process may be the setting of a vision or visioning statement by key player(s). If HR is to remove its reputation of being the bridesmaid, rather than the bride, then it needs to adopt strategic positioning, understand the business completely (business partnership), and adopt a leadership role (business leader).

 HM REVENUE AND CUSTOMS (HMRC)

CASE STUDY 6.2

In an article from *The Times* (2010), Chris Mills argues that the radical change encountered by HMRC resulted in ineffective change management, attributed to the leadership rather than general competence.

Mills goes on to say that since the merger of the Inland Revenue, and Customs and Excise since 2003, the organisation focused more upon tax-raising at strategic level, but lost the sense of purpose lower down. The lack of involvement of operational staff, where they drive the process quickly and effectively, was lacking. What is required includes strategic goals and a 'comprehensively thought-through model of the entire organisation, which encompasses vision, strategic performance measures, organisational structures, projects and business-as-usual activities, together with the right combination of skills, competencies and behaviours needed by all staff'. Mills continues this line of argument by stating that the need to demonstrate clear alignment between all of these factors is crucial. The extent to which senior managers are more likely to be focused on building the profile of their

own area (and themselves) may contaminate the effectiveness of the change process, despite having an overarching strategy and vision.

Another potential compounding factor is the Government's Efficiency Agenda, which attempts to maximise resources and ultimately save costs. Mills posits that senior civil servants are often criticised for their apparent inability to translate good strategies into effective action, and sometime overuse consultants and other external staff in order to make things work, rather than providing the bursts of expertise for which they are better suited.

Source: Mills (2010)

Question

1   Consider how the use of a change intervention, such as OD or systems intervention strategy, can assist in ensuring the strategic to operational alignment required to bring about effective change at HMRC.

HR VALUE ADDED AND CHANGE

Can HR establish and maintain a strategic-level involvement in organisations? The danger of pigeon-holing functions is that some form of reductivism may result. If strategy was determined at a resource and capability level, then HR could perhaps fit more readily within strategic decision-making in organisations. However, Warren (2009) argues that OD needs to start with the business and HR's role is to facilitate it. HR and OD should be one and the same. It depends upon the level of importance that OD has within organisations as to whether OD impacts (and possibly guides) upon strategic planning.

For HR partners to take a leadership and proactive role, they will need to contribute towards key strategic decisions, and to do this, understanding of strategic change and change interventions is critical.

When bridging the strategic and tactical level, we can identify various ways in which HR professionals can endeavour to secure a successful role in the contribution made to change projects, namely:

- involvement at the initial stage in the project team
- advising project leaders in skills available within the organisation – identifying any skills gaps, training needs, new posts, new working practices, etc
- balancing out the narrow/short-term goals and broader strategic needs
- assessing the impact of change in one area/department/site on another part of the organisation
- being used to negotiating and engaging across various stakeholders
- understanding stakeholder concerns to anticipate problems
- understanding the appropriate medium of communication to reach various groups
- helping people cope with change, performance management and motivation.

There are perhaps many other areas where HR should impact upon change in organisations, such as learning from change, capturing appropriate knowledge and knowledge share. Similarly, HR can facilitate team building. Arrata *et al* (2007) argue that three critical elements are crucial to any change programme: thoughtful design; careful recruitment and development of personnel; and close integration between the change agent team and the organisational areas targeted for change. Successful communication underpins the effectiveness of the change team.

 REFLECTIVE ACTIVITY 6.4

Concepts such as engagement and communication are vital within strategic and organisational change. It could be argued that HR has a central role in the day-to-day running of both of these concepts. In some cases, HR takes a leading role in implementing a range of change initiatives.

1   To what extent are there tensions for HR when managing change at both strategic and operational levels?

2   As a counter-argument, should line managers be largely responsible for engagement and communication within their respective divisions or departments?

 CHANGE: THE FINANCIAL INDUSTRY IN 2007

CASE STUDY 6.3

Paralysis within the financial sector following the 'credit crunch' of 2007 saw the first run on a major British bank in more than a century, which eventually led to Northern Rock being nationalised the following year. Nearly a year later, the US banking sector experienced a tumultuous weekend in September 2008 when Merrill Lynch was acquired and 'saved' by the Bank of America, while Lehman Brothers was left to its own demise by the US Treasury and went into liquidation.

The consequences of these events would be felt all over the world, as governments provided unprecedented financial rescue packages to stabilise the global banking sector and support their economies. However, this rescue attempt could not prevent many developed countries slipping into recession in 2008 while politicians and media commentators debated how long the recession would last. In 2013 many developed economies were still 'flat-lining' with gloomy growth forecasts for subsequent years, so the events of 2007 and 2008 had indeed cast a long shadow.

In the UK and in many other countries, the cost of the financial meltdown has been, and is still being, shared by businesses, public sector services and taxpayers. Since the financial crisis, many companies have struggled to survive and have responded by cutting costs, wages and jobs. Public sector budgets have been cut as governments attempt to manage the enormous budget deficit acquired as a result of the bank bail-outs.

The financial crisis was a dramatic and major change, but it is important to recognise that it is still only part of a continuum of change, which, at any moment in time has historical lineage, current context and future implications.

This recent episode in change also serves to illustrate how the business environment is shaped by external factors outside the control of most organisations, and even outside the control of institutions who thought they were in control!

There are not many organisations that will remain unscathed by the fallout from the events described above. In order to survive and sustain, organisations will have to respond to the dynamic business environment they operate in by managing change.

Managing change is nothing new to organisations, but the scale and speed of change in the business environment may present situations and challenges that are difficult to respond to, as was the case for Lehman Brothers in 2008. Lehman Brothers found that in the rapidly changing environment in which it was engulfed, it could not exert control or manage change to sustain the organisation.

The causes of the financial crisis were a complex combination of political, economic, social and technological factors which shaped the external business environment.

These drivers of change had their roots in the USA, going back to 2002 when the relaxation of financial regulations, available cheap debt and the desire of individuals to own or improve their homes all came together to shape a business environment that provided opportunities for financial institutions to create and sell new loan products known as sub-prime mortgages. These mortgages were sold to many individuals with poor credit standing who had little chance of repaying their loans.

Complex computer software programs and global communication networks enabled this sub-prime debt to be repackaged and sold on as investments on the global mortgage bond market.

The difficulties incurred by banks which either sold these mortgages or invested in the repackaged sub-prime mortgage debt led to what became known as the 'credit crunch'. The financial institutions had failed to identify the risk to which they were exposing themselves because they did not fully understand the nature of the business environment in which they were operating. In other words, they did not recognise the external factors that would eventually impact on their business.

Had the financial institutions understood the risk they were engaging in, they may have made smarter decisions and avoided the difficulties they got into, or could have taken steps to manage the risk better. With improved knowledge and understanding of the business environment, organisations can make better informed strategic decisions in order to minimise risk and optimise performance. In other words, good information and how to use it makes for better decision-making and management control.

There were a number of key internal factors involved in the financial crisis of 2007, which, when combined with the external drivers described above, provided an inevitable path to disaster for many of the organisations involved, as outlined below.

First, there was the decision of the banks to repackage sub-prime mortgages as collateral debt obligations (CDOs), a type of asset-backed security, and sell these as investments on the mortgage bond market, which represented a new business model for dealing with mortgages. This had the effect of spreading high-risk investments amongst the financial institutions who decided to engage in this business model – but not in a good way. The CDOs were so complex that the banks who had bought these were unable to

gauge the amount of risk they were exposing themselves to.

Internal management decisions were taken by: (a) the banks providing the mortgages to take advantage of a business opportunity they saw as a new marketing strategy; and in turn (b) other banks and financial institutions to invest in CDOs as an investment strategy.

Another major internal driver of change in the financial crisis was the practice of incentive schemes based on large cash bonuses to reward employees for selling and investing these products. This powerful driver encouraged the proliferation of these activities.

Questions

1   What were the triggers for change within the context described?

2   To what extent was the change depicted a 'Big Bang' approach to change?

CONCLUSION

Lloyd and Maguire (2002, p149) argue that, 'In future, the critical focus for sustainable organisational success will build on what the organisation knows about itself and its environment, and not on the transient structure and detailed processes. The successful organisations of the future will not be managing change but rather facilitating conversations for organisational learning and individual responsibility'. Hence the emphasis here is upon individual and team development, which sits comfortably within the scope and domain of HR.

'Change is ultimately about people – if they do not change, nothing significant happens' (Miller 2004, p10). Perhaps the argument for organisations having stronger and more sophisticated OD processes can never be understated. A positive employee attitude towards change is vital to a successful outcome. Tan and Tiong (2005) found that the highest correlated success factor was optimism, which they define as attitude towards change. HR, in partnership with line management, need to ensure that organisational change is planned, communicated and executed successfully on an ongoing basis in order to sustain business survival.

KEY LEARNING POINTS

- There are numerous ways in which change can be analysed as far as the scope and nature of change is concerned.
- HR professionals need to have an appreciation of the complex nature of several (sometimes contradictory) change interventions operating concurrently.
- The context of change needs to be analysed in order to decide upon whether and which type of change intervention is needed or appropriate.
- OD is a change intervention particularly suited to changing employees' values and organisational culture.
- HR has a significant contribution to make to strategic change interventions, particularly when collating knowledge and learning emanating from change interventions, which can then be used on subsequent change interventions.
- Change agents typically have to exhibit a range of skills and competences in order to demonstrate their credibility as a change agent, and simultaneously be aware of the political context within which they operate.

REVIEW QUESTIONS

1   Discuss the extent to which a vision and mission statement is important when an organisation is going through cultural changes.

2   Consider a change intervention with which you are familiar and consider what some of the barriers to change were, and where resistance to change was encountered. Try and classify these barriers and resistance factors into key categories.

3   What are some of the key skills that a change agent needs to exhibit? To what extent are these skills context specific?

4   Think about how you could apply Lewin's change model to a change scenario of your choice. To what extent were there critical moments that defined the unfreezing, movement and refreezing?

EXPLORE FURTHER

Hughes, M. (2010) *Change Management: a critical perspective*. 2nd edition. London: CIPD Publications. A sound textbook presenting a range of approaches to change.

Price, D. (ed.) (2009) *The Principles and Practice of Change*. Basingstoke: Palgrave Macmillan. Provides a range of different perspectives on change by presenting some key articles and works on change.

Senior, B. and Swailes, S. (2010) *Organisational Change*. 4th edition. Harlow: FT Prentice Hall. The chapters on systems change and OD are particularly useful reading.

CHAPTER 7

Flexibility and the Psychological Contract

Simon Turner

LEARNING OUTCOMES

After reading this chapter, you should be able to:

- define flexibility and understand the different meanings attached to this concept

- evaluate the importance of the psychological contract on employees' behaviour

- understand how flexibility and the psychological contract are inter-related; and

- explain how psychological contracts and flexibility can link with improved organisational performance.

OVERVIEW

This chapter aims to explore the connections between organisational performance and two topics in the current HRM spotlight: the notion of flexibility, and the ways in which organisations respond to the need for greater flexibility within a context of continuous improvement; and the slippery concept of multi-faceted psychological contracts which might help us to make sense of workers' commitment and associated attitudes towards the employer.

There are connections between these topics. The level of commitment displayed by workers can be related to their psychological contract, and the state of the contract in turn influences workers' attitudes towards providing flexibility. Employers' desires for these concepts to be 'got', or controlled, are linked with the creation of HR policies designed to improve organisational performance. There is much debate in the HR field surrounding the approaches and activities designed to secure improvements in outcomes and performance, including recommendations by the CIPD, the UK professional body. It has been observed (Marchington *et al* 2009) that there is a tendency for these concepts to become conflated with their anticipated results, so that the descriptions become prescriptions, accepted as conventional wisdom.

We also find tensions within this field. The desire for organisations to integrate HR policies with business objectives may sit uneasily with the move towards Atkinson's (1984) flexible firm, with decentralised responsibilities and externalised workers. The client organisation in an outsourcing arrangement may find it difficult to manage, or influence, the policies of the supplier of labour. Gilmore (2012) records that flexible approaches to workforce deployment have often been coupled with an increase in part-time working, fixed-term contracts and outsourcing, making it potentially more difficult to secure organisational commitment. It has been noted that in much of the HR management literature, the typical focus is on the remaining core activities and not on how non-core activities are provided (Marchington *et al* 2009).

The concepts set out and discussed in detail in this chapter are central to the core themes of the book, based around effective leadership and management of people. As such, material presented in this chapter is linked with themes and topics introduced elsewhere in the text. To take one example, the broad term 'flexibility' encompasses organisational and individual elements. In Chapter 8 we will see how people's experiences of work are affected by the organisational structure in which they operate, and of course, by the nature of work they do. In an important sense, therefore, organisational and job design lay out the context within which flexibility can be achieved. At the same time, the individual aspect of flexibility must be understood with reference to the subject of motivation, which we address in Chapter 12.

Meanwhile the promotion of all aspects of high-performance working, including flexibility, was addressed in Chapters 2 and 3. What can be said is that flexibility operates on both an organisational and individual level and that organisations and individuals (including managers and leaders) will have a keen interest in the topic.

We have, finally, an interesting issue regarding terminology and language throughout this chapter. How we choose to refer to the people – as employees, workers, or individuals – is context-bound, and arguably influences (or is influenced by) our thinking. Much of the current literature focuses on employees inside the organisation, yet as we will see, so-called networked organisations rely also upon people outside: agency and outsourced workers, and the pseudo-employed.

INTRODUCTION

It is frequently stated that the management of people in organisations has recently been carried out against a backdrop of a rapidly changing and turbulent environment (CIPD 2012b, Holbeche 2013). In many advanced economies there has been a move away from mass production of standardised products or even routine white-collar administrative work, with many such jobs moving to countries such as China and India. Concurrently it has been suggested that people in organisations increasingly aspire to work more flexibly and wish to work in more autonomous and creative roles. A search for work–life balance by many employees results in a need for support from employing organisations in order to prevent burnout and maximise their work performance (French *et al* 2011). Accelerating globalisation and technological advance has meant that the environment of organisations – both in the private and public sectors – has changed rapidly, resulting in a need for greater flexibility from organisations, their leaders and other workers (Thomas 2009, Thompson and McHugh 2009).

In this chapter we will examine a range of terms which have emerged as both diagnoses of current work practices and solutions to problems of managing people in the current competitive environment. Words and phrases such as 'flexibility', 'work–life balance' and 'work intensification' will be defined, analysed and their benefits and disadvantages highlighted. The debate on flexible responses to trends such as globalisation, technological advance and the 'marketisation' of public sector provision now has an established body of knowledge from Atkinson's (1984) notion of the flexible firm through to the CIPD report on sustainable organisation performance (CIPD 2010a). The area under consideration in this chapter continues to be academically relevant, topical and of personal interest to many of us.

REFLECTIVE ACTIVITY 7.1

KPMG avoids redundancies through flexible working

Writer and researcher Charlotte Wolff notes how international professional services firm KPMG was particularly concerned to avoid employee redundancies following the economic downturn of 2008. David Conder, Head of People at KPMG, noted that: 'When we made redundancies alongside other, similar, firms in 2002/3, it constrained growth when the upturn came and it was also a very painful process for the organisation to go through'. KPMG's strategy now is to do the right thing for its clients, its people and the business. This means retaining talent, intellectual capital and the motivational level of its teams, thus ensuring continuity and top quality service.

KPMG's strategy now includes a 'flexible futures' programme using reduced hours and sabbaticals to manage the workforce flexibly during times when business is quiet.

Source: Wolff (2008)

Question

1   Provide three reasons why we might reasonably anticipate that redundancies would hinder an organisation's performance following an economic upturn.

FLEXIBILITY

Flexibility has been frequently identified as a key HR policy goal, along with strategic intention, quality and employee commitment, in order to ensure an adaptable organisation structure (Guest 2004). These HR goals are in turn held to generate:

> … a range of positive organisational outcomes, such as high job performance, high quality problem solving, successful change, lower turnover, absenteeism and grievance levels and high cost-effectiveness. (Iles *et al* 1996, p18)

On the one hand employers, encouraged by governments and non-governmental bodies, such as the International Monetary Fund and the World Bank, press the case for workforce flexibility in the hunt for efficiency, and on the other hand it is claimed that individual employees look for flexibility in working hours as they attempt to juggle the demands of home and work lives. It seems that the two agendas might meet in a unitary, though stressful, work–life balance (CIPD 2012d, Taylor 2002, Pollitt 2003) where employers' flexibility requirements can coincide well with the wants and needs of a great many employees. Truss *et al* (2006) found that workers who were on flexible contracts tended to be more emotionally engaged, more satisfied (with their work) and more likely to speak positively about their organisation. In addition, these workers were also less likely to quit.

Four main types of flexibility can be identified (after Blyton and Morris 1992):

1   Task or functional flexibility, where employees may be multi-skilled.

2   Numerical flexibility, using different types of employment contracts and sub-contracting, as in Atkinson's (1984) core-periphery concept.

3   Temporal flexibility, where the number and pattern of hours worked varies, for example zero hours, and annual hours.

4   Wage flexibility, where wages are individualised, and may be performance-related.

A notable early contribution to an understanding of contemporary attempts to change work and workers allocation was Atkinson's (1984) flexible firm model. This painted a heroic picture with committed core employees being highly regarded, well paid, with improved career prospects, and who offer in return functional flexibility, often through multi-skilling. On the periphery are the distanced externals: the 'atypical', 'non-standard' or 'non-core' workers (described in negative terms) with low security to ease the organisation's needs for adjustments to market forces. There are important ethical undertones to such a distinction, with Clegg *et al* (2011) suggesting that the periphery itself comprised two sub-groups. These were firstly workers who were semi-skilled operating in the lower rungs of the supply chain and who could be easily dismissed and re-employed according to cost and demand fluctuations. The other sub-group was an underclass working (possibly illegally) in poor conditions outside the formally recognised labour market. Such workers do not show up in official statistics or most research studies so remain outside the scope of most discussions of worker flexibility – but are real nonetheless. Later in the chapter we look again at the dark side of flexible working.

Current observations are that organisational forms are changing, with bureaucracies being dismantled and replaced by looser, networked organisational forms and processes, featuring partnerships and contracting-out of activities. 'In the name of right-sizing, de-layering and concentrating upon core competencies, the outsourcing of services continues to expand' (Marchington *et al* 2005, p2) as organisations move from vertical towards horizontal integration. With this, come changes in the employment relationship. Marchington *et al* present an additional dimension to the understanding of employment flexibility, namely the extent to which the employment contract is under the influence of a single employing organisation or subject to control or influence by multiple employers, as might be the case with agency workers (see Figure 7.1). This axis is added to the previously accepted continuum depicting variations in the internalisation or standardisation of the employment contract (as in the core-periphery concept).

As the authors describe, the internalised, standard employment relationship is seen in the bottom left-hand corner. In the top right-hand corner is self-employment, 'where there is no contract of employment and where the self-employed individual sells his or her skills to a range of organisations and is, therefore, not dependent on a particular organisation for income' (ibid, p18).

The horizontal axis, from employees to non-employees, depicts the shift away from internalised full-time employees to a diversification of contracts including part-time, casual, temporary, and self-employed workers. 'Part-time work might be considered to be close to the standard contract as there is nothing in principle stopping part-time work being organised on the same basis as internalised, full-time work with the same social rights and same regularity of employment' (ibid, p18). At the extreme of where the guarantees of employment and income are, at best, short term, are the so-called pseudo self-employed workers, who often work at a distance from the employer – such as home-workers and freelancers – 'but who may be highly dependent upon one employer, even if there is no formal contractual guarantee of continuous employment or minimum income' (ibid, p19).

In the centre of the field we find temporary agency workers, in ambiguous circumstances: self-employed yet employed, where the agency is commonly regarded as the legal employer, even though it is the client who exercises control.

Figure 7.1 The twin dimensions of employment flexibility

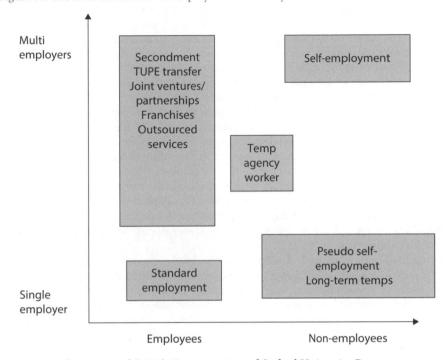

Source: Marchington *et al* (2005). By permission of Oxford University Press

> The employing organisation, which acts as host to the temporary agency workers, directs their work activities side-by-side with those of direct employees on similar tasks … This employment relationship … [involves] both deviations from the status of direct employees, and control from more than one employing organisation (ibid, p19).

The top left-hand side 'covers an area where employment is internalised but where there is more than one employing organisation that can be considered party to the relationship.' Here 'there is a direct employment relationship but other employers – acting as agents or suppliers – may be involved in the employment experience, and even in controlling the employment relationship' (ibid, pp18–19).

WORK INTENSIFICATION AND WORK–LIFE BALANCE

Recent years have seen an increasing number of organisations in the UK offering a range of flexible working options to their employees. For many employers this has been a response to increasing interest in work–life balance, the need to be competitive in the labour market, and the introduction of legislation giving parents of young or disabled children and, more recently, carers, the right to request flexible working arrangements (Kelliher and Anderson 2010).

In a more critical vein, attention is drawn to other aspects of the work–life balance concept by Eikhof *et al* (2007) where 'beyond working time and the provision of flexible working practices to enable child care, there is little in the debate about the need to change work per se.' These authors also comment that the work–life debate 'narrowly perceives "life", equating it with women's care work, hence the emphasis again of family-friendly policies' (ibid, p326).

We can detect that flexibility, lying at the heart of the wage–work bargain, means different things to the different parties to the deal. Whilst conventional definitions are expressed from the point of view of the employer or organisation, descriptions of the consequences for the worker are required in the interests of balance.

It is possible to glimpse an unanticipated consequence of adopting flexible working practices – that of work intensification. Whilst reporting evidence that flexible workers record higher levels of job satisfaction and organisational commitment than their non-flexible counterparts, Kelliher and Anderson (2010) also report evidence of work intensification being experienced by both those who work reduced hours and those who work remotely. It is suggested that the apparent paradox of high job satisfaction and organisational commitment alongside work intensification can be explained by employees trading flexibility for effort. Employees respond to the ability to work flexibly by exerting additional effort, in order to return benefit to their employer.

Three means by which intensification may take place have been identified (ibid, p86). Increased effort may be imposed (as when workloads may increase following downsizing) or enabled (because flexible working patterns facilitate the exercise of increased effort), or it may be a reciprocal act on the part of employees in exchange for discretion over working arrangements.

Intriguingly, Kelliher and Anderson (2010, p99) suggest that in contemporary workplaces, with a 'prevailing rhetoric of greater personal autonomy', employees often see themselves as responsible for their own work intensification. To some extent the professional workers saw themselves as partly responsible and therefore did not voice opposition. However, other studies have also found that employees do not always respond negatively to intensification, especially where they believe they will gain some benefit as a consequence (ibid, p99).

REFLECTIVE ACTIVITY 7.2

Current research: experiences of intensification

Kelliher and Anderson's (2010) interviewees, from a number of UK private sector organisations, vividly illustrate the three means of intensification.

Imposed intensification

Workers describe why imposed flexible working on reduced hours contracts has resulted in work intensification. Their workloads did not decrease in line with their hours when they moved to a reduced hours contract and consequently they were doing something akin to a full-time job, but in fewer paid hours. This could result in both increased extensive and intensive effort.

One interviewee commented: 'There is enough workload to keep me busy for five days, but I only have three days to do it in, so I either work late, which I do sometimes, or I try and delegate some of it.'

Others described that they felt the need to be available at times when they were not scheduled to be working, but when the business was operating. This took the form of being prepared to take phone calls and checking emails at times when they were not working.

For example one interviewee reported: 'On a Monday, when I'm not at work, I'll typically put in 40 minutes to an hour just checking my emails to make sure that I'm on top of any issues that come up, or that came up over the weekend … so I check the email at least once if not twice during the Monday.'

Enabled intensification

By contrast, others, typically remote workers, describe that working flexibly enabled them to work more intently, exercising both greater intensive and extensive effort. For example: 'It's much easier to maintain your energy levels and enthusiasm if you're working for three days or four days, than if you're working for five days ... and keep your efficiency up if you're just maintaining it over three or three and a half days, rather than five.'

Intensification as reciprocation and exchange

Commitment levels of remote and reduced hours workers are reportedly higher than those who did not work flexibly. The impact of commitment on effort is illustrated by this worker who reported greater extensive effort when she worked from home:

'So you have this kind of loyalty I guess, which is very deep-seated to be honest, if people are prepared to treat you as a human being more ...

I'm not some kind of machine that has to be at the office at nine and five thirty, I actually do see myself in a more human way, which is around the commitment ... When companies support you, you are naturally more loyal and more committed.'

Source: Kelliher and Anderson (2010)

Question

1 As an HR manager, how would you respond to employees who have complained to you about their work intensification, and the impact that it was having upon their performance levels?

THE BUSINESS BENEFITS OF FLEXIBLE WORKING

We commonly hear managerial descriptions, in unitary terms, of flexible working arrangements featuring options which allow employees to strike a work–life balance which fits with their needs, and yet gives the employer a say in the decision-making process (Wight 2007). Elsewhere we find descriptions of flexible working delivering improved business performance on service delivery and customer satisfaction, efficiency savings, and reduced recruitment and retention costs (Thomson 2008). Examples of this flexible working include part-time work, job-sharing, flexi-time, working school hours, nine-day fortnights, mobile working, and team rotas, which are claimed to give the employees choice in how, when and where they work (see Case Study 7.1).

CASE STUDY 7.1

BENDING THE RULES: SURREY COUNTY COUNCIL EMBRACES FLEXIBLE WORKING

Surrey County Council has taken steps to ensure that its workers can complete their daily tasks from spaces other than their desk at the office. There have been investments in technology which allow workers to log in at any PC or any telephone on a certain network, and all social workers have a tablet PC to carry when out of the office. Anything the social worker records on the tablet is instantly added to a database back at the office and is therefore accessible to other staff. Staff are able to check their work emails from home, allowing the option of working from home, and also reducing the dependence on physical office space. Working from different offices or at home, working while

travelling, and hot-desking in an office environment can all add flexibility to the working day.

The importance of giving the employees choice in how, when and where they work has led to an improvement in Surrey Council in terms of productivity, reduced sickness levels and financial gains. There has been a 4 per cent reduction in staff turnover, and there are now 700 fewer full-time posts, leading to a decrease in staff costs. The council has been able to rationalise its property portfolio and standardise IT systems. It has also seen an increase in morale amongst employees as they are given more freedom to choose their working hours, and it shows trust in the employees that they will manage to strike a successful work–life balance.

Taking a broader view, the issue of flexible working has become an increasingly important topic as the Government re-evaluates the employment laws in the UK. All employees, regardless of circumstance, have a right to request a flexible working pattern from an employer. The employer has to weigh up the effect the application would have on the business as a whole. The employer has the right to reject an employee's flexible working request if it would be of detriment to the business.

Source: Wight (2007)

Questions

1   Give examples from your own experience of flexible working.

2   Were your feelings towards flexible working positive or negative – or a mix of the two – and why?

3   How can organisations balance greater employee freedom within flexible working with customer requirements?

FLEXIBLE WORKING AND PERFORMANCE

It is widely argued (see, for example, DTI 2005) that flexible working arrangements (FWAs) are good for business and the health and well-being of the working population. For decades researchers have attempted to assess the impact of FWAs on worker performance. A recent review of the literature on the link between FWAs and performance-related outcomes suggests that, taken together, the evidence fails to demonstrate a business case for the use of FWAs (de Menezes and Kelliher 2011). Whilst support for a link with performance has been most commonly found in relation to some aspects of performance such as absenteeism and job/work satisfaction, concerning other aspects of organisational performance (such as financial performance indicators, retention, individual productivity, organisational commitment, and health or well-being), the most common finding was no association. The authors conclude that, with the evidence to date, making causal inferences on this aspect of people management is problematic.

NEGATIVE ASPECTS OF FLEXIBILITY

We have already drawn attention to the dark side of flexible working and this was highlighted in the UK context by Toynbee (2008); see below.

Appalling conditions

Labour MPs representing the poorest parts of the country see how appalling conditions under bad employers can be. They see where agency workers are brought in to undercut existing wages – remember Gate Gourmet (the airline catering firm that was involved in a high-profile dispute with employees at London Heathrow airport in 2005)? Or where workers who want to be taken on permanently are fired and rehired to prevent them acquiring rights. They see outsourced NHS cleaners, and workers throughout the public sector being denied the chance they once had to work their way up. Agencies don't train people to fill higher-level jobs for which they are not contracted (Toynbee 2008).

An alternative to the conventional wisdom regarding the economic necessity of flexibility, at both global and individual levels, is provided by Giles *et al* (2010) in the following case study.

THE FAILINGS OF FLEXIBILITY

For years, it has been the settled view in economics that, in most cases, flexible labour markets are best. More jobs might be lost in a downturn, but this cost is far outweighed by the benefits of flexible pay and the ease of reallocating jobs from dying industries to dynamic ones. Nobody was more closely aligned with such recommendations than the Organisation for Economic Co-operation and Development, the Paris-based group of developed nations.

But now the OECD is modifying its view. 'We have been promoting flexibility, not for the sake of it, but for economic performance and for workers to get into new jobs,' says Stefano Scarpetta, the OECD's head of employment analysis.

This motivation is allowing a change of view. 'Judging from the outcomes so far, short-time working schemes [such as in Germany, in which people work fewer hours while the government tops up their pay, although there are questions about whether this merely delays job losses] seem to have been rather successful in containing the job haemorrhage,' he says, adding that even his organisation is 'a little bit more positive on public works programmes: we argue that as part of a labour market approach, they might be worthwhile'.

While this is not a wholesale repudiation of the OECD's former views, it reflects the fact that, according to the organisation's own analysis, the gains in employment flexibility of recent years have failed to protect employees from the economic crisis. 'There do not appear to be any clear grounds for concluding that workers, generally, are any better or worse prepared to weather a period of weak labour markets than was the case for the past several recessions,' the OECD concluded in its latest Employment Outlook.

Some top economists argue that the theory of superiority of flexible labour markets applies only at full employment. It will not work well when there has been a large shock to demand, output is well below potential and jobs are effectively rationed. In these circumstances, German-style institutions that cushion and spread the pain are probably superior.

Source: Giles *et al* (2010)

Question

1   Identify the stated view taken on flexible labour markets by the main UK political parties. Can you identify significant differences between them?

THE BENEFITS OF BEHAVIOURAL FLEXIBILITY

Most attention has been given to organisational and labour market flexibility rather than personal flexibility. For firms to be flexible they depend on the flexibility of the workforce: an orientation, attitude, or style among employees, including team-oriented, lateral and autonomous perspectives (Iles *et al* 1996, p21). Anell and Wilson (2000, p168) suggest the following qualities might be required in employees:

a desire to seek feedback on performance, a desire to improve, an ability to see multiple perspectives, a broad vision, an ability to visualise relationships, a readiness to accept responsibility for decisions, self-confidence, proactivity, a liking for change and a desire for co-operative independence.

Among senior managers, personal and strategic flexibility and internal characteristics such as problem-solving or creative thinking are desirable. These authors describe elements of 'behavioural flexibility' in managers in terms of the ability to manage complexity and uncertainty, adaptability, tolerance of ambiguity, openness, empathy, non-judgementalism, interest in others, and willingness to acquire new behaviours and attitudes. Sennett refers to 'a particular strength of character – that of someone who has the confidence to dwell in disorder … who flourishes in the midst of dislocation' (1998, p62).

In his book, *The Corrosion of Character* (1998), Richard Sennett examines the consequences for workers of the need for organisations to operate in highly competitive markets. He suggests that the flexibility they need to display, the willingness to accept change, and the loss of security that results, can have damaging effects on personal character.

Character, he argues, is an emotional experience that involves loyalty, mutual commitment and the pursuit of long-term goals. As society pursues immediate needs and businesses seek to respond to the consequent short-term goals, organisations find themselves regularly needing to restructure and redesign. In such a new economy he suggests that character traits are damaged with negative effects on workers' morale and motivation. People thus co-operate but without any underlying commitment: 'superficial co-operativeness'.

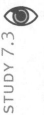

CASE STUDY 7.3

PWC INCREASES EMPLOYEE FLEXIBILITY

Professional-services firm PricewaterhouseCoopers (PWC) is described as a knowledge-driven organisation. When its employees leave, the firm not only loses the training and knowledge they have built up, but also the client relationships they have developed.

PWC now has a strategy based around choice for its employees, whose average age is only 27. There is a generous scheme of maternity and paternity leave, childcare vouchers for returning mothers and other benefits. Moreover, most employees are equipped to be able to work from home, and almost all of them choose to do this at least once a month.

The company has launched an in-house concierge service. Employees are offered a wide range of domestic services at discount price. They include activities (such) as waiting in for plumbers, builders and electricians.

Take-up appears to be greatest among company consultants, who often work offsite for months.

PWC has also introduced the notion of 'paid time off', rather than the more restrictive 'annual leave'. Employees can use their paid time off allocation for short-term illness, child care and jury service, as well as holiday.

According to the author, the strategy appears to be successful. Despite skill shortages in the consultancy sector, staff retention at PWC has improved by 4–5 per cent over the previous year.

Source: Perry (2001)

Questions

1   What does this case show us about the benefits of flexibility to organisations and staff?

2   Is this type of flexibility restricted to the type of professional worker employed

by PWC or could and should it
have wider application?

The parties' responses to each other's requests for flexibility within the wage–work bargain, worker and 'employer', are likely to be inextricably interlinked. The concept of the psychological contract provides us with a suitable lens through which to view this aspect of leading and managing people.

THE PSYCHOLOGICAL CONTRACT

Although questions have been raised about its meaning and value (Guest 1998), the concept of the psychological contract has become a central theme of people management. It describes the employment relationship in terms of mutual expectations or obligations, in order to make sense of the range and degrees of commitment that flow in both directions. It is here that organisational policy and procedures mix with individual managerial and employee attitudes and behaviours, with complex outcomes.

There are two main definitions of the psychological contract (Marks 2001). The first is derived from the work of Argyris (1960) and Schein (1978) and refers to the perceptions of mutual obligations held by the two parties in the employment relationship, the organisation and the employee (or worker). The second definition, which is based on the work of Rousseau (1995, p9), asserts that the psychological contract is formulated only in the mind of the employee and is therefore about 'individual beliefs, shaped by the organisation, regarding terms of an exchange between individuals and their organisation'.

According to Rousseau (1995, p1) the ideal contract details expectations of both the employee and the employer, but these contracts are incomplete and so become 'self-organising'. A contractual continuum is commonly offered, from transactional (covering incentive pay and well-specified performance levels) to relational (including loyalty and concern for employee well-being). Transactional terms are exemplified by 'a fair day's work for a fair day's pay' and focus on short-term (and usually monetary) exchanges. The relational contract 'focuses on open-ended relationships involving considerable investments by both employees (company-specific skills, long-term development) and employers (extensive training)' (ibid, p91).

A useful typology is offered by Rousseau (see Figure 7.2), using the dimensions of timeframe and performance requirements, who says that four types of contract emerge 'with distinct behavioural implications for workers' (1995, p98):

- transactional contracts – of limited duration with well-specified performance terms
- transitional or 'no-guarantees' contracts – essentially a breakdown in contracts, reflecting the absence of commitments regarding future employment as well as little or no explicit performance demands or contingent incentives
- relational contracts – open-ended membership but with incomplete or ambiguous performance requirements attached to continued membership
- balanced contracts – open-ended and relationship-oriented employment with well-specified performance terms subject to change over time.

Figure 7.2 Types of psychological contract

Performance terms

	Specified	Not Specified
Duration Short term	Transactional (eg retail checkout operators employed during Christmas season) • Low ambiguity • Easy exit/high turnover • Low member commitment • Freedom to enter new contracts • Little learning • Weak integration/identification	Transitional (eg employee experiences during organisational retrenchment or following merger or acquisition) • Ambiguity/uncertainty • High turnover/termination • Instability
Long term	Balanced (eg high-involvement team) • High member commitment • High integration/identification • Ongoing development • Mutual support • Dynamic	Relational (eg family business members) • High member commitment • High affective commitment • High integration/identification • Stability

Source: Rousseau (1995)

In other words, the 'psychological contract' is a term for describing what is implicit in terms of reciprocity and exchange within the employment relationship.

It is suggested (CIPD 2012e) that employers have been encouraged to take the psychological contract seriously due to changes ranging from there being more employees on part-time and flexible work, to the survivors of down-sizing having to do more, and 'human capital' becoming more critical to business performance.

IMPLICATIONS FOR THE MANAGEMENT OF PEOPLE

The CIPD (2012e) asserts that organisations have to 'get the most out of this resource (employees)' by knowing what employees expect from their work, by using the psychological contract as 'a framework for monitoring employee attitudes and priorities', and draws attention to the importance of the line manager role, in these terms:

> In order to display commitment employees have to feel that they are being treated with fairness and respect. Many organisations have concluded that they need to create a corporate personality or identity with a set of corporate values or a stated mission – an 'employee value proposition' or 'employer brand' – which employees will recognise and relate to. In practice the employer brand can be seen as an attempt by the employer to define the psychological contract with employees so as to help in recruiting and retaining talent.

Recent work has emphasised the notion of engagement. This is defined by the CIPD (2012f) as 'employees internalising and emotionally connecting to the organisation's core purpose'. This CIPD survey emphasised the role of line managers in motivating via an engaging team-management style.

There is no doubt that increasing competition and changing expectations among employees have prompted a growing disillusionment with the traditional psychological contract based on lifetime employment and steady promotion from within. Consequently, companies must develop new ways to increase the loyalty and commitment of employees.

For instance, given the pressure to do things better, faster and cheaper, reward systems should recognise contribution rather than position or status. Reward strategies may also be used to rebuild commitment for survivors in downsizing organisations.

In addition, considering the shift towards decentralisation and empowerment, it is essential that individuals and groups are given more responsibility over salary decisions. Furthermore, rewards should be based on continuous performance and continuous improvement, rather than single events or past achievements.

CONTRACTS

Theories of the psychological contract have been built around full-time permanent employment and there is discussion about the extension of the concept to incorporate the experience of contingent workers. As Marchington *et al* (2005, p78) point out:

> temporary agency workers attempt … to satisfy their obligations simultaneously to two employers – the agency and the client. This simultaneity raises questions about organisational commitment and loyalty.

'Forced' changes to contracts

Earlier in this chapter, 'imposed intensification' of work was noted when employees were subjected to reduced hours contracts. Saunders and Thornhill (2006) explore the implications for employees' psychological contracts in conditions of a forced change from permanent to temporary employment status for some employees within an organisation. They suggest that permanent employees generally continue to exhibit relational forms of attachment to the organisation. These, 'the employees believe', are reciprocated by the organisation. Reactions from forced temporary workers are more varied. After a period of denial, some develop a more calculative approach to their interactions. Others maintain aspects of their previously developed relational attachments. Only some temporary workers appear to recognise that their future direction is no longer a concern of the organisation. Although only based upon one organisation, Saunders and Thornhill suggest that the process of psychological contract adjustment is likely to emerge through gradual reinterpretation, rather than through renegotiation.

Since commitment within the psychological contract is assumed to be based on 'volition', then a lack of volition, and conflicts of loyalty, will have an effect on psychological contracting among contingent workers. We might expect non-permanent staff to show a more transactional approach, and show less commitment, than permanent staff. Research evidence provides ambiguous results. In a call centre environment, Biggs and Swailes (2006) found that agency workers had a significantly lower level of organisational commitment compared with permanent workers. However, this is not necessarily the case according to MacDonald and Makin (2000, p89), who suggest 'the observance and commitment to the norms, symbols, and rituals of desirable groups is often higher among those just outside, but wishing to join, the group than it is among established members.' From the same authors we hear of higher levels of organisational commitment and job satisfaction among some temporary staff.

One possible explanation, it is suggested, may lie in the short tenure of non-permanent staff within the organisation.

Contract breach

To what extent can we come to understand the concept of the psychological contract through examining its being breached or violated? Coyle-Shapiro and Kessler (2000) describe a situation in which the majority of employees have experienced contract breach, in a large local authority directly responsible and accountable for a range of public services including education, environmental health and social care to the local population. This view was also supported by managers, as representatives of the employer, who further indicated that the organisation, given its external pressures, was not fulfilling its obligations to employees to the extent that it could. Overall, the results indicate that employees redress the balance in the relationship through reducing their commitment and their willingness to engage in organisational citizenship behaviour when they perceive their employer has not fulfilled its part in the exchange process.

Workplace transitions are thought to result in a fundamental shift in the employment relationship, and the impact of organisational change can be seen in terms of Rousseau's types of psychological contracts (PCs) (see Figure 7.2). Chaudhry *et al* (2011) suggest that the ways in which employees make sense of organisational change influence whether employees revise their PCs. In their study, transactional and balanced PCs appear to be less affected by the contextual and cognitive factors related to the change, while changes occur in relational PCs.

A range of individual responses

There is a 'complexity of feelings' towards, and reactions resulting from, becoming a temporary worker, according to Saunders and Thornhill (2006, p452), where the attractions associated with obtaining greater freedom have also been associated with greater insecurity, potentially lower control over hours of work and working patterns, and a continuing need to find new work. These ideas of preference for temporary work have been linked to workers' skill and knowledge levels to produce a typology of temporary contracts (Marler *et al* 2002 cited in Saunders and Thornhill 2006, p452):

● boundaryless worker: high preference for temporary work and a high skills/knowledge level
● permanent temporary worker: high preference for temporary work and a low skills/ knowledge level
● transitional worker: low preference for temporary work and a high skills/knowledge level
● traditional worker: low preference for temporary work and a low skills/knowledge level.

This typology 'implies that personal preferences for temporary work are likely to influence feelings towards different types of psychological contracts. In particular, high preferences for temporary work would seem likely to accentuate positive feelings towards transactional-oriented psychological contracts, whereas low preferences for temporary work would accentuate negative feelings towards transactional-oriented psychological contracts' (ibid, p452).

There is interest in the state of the psychological contract during public sector restructuring and associated changes in employment relationships. Research (Wang *et al* 2010) into the effect of the 'transfer' process on employees' psychological contracts within the context of the move to a new employment relationship, as part of a public–private partnership, highlights that supervisors in particular have a strong influence on employees' attitudes and behaviour.

Table 7.1 The distinction between 'old' and 'new' characteristics of psychological contracts

Old contract	New contract
Organisation is 'parent' to employee 'child'	Organisation and employee enter into 'adult' contracts focused on mutually beneficial work
Employees' identity and worth are defined by the organisation	Employees' identity and worth are defined by the employee
Those who stay are good and loyal; others are bad and disloyal	The regular flow of people in and out is healthy and should be celebrated
Employees who do what they are told will work until retirement	Long-term employment is unlikely; expect – and prepare for – multiple relationships
The primary route for growth is through promotion	The primary route for growth is a sense of personal accomplishment

OLD AND NEW PSYCHOLOGICAL CONTRACTS

The terms of the new contract are still unclear, though the material so far in this chapter has provided us with insights; Maguire (2002) presents a number of distinctions between the old and new psychological contract, which are shown in Table 7.1.

As Maguire (2002, p8) puts it:

The key differences between the 'traditional' and the 'new' psychological contract relate to the decreased expectation of paternalistic human resource practices, the replacement of the concept of organisational worth with 'self-worth', the substitution of personal accomplishment for promotion as the route to growth, and the decreased importance of tenure.

REFLECTIVE ACTIVITY 7.3

Thinking about the organisation you work for, or one with which you are familiar, to what extent is employment characterised by 'old' or 'new' contracts?

To what extent do you envisage your career developing with multiple employers? If you find this picture realistic, will your loyalty to any one employer be diminished?

The CIPD suggests (2012e) that in many ways the 'old' psychological contract is in fact still alive, and that employees still want security: interestingly, labour market data suggest that there has been little reduction in the length of time for which people stay in individual jobs. They are still prepared to offer loyalty, though they may feel less committed to the organisation as a whole than to their workgroup. In general they remain satisfied with their job.

It is commonly heard that the 'old' psychological contract, with its emphasis on employment security, has been held to have been violated because of extensive downsizing among white-collar employees from the late 1980s and early 1990s (Mumford 1995). This proposition has been examined by Beaumont and Harris (2002), using data from UK manufacturing industries for the years 1978–95. The authors call into question the view that historically high and sustained downsizing among white-collar employees was a leading cause.

Examining the psychological contract in terms of the parties' fulfilment of their obligations to each other highlights gaps in what employees expect and receive from their employer as well as what employees feel they owe the employers and actually give. This is illustrated in Simon Caulkin's findings set out below.

Loyalty of young workers: the new psychological contract?

Simon Caulkin reports on research by the Work Foundation on the motivation of the newest generation of workers, the 18- to 24-year-olds.

'Employers need to understand better how Generation Y, as the Work Foundation researchers term them, differs from previous cohorts of workers, and what that means for employment policies. For young workers, the new implicit contract of employability, rather than a job for life, is the only one they have known. And they have learned its lessons fast. Accordingly, they have developed a much more instrumental approach to employment than their predecessors. They have high expectations of careers development and gaining early responsibility and attach substantial importance to the employer's "brand" – not just out of desire to work for a company that matches their own values, but also with an eye to improving their CV.

'The Work Foundation terms this "gold-dusting": buffing their record to attract other employers. Loyalty to the organisation lasts only as long as they are achieving personal goals.'

Source: Caulkin (2003)

We can conclude that contextual factors are key to understanding the psychological contract. If the employer is felt to have breached the contract, should we automatically assume that employee behaviour will necessarily be affected negatively? It seems that, in times of high job insecurity, employees may be less inclined to display negative behavioural outcomes due to the power disparity between the employer and employee, or to fear of redundancy, though attitudes towards the employer will be changed, if not translated into action.

 THE PSYCHOLOGICAL CONTRACT AND RETENTION

CASE STUDY 7.4

Roger Eglin, writing in the *Sunday Times*, suggests that emotional ties – rather than just money – are vital in getting good managers to stay with their employers.

A group of 476 Henley alumni were questioned about their relationship with their employers. Of the replies, 11 per cent were couched in what are described as transactional terms, while a compelling 52 per cent came down in favour of a relationship contract. 'They want a more effective relationship with issues such as aspiration, equity and community remaining important ... For those who have the talent and can make a choice this is what counts.'

With some jobs set to move to India, Barclays Bank has struck a deal with the Unity trade union to help those affected. But rather than losing people through redundancy, Barclays is offering them training-and-development opportunities to make them more 'marketable' within the bank.

Source: Eglin (2004)

Question

1   Would you characterise your relationship with your current or previous employer as

> transactional, or is it based
> upon emotional ties?

FLEXIBILITY, PSYCHOLOGICAL CONTRACTS AND PERFORMANCE

The concepts of flexibility and the psychological contract are essentially transactional involving reciprocal views concerning the quality of relationship between employee and organisation. It is now appropriate to revisit the links between people management and organisational performance.

Organisations seek to identify the link between people and performance (Purcell *et al* 2003), and the concept of high-performance working (HPW) (CIPD 2004a, 2004b, DTI 2005) is characterised by references to flatter, non-hierarchical structures, moving away from reliance on management control, towards teamworking and autonomous working based on high levels of trust, communication and involvement. Whether the focus is on profit and shareholder value in the private sector, or on outputs and service levels in the public sector, performance is the topical currency.

Purcell *et al*'s (2003) study on the impact of people management on organisational performance was intended to show the way in which HR practices – or what the CIPD terms 'people management', meaning all aspects of how people are managed – impact on performance. The study was conducted within a framework which claims that performance is a function of people's ability (knowledge and skills), their motivation, and the opportunity they are given to deploy their skills (referred to as AMO). The authors concluded that a range of 11 HR policies and practices are required to turn this into action and a model was devised, covering recruitment and selection, training and development, career opportunity, communications, involvement in decision-making, teamworking, appraisal, pay, job security, job challenge/job autonomy, and work–life balance.

> These performance-related HR policies encourage people to exercise a degree of choice on how and how well they do their job. In other words, they help induce discretionary behaviour which makes people work better and improve performance. This happens because the HR policies and practices develop positive employee attitudes or feelings of satisfaction, commitment and motivation. (Purcell *et al* 2003, pix)

This material is taken from *Bringing Policies to Life: The vital role of front line managers in people management* by Sue Hutchinson and John Purcell (2003), with the permission of the publisher, the Chartered Institute of Personnel and Development, London.

Figure 7.3 The people and performance model

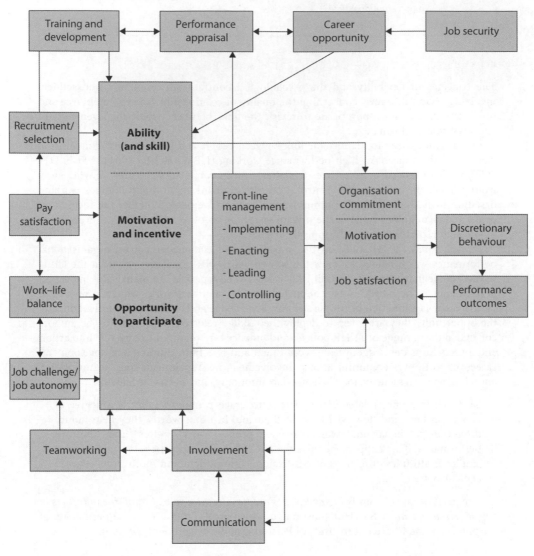

Some HR policies and practices were shown to be particularly important in terms of influencing employee outcomes like commitment, job satisfaction and motivation. These were those concerned with career opportunities, job influence, job challenge, training, performance appraisal, teamworking, involvement in decision-making, work–life balance, and having managers who are good at leadership and who show respect.

Among the implications for HR policy and practice is 'operational measurement' rather than 'remote' measures of profit:

> Proving that HR contributes to performance is not a major issue, and measures which use profit or shareholder values are too remote from the practice of people management to be useful. What is important is operational measurement where a close link can be observed, and the regular collection of these measures covering

people, operational, financial and customer areas is commonly done in the best firms. (Purcell *et al* 2003, p72)

We can conclude that the responsibility for enacting the policies rests with front-line managers, since these are the people with whom workers theoretically interact. In Hutchinson and Purcell's (2003) framework, 'organisation process advantage'– the way these policies are implemented – is what makes a difference. Put another way: it's not what you do, it's the way that you do it.

FRONT-LINE MANAGERS AND THE HRM–PERFORMANCE CHAIN

A suggested causal chain linking policy inputs to performance outcomes (Purcell and Hutchinson 2007) draws attention to employee discretionary behaviour, sometimes referred to as organisational citizenship behaviour (OCB), being a consequence of HR practices and front-line manager (FLM) leadership behaviours:

> It is often observed that there is a gap between what is formally required in HR policy and what is actually delivered by FLMs. The way FLMs undertake their HR duties of selecting, appraising, developing, communicating, involving, etc, is inextricably linked to a wider set of what are increasingly called leadership behaviours, which aim to influence employee attitudes and behaviour and give direction. These two aspects of FLMs' roles can be brought together in the term 'people management' (ibid, p3).

Additionally, there is recognition that independent of FLM leadership behaviour, the HR practices as perceived by the employees will be related to organisational commitment and job experiences, and that the outcome effect on employee attitudes will be greater when both are positive. A possible people management-causal chain emerges, which seeks to clarify the distinction between policies, practices and employees' experiences of them. It is seen as follows (ibid):

- intended practices; designed by the organisation
- actual practices; and style of leadership behaviour
- perception of practices; in terms of satisfaction, fairness and legitimacy
- employee attitudes; in reaction
- employee behaviour; observable responses including OCB and attendance
- unit-level outcomes; organisational effectiveness and performance.

The authors conclude that the crucial link is between the employee experiences of people management, the formation or modification of attitudes towards the employing organisation and the job, and the inducement these provide to engage in certain types of discretionary behaviour (ibid, p16).

LEADERSHIP AND MANAGEMENT STANDARDS

The CIPD (2007a) Standards for Leadership and Management are placed in the language of performance infrastructure ('critical failure factors') and differentiators ('critical success factors'). The former describes what is needed to do things right (efficiency) and deliver acceptable levels of behaviour and legal compliance, although it is observed that mere adherence to process seldom generates high-performance outcomes. The latter describes what is needed to do the right things (effectiveness) and, the proponents claim, deliver 'genuine' people involvement, commitment, engagement and added-value contribution. There are connotations of Herzberg's two-factor theory of motivation, which we discuss in Chapter 12, here: 'infrastructure' linking with hygiene factors and 'differentiators' involving motivators. The 11 policy areas (Purcell *et al* 2003) are seen as the performance infrastructure requirements, while the ways in which front-line managers deliver the policies – implementing, enacting, leading and controlling – are seen as the differentiators. It is claimed that these are 'directly related to the levels of commitment, motivation and satisfaction that employees report, and this, in turn, is linked to the vital area of discretionary behaviour' (Hutchinson and Purcell 2003, p3).

In 2010, the CIPD's report on sustainable organisational performance concluded that sustainable organisations would need to have a balanced short- and long-term focus and, crucially, agility to adapt to challenges and opportunities. It is clear that the notion of flexibility coupled with the need to ensure engagement via positive psychological contracts is crucial in this regard. The same report emphasised the need for leaders who regard employees as a core asset. We have seen that the management of flexible working should have at its centre a preoccupation with the people involved and should both be implemented and reviewed through consultation with those most closely involved.

There are very clear and important links between understanding the concepts, putting them into operation via effective management and subsequent organisational performance.

CASE STUDY 7.5

CHILDCARE AND PARENTAL LEAVE

One million mothers would rather leave the workforce than stay in it, says Mintel, and only 20 per cent return to work within a year of childbirth. Childcare costs, and the squeezed working and financial situation many parents report, all cause huge strain on the family dynamic, forcing men into a breadwinning role that society had been slowly easing them out of and, say the likes of Gillian Nissim (see below), putting parents at 'loggerheads'. Most importantly, it is setting back diversity and, if it does force parents out of the workforce in significant numbers, has profound implications for the future health of the British workplace.

The effects are seen across both the much-discussed 'squeezed middle' of working professionals and in lower-paid positions where the economic benefits of work are lessening.

Gillian Nissim, founder, Working Mums

Your organisation started life in 2006. What's changed since?

A core of businesses have always seen the benefit of the family and flexible working, but the last few years have

seen a rise in the rate of discrimination against mothers. If workplaces were so brilliant, Working Mums wouldn't need to exist.

Do working women suffer more when they become parents?

Not always. But the real problem for working mothers is that they often don't go back to the same field, which means a life-long loss of earnings. Many are working, at a loss, just to keep their toe in the door. Mothers should be able to get back to their careers.

We're seeing more men involved with parenting, but more could be working flexibly to alleviate pressure on mums. Government policy to extend paternity leave, and allow couples to divide their total leave, will put things on more of an equal footing, but men are not taking up their paternity entitlement.

Because childcare is still seen as a woman's role?

Maybe. I fear childcare is forcing family life to swing back to being female-led because of changes to child tax credits. We're hearing mothers really question their ability to continue working. It's got to the point where they're having to decide whether it's cheaper for them to stay at home. That will be bad news for families long term, as women will re-enter the workforce doing lower-skilled work.

Despite legislation, there won't be wholesale changes to family dynamics overnight. Families are at loggerheads. In an ideal world it shouldn't be one person staying at home and the other not – it should be more of a conversation. Only when both parents have a choice will the work/family dilemma be solved.

What should employers be doing?

They must focus more on the benefits of a diverse workforce. More work is also needed around job design. Mothers feel they have no way of resuming their roles after having a family. But women won't be able to work and have a family if there aren't more women in the pipeline.

Men need to demand more of a role in family life too, and there's nothing to be ashamed of for them in being a parent. HR shouldn't see flexibility as about gender – it's more about when and where all parents work.

Parental leave: What's next?

The changing legislative landscape explained

Since 2011

A father can take up to 26 weeks' additional parental leave on top of his two weeks' ordinary leave, but it can only be taken 20 or more weeks after the child's birth and after the mother has gone back to work, and in a single block. He must have been on a continuous contract with his employer for at least 26 weeks by the end of the 15th week before the baby is due.

From 2015

Employed mothers (who will still be eligible for 52 weeks' maternity leave) will be able to return to work after two weeks if they want to (four weeks for manual workers). Couples will then be able to share the remaining time between them by either taking it in turns to stay at home or by taking leave together (provided the total does not exceed 52 weeks). They will need to be 'open' with their employers and give 'proper notice' (expected to be eight weeks).

From 2018

Ordinary paternity leave (two weeks) is scheduled to be reviewed.

Source: Crush (2013)

Questions

1   What impacts on employee attitudes and organisational performance might we see as a result of this dilemma?

2   How might the HR professional intervene in the interests of employee and organisation alike? How might the dilemma be resolved?

CONCLUSION

Organisations concentrate upon meeting the needs of their stakeholders: shareholders and customers in the private sector; government and service users – now increasingly 'consumerised' – in the public sector. Responsiveness to the 'whip' of the market, previously a private sector concern, is also now increasingly required in the public sector as it becomes 'marketised'. The organisation and its workers, internal or external, core or contingent, are required to focus on performing.

Agile response is the order of the day as timeframes are shortened, and so flexibility is sought, from collective and structural flexibility, to individual and behavioural. As organisations are re-engineered and downsized, and spans of control are increased, management attention is devoted to the increasingly autonomous worker, without losing control. To better understand the discretionary element of employment relationships, the psychological contract, and its management, has become a focus of attention.

It seems that the air is filled with managerial information and messages, suggesting what might or should be done. There are confident, sometimes strident, assertions and claims, based on research findings and examples of what appears to be best practice, and some of these might remind us of Pollert's (1991) 'desperate search for panaceas'. Amongst this traffic it is possible to detect strengthening signals, describing increasing intensification of work and workers feeling pressurised. Where there is not a readily available pathway for workers to transmit signals of this sort, the alternative is to send messages through changed behaviour or attitudes. The reader, and the HR practitioner, then has the difficult task of listening and making sense of the sometimes conflicting information at his or her disposal.

KEY LEARNING POINTS

- Developments in the global economy have resulted in a need for greater flexibility from organisations.
- There are different types of flexibility including task, numerical, temporal and wage flexibility.
- There are documented examples of unintended consequences of flexible working, and negative aspects of this notion more generally.
- Managers can usefully be aware of the concept of the psychological contract, in order to enhance worker commitment and engagement.
- A number of HR policies and practices, frequently carried out by line managers, influence worker commitment, loyalty and engagement.

REVIEW QUESTIONS

1   Critically assess the respective advantages and disadvantages to organisations and to employees of the different forms of workplace flexibility.

2   Identify and evaluate the specific actions that managers can take that will improve employees' psychological contracts with the organisation.

3   Evaluate the role of front-line managers in influencing the discretionary performance of individuals within the organisation.

4   How might the performance of outsourced workers be managed or controlled in order to sustain satisfactory outcomes for customers and service users in 'networked' private and public sector organisations?

EXPLORE FURTHER

Guest, D. (2004) Flexible employment contracts, the psychological contract and employee outcomes: an analysis and review of the evidence. *International Journal of Management Reviews.* Vols. 5/6, No.1, pp1–19. This article provides a thorough review of evidence about the characteristics and consequences of flexible employment contracts and the role of the psychological contract.

Rousseau, D. (1995) *Psychological Contracts in Organisations: Understanding written and unwritten agreements.* London: Sage. Readers are referred to this publication for a comprehensive account of the psychological contract.

Sennett, R. (1998) *The Corrosion of Character: The personal consequences of work in the new capitalism.* London: Norton. Sennett's account of the social consequences of flexibility is recommended to all readers.

PART 4

MANAGING PEOPLE: EFFECTIVE PRACTICE

CHAPTER 8

Organisational and Job Design

Ray French

LEARNING OUTCOMES

After reading this chapter, you should be able to:

- assess the potential importance of organisational design and job design as part of the process of leading, managing and developing people

- recognise the contribution both concepts can make to the development of flexible and committed employees

- identify the possible negative impacts and/or unintended consequences of organisational design and job design

- point to the prevalence of post-bureaucratic structures and 'enriched' jobs in reality within the twenty-first-century global workforce.

OVERVIEW

In this chapter we examine organisational arrangements, in particular the ways in which organisations can be structured and jobs designed. These are important topics with significant relevance to leading, managing and developing people. As we will see organisations and jobs can be designed in very different ways and anyone involved in these activities can therefore exercise a significant degree of choice. It is important therefore to understand contrasting models of structure and job design in order to make informed choices in these areas.

These topic areas contain insights derived from classical studies; some dating from early in the twentieth century. However, thinking continues to evolve and there is a need to consider new and evolving thinking. In the area of job design, for example, a recent report on 'smart working' identified a new paradigm in some organisations, in which employees would be given ever greater flexibility in job design with decisions on job content placed in the hands of the job holder (CIPD 2008a). We deal with this topic in more detail later in the chapter.

It is also the case that topics covered in this chapter can go beyond the confines of a single organisation and even become a matter of public concern. Thus, in a much publicised case, the BBC's organisation structure came under critical review in 2012 and 2013 following several scandals affecting the corporation. A *Daily Telegraph* article on 22 February 2013 reported the conclusions of a report into the Jimmy Savile allegations which pointed to structural problems, noting that staff in different BBC departments were 'on different planets' and that senior leaders did not have scheduled meetings with each other (Rayner and Swinford 2013). It is important, both as practitioners and informed citizens, to keep abreast of new thinking and current events in order that our insights and recommendations are valid.

In practical terms there is evidence that structural arrangements and the design of jobs will have a strong influence on *organisational performance*. Mullins (2013) summarises the classical work of Drucker (1989), who argued that a poor structure would diminish an organisation's performance – even where one found good managers – and Child (2005), who also posits a link between the way an organisation is set up and strong economic performance. Child in fact goes further in concluding that the way organisations are structured also sends messages to the wider society about how people are and should be treated, so in common with other parts of this book there is an ethical component to the subject (see Chapter 4).

Returning to the theme of performance, much of the literature on job design also posits a link between the ways in which people's jobs are designed and their productivity. In this chapter we will see how people's attitudes and behaviour are shaped by their overall working context – including structure and job design. These attitudes and behaviour will have an impact on their motivation and engagement (see also Chapter 12) (CIPD 2012f).

From the perspective of leading, managing and developing people, organisational and job design are key concepts if people's experience of work can be shown to be strongly affected by the structure within which they operate and, of course, the nature of the work that they carry out. French *et al* (2011) locate this idea within their concept of a *performance equation*, which states that in order to perform well workers must firstly have the requisite attributes (skills and abilities). High performance is, secondly, conditional on people wanting to excel (levels of motivation). However, workers' performance is also affected by a third dimension, namely the organisational support provided for them. This last part of the equation deals with the backdrop to effective working. It encompasses the infrastructure of work, including the ways in which organisations are set up and jobs designed.

The topics examined in this chapter can appear abstract, maybe even 'dry', and less engaging than areas such as leadership and ethical considerations. However, organisational and job design are important concepts on several levels. If two friends, one working in a classical bureaucracy, the other in an 'adhocracy' (we will define these terms in more detail), compare their everyday experiences of work they will find that their working lives are indeed very different. As we will also see, organisation and job design are core principles underlying strategies of people management, so they are of interest to existing and future HR managers as well.

It is important to recognise that attempts to enhance performance through the application of design principles can founder through the law of unintended consequences. Linstead *et al* (2009) and Watson (2012), for example, both highlight what are termed 'dysfunctions' of bureaucracy. Bureaucratic structures are intended to foster efficient working through stability, predictability and fair treatment (both of employees and clients or customers). Bureaucracy is essentially conceived as a rational system of organisation. The very features which are supposed to aid efficiency can result in reality in negative behaviour; for example defensive or even 'jobsworth' style behaviour among employees, resulting from over-adherence to rules, and moderate or 'get-by' performance as a consequence of slow and rigid promotion procedures. In this chapter we will advise against any assumption that implementing changes in organisation or job design will automatically result in positive outcomes. Notwithstanding this point, organisation and job design can be powerful tools for change.

We will, finally, show how recent work in organisation and job design has often sought to use these ideas to promote flexible working – an important theme within leading, managing and developing people in the twenty-first century. Gilmore (2012) notes that flexibility as a theme has come to permeate discussion about employment in general terms, and labour utilisation more specifically. The emerging concept of post-bureaucratic organisation is also underpinned by the idea of flexibility. The same author also notes that flexibility is associated with interesting tensions arising in the employment relationship. It is not a neutral or anodyne concept. Preece (2012) records that one reason for organisation redesign – in the form of post-bureaucratic structures – is to allow the job of managing human resources to focus on maximising benefits of working with a more flexible, temporary workforce. It is also very important to ensure that workers' knowledge and skills are deployed in ways that add value to the firm. The links between organisational design, job design and flexibility will be further drawn out in this chapter.

INTRODUCTION

We begin this section with a definition of some of the key terms which form the basis for an understanding of organisational arrangements.

ORGANISATIONAL DESIGN

Organisational design (OD) is defined as a planned activity in which designers, usually managers, maybe in conjunction with specialised consultants, attempt to adjust the formal shape of their organisation. There are many types of organisation and consequently many choices in organisational design (Wood *et al* 2010). OD is defined by French *et al* (2011, p291) as 'the process of choosing and implementing a structural configuration for an organisation'. We see therefore that organisational design and structure are not synonymous but in a fundamental sense are linked concepts. OD creates organisational structure, defined as the intended pattern of tasks, responsibilities, lines of authority and networks of communication in an organisation.

It can be seen from this categorisation of structure that we are in essence dealing with formalised features of organisations. The classic way to depict an organisation's structure is via scrutiny of a chart or other diagram, in effect taking an impersonal view of what *should* happen in that organisation. The term *informal organisation*, contrastingly, denotes what actually happens in a workplace, which can deviate from what should occur within formal arrangements – for example, if people habitually ignore a bureaucratic rule or procedure.

'Organisation structure' as a term has several different sub-components within this overarching definition. These are set out below:

Formalisation

Formalisation refers to the extent to which an organisation stipulates the way work or particular roles comprising a job should be carried out. One guide to ascertain the degree of formalisation is the existence of procedural manuals or job descriptions pre-ordaining working styles and practices.

Specialisation

This aspect of structure refers both to the extent to which work roles involve a range of specialist activities and to the ways in which workers with similar or related roles and tasks are grouped together. Many organisations have historically operated in a highly specialised manner, typically by setting up discrete, functionally based departments.

Vertical differentiation

This sub-set of structure links to power and authority. An organisation could specify many levels within a hierarchy, each with distinct reporting responsibilities, or it might be designed as a relatively 'flat' organisation, with few hierarchical levels. The concept of span of control in which the ratio of workers reporting to managers is prescribed is also relevant here.

Centralisation

This deals with decision-making, in particular whether responsibility in this regard rests with senior managers, rather than it being cascaded throughout the organisation. Closely associated with this central idea is the degree to which tight control is exercised by a head office or whether, contrastingly, greater autonomy is granted to operating units or divisions.

Line and/or staff functions

In this element of structure there is a distinction between line functions, which are intimately connected with the primary purpose of the organisation, and contrasting (although complementary) staff functions, which supplement and further the aims of the organisation through the provision of ancillary services. In a large college, for example, the organisation's prime objective will be the education of students – so that lecturers form part of the line, while an HRM department may be categorised as a staff function. We have looked at the implications of this distinction for HR in Chapter 2. The relationship between line and staff (and their relative importance) raises issues of horizontal (as opposed to vertical) co-ordination and control.

Later in this chapter we will examine the ways in which organisational design – and hence structure – can be utilised in a positive way within the overall project of leading, managing and developing people.

REFLECTIVE ACTIVITY 8.1

Look again at the elements of organisational structure listed above. How formal, centralised and vertically differentiated do you imagine the following types of organisation should be?

- the British Royal Navy
- an animal welfare charity
- a web design and creative agency.

JOB DESIGN

Job design as defined by French *et al* (2011, p244) is 'the planning and specification of job tasks and the work setting in which they are to be accomplished'. The authors elaborate on their definition by proposing that much contemporary writing on the subject views the objective of job design as facilitating meaningful, interesting and challenging jobs and that, within this perspective, a manager's responsibility is to design jobs that will motivate an individual employee. This finding underpins much academic research in this area, which often posits a link between aspects of jobs and employees' psychological well-being. We will examine several examples of work within this tradition in this chapter. However, job design, as we will see, does not presuppose the design of enriched jobs – it can also lead to the splitting of tasks into routine, repetitive and unskilled work.

Watson (2006) draws a distinction between the terms job design and work design. He notes that job design refers to task patterns that could occur in any part of a work organisation, while work design is underpinned by more broadly defined principles which could reflect that organisation's culture and structure. This refining of terminology is useful in that it highlights the role of managerial choice in devising principles for organising work. Thus job design, and beyond this, work design, can form part of a more strategic approach to managing people. Watson makes the distinction in this context between *direct* and *indirect* control principles. In the former case, there is a stress on prescribed task procedures with only a minimal level of commitment required from employees. In contrast, indirect control principles emphasise far greater discretion for employees in the way they perform tasks; this is in turn dependent on their higher levels of commitment, leading to mutual trust between members of the organisation in question.

It would be true to say that for much of its history job design, and the broader concept of work design, has been associated with principles of direct control. In reading earlier work on this subject, one finds particular resonance of these ideas in the work of Frederick Taylor and his model of *scientific management*, often subsequently referred to as 'Taylorism'. As we will see, Taylor's work, together with principles associated with Henry Ford, contain assumptions that jobs can be designed on a rational basis in order to maximise workers' efforts with a view to quicken production, radically reduce costs and increase output to a very significant extent. It can be argued that mass production and consumption patterns have been predicated on these principles. At the time of the millennium several commentators promoted the case for Ford as one of the key influential figures of the twentieth century, in part because of his impact on social trends due to the production of affordable cars, but also because many millions of people worked in jobs that bore the stamp of his (and Taylor's) vision. This tradition within job design has either minimised the issue of workers' motivation or put forward a model of needs at work which centre on maximising income, for example the concept of rational economic man.

Leach and Wall (2004) link different views of job design with specific epochs, making the distinction between traditional job design, which emphasises the design of jobs in order to minimise skill requirements and training times, with more contemporary *job redesign*, which, contrastingly, recommends increasing the number of tasks carried out by an individual worker such as through job rotation and 'enlarging' and/or 'enriching' individual jobs. We will explore these concepts in greater detail later in the chapter.

FLEXIBILITY

We have referred to this concept on several occasions already in this book and examine it in greater detail and depth in Chapter 7. This broad term refers to several discrete areas of business operations. It can be applied firstly to flexible forms of organisational structure – implying a move away from a rigid bureaucratic form to one that can respond more speedily to demands emanating from its environment (Daft *et al* 2010). At the same time it refers to attempts to enrich workers' jobs through multiskilling, greater autonomy and responsibility with the general aim of fostering both better performance and greater commitment to the employing organisation. We will primarily examine the notion of flexibility with reference to these twin themes.

The term flexibility is also, however, used in the area of employment itself, resulting in greater prevalence of such arrangements as part-time and fixed-term working, casual employment, outsourcing and teleworking. For some commentators, eg Bratton and Gold (2012), increasing flexibility of employment has led to heightened distinctions between a core and peripheral workforce.

A CIPD survey (2013b) included data on why employers chose to outsource parts of their employee resourcing activities, such as recruitment advertising and candidate sourcing and screening. Some of the more oft-cited reasons given for outsourcing included: increasing efficiency; reducing costs; freeing up HR managers to concentrate on more strategic activities; and increasing resourcing flexibility to meet peaks and troughs of demand.

One can see that there are powerful reasons for outsourcing work beyond individual organisations. However, some of the same reasons given for outsourcing, particularly increasing efficiency and reducing costs, were given as a justification for keeping activities in-house. There are no right answers and individual circumstances intervene; for example, a particular relationship with an external provider might make it advantageous to outsource.

MODELS OF STRUCTURE

Having defined the key terms used in this chapter, we now turn to look more closely at the topic of organisational structure, which is an essential component of OD.

BUREAUCRACY

Bureaucracy has been a highly influential and long-lasting form of organisation structure: some writers see examples of it as far back as ancient Greek and Roman civilisations. In modern times, its key features were articulated by the sociologist Max Weber, who constructed an ideal type of bureaucracy, ie what it would look like in an extreme or idealised form.

WEBER'S MODEL OF PURE BUREAUCRACY

- Tasks are allocated according to certified expertise, with resultant specialised (for example, departmental) structure.
- Jobs are defined through clear and often simplified routine tasks.
- Control is exercised through a hierarchical structure, typically with many layers denoting levels of authority.
- Rules and procedures are clearly set out in the form of written documentation.
- There are pre-set formal systems of communication via specified channels with hierarchical authority paramount.
- Employees are appointed and, where appropriate, promoted on the basis of clear criteria often relating to their qualifications.
- Managers are salaried officials and do not have a financial stake in the organisation.
- Rules are set and all decisions made rationally in an attempt to eliminate non-rational elements such as emotional involvement or personal preference.

In the late nineteenth century Weber claimed that organisations (in Europe) came to lay particular stress on rational decision-making. It was claimed that this distinguished them from the ways in which previous communities' workplaces operated more on the basis of traditional authority. Watson (2006, p38) states that, 'Out of this major cultural shift came bureaucracy. And bureaucracies are what modern organisations are.'

ALTERNATIVES TO BUREAUCRACY: ADAPTING TO 'CONTINGENCIES'

From the 1950s onwards, a wave of critical comment emerged centring on a perceived inability of bureaucratic structures to cope well in the face of changing circumstances. The underlying idea that organisation structures are influenced by 'external' factors, to which they must be adapted to ensure high performance, is commonly referred to as *the contingency approach*. Before examining the factors that have been identified as relevant situational events or contingencies, it is timely to look at some alternative structures which are either extensions of bureaucracy or radical alternatives.

Project team structures

Project teams are normally seen as temporary structures set up for a specific purpose where cross-functional expertise is required (see Needle 2010, for further detail). In some sectors – for example, consultancy – such structures could be seen as the norm, groups of employees from different functional areas routinely being assembled to provide an integrated service for a particular client. Another possible scenario in which such a structure would be relevant is where a project group comprising potential users of a new IT system, including representatives from different functional departments, work together to consider the implications of a new system for their own sub-unit. One advantage of such a structure is that it encourages workers to consider their contribution to organisational goals from a variety of perspectives and can therefore facilitate cross-fertilisation of ideas.

The matrix

Matrix structures are by no means recent phenomena, having been identified in significant numbers from the 1970s onwards. The key defining point of a matrix structure is multi-reporting, in that employees are required to consider at least two aspects of their job – typically their functional specialism and the products or services provided as part of their work. We have already referred to the distinction between line and staff functions, which is addressed directly in the matrix form, the notion of facing in different directions being reinforced in the structure of the organisation itself. Many students and academics reading this book will be familiar with the idea of the matrix since it is by no means uncommon in the higher-education sector (the author can identify examples from a number of different countries). A lecturer may form part of an academic department based on his or her academic subject area, but also have to report to senior managers whose remit could be courses (the product), or quality assurance, or international developments, or knowledge transfer. In such a case the individual lecturer could report to five separate managers.

The advantages of matrices are similar to those put forward for project teams in that they allow for easier collaborative working – and even synergy. On the other hand, the major criticism of matrix structures has centred on their potential for ambiguity and even outright confusion in reporting. The matrix idea could readily lend itself to transnational or global working, and this aspect is pursued more fully later in this chapter. The concept of a matrix is indeed similar to the ideal type of the 'global firm' based on divisional structure.

Divisional structure

The divisional form of structure, also known as the multi-functional model, was originally conceived as an alternative to the functional bureaucracy. In this form, entire divisions are set up to deal with all aspects of a product or service. It can be argued that the focus of such a structure is on *outputs* – that is, the end product – rather than on the inputs (all resources including human skills, knowledge and effort) needed to turn the end product into a tangible entity. General Motors (GM) for many years provided an example of this type of strategic approach to structure. GM's divisions were based on brand names and associated products. Individual divisions were largely self-contained and operated as profit centres. However, headquarters – sometimes known as 'the centre' – co-ordinated overall strategy and centralised other activities. The divisional nature of this multinational company became evident in 2009, when GM, following financial problems caused by global economic turbulence, sold off whole divisions of the company hosted outside the USA.

Organic structure and 'adhocracy'

The organic model was originally put forward by the researchers Burns and Stalker (1961) as an idealised counterpoint to the classic bureaucratic structure. As we shall see in the following section examining the impact of contingent factors on organisational form, Burns and Stalker found that this type of structure, or rather its component features, would be effective when organisations operated in a turbulent environment of rapidly changing technology, fierce competition and uncertain customer demand. The features of this abstract model were:

- network (as opposed to hierarchical) structures of control and communication
- knowledge spread throughout the organisation (rather than located at the top)
- employee commitment to their tasks (compared with loyalty to the organisation)
- knowledge, skills and experience applied to diverse tasks (compared with long-term specialisation)
- communication flowing up, down and across the organisation rather than being essentially top–down.

Burns and Stalker's organic structure is overall characterised by informality and flexibility. Originally applied to the fast-changing microelectronics sector of the 1960s, it has increasingly been advocated in other areas of the private and public sectors because their environments are perceived as more turbulent as a result of economic, political and technological change.

The adhocracy shares important features of the organic form. However, it may go further in that it can be defined as an organisational type that is not planned in the first instance, rather it develops spontaneously or in an *ad hoc* manner, hence the name (Clegg *et al* 2011).

Virtual network structure

When defining types of structure in the preceding paragraphs it became evident that organisations may not simply structure their operations so that they are bounded within a single entity. Rather, as we saw in the case of divisional structure, individuals might operate separately from headquarters in important respects. Virtual network structures take this principle further with organisations 'farming out' activities to other companies. This phenomenon is often referred to as *outsourcing*. Whole areas of activity can be outsourced to another organisation, including accounting, marketing, design and, interestingly for our purposes, HRM. In some cases the organisation may not do what it is most famous for – Daft *et al* (2010) record that the fashion-wear company Nike may produce very little or at times none of its own clothing.

Virtual network structures may involve the 'hub' organisation imposing its own patterns of structure on its partners or, contrastingly, might enable partner organisations to devise their own structure and indeed ways of designing workers' jobs.

Key relationships in the network structure are those running *across* organisations and managing such relationships effectively becomes paramount. Relationships can be contractual in nature, with deterrents put in place to avoid betrayal and other negative behaviour, or might be based on trust-based links, underpinned by knowledge of the partner organisation. In some cases the relationship can come to be based on goodwill and mutual obligation – akin to a successful personal relationship.

CONTINGENT FACTORS

There are many potentially distinctive forms of organisational structure: we have only outlined some general principles here. As suggested earlier, the essence of the contingency approach is that particular types of structure should be *designed* in the light of the contingent factors acting on the organisation in question. Although contingencies are by definition framed by unique circumstances, the overarching factors usually put forward are listed below.

Technology

The work of Joan Woodward, published in 1965 (but based on research carried out in the mid-1950s), identified a link between technology – here referring to production methods – and the ways in which the companies she studied were organised. Woodward's conclusion was that the production systems used by the companies she researched resulted in differences in those companies' structures. Woodward, in addition to demarcating forms of structure and linking them to technology, also, and very importantly, concluded that there was an optimal situation in which organisations that aligned their structures according to the technologies they used would be the most efficient. In other words, the structure would have to fit with this particular contingent factor.

Size of organisation

A research team from Aston University in England proposed that an organisation's size would be the most important determining factor in terms of its optimal structure (see Pugh and Hickson 1976, for an account of the research by members of the original group). The Aston researchers examined the extent of specialisation, the degree to which formal policies influenced work in reality, and standardisation in terms of procedures. The Aston academics then identified a number of points for comparison, all deriving from Weber's ideal type of bureaucracy, finally correlating these with statistical data from their own research sample. Their conclusion was that the independent variable which most strongly impacted on the dependent variable of organisational structure was size. The *post hoc* logic which purports to explain these findings was fundamentally that as organisations grow in size there is considerable pressure for them to become more bureaucratic– see also Chapter 3. Once again the influence of a contingent factor pointed to an ideal structure depending on the nature of the specific organisation.

Organisational environments

As we have already noted, Burns and Stalker (1961) proposed their dichotomy of *mechanistic and organic structures*. The mechanistic category is very similar to Weber's model of bureaucracy, while the diametrically opposite organic form is flexible, is network-based and requires commitment – in addition to compliance and loyalty – from employees within this structure. The key contingent variable for Burns and Stalker was the particular environment facing the organisation. The more turbulent the environment, in terms of technological advance, competition and customer or client demand, the more organic the organisation should be, if it were to prosper and even survive in such a challenging milieu. Burns and Stalker identified organisations that had failed to adapt via changed structures, thus adding weight to their central proposition.

In conclusion, organisational design offers a degree of choice to decision-makers who should consider the contingent factors faced by their organisations before deciding on structural arrangements. Nonetheless, such choices are themselves constrained as it has been shown that different structures tend to be more effective in particular circumstances, ie depending on factors such as size, technology and environment.

One should also be wary of assuming that organisations can only respond to contingent factors in a highly constrained way. There is a danger of interpreting the contingency model, which was conceived as a flexible idea, very much an antidote to the 'one best way' approaches of the 1950s, in an over-deterministic way. Child (1972) introduced the important idea of strategic choice, whereby managers or other senior figures within organisations make informed decisions about the conditions in which they *chose* to operate.

Child proposed that in reality large organisations could select and manipulate their environments. Daft *et al* (2010) use the example of the retailer Wal-Mart to illustrate this point, concluding that Wal-Mart had successfully lobbied the World Trade Organisation and UK and Chinese governments for a reversal of policies on large store openings. This enabled them to maintain their global structure, whereas if they had simply adapted to their environment they might have merely complied with government diktat or conceivably not operated in those countries at all.

Child also proposed that structural responses to changes in technology could equally be viewed as the result of decisions on which tasks decision-makers wished to be involved in, while it was possible to break down large operating units into smaller sections, thereby making a positive choice on structure.

Notwithstanding the validity of Child's work, the contingency view of organisational design remains dominant in management thinking and it contains many valid insights.

 TAMING A LIFE-THREATENING ILLNESS

CASE STUDY 8.1

A few years ago a patient was admitted to a UK hospital for transplant surgery. The operation was deemed life-saving, so the oft-repeated cliché of work not being a matter of life and death did not apply. The 10-hour procedure was successful and the patient embarked on a lengthy recovery which began by lying in his hospital bed. As one can imagine, this rest period afforded an opportunity for deep reflection on a range of topics.

Our patient was a Professor of Sociology, and his reflections came to encompass both his professional training and his deeply personal concerns. So he began to ponder on how the human and social endeavour involved in saving his life had come to be. He could see: 'social acts of great learned skill and scientific knowledge, myriad social acts of humane and loving care, multiple social acts of practical activity – cleaning the floors, pushing trolleys with patients, providing food, keeping the plumbing going, welcoming the outpatients, organising beds, orchestrating a million little daily routines.

In the course of its daily work, the hospital relied on so many roles: nurses, doctors, porters, ambulance drivers, social workers, phlebotomists, physiotherapists, transplant co-ordinators, administrators and ward managers. There are of course many more. Thousands of workers were organised through structure and job design in a massive division of labour in order to save people's lives.

Source: Plummer (2010), p5

Questions

1   Hospitals are often categorised as bureaucratic organisations. What are the advantages of such a structure in a hospital setting?

2   Identify the contingent factors that impact on a hospital and show how they influence hospital structure. Could one ever envisage a non-bureaucratic hospital? Give reasons for your answer.

APPROACHES TO JOB DESIGN

Traditionally, job design principles have emphasised job simplification (Taylor 1911), interpreted critically by some writers as deskilling, while more recent contributions to the subject area have typically recommended expanding jobs in order both to increase employee job satisfaction, or at least to reduce boredom, and to engender greater *flexibility* in a workforce (Hackman and Oldham 1980). It is often proposed that such flexibility is desirable in view of changes in the wider business environment. In the UK context, Hutton (2004, p1) introduced this argument some 10 years ago as follows: 'Britain's fundamental economic structures are changing; industries and services built around knowledge are growing, while those built around mass industrial production and raw muscle power are declining. Work is becoming more intelligent and an intelligent workforce is going to be one that wants to be intelligent about how it organises itself. The more autonomy and control it can have, the more content it will be.'

One should be wary of assuming that there is, or will shortly be, a proliferation of 'intelligent' work. On the contrary, the emergence of increasing numbers of workplaces such as fast-food outlets and call centres have mainly been associated with standardised repetitive 'Taylorist'-style jobs. Beyond such work with its associated routine tasks, one also finds what Clegg *et al* (2011) refer to as 'grunge jobs' comprising both work carried out in the lower reaches of the supply chain supporting global business, and that performed by an underclass of sometimes illegal workers operating in very poor conditions outside the formally recognised and regulated job market.

Nonetheless there is also evidence that increasingly many workers will be required to act as thinking performers and this segment of the workforce will form the main focus in this chapter. In such an environment it is posited that organisations seeking distinctive high performance should be involved in job design which contributes towards a positive psychological contract between employer and worker. This, it is suggested, can also aid and reinforce successful organisational performance. We have discussed both the issue of flexibility and the psychological contract in more detail in Chapter 7.

It is also necessary for all organisations to engage in job design as an 'infrastructure' task, to ensure that work is allocated into suitably sized role descriptions capable of being carried out effectively. At the same time, it is essential to ensure suitable demarcation of roles both vertically (in terms of skill, knowledge and hierarchical level) as well as horizontally (in functional terms). This aspect of basic job design is a pre-requisite for minimal threshold standards of performance by organisations and is needed to avoid fundamental problems relating to the nature of work and roles.

REFLECTIVE ACTIVITY 8.2

Read the statement below which appears on Tesco's corporate website and answer the question which follows.

Making Tesco A Great Place to Work

We know that our people want four things from us at Tesco:

- *to be treated with respect*
- *a manager who helps me*
- *an interesting job*
- *an opportunity to get on.*

Source: Tesco (2013): www.tesco-careers.com/home/working/why-join-tesco

It might be thought that the aim of securing interesting jobs in the supermarket context is the most challenging of the four aims set out above. In the 'Meet Our People' section of Tesco's website we hear from a customer assistant who says:

'... to be honest I got a job at Tesco because I needed some money, but working here has been far more enjoyable and rewarding than I could ever have thought it could be.'

At the start of your study of this topic and without referring to material set out later in this chapter, suggest ways that Tesco's managers could provide interesting jobs for store workers.

Answer from your knowledge of large supermarkets, as a shopper if you have no personal experience of store working.

It is possible to locate key developments in the approach to job design, although while these have been developed in particular epochs, each can still be applied to current work situations. It is now time to look at these approaches in more detail.

SCIENTIFIC MANAGEMENT

As indicated earlier, for its most famous proponent, Frederick Taylor, scientific management involved organising tasks into highly specialised jobs. Managers should take on responsibility for planning, co-ordinating and monitoring work, with the task worker restricted to the level of operative. Recruitment and training are simplified and workers are grouped together in large units such as factories or call centres, enabling a high volume of chiefly standardised goods or services. One example is the Fordist production line system, which, in addition to demarcating jobs, also controlled the speed of work. It is difficult to over-emphasise the significance of this model of job design. Henry Ford, in laying the conditions for mass production of cars, was able to reduce costs very substantially, which in turn led to greatly increased levels of car ownership in the USA. This led to him being considered one of the pivotal figures of the twentieth century in the industrialised world.

   Scientific management as a driver for job design has attracted much controversy and a good deal of criticism for the following reasons:

- it can lead to product inflexibility
- it has been criticised as dehumanising and for failing to recognise 'higher order' human needs such as self-actualisation
- it may foster compliance and an instrumental view of work as a means to an end, as opposed to engendering commitment and loyalty
- monotony and boredom can result in reduced performance outcomes.

REFLECTIVE ACTIVITY 8.3

Scientific management is perceived by some commentators as a particular direct form of control of work and workers by management. Braverman (1974) is prominent among writers who go on to assert that this concept of job design is fundamentally associated with an attempt to deskill workers. The notion of deskilling derives from the work of Marx – see McLellan (2000) in which owners and managers seek to maximise surplus value from workers, in essence exploiting them.

Managers as a group are, in the nature of their role, concerned to control and regularise jobs and work. Nonetheless, not all jobs have been subject to this version of job and work design and the ability of particular groups of workers to retain or even enhance skill levels remains an important factor in job design.

Question

1   How valid do you find the deskilling thesis, both as a theory and explanation of reality in work organisations?

Adler (1999) has put forward an interesting restatement of the impact of simplified 'Taylorist' jobs on employees' attitudes to their work situation. His research indicated that under conditions of scientific management, employees could still be motivated by a sense of a 'job well done'. For example, they were found to respond positively to managers encouraging them to compete with co-workers, both in terms of quality and output. When they were respected and trusted by managers, the workers under study reciprocated with commitment and loyalty.

JOB REDESIGN

Job redesign emerged in part as a reaction to the perceived negative effects of scientific management. Its academic roots lie in the so-called 'human relations' school, which emphasised people's social needs which, it was claimed, could and should be met in the workplace. Herzberg's two-factor theory of motivation proposed that pure motivation derived from the content of work as opposed to hygiene factors such as pay, physical working conditions and quality of supervision. Hygiene factors, for Herzberg, were sources of dissatisfaction which could be lessened if, for example, pay was improved. However, workers would only be truly motivated if their job or work met their needs for recognition, autonomy and achievement. Herzberg's view was that virtually all human beings would respond to work which was rich in motivating factors, if they had the ability to do the job and the opportunity to carry out meaningful work. We will, however, question this near-universal perspective later in this chapter.

In a highly significant contribution to this topic area, Hackman and Oldham (1980) proposed, on the basis of research, that five key characteristics could be used to identify the extent to which a job would, in reality, be motivating.

- skill variety – if different and diverse activities demanded the exercise of a range of skills and abilities
- task identity – the extent to which a job involves a whole and identifiable piece of work with a tangible end result
- task significance – the perceived value and effect of a job on other people
- autonomy – where a worker is free to schedule the pace of his or her work, have some choice in how the work is carried out and is relatively independent of supervision
- feedback – the degree to which a worker gets information about the effectiveness of their performance. This feedback could be gained through observation of their work outcomes.

It is argued that each key characteristic is linked to a positive psychological state which, in turn, leads to desirable work outcomes. For example, task significance could result in a feeling of satisfaction in the meaningfulness of work undertaken, with positive outcomes of work motivation and effectiveness following on from this psychological state. In summary, Hackman and Oldham stated that intrinsic motivation is dependent on individuals experiencing *three* critical psychological states: experienced meaningfulness (as noted above); experienced responsibility for work; and knowledge of the results of work activities.

Hackman and Oldham recognise that individuals can respond to the characteristics differently; they are after all a function of the individual's perception, so the motivating potential of a job may vary between people. Several factors will influence the manner in which any one individual will respond to changes in their job design.

- *Growth-need strength*. It is suggested that people vary in the extent to which they desire accomplishment and autonomy at work. People high in this category will therefore respond positively to enriched jobs; contrastingly, other workers might find newly enriched jobs a source of anxiety.

- *Knowledge and skill.* People who perceive they can perform adequately (known as a sense of self-efficacy) respond more positively to enriched jobs. This highlights the importance of individuals' perceptions and also the development of knowledge and skills at work.
- *Context satisfaction.* Hackman and Oldham found that employees who were more satisfied with contextual factors such as pay and working conditions would be more likely to respond positively to job enrichment than fellow workers dissatisfied on these measures.

However, despite recognising potential differences in the ways particular workers might respond to job enrichment, in overall terms Hackman and Oldham's model sets out a clear agenda for managers and others to devise meaningful and varied jobs.

REFLECTIVE ACTIVITY 8.4

How can Hackman and Oldham's model be applied to the following jobs:

- dentist
- railway ticket collector
- university lecturer
- tiler
- your current or previous job (assuming this is not one of the above)?

The job redesign approach attempted to put forward a model which, through increasing the scope of jobs, could result both in greater efficiency and output (however defined) while also increasing the motivation of a workforce. Hackman and Oldham, while stressing the importance of 'moderating factors' which depress levels of motivation, for example lack of knowledge or skill, 'low growth need strength' and other negative factors in the work context, clearly advocate the design of jobs which can lead to psychological well-being among the people who perform them.

We have noted that Hackman and Oldham question whether, and to what extent, job-holders are likely to respond positively to jobs that are redesigned in this way. Their approach in addressing this issue is essentially a psychological one focusing on presumed needs and other psychological characteristics of human beings which could vary. It may be, however, that individual workers can also *choose* work that, although comparatively meaningless, may offer the prospect of other desired rewards including pay, for wider reasons based on their calculation of costs and benefits. Support for this notion is provided by the work of Goldthorpe and Lockwood (1968), who identified a category of workers who took an instrumental attitude or *orientation to work*. Formed outside the workplace and influenced by, among others, family and peers, the instrumental orientation regards work as a means to an end, and workers within this category often make a conscious decision to enter psychologically unfulfilling but highly paid work. Thus many workers meet their higher-order needs off the job. With 168 hours in every week, work rarely consumes more than a third of this time for most people. There is ample opportunity for individuals with strong growth needs to find satisfaction beyond their place of work

This is not to say that decision-makers should make no attempt to design satisfying work for job-holders; there may be considerable practical benefits in so doing. It is useful, however, to adopt a contingency perspective in this area; that is to understand that the nature of job design may depend on a variety of factors including the work itself and the chosen orientations to work as well as the psychological needs of the workforce.

It should finally be noted that enriched work with its hoped-for concomitant high commitment can itself be regarded as a form of subjugation due to the demands it imposes on employees working within its precepts. Grey (2009, p82) notes that: 'what now appears quite normal and natural is that managers will work long hours, do whatever needs to be done to get the job done and are motivated to do so by the intrinsic interest of their work, the payment they receive and, in general, a sense of responsibility and professionalism'. Grey goes on to paint a picture of managers stressed out by endless demands and locked into a particular set of corporate imperatives which, while in many respects preferable to that endured by workers in less enriched and self-managed jobs, themselves involve considerable sacrifices in many respects.

LESSONS FROM JAPAN

Any overview examining how job design has developed as a concept would not be complete without acknowledging the influence of ideas originating in, and imported from, Japan. The purpose here is not to provide an account of how Japanese techniques came to be commended to UK organisations from the 1980s onwards. Neither will we undertake a detailed analysis of what is a highly complex concept of management underpinned by deep assumptions within Japanese society. Rather, we will concentrate on how Japanese management principles have impacted on the specific area of job design, where it is claimed the following factors are particularly relevant:

- *Teamwork.* Japanese management techniques have often advocated the grouping of workers into teams, even in areas of work which would otherwise be organised on an individual basis. This concept can be extended to encompass task decision-making, for example, through quality circles.
- *Multiskilling.* The physical grouping of workers can also be extended to enable more similar job descriptions, that is setting a context of work in which employees are required to have generalised job skills. It follows that these jobs are minimally demarcated. We see here an early embodiment of the principle of flexibility.
- *Total Quality Management (TQM).* For our purposes the key element of TQM is the principle that quality control should be the concern of all workers and therefore form part of every employee's job role. This could be seen as one manifestation of job enlargement, building both additional duties and responsibilities into their jobs.

REFLECTIVE ACTIVITY 8.5

TQM

Derived from Japanese management methods, and in contrast to other methods of monitoring the quality of a business's output, such as inspection and quality control, TQM is said to be a means of ensuring customer satisfaction through a process of continuous improvement of all work operations. Importantly for the study and leadership of people, to be successful its advocates point to the need for all employees to be involved in TQM. It requires creative thinking and the use of teamwork to solve problems and meet customers' needs. From this standpoint, competitive advantage and differentiation can be achieved through recognising the, often untapped, resource that organisations have in their workforces.

Question

1 To what extent could your own job – or one with which you are familiar – benefit from TQM applications? Give reasons for your conclusions.

Japanese work design principles have been incorporated within a wider philosophy including 'single status' employment conditions and lifetime, or at least long-term, tenure of employment. Some elements are not unique to the Japanese context, for example Swedish car-makers had also (quite independently) introduced small-group working into their production processes along with aspects of job enlargement. Nonetheless the Japanese system, as described, can be said to be a distinctive and coherent view on job design, the latter perhaps being seen as a differentiating factor. There have been well-publicised instances of Japanese practices being introduced to the UK, for example in the Nissan and Toyota car production facilities. Some of the principles outlined here have been widely adopted. While the economic difficulties experienced by Japan since the 1990s have cast some doubt on the extent to which they can be regarded as a panacea, many employers now assume that quality issues should be the concern of all workers and that this should be operationalised through job design.

One should take a realistic view of the extent of improvements emanating from such approaches to job design. These, it is claimed, centre on the twin benefits of greater productivity and more positive attitudes among job-holders. Important and commendable as they are, these benefits will not outweigh other factors affecting the organisation. One example is provided by figures indicating the comparatively strong productivity of Japanese-owned car plants in the UK. Rhys Murray-West (2002), in acknowledging their excellent productivity, noted nonetheless that measuring performance by productivity was 'using only a Soviet Union measure of performance. Productivity is a necessary condition of performance, but it is in no way sufficient to guarantee profitability. It hasn't stopped Nissan slipping into loss-making, which indicates the pressure they are under from the strength of sterling.' He also referred to the crucial importance of the desirability of the product itself!

BUSINESS PROCESS RE-ENGINEERING

Business process re-engineering (BPR), we will argue, should also be examined when considering approaches to, and influences on, job design. BPR emerged in the 1990s and is associated with Hammer and Champy (1993) and Davenport (1993). These writers advocate a radical approach to OD. In effect, they recommend ignoring past and current practice when considering how to both structure an organisation and design work. They place a strong emphasis on processes, and attention to these at the same hierarchical level. Such chains of process are thus horizontal and often cross traditionally functional boundaries.

The focus on an absolute need to serve the customer can result in very dramatic changes to work processes and jobs. Buchanan and Wilson (1996) conducted a 'patient trail' in a British hospital. They found that a hospital patient might routinely have dealings with between 50 and 150 different members of the hospital's staff, becoming at different times the responsibility of most of the hospital's functional departments in the course of diagnosis, on-site treatment and aftercare (see also Case Study 8.1). Problems that arose from this complex process were attributed to hospital staff being quite naturally concerned primarily with what happens at their own stage of the patient's journey. Staff working within such a fragmented environment were not always aware either of what had gone on before or what would subsequently happen to the patient.

Examples such as that given above suggest that organisations should restructure away from vertical or functionally based departmental structures if there is to be a true focus on the customer (this ignoring the debate as to whether patients can be truly thought of as customers). But in addition to organisational restructuring, BPR also implies that jobs themselves should also be reorganised around principles of customer care and that employees should increasingly be empowered to make the decisions affecting a customer's relationship with the organisation.

GOAL-SETTING AND JOB DESIGN

Mullins (2013) notes that seemingly diverse methods of job design can in reality be inter-connected with some extent of overlap between them. He also brings the concept of goal-setting into view as another approach to job design. This conclusion was also drawn by French *et al* (2011), who suggest that as goal-setting involves developing, negotiating and formalising employees' targets and objectives, it can readily be expanded to encompass goal-setting results in specific task goals. Locke's work on goal-setting suggested that specific and difficult goals supported by task feedback are more likely to lead to higher performance, although they should not be seen as too difficult or impossible and they would in any case only be effective if the worker had a feeling of self-efficacy.

SMART WORKING

At the start of this chapter we noted that the topic areas of organisational and job design continue to be debated, with new thinking and research findings put forward for our consideration on a regular basis. A CIPD report (2008a) summarises several recent trends in these areas under the heading of *smart working*.

Smart working is defined as 'An approach to organising work that aims to drive greater efficiency and effectiveness in achieving job outcomes through a combination of flexibility, autonomy and collaboration, while optimising tools and working environments for employees' CIPD (2008a, p7). Smart working is, furthermore, identified as a new paradigm in which a critical mass of workers (in the developed world) experience increasing autonomy at work. The report goes on to identify a collaborative work experience in many organisations in which a customised work experience is developed for groups of workers informed by their individual needs and aspirations.

This recent contribution to the literature identifies trends in the wider work environment which have helped promote the trend of smart working. These include the advent of home-working, enabled by developments in technology and a sense that with less expectation of long-term employment with an individual employer, workers are more prepared to switch jobs if they feel that job design is neglected.

This is an optimistic note on which to end the main body of this chapter and it is hoped that the experience of organisations and jobs will become a happier one for more and more of us – not just a fortunate few. Nonetheless, the smart working report records that the job characteristics model – outlined earlier in this chapter – in which people are subordinate to a pre-existing job (which may be more or less autonomous and responsible) is still relevant. Moreover, it should be stressed that the report did not deal with jobs and workplaces in the developing world where the picture can be a lot less rosy. In 2013, a lethal accident at a Bangladesh factory making clothing for several well-known UK fashion labels revealed jobs and management structures that were way below the standards aspired to in smart working or similar models (Nelson and Bergman 2013).

WORKING AT CAPGEMINI

CASE STUDY 8.2

Capgemini is a global leader in consulting, technology, outsourcing and local professional services. Headquartered in Paris, the organisation operates in more than 30 countries with 82,000 people across the globe.

Capgemini's consultants need to be able to work effectively from any location. Therefore all new recruits are provided with powerful lightweight laptops with wireless connectivity, mobile phones with email and Internet capability, easy access to teleconferencing facilities and the ability to access the intranet remotely. Although consultants are often based on-site with clients and – as we have seen – frequently work remotely, there is office accommodation too. However, this is intentionally unusual, and the Soho office in London comprises 'hot desks' and collaborative work areas and flexible zones intended to foster 'accelerated decision-making and open and honest discussion.'

Capgemini provides people with a great deal of autonomy in their daily work. Consultants are often responsible for the planning and definition of projects in line with customer requirements and operate as self-managed individuals. Consultants refer to mentors and 'reviewers' (a colleague who is a grade above) on development matters. Leaders should be approachable, know their people on a personal level and

Capgemini aim for a 'low politics environment'.

Capgemini's structure complements this context of work. The business operates a flat structure with six grades of consultants throughout the business. Performance is assessed against defined objectives and client expectations. Each grade has a set of behavioural competencies aligned with learning interventions, feedback and self-analysis tools.

The way in which jobs and structures are set out at Capgemini is underpinned by a distinctive organisational culture. Values of fun, modesty, solidarity, freedom, trust, boldness and honesty are celebrated and reinforced through recruitment, performance, recognition, learning and other processes and role-modelled by leaders.

Questions

1   Would Capgemini's structure and work arrangements be suitable in your own job (or in one you are familiar with)? Explain your answer.

2   Which element of Capgemini's strategy is more important – its structure or its culture? Why have you reached your conclusion?

CONCLUSION

The argument for linking principles of organisational design and job design to high performance and commitment workplaces can be summarised as follows:

- OD can achieve an organisational structure best suited to deal with that organisation's circumstances or contingent factors.
- A constantly changing and ever more competitive business environment means that work organisations in all sectors require multiskilled, proactive and customer-focused

staff in order to be successful. These staff can be characterised as thinking performers – or possibly smart workers.

- An increasingly educated workforce, used to exercising discretion and choice in other areas of their lives will, in any case, demand jobs which are psychologically fulfilling.
- High-performance work organisations will therefore increasingly need to design (or enable their workers to design, jobs that provide variety, scope for initiative and autonomy and empower job-holders.

Noon and Blyton (2002) group these arguments under the heading of the 'upskilling thesis'. These writers go on, however, to question the extent to which this thesis is borne out in practice, proposing that there remain very wide differences both in terms of the range of tasks undertaken by workers and the degree of autonomy experienced across the labour market.

A contingency approach to the area, while recognising the value of 'humanising' jobs, would suggest that different models of job design are appropriate in different situations. For example, we should critically address the proposition that work has largely become more 'intelligent'. A large-scale research project carried out by Professor Peter Nolan into work patterns in the UK identified a more complex and subtle picture in the early years of the twenty-first century. Nolan (quoted in Wignall 2004) records that: 'we still have 10.5 million manual workers in this country. That's 40 per cent of the workforce. They're in warehouses, filling envelopes, filling shelves. Stacking shelves is something like the eighth quickest growing occupation... people think we now have a service economy where everyone sits at a computer, and that's just not true. Jobs are being created by new technologies, but those jobs are the same kind of jobs that people were doing before.'

It is not the intention here to dismiss the possibility that all jobs can be enriched or made more customer-focused; this is certainly true to an extent and managers should develop ways in which this may be achieved. However, one should recognise the role of rhetoric – or even hyperbole – in some literature in this subject area, and the relatively unchanging nature of many people's work.

One can also put forward a view that organisational effectiveness can be achieved through different models and indeed conceptions of organisational design. The fast-food sector provides a notable example of continuing simplification of tasks, albeit within a teamworking framework. Here, we have classical contingency principles operating – that is, the optimal structure of the organisation will all depend on the level of predictability required (both product and service), hierarchical relationships and the expectations of a workforce, many of whom in this case may have only short-term plans regarding their work and employment. In contrast, the nature of organisations and work in other sectors may lend itself far more easily to flat structures or even adhocracies, encouraging greater initiative and autonomy on the part of job–holders. Organisational design remains an important area; as Clegg et al (2011, p528) note: 'Organisation design matters just as much as any other kind of design ... ugly organisation design produces bad managing.'

As we saw in Chapter 7 it has been argued that organisations should seek to implement and maintain functional flexibility, this concept encompassing job rotation, multiskilling and, where appropriate, teamworking as part of an overall strategy of flexibility or adaptability. Other aspects of flexibility included numerical flexibility, the precursor of many instances of downsizing, and financial flexibility, which, in an attempt to control salary costs, has seen numerous examples of sub-contracting work, zero hours contracts and even the wholesale movement of jobs to other parts of the world. However, even this seemingly inexorable logic may be contingent on particular circumstances. Clark (1993) suggests that there might be instances where workers' specialist knowledge is perceived as sufficiently important to justify retaining and bolstering it. The same author also notes that a worker's commitment to high-quality work can emanate from a feeling of ownership of that work or job. There is, in conclusion, a range of strategic choices available to organisational decision-makers when approaching the area of both organisational and job design.

- People's experience of work is affected by the organisational arrangements in which they operate and the nature of the work they do.
- A variety of organisational structure models have been put forward in order to enhance performance.
- Job redesign emphasises increasing the scope of jobs in order to increase efficiency and foster high levels of worker motivation.
- Large numbers of people continue to work in jobs designed under principles of 'Taylorism' or scientific management.
- A contingency approach to both organisational and job design, stressing the importance of recognising situational factors, is recommended.

REVIEW QUESTIONS

1   List five advantages of the bureaucratic model of structure and five disadvantages. Do the advantages outweigh the disadvantages or *vice versa*?

2   With reference to real-world examples, assess the usefulness of the contingency approach to organisational design.

3   Assess the importance of job design within the overall process of managing people. Give reasons for your answer.

4   How strong is the evidence that meaningful work will motivate a workforce?

EXPLORE FURTHER

Daft, R., Murphy, J. and Willmott, H. (2010) *Organization, Theory and Design.* Andover: Cengage. The authors cover material dealt with in this book, so this is valuable as an alternative perspective on the two central topics. A range of case studies illustrate the concepts' inherently practical nature.

Grey, C. (2013) *A Very Short, Fairly Interesting and Reasonably Cheap Book About Studying Organizations.* 3rd edition. This book provides a thought-provoking and entertaining account of the development and application of many of the principles dealt with in this chapter.

Hackman, J.R. and Oldham, G.R. (1980) *Work Redesign.* New York: Adison-Wesley. Read this source text for an in-depth discussion of how job characteristics can affect workers' attitudes.

CHAPTER 9

Recruitment and Selection

Sally Rumbles and Ray French

LEARNING OUTCOMES

After reading this chapter, you should be able to:

- comprehend the potential importance of recruitment and selection in successful people management and leadership

- identify aspects of recruitment and selection which are needed to avoid critical failure factors

- understand recruitment and selection policies and procedures which are said to be associated with high performance, commitment and successful organisational outcomes

- evaluate selection methods according to criteria of professionalism including reliability, validity and fairness

- appreciate the links between recruitment and selection and other activities which integrate workers within an organisation and ensure their longer-term successful working.

OVERVIEW

In this chapter we examine the important role of recruitment and selection within the process of leading, managing and developing people. Recruitment and selection is pivotal in this regard in certain important respects. At the most basic level our focus in this book is on people management within the employment relationship. Those charged with recruiting people to posts in work organisations take a crucial 'gatekeeper' role; only those people selected for employment can be led, managed and developed. So in the most fundamental sense the decision to employ (or not) underpins the whole area of managing people. Issues associated with exclusion from the workplace also highlight the need for professionalism, fairness and ethical behaviour on the part of those engaged in this activity.

Recruitment and selection also has an important role to play in ensuring worker performance and positive organisational outcomes. It is often claimed that selection of workers occurs not just to replace departing employees or add to a workforce, but rather aims to put in place workers who can perform at a high level and demonstrate commitment (Pilbeam and Corbridge 2010). We will elaborate on the sometimes complex linkages between recruitment and selection and performance later in this chapter.

Recruitment and selection is characterised finally by potential difficulties and it is necessary to keep abreast of developments in research in the field. Research from the CIPD (2009a), for example, concluded that organisations should increasingly be inclusive in their employment offering, as younger generations have grown up with the notion of flexible working, while older people have an interest in flexible working as an alternative to retirement. This is just one example of how current research can inform practice and also shows the critical importance of the social context in which recruitment and selection takes place.

INTRODUCTION

Recruitment and selection forms a core part of the central activities underlying human resource management, namely the acquisition, development and reward of workers. It frequently forms an important part of the work of HR managers or designated specialists within work organisations. However, and importantly, recruitment and selection decisions are often for good reason taken by non-specialists, or line managers. There is therefore an important sense in which it is the responsibility of all managers, and where HR departments exist, it may be that HR managers play more of a supporting advisory role to those people who will supervise or in other ways work with the new employee. As Mullins (2013) notes, if the HRM function is to remain effective there must be consistently good levels of teamwork, plus ongoing co-operation and consultation between line managers and the HR manager. This is most definitely the case in recruitment and selection as specialist HR managers (or even external consultants) can be an important repository of up-to-date knowledge and skills, for example on the important legal dimensions of this area.

Recruitment and selection is often presented as a planned rational activity, comprising certain sequentially linked phases within a process of *employee resourcing*, which itself may be located within a wider HR management strategy. Bratton and Gold (2007, p239) differentiate the two terms while establishing a clear link between them in the following way:

> Recruitment is the process of generating a pool of capable people to apply for employment to an organisation. Selection is the process by which managers and others use specific instruments to choose from a pool of applicants a person or persons more likely to succeed in the job(s), given management goals and legal requirements.

In setting out a similar distinction in which recruitment activities provide a pool of people eligible for selection, Foot and Hook (2011, p161) suggest that:

> … although the two functions are closely connected, each requires a separate range of skills and expertise, and may in practice be fulfilled by different staff members. The recruitment activity, but not normally the selection decision, may be outsourced to an agency. It makes sense, therefore, to treat each activity separately.

Recruitment and selection, as defined here, can play a pivotally important role in shaping an organisation's effectiveness and performance, if work organisations are to be able to acquire workers who already possess relevant knowledge, skills and aptitudes, and to make an accurate prediction regarding their future abilities. If we accept this premise (which will be questioned to some extent in this chapter), then recruiting and selecting staff in an effective manner can both avoid undesirable costs – for example, those associated with high staff turnover, poor performance and dissatisfied customers – and engender a mutually beneficial employment relationship characterised, wherever possible, by high commitment on both sides.

Recruitment and selection is a topical area. While it has always had the capacity to form a key part of the process of managing and leading people as a routine part of organisational life, it is suggested here that recruitment and selection has become ever more important as organisations increasingly regard their workforce as a source of competitive advantage. Of course, not all employers engage with this proposition even at the rhetorical level. However, there is evidence of increased interest in the utilisation of employee selection methods which are valid, reliable and fair. For example, it has been noted that 'over several decades, work psychology has had a significant influence on the way people are recruited into jobs, through rigorous development and evaluation of personnel selection procedures' (Arnold *et al* 2010, p136). In this chapter we will examine several contemporary themes in recruitment and selection including the so-called competency approach and online recruitment.

Recruitment and selection does not operate in a vacuum, insulated from wider social trends, so it is very important to keep abreast of current research. The CIPD annual survey report *Resourcing and Talent Planning* (2012g) found that:

- Changes in resourcing reflected a stronger focus on costs and reductions in budgets: 47 per cent of organisations reported a reduction in resourcing budgets; 25 per cent reduced new hires; and 19 per cent had implemented a recruitment freeze.
- 82 per cent of organisations reported having difficulties in filling at least some vacancies.
- More organisations focused on developing and retaining in-house talent.
- Conversely, over two-thirds of organisations reported that they had experienced some difficulty in retaining staff, particularly managers and professionals.

These specific findings epitomise the very close link between recruitment and selection and their wider social and economic context.

This aspect of employee resourcing is characterised, however, by potential difficulties. Many widely used selection methods, for example interviewing, are generally perceived to be unreliable as a predictor of job-holders' performance in reality. Thus it is critically important to obtain a realistic evaluation of the process from all concerned, including both successful and unsuccessful candidates. There are ethical issues around selecting appropriate, and by implication rejecting inappropriate, candidates for employment. Many organisations seek to employ people who will fit in with their organisation's culture (French *et al* 2011; and see also Case Study 9.1 below). This may be perfectly understandable, but it carries important ethical overtones; for example whether an employing organisation should be involved in shaping an individual's identity. We put forward the view in this chapter that, notwithstanding the moral issues and practical difficulties outlined here, recruitment and selection is one area where it is possible to distinguish policies and practices associated with critical success factors and performance differentiators which, in turn, impact on organisational effectiveness in significant ways.

WHY WORK AT IKEA? (PART ONE)

The following extracts are taken from the IKEA Group corporate website 'Why work at IKEA?' section. The central importance of values and culture continue to be stressed in IKEA recruitment materials.

Because of our values, our culture and the endless opportunities, we believe that it's important to attract, develop and inspire our people. We are continuously investing in our co-workers and give them sufficient opportunities and responsibility to develop.

What would it be like to work at IKEA?

You'd be working for a growing global company that shares a well-defined and well-communicated vision and business idea.

You'd be able to develop your skills in many different ways, becoming an expert at your daily work, by taking new directions in other parts of the company, or by taking on greater responsibility, perhaps even in another country.

Human values and team spirit are part of the work environment. You'd not only have fun at work, you'd be able to contribute to the development of others.

At IKEA you'd be rewarded for making positive contributions.

You'd have the chance to grow and develop together with the company.

Values at the heart of our culture

The people and the values of IKEA create a culture of informality, respect, diversity and real opportunities for growth. These values include:

Togetherness and enthusiasm

This means we respect our colleagues and help each other in difficult times. We look for people who are supportive,

work well in teams and are open with each other in the way they talk, interact and connect. IKEA supports this attitude with open plan offices and by laying out clear goals that co-workers can stand behind.

Humbleness

More than anything this means respect. We are humble towards our competitors, respecting their proficiency, and realising that we constantly have to be better than they are to keep our market share. It also means that we respect our co-workers and their views, and have respect for the task we have set ourselves.

Willpower

Willpower means first agreeing on mutual objectives and then not letting anything actually stand in the way of actually achieving them. In other words, it means we know exactly what we want, and our desire to get it should be irrepressible.

Simplicity

Behind this value are ideas like efficiency, common-sense and avoiding complicated solutions. Simple habits, simple actions and a healthy aversion to status symbols are part of IKEA.

Source: www.ikea.com. Used with the kind permission of IKEA.

Questions

1   In what ways could an employer seek to assess qualities of supportiveness, humility, willpower and simplicity among candidates in the course of a recruitment and selection process? How accurate do you think judgements made along these measures are likely to be?

2   What selection methods could IKEA employ to assess whether

potential workers can 'develop skills' and 'take on new directions and responsibilities'?

3   To what extent should an organisation like IKEA attempt to recruit and select workers who embody their

organisational culture? Give reasons for your answer. Identify some possible negative outcomes of aligning selection with organisational culture.

EFFECTIVE RECRUITMENT AND SELECTION

We have already referred to the potential importance of recruitment and selection as an activity. Pilbeam and Corbridge (2010, p155) provide a useful overview of potential positive and negative aspects, noting that, 'The recruitment and selection of employees is fundamental to the functioning of an organisation, and there are compelling reasons for getting it right. Inappropriate selection decisions reduce organisational effectiveness, invalidate reward and development strategies, are frequently unfair on the individual recruit and can be distressing for managers who have to deal with unsuitable employees.'

REFLECTIVE ACTIVITY 9.1

Getting it wrong

In an attempt to check the robustness of security procedures at British airports, Anthony France, a reporter for *The Sun* newspaper, obtained a job as a baggage handler with a contractor subsequently named by the newspaper. In the course of his selection, France gave bogus references, and provided a fake home address and bank details. Throughout the selection process he lied about his past while details of his work as an undercover journalist were available on the Internet.

France then proceeded to take fake explosive material onto a holiday jet airliner at Birmingham International Airport.

This case provides a good, albeit extreme, example of the possible consequences of

flawed selection procedures, or as happened here, when agreed practices, such as checking personal details, are not put into effect. Such consequences are potentially wide-ranging and veer from the trivial and comic to possibly tragic outcomes. One can certainly reasonably anticipate many of the negative outcomes listed below to follow when the predictions made about a candidate for employment fail to be borne out.

It is undoubtedly true that recruitment and selection strategies and practices have important consequences for all concerned, so what are the keys to maximising the chances of effective recruitment and selection? Some important factors are listed below.

RECOGNISING THE POWER OF PERCEPTION

Perception is defined as the process by which humans receive, organise and make sense of the information they receive from the outside world: Huczynski and Buchanan (2013), French *et al* (2011) and Mullins (2013). The quality or accuracy of our perceptions will have a major impact on our response to a situation. There is much data suggesting that when we perceive other people – particularly in an artificial and time-constrained situation like a job interview – we can make key mistakes, sometimes at a subliminal level.

One key to enhancing effectiveness in recruitment and selection therefore lies in an appreciation of some core principles of interpersonal perception and, in particular, some common potential mistakes in this regard.

- *Selective perception.* Our brains cannot process all of the information which our senses pick up so we instead select particular objects – or aspects of people – for attention. We furthermore attribute positive or negative characteristics to the stimuli, known as the 'halo' and 'horns' effect respectively. For example, an interviewee who has a large coffee stain on their clothing, but is otherwise well presented, may have difficulty creating an overall positive impression despite the fact that it might be that their desire for the new job resulted in nervousness and clumsiness.
- *Self-centred bias.* A recruiter should avoid evaluating a candidate by reference to themselves as this may be irrelevant to the post in question and run the risks of a 'clone effect' in a changing business environment. The phrase 'I was like you 15 years ago' may be damaging in a number of respects and should not be the basis for employment in most situations.
- *Early information bias.* We often hear apocryphal stories of interview panels making very early decisions on a candidate's suitability and spending the remaining time confirming that decision. Mythical though some of these tales may be, there is a danger of over-prioritising early events – a candidate who trips over when entering an interview room may thus genuinely be putting themselves at a disadvantage.
- *Stereotyping.* This is a common shortcut to understanding an individual's attributes, which is a difficult and time-consuming process, as we are all unique and complex beings. The logic of stereotyping attributes individuals' characteristics to those of a group they belong to; for example the view that as Italians are considered to be emotional, an individual Italian citizen will be too. Stereotypes might contain elements of truth; on the other hand, they may be entirely false. Stereotyping may well be irrelevant and, if acted on, also discriminatory.

It should be stressed that these, and other, perceptual errors are not inevitable and can be overcome. Many HR professionals study subjects like organisational behaviour as part of their career qualifications in which they are made aware of the dangers of inaccurate perception. Nonetheless, it remains the case that an understanding of this subject area is an important building block to effective recruitment and selection.

TAKING A STAGED APPROACH

Much prescriptive writing on recruitment and selection advocates viewing the process as sequential with distinct and inter-linked stages. This model is referred to as the *resourcing cycle*. The resourcing cycle begins with the identification of a vacancy and ends when the successful candidate is performing the job to an acceptable standard, ie post-selection. It is a two-way process. Organisations are evaluating candidates for a vacancy, but candidates also observe the organisation as a prospective employer. In recent years there has been an increasing focus on employer branding and image in attracting candidates. Organisations that gain a reputation for treating people well, offering stimulating, secure employment with the potential to progress, stand a far greater chance of attracting, recruiting and retaining good people. Conducting the process in a professional and timely manner is necessary in helping to ensure that not only is the best candidate attracted to apply and subsequently accept the post, but also that unsuccessful candidates can respect the decision made. If an unsuccessful applicant gains a favourable impression of the organisation, they may then possibly apply for future vacancies.

The first step in the recruitment process is to decide that there is a vacancy to be filled. Increasingly, a more strategic and questioning approach may be taken. If, for example, the vacancy arises because an employee has left, managers may take the opportunity to review the work itself and consider whether it could be processed in an alternative way. For example, could the work be done on a part-time, job-share or flexi-time basis? Alternatively, the job could be automated. The financial services sector in the UK provides one example of where technological developments have resulted in both significant job losses and changed patterns of work since 1990; see Chapter 1.

On the assumption that a post does need to be filled, it will be necessary to devise specifications. Whether a competency-based approach (this concept will be defined later in the chapter) or the more traditional method of formal job descriptions and person specifications is chosen, a CIPD report (2007b) notes that specifications need to reflect the duties and requirements of the job along with the skills, aptitudes, knowledge, experience, qualifications and personal qualities that are necessary to perform the job effectively. Consideration should also be given to how the recruiter intends to measure and elicit information regarding those skills. Are they essential to job performance or merely desirable and can they be objectively measured?

ATTRACTING CANDIDATES

The next stage in the recruitment cycle is the attraction of candidates, as one important objective of a recruitment method is to realise an appropriate number of suitable candidates within reasonable cost constraints. Pilbeam and Corbridge (2010) note that there is no ideal number of applications and no intrinsic value in attracting a high volume of candidates, and neither is there a single best way to recruit applicants. The chosen recruitment medium needs to ensure that there are a sufficient number of suitably qualified candidates from which to make a selection without being overwhelmed with large numbers of unsuitable applications. Using a recruitment agency to find a small number of suitable candidates, particularly for senior or specialised posts, may prove a significantly more cost-effective and efficient method than a major web-based advertising campaign which generates a large response from unsuitable candidates. The choice of method will also be influenced by the availability of candidates, that is, is there likely to be a shortage or surplus of candidates? This is particularly relevant in the current UK labour market, where there are significantly more applicants than vacancies. For example, in the highly competitive graduate recruitment market organisations will match the choice of methods to the nature of the vacancy, the university or course being targeted and the specific sector and other relevant factors. Small employers are more likely to carry out a targeted recruitment, while a large organisation (with a high-profile employer brand) will utilise a variety of methods to attract talent, in so doing accepting that they will receive a large volume of speculative applications (Suff 2012a).

REFLECTIVE ACTIVITY 9.2

According to the CIPD (2012g) the most effective methods for attracting applications are the company website (61 per cent) and recruitment agencies (53 per cent). The public and voluntary sectors are more likely to use local newspapers for attracting candidates whilst almost all large organisations (97 per cent) had their own corporate careers' website that were accessible using mobile phone technology (41 per cent) (Suff 2012b). Word of mouth and personal recommendations are seen as the most effective and popular methods used by SMEs (Bergman 2012).

Look at the recruitment section of your local newspaper and a good quality broadsheet. What sort of vacancies is typically advertised there? Compare and contrast these with the types of vacancies advertised in online 'job boards' or recruitment websites. What indicators are there in the wording of advertisements as to whether there is a surplus or shortage of candidates? What indications are there that online recruitment methods are replacing more traditional ways of attracting candidates?

Which method of recruitment should be adopted? There is no single best way, and a contingency approach involving an analysis of what might be effective in particular circumstances is advocated, ie 'it all depends'.

HR professionals should carefully consider and review which methods have been most effective in the past and which would be most appropriate for the current vacancy. They should also, critically, keep methods under review.

SELECTION

One of the last stages in recruitment and selection is selection itself, which includes the choice of methods by which an employer will reduce a shortlisted group following the recruitment stage, leading to an employment decision. For most people, this is the only visible stage of the resourcing cycle as their experience of it is likely to be as a subject or candidate rather than involvement in planning the entire process. While recruitment can be perceived as a positive activity generating an optimum number of jobseekers, selection is inherently negative in that it will probably involve rejection of applicants.

It would be prudent to argue that selection decisions should be based on a range of selection tools as some have poor predictive job ability. While it is almost inconceivable that employment would be offered or accepted without a face-to-face encounter, many organisations still rely almost exclusively on the outcome of interviews to make selection decisions.

To have any value, interviews should be conducted or supervised by trained individuals, be structured to follow a previously agreed set of questions mirroring the person specification or job profile and allow candidates the opportunity to ask questions. The interview is more than a selection device. It is a mechanism that is capable of communicating information about the job and the organisation to the candidate, with the aim of giving a realistic job preview, providing information about the process, and thus can minimise the risk of job offers being rejected. Organisations seeking high performance in their selection processes should therefore give considerable attention to maximising the uses of the interview and, ideally, combine this method with other psychometric measures where appropriate.

VALIDITY OF SELECTION METHODS

It may appear self-evident that organisational decision-makers will wish to ensure that their recruitment and (in this case) selection methods are effective. We have already suggested, however, that making judgements on an individual's personal characteristics and suitability for future employment is inherently problematic and that many typical selection methods contain significant flaws. There is also the question of what is meant by the terms 'reliability' and 'validity' when applied to recruitment and selection.

'Reliability' in the context of workforce selection can refer to the following issues:

- Temporal or 're-test' stability where the effectiveness of a selection tool is assessed by consistency of results obtained over time. An individual could, for example, complete a personality inventory or intelligence test at different times over a period of several years, although in the latter case it would be important to isolate the impact of repeated practice on results.
- Consistency, that is, can the test measure what it sets out to? Some elements of IQ tests have, for example, been criticised for emphasising a person's vocabulary which might in

turn be influenced by their education and general background rather than their innate intelligence.

'Validity' in this area is typically subdivided into the following aspects:

- Face validity has an emphasis on the acceptability of the selection measure, including to the candidate him or herself. For example, it is possible (although extremely unlikely) that there is a correlation between a person's hat size and their job competence. However, you would be reluctant to measure candidates' heads as part of their selection due to their probable scepticism at the use of this measure.
- Content validity refers to the nature of the measure and in particular its adequacy as a tool. For example, the UK driving test could be criticised for not assessing ability in either night driving or travelling on motorways.
- Predictive validity centres on linkages between results or scores on a selection measure and subsequent outcome – most commonly, job performance at a future point. Here it is important to identify when the comparison will be made, ie immediately in the case of a simple job requiring little training, or more commonly at an intermediate point, possibly after a suitable probationary period.

We argue here that validity, along with fairness, should be the overriding indicator of a selection method for high-performance organisations and that it is important to obtain sophisticated data on validity in all its forms. Pilbeam and Corbridge (2010, p189) provide a summary of the predictive validity of selection methods based on the findings of various research studies.

1.0	Certain prediction
0.9	
0.8	
0.7	Assessment centres for development
0.6	Skilful and structured interviews
0.5	Work sampling
	Ability tests
0.4	Assessment centres for job performance
	Biodata
	Personality assessment
0.3	Unstructured interviews
0.2	
0.1	References
0.0	Graphology
	Astrology

However, they suggest that these validity measures should be treated with caution as they can be affected by the performance indicators used, and also the way the tools were applied. They indicate nonetheless both variability between measures and some overall degree of uncertainty when predicting future work performance during the selection process.

While it is recommended that validity should be the prime factor in choosing selection tools, it would be naïve not to recognise that other factors such as cost and applicability may be relevant. How practical, therefore, is it to conduct any particular measure? As indicated earlier, an organisation aiming for high performance is recommended to adopt valid measures as opposed to merely practical or less costly ones. Again, one should recognise that recruitment and selection is contingent upon other factors such as the work itself. A high-performance organisation in the fast-food industry may legitimately decide not to adopt some relatively valid but expensive methods when selecting fast-food operatives. It should be noted that the oft-derided method of interviewing can in reality be a relatively valid method if conducted skilfully and structured.

RECRUITMENT AND SELECTION: ART OR SCIENCE?

Systematic models of recruitment and selection based on a resourcing cycle should not necessarily imply that this process is underpinned by scientific reasoning and method. As we have seen, Pilbeam and Corbridge note that even the most valid methods fall some way short of complete predictive validity. Thompson and McHugh (2009, p285) go further, taking a critical view on the general use and, in particular, the validity of employee selection methods. In commenting on the use of personality tests in selection, they state that, 'in utilising tests employers are essentially clutching at straws and on this basis will probably use anything that will help them make some kind of systematic decision'. They identify now-discredited selection methods, such as the use of polygraphs to detect lying and other methods, such as astrology, which are deemed more appropriate in some cultures rather than others. It is indeed important to keep in mind that today's received wisdom in the area of recruitment and selection, just as in the management canon more generally, may be criticised and even widely rejected in the future.

The process of recruitment and selection continues nonetheless to be viewed as best carried out via sequential but linked stages of first gathering a pool of applicants, then a screening-out process, followed by the positive step of actual selection. This apparently logical ordering of the activities is largely viewed as essential to achieve minimum thresholds of effectiveness.

INDUCTION AND TRANSITION

It is not always the case that selected employees are immediately capable of performing to the maximum level on their allotted job(s) and important stages in the resourcing cycle occur post-selection. Many organisations when selecting are making a longer-term prediction of a new employee's capability. This accounts for many organisations imposing a probationary period in which employees' performance and future potential can be assessed in the work setting. The resourcing cycle extends into this post-selection phase and the induction period and early phases of employment constitute a critically important part of both successful integration into the workplace culture and development as a fully functioning worker. The final stage of the resourcing cycle involves evaluation of the process and reflection on lessons learned from the process and their implications for the future.

RECRUITMENT COSTS

A concern with effectiveness in recruitment and selection becomes all the more important when one considers the costs of getting things wrong. We begin with apparent costs which centre on the direct costs of recruitment procedures, but one might also consider the so-called opportunity costs of engaging in repeated recruitment and selection when workers leave an organisation. An excessive preoccupation with recruitment and selection will divert a manager from other activity he or she could usefully be engaged in. It is also useful to consider the investment, including training resources, lost to the employer when a worker leaves prematurely. According to the CIPD Resourcing and Talent Planning

Survey (2012g), the median recruitment cost of filling a vacancy is £8,000 for senior managers/directors and £3,000 for other employees. An alternative survey conducted by Bersin and Associates (2011) estimates the UK cost at £5,311 compared to only £2,226 in the USA. Much of the difference in costs can be attributed to the UK's continued heavy reliance on recruitment agencies, who typically charge 20–30 per cent of starting salary as a fee (Woods 2011).

Implicit costs are less quantifiable and include the following categories:

- poor performance
- reduced productivity
- low-quality products or services
- dissatisfied customers or other stakeholders
- low employee morale.

These implicit costs are in themselves clearly undesirable outcomes in all organisations. In high-performing organisations average or 'adequate' performance may also be insufficient and recruitment and selection may be deemed to have failed unless workers have become 'thinking performers'.

CONTEMPORARY THEMES IN RECRUITMENT AND SELECTION

THE COMPETENCY APPROACH

Typically, decisions on selecting a potential worker are made primarily with a view to taking on the most appropriate person to do a particular job in terms of their current or, more commonly, potential competencies. In recent years this concept has been extended to search for workers who are flexible and able to contribute to additional and/or changing job roles. This approach contrasts with a more traditional model which involves first compiling a wide-ranging job description for the post in question, followed by the use of a person specification, which in effect forms a checklist along which candidates can be evaluated on criteria such as knowledge, skills and personal qualities. This traditional approach, in essence, involves matching characteristics of an 'ideal' person to fill a defined job. There is a seductive logic in this apparently rational approach. However, there are in-built problems in its application if judgments of an individual's personality are inherently subjective and open to error and, furthermore, if these personal characteristics are suited to present rather than changing circumstances.

The competencies model, in contrast, seeks to identify abilities needed to perform a job well rather than focusing on personal characteristics such as politeness or assertiveness. The CIPD defines 'competency' as the behaviours that employees must have, or must acquire, to apply to a situation in order to achieve high levels of performance, while 'competence' relates to a system of minimum standards or is demonstrated by performance and outputs (CIPD 2012h). Torrington *et al* (2008, p170) identify potentially important advantages of referring to competencies in this area, noting that:

> they can be used in an integrated way for selection, development, appraisal and reward activities; and also that from them behavioural indicators can be derived against which assessment can take place.

Competency-based models are becoming increasingly popular in graduate recruitment where organisations are making decisions on future potential. Farnham and Stevens (2000) found that managers in the public sector increasingly viewed traditional job descriptions and person specifications as archaic, rigid and rarely an accurate reflection of the requirements of the job. There is increasing evidence that this popularity is more widespread. A CIPD report (2007b) found that 86 per cent of organisations surveyed were now using competency-based interviews in some way, and in another, over half of employers polled had started using them in the past year (William 2008). The use of competencies for recruitment and development may also attract good candidates. PWC, for example, use their 10 core competencies to market their organisation to prospective candidates on their website, encouraging them to 'buy in' to their corporate philosophy. It is suggested that the competence-based model may be a more meaningful way of underpinning recruitment and selection in the current fast-moving world of work and can accordingly contribute more effectively to securing high performance.

FLEXIBILITY AND TEAMWORK

Many commentators refer to significant changes in the world of work and the implications these have for the recruitment and selection of a workforce. Searle (2003, p276) notes that:

> Increasingly employees are working in self-organised teams in which it is difficult to determine the boundaries between different job holders' responsibilities. The team undertakes the task and members co-operate and work together to achieve it. Recruitment and selection practices focus on identifying a suitable person for the job, but ... isolating a job's roles and responsibilities may be difficult to do in fast-changing and team-based situations.

There is here an implication both that teamworking skills could usefully be made part of employee selection and also that an individual's job specification should increasingly be designed and interpreted flexibly. It can plausibly be posited that we now inhabit a world of work in which unforeseen problems are thrown up routinely and on an ongoing basis and there is seldom time to respond to them in a measured fashion (Linstead *et al* 2009). In this type of business environment, decisions made can be rational in terms of past practice and events, but may in fact be revealed to be flawed or even obsolete when they are made in the new context.

If we accept this analysis of work in the twenty-first century, there is therefore an implication that organisations aiming for high performance may need to use selection methods which assess qualities of flexibility and creative thinking (irrespective of whether they are using a traditional or competency recruitment and selection model). Of course, many jobs may still require task-holders to work in a predictable and standardised way, so one should exercise caution when examining this rhetoric. Interestingly, however, recruitment and selection practices should themselves be kept under constant review if we accept the reality of a business world characterised by discontinuous, rather than incremental, change. Organisations also need to ensure they do not infringe upon discrimination laws when trying to create the right teams for their organisation.

 ABERCROMBIE & FITCH

CASE STUDY 9.2

How far should organisations go to attract the right candidates?

When US-based clothing store Abercrombie & Fitch (A&F) planned to open a store in Aberdeen in 2010, the company found itself at the centre of a discrimination row after posters were put up outside the store asking for

'cool and good looking people [to] come and represent our brands'. This came just months after the company was found guilty of the harassment and unfair dismissal of Riam Dean, a disabled employee.

Audrey Williams, employment law partner at Eversheds, told *Personnel*

Today that 'the advert opens up the organisation to legal complaints. "Cool" is a subjective measure, but can stereotypically describe someone who is younger. "Good looking" could become an issue if someone with facial disfigurements applied for the job and was subsequently rejected. While the advert may get candidates through the door, the firm is potentially cutting off talented staff ... and experienced retail staff would be put off from applying or the firm would reject talented people because of their looks.'

The problem is that the nature of A&F's advertising could discourage applicants from applying. Moreover, the brand has seemed to influence the company's recruitment and selection practices. For example, in 2003 it was the subject of a multi-million-dollar lawsuit for discrimination in the USA on the grounds of race, and as recently as 2012 it was still falling foul of discrimination law when Michael Bustin, the pilot of the corporate jet, was dismissed for being 'untrendy' and too old.

The clothing retailer has developed a highly successful market base by attracting (primarily) teenagers into its stores using sophisticated and targeted marketing. This involves the use of young, beautiful and predominantly white models and employees to attract younger customers.

Source: adapted from Peacock (2010)

Questions

1   Is there really anything wrong with targeting good-looking and cool prospective employees?

2   Would older workers genuinely want to work in an environment where the customers are predominantly teenagers?

RECRUITING IN THE VIRTUAL WORLD

Increasing use of the Internet is probably the most significant development in the recruitment field in the early twenty-first century. Whilst figures vary, recent surveys on recruitment practice (CIPD 2012g and Suff 2013a) continue to show that it is both the most popular and effective method for attracting applicants to organisations. There is mixed evidence that the Internet produces better quality candidates, but it does deliver more of them and more employers report that online recruitment made it easier to find the right candidate (Crail 2007; Suff 2013a).

In November 2012 Facebook launched its jobs search 'app' in the USA, which included around 1.7 million job listings. It was set up in conjunction with the US Department of Labor and three non-profit labour organisations as part of its social jobs partnership initiative. Facebook's entry into the 'jobs board' market is a reflection of the growing influence that these professional job site are having on recruitment activities. In the UK, 80 per cent of employers use job boards to help fill their vacancies, with Total Jobs, Reed, and Monster being most popular with employers (Suff 2013b). Job boards, at 36 per cent, were seen as the fourth most effective method of recruitment (CIPD 2012g). The effectiveness and use of professional networking sites (such as LinkedIn) are increasing, but wider social networking sites such as Facebook and Twitter are seen as being of limited effectiveness by employers (8 per cent).

The benefits of online recruitment to employers include speed, reduced administrative burden and costs, and no geographical limits. Suff (2013a) also comments that applicants are more likely to know something about the organisation and its work if they use employers' websites. Employers also value online recruitment because it facilitates company branding.

The benefits to applicants are that it is easier, faster and more convenient to post a CV or search a job site online than to read a selection of printed media (Whitford 2003). This is all very well for jobseekers whose skills are high in demand, but if employers are preferring to post vacancies on their own websites then candidates still have to trawl the web in order to find vacancies, and even 'web savvy' applicants might be deterred by the perceived impersonal nature of online recruitment. There are, of course, still some people who are either not comfortable using the Internet or do not have ready access to a computer; thus there is still a role for conventional advertising (IDS 2006).

Whatever the pros and cons, online recruitment continues to expand and employers are now combining more traditional methods with online recruitment to attract suitable candidates. Other employers, such as Microsoft, are enhancing brand visibility and credibility by having a wider Internet recruitment presence. Microsoft uses its online tools to impact and influence its public image and reach a broader audience in order to help create a diverse workplace with varied skills and talents. One initiative is the introduction of corporate recruitment blogs. The idea is that potential job candidates may be attracted to the company through what they see on the blog and make contact through the specific blogger, who will initiate the recruitment process on behalf of the company (Hasson 2007).

The Internet is also being used more widely to attract applicants not only to organisations and their brand, but also careers, as Reflective Activity 9.3 demonstrates.

REFLECTIVE ACTIVITY 9.3

My Marriott Hotel – a new way to attract applicants?

In June 2011 the first ever culinary social media game, My Marriott Hotel, was launched on Facebook to promote Marriott International Inc. Developed in conjunction with Evviva Brands, a specialised brand consultancy, the game was designed as a tool for reaching employment candidates in countries such as China and India, where the service industry is growing, but hospitality is not a highly sought-after career. By managing a virtual hotel kitchen, players are given insights into the world of hotels and a culinary career at Marriott. Three weeks after the launch of the game, the Marriott jobs and careers page on Facebook received over 10,000

'likes' and the game was being played in over 101 countries. Existing employees were also encouraged to share and promote the game within their own social networks.

The game was developed in response to feedback from surveys and focus groups that suggested that the company needed to enhance its online profile. Despite ranking in Fortune's 'Best Place to Work', its brand recognition was low in many countries.

Have a look at the game for yourself (apps.facebook.com/mymarriotthotel). Would you be attracted to a career in hospitality management as a result of playing this game?

Source: adapted from Freer (2011)

FAIRNESS IN RECRUITMENT AND SELECTION

One factor shared by traditional and competence models of recruitment and selection is that both are framed by an imperative to take on the most appropriate person in terms of their contribution to organisational performance. This is, of course, unsurprising given the preoccupation of organisations in all sectors with meeting objectives and targets. However, when we consider what is meant by making appropriate selection decisions, other factors, including fairness, can also be seen to be important.

Decisions made in the course of the recruitment and selection process should be perceived as essentially fair and admissible to all parties, including people who have been rejected. There is evidence to support the view that applicants are concerned with both procedural justice (ie, how far they felt that selection methods were related to the job, and the extent to which procedures were explained to them) and distributive justice (where their concern shifts to how equitably they felt they were treated and whether the outcome of selection was perceived to be fair) (see Gilliland 1993).

Fairness in this regard can be linked to the actual selection methods used. Anderson *et al* (2001) found that interviews, resumes, and work samples were well-regarded methods, while handwriting tests (graphology) were held in low regard. Personality and ability tests received an intermediate evaluation. This is linked to the concept of face validity: how plausible and valid does the method used appear to the candidate under scrutiny? It is reasonable to suggest that employers should take care in choosing selection methods in order to maintain credibility among applicants as well, of course, as assessing the predictive value of the methods.

Fairness in selection also extends to the area of discrimination and equal opportunities, as we saw in Chapter 4. In the UK, for example, current legislation is intended to make unlawful discrimination on the grounds of age, race, nationality or ethnic origin, religion or belief, disability, sex, marital status and sexual orientation. The law identifies both direct discrimination, where an individual is treated less favourably on the sole grounds of their membership of a group covered in the relevant legislation, and indirect discrimination, which occurs when a provision applied to both groups disproportionately affects one in reality. The Equality and Human Rights Commission highlights headhunting as one area in which indirect discrimination may occur. Headhunters may, in approaching individuals already in jobs, contravene this aspect of the law if existing jobs are dominated by one sex or ethnic group, for example. Compliance with equal opportunities legislation provides one example of performance infrastructure and would, it is surmised, reap business benefits, ie recruiting from the truly qualified labour pool and avoiding negative outcomes such as costly and reputation-damaging legal processes.

High-performance organisations may seek to go beyond the compliance approach and work towards a policy or even strategy of managing diversity (see also Chapter 11). As defined by the CIPD (2006), a managing diversity approach:

> is about ensuring that all employees have an opportunity to maximise their potential and enhance their self-development and their contribution to the organisation. It recognises that people from different backgrounds can bring fresh ideas and perceptions, which can make the way work is done more efficient and make products and services better. Managing diversity successfully will help organisations to nurture creativity and innovation and thereby to tap hidden capacity for growth and improved competiveness.

It is thus important to ensure such a policy is operationalised in the field of recruitment and selection, as staff involved in this activity can be said to act as gatekeepers of an organisation.

OPPORTUNITIES FOR ALL AT ASDA

The following statement is an extract from the 'Opportunities for All' section of Asda's corporate website, accessed September 2004.

At Asda we endeavour to discriminate only on ability and we recognise that our organisation can be effective if we have a diverse colleague base, representing every section of society.

We want to recruit colleagues and managers who represent the communities in which we operate and the customers we serve.

Ethnic minorities

We have been working at all levels to make sure that ethnic minorities are represented across all levels of our business and we operate a policy of Religious Festival Leave so that any colleague can apply to take up to two days' unpaid leave to attend their Religious Festival.

Women

We recognise that there are mutual benefits in making sure we employ women in our workplace. Besides our equal opportunities recruitment policy we have a number of other initiatives which support our commitment particularly our flexible working practices which include job shares and part time working at all levels, parental leave, shift swaps and career breaks.

Disability

It is our aim to make sure that our stores are accessible for disabled people to both work and shop in. As a company we have been awarded the Two Tick symbol and we have a good working partnership with Remploy and we work together to help disabled people get back into the work place. We offer people with disabilities a working environment which is supportive and we operate an equal opportunities policy on promotion.

If due to your disability, you need some help whether completing your application form or during the interview process, please contact the people manager in your local store or depot who will be pleased to help.

Age

The proportion of older people in the population is steadily increasing and we're seeing this reflected in the age profile of our workforce. We want to encourage the recruitment and retention of older, experienced colleagues many of whom welcome the opportunity to work beyond the traditional retirement age, to work flexibly and enjoy a phased retirement.

We've been encouraging stores and depots to recruit more mature colleagues or 'Goldies' and in one new store in Broadstairs we opened with over 40 per cent of our colleagues aged 50 or over. And we have seen a reduction in both labour turnover and absence well below average in the store.

To further reinforce our commitment we also offer a number of flexible working schemes such as Benidorm Leave where older colleagues can take three months' unpaid leave between January and March or grandparents' leave where colleagues who are grandparents take up to a week off unpaid to look after a new arrival.

Source: used with the kind permission of ASDA Ltd.

Questions

1   To what extent does this statement from Asda's website indicate that this organisation has a strategy for diversity

management? What has led you to your conclusion?

2   How does Asda seek to safeguard its 'Opportunities for All' policy in the area of recruitment and selection?

3   Produce a statement for use by companies setting out

employment policy in the area of age discrimination and indicate how this could take effect in the recruitment and selection of workers.

THE EXTENT OF PROFESSIONAL PRACTICE

SMALL AND MEDIUM-SIZED ENTERPRISES

There is evidence to suggest that many HRM practices often prescribed in the academic literature are more common in some sectors of business than others and that the small and medium-sized enterprises (SME) group, in particular, is less likely to have in-house HR expertise and sophisticated systems in place (Cully *et al* 1999). A study carried out by Cassell *et al* (2002) in SMEs in the north of England, focused on both the use and perceived value (by employers) of a range of HRM procedures. In the area of recruitment and selection, only 31 per cent of firms in the sample used wide-ranging employee development and recruitment and selection procedures. Interestingly, 38 per cent of the sample questioned said that they did not use recruitment and selection procedures at all. In the companies that did make use of them, 50 per cent found that the procedures helped 'entirely' or 'a lot' in over half of the instances in which they are used. This is some way from the picture of widespread usage and the assumed universal benefits conveyed in some sources.

The reality of the context faced by managers of SMEs will frame their responses in an entirely understandable way, and prescriptive 'textbook style' approaches may be viewed as inappropriate. It would, of course, be as damaging for SMEs as for any other organisation if a lack of high-quality practices in recruitment and selection were seen to inhibit performance and, indeed, SMEs have often been criticised for a lack of a proactive and integrated approach to managing people. However, any assumption that universally applicable approaches to recruitment and selection are needed may ignore the distinctive processes and practices faced by particular organisations.

REFLECTIVE ACTIVITY 9.4

Lack of skills a major factor in UK recruitment and selection difficulties

A CIPD survey (2008b) reported that 86 per cent of British organisations were having difficulty filling vacancies in spite of the financial and economic crisis that hit in that year. In part this was the result of a 'skills crunch', with 70 per cent of the research sample citing a lack of necessary candidate skills as the main reason for recruitment difficulties. However, only half of the surveyed companies had a formal

resourcing strategy to counter the skills-gap problem and struggled to recruit top talent.

Deborah Fernon of the CIPD also pointed to the importance of retention of talented workers, noting that, 'Organisations should have a look at their learning and development strategies, which can help meet business demands in two ways. Firstly those employers who have development opportunities are more likely to stay, which reduces turnover. Secondly, a good learning and development culture will foster a strong employer brand, helping to attract key talent.'

This research highlights the importance of referring to contemporary evidence when

analysing recruitment and selection in general terms and also points to the importance of the post-selection phase in retaining staff.

REFLECTIVE ACTIVITY 9.5

Employers are from Mars, young people are from Venus

Stevens (2013) summarises a CIPD report highlighting a mismatch between the expectations of employers and young people in the recruitment process. This conflict of understanding hinders entry to the labour market for young jobseekers and contributes to high rates of youth unemployment, according to the report. The mismatch also fuels a 'ticking timebomb' of skills shortages for UK businesses, who might be unwittingly limiting their access to a diverse group of talent in the 16–24 age group.

Specific problems identified by the report were:

● 'scattergun' applications from young people who had not researched the organisation and/or tailored their submissions

● a vicious cycle of employers asking for workplace experience in entry-level roles
● lengthy and untransparent recruitment and selection procedures meaning that young applicants were unaware of the stages involved
● poor careers advice and guidance in schools with resultant lack of awareness on how to improve chances of finding a job.

Questions

1   What steps can be taken to reduce the mismatch between employers and younger job applicants?

2   To what extent is it part of the role of HR managers to address a social problem such as the one identified in this report? Refer to both Chapters 4 and 9 of this book when devising your response.

RECRUITMENT AND SELECTION: A CONTINGENCY APPROACH

The underlying principle that organisational policies and practices need to be shaped within a particular context is often referred to as the 'contingency approach'. This puts forward the argument that successful policies and strategies are those which apply principles within the particular context faced by the unique organisation.

One example of a 'contingent factor' which can impact upon recruitment and selection is national culture. French (2010) draws attention to important cross-cultural differences in the area For example, different cultures emphasise different attributes when approaching the recruitment and selection of employees. It is also the case that particular selection methods are used more or less frequently in different societies – see also Perkins and Shortland (2006). So in individualistic cultures such as the USA and UK, there is a preoccupation with selection methods which emphasise individual differences. Many psychometric tests can indeed be seen to originate from the USA. Furthermore, in a society which emphasises individual achievement as opposed to ascribed status (eg through age or gender), one might expect a raft of legislation prohibiting discrimination against particular groups. Here the expectation is that selection should be on the basis of individual personal characteristics or qualifications. This may contrast with more collectivist societies, for example China, where personal connections may assume a more prominent role. Bjorkman and Yuan (1999) conducted one of several studies which reached this overall conclusion. It may also be true that selection methods are given varying degrees of face validity in different societies. A CIPD survey (2004c) on graphology discovered that, while relatively few companies in the UK used graphology as a trusted method of selecting employees, its adoption was far more widespread, common and therefore accepted in other countries, including France.

In summary, the contingency approach with the underlying message that managing people successfully depends on contextual factors – 'it all depends' – can readily be applied to the area of recruitment and selection. The increasingly large number of organisations operating across national boundaries, or who employ workers from different cultural backgrounds, can benefit from formulating policies within an awareness of cultural difference.

RECRUITMENT AND SELECTION AND ORGANISATIONAL CULTURE

It is unsurprising that the culture of a particular work organisation will influence selection decisions, with recruiters both consciously and unconsciously selecting those individuals who will best fit that culture. In some organisations recruitment policy and practice is derived from their overall strategy, which disseminates values into the recruitment and selection process. Mullins (2007) provided the example of Garden Festival Wales, an organisation created to run for a designated and short time period. This organisation's managers were particularly concerned to create a culture via the recruitment of suitable employees. This is an interesting example as this organisation had no prior history and it indicates the power of recruitment and selection in inculcating particular cultural norms.

Other research has demonstrated that individuals as well as organisations seek this best fit, providing evidence that many individuals prefer to work in organisations that reflect their personal values. Judge and Cable (1997) and Backhaus (2003) found that jobseekers may actively seek a good 'person–organisation fit' when considering prospective employers. This, of course, provides further support for the processual two-way model of recruitment and selection. However, justifying selection decisions on the basis of cultural fit means that there are ethical issues to consider in terms of reasons for rejection: are organisations justified in determining who does and does not fit? It may be that practical concerns also emerge, for example in the danger of maintaining organisations in the image of current role models – which may be inappropriate in the future. Psychologists have also long recognised the threat posed by 'groupthink', where innovation is suppressed by a dominant group and a 'king's new clothes' syndrome develops, with individuals reluctant to voice objections to bad group decisions.

CONCLUSION

This chapter highlights the importance of recruitment and selection in successful people management and leadership. An awareness of issues and concepts within this area are important tools for anyone involved with leading, managing and developing people – even if they are not HR managers *per se*. A recognition of the importance of this aspect of people management is not new and success in this field has often been linked with the avoidance of critical failure factors including undesirable levels of staff turnover and claims of discrimination from unsuccessful job applicants.

It has been argued here that it is also possible to identify aspects of recruitment and selection which link with critical success factors in the twenty-first-century context, differentiating organisational performance and going some way to delivering employees who can act as 'thinking performers'. It is proposed, for example, that a competencies approach focusing on abilities needed to perform a job well may be preferable to the use of a more traditional matching of job and person specifications. In addition, many organisations may increasingly wish to identify qualities of flexibility and creative thinking among potential employees, although this may not always be the case; many contemporary jobs do not require such competencies on the part of job–holders. It is also the case that organisations should be preoccupied with the question of validity of selection methods, ideally combining methods which are strong on practicality and cost, such as interviewing, with other measures which are more effective predictors of performance. It is proposed finally that a managing diversity approach, welcoming individual difference, may enhance organisational performance and create a climate in which thinking performers can emerge and flourish.

However, it is proposed that a contingency approach to recruitment and selection, recognising that organisational policies and practices are shaped by contextual factors, remains valid and that effectiveness in recruitment and selection may vary according to particular situational factors. In this regard it is noted that cultural differences could be an important factor in predicting the relative success of recruitment and selection measures.

 WHY WORK FOR IKEA? (PART TWO)

CASE STUDY 9.4

Return to Case Study 9.1 at the start of this chapter.

IKEA puts great stress upon recruiting employees who will complement its organisational culture.

Questions

1   What are the potential benefits of selecting a workforce in terms of an organisation's culture?

2   What are the philosophical and practical arguments against selection based on values and work culture?

KEY LEARNING POINTS

- Managers involved in recruitment and selection of workers have a key gatekeeper role in giving or denying access to work.
- Effective recruitment and selection is characterised by knowledge of social-science topics such as perception.
- A staged logical approach to recruitment and selection, ie seeing it as a process, is recommended.
- We should examine the validity of different selection methods.
- Fairness is a fundamentally important principle reflecting the ethically loaded nature of the activity.

REVIEW QUESTIONS

1   Indicate with examples three ways in which recruitment and selection policies and practices can be used by an organisation aiming to develop staff as part of a talent management strategy.

2   Evaluate the evidence regarding the potential validity of biodata and personality assessment as tools for selecting employees.

3   What do you understand by the contingency approach to recruitment and selection? Provide two examples, from academic sources or your own experience, to illustrate this approach.

4   Evaluate the effectiveness of social media and online recruitment methods in comparison to more traditional methods. In what circumstances might more traditional methods be a more effective way of attracting applicants?

EXPLORE FURTHER

Arnold, J., Cooper, C.L. and Robertson, I.T. (2010) *Work Psychology: Understanding human behaviour in the workplace*. 5th edition. Harlow: FT/Prentice Hall. Chapter 5 provides a clear and interesting discussion of different selection techniques and their validity.

Gilmore, S. and Williams, S. (2012) *Human Resource Management*. Oxford: Oxford University Press. Chapter 5 takes a themed approach to the topic of employee selection.

Thompson, P. and McHugh, D. (2009) *Work Organisations: A Critical Approach*. 4th edition. Basingstoke: Palgrave Macmillan. In Chapter 19 entitled 'Masks for Tasks', the authors take a critical perspective on the topics of how we assess others' attributes and how such perceptions are used in employee selection.

CHAPTER 10

Developing Employees

Alex Tymon and Margaret Mackay

LEARNING OUTCOMES

After reading this chapter, you should be able to:

- explain the terms:
  - human resources development
  - learning, training and development
  - career management and career development
  - continuing professional development
- understand the organisational and economic need for development activities referring to contemporary debates and research
- identify where responsibility for development lies and why this is contested
- critique some of the more frequently used development techniques
- explain the difference between career management and career development using three models
- identify the rationale for career development from an organisational and individual view
- evaluate the practice of continuing professional development.

OVERVIEW

The business case for investment in employee development is built on the need to sustain organisational performance, and to adapt to a dynamic environment. The impact of a knowledge economy and resultant demand for a skilled workforce underpins the workplace as a critical learning environment. Proactive support for employee development differentiates an organisation's knowledge and skill capability. Such support can be viewed as an offensive strategy for organisational growth, industry leadership and engagement of superior employee performance.

This chapter focuses on how individuals can adapt through learning, and expand their skill capability to deliver innovative practices, products and customer commitment. We begin by defining key concepts, before going on to highlight the evolving emphasis on work-based and individual learning – in contrast to more formal traditional training approaches. In this chapter, we also review perceptions of learning responsibility and talent development. In this regard we note a shift from corporate career management to individual career development. The chapter ends by considering the promotion of continuing professional development as key to building flexibility and agility.

INTRODUCTION

CREATING THE FUTURE AND ADAPTING TO CHANGE

Despite the tough operating conditions in the ongoing recession, it is interesting to note that many successful and well-known organisations continue to maintain or even increase their investment in learning, training and development (Freifeld 2009), with a mean training budget of 4.52 per cent of payroll (*Training Magazine* 2012). This tells us that developing employees is regarded as an essential organisational activity for success. According to Cho *et al* (2009, p263), 'The success of tomorrow's most effective organisations will lie in their capacity to learn.'

The ways in which organisations develop their employees evolve in response to changes in the world of work, and these changes are making the task of developing employees increasingly challenging. In 2004 the former US Secretary of Education Richard Riley predicted the top 10 jobs which would be in demand in 2010, noting that these did not even exist at the time of his prediction. There is much debate on the validity of Riley's prediction, but it is safe to say that we are going through a period of very significant change in employment. It is hard to predict what might be needed in 2020. We saw that from 1998 to 2008 there were 12 jobs created in knowledge industries for every one job created elsewhere (DCSF 2009). Thus, organisations and employees today will almost certainly need additional and radically different skills in the future.

However, it is not just organisations that need to be flexible and adaptable in their approach to learning and development. The Leitch Report (2006) highlighted major issues with skills shortages in the UK and the potential impact these could have on the economy and therefore society as a whole, suggesting that skilled and knowledgeable individuals who are able and willing to contribute were essential.

Above all, it will be the individual person for whom development is most important in the future. It is estimated that a school–leaver in 2010 will have had between 10 and 14 jobs by the time they are 38 years old, and by 2020 there will be 5 million fewer lower-skilled jobs in the UK (DCSF 2009). Thus it will be increasingly rare for individuals to remain in the same occupation for their whole working life and certainly not in the same organisation. The employment security and success of individuals will increasingly depend upon continuous lifelong learning and skills flexibility. Learning agility and taking responsibility for one's own development will be a necessity, with career management and continuing professional development growing in importance (Ashford and DeRue 2012, Day and Sin 2011, Povah and Sobczak 2010). It is therefore this overriding need to be adaptable and flexible in learning that we have chosen to focus upon in this chapter.

DEFINITIONS OF KEY TERMS

We begin this chapter by defining some of the key terms which underpin developments and debates in the area of employee development.

HUMAN RESOURCE DEVELOPMENT

In simple terms, human resource development (HRD) can be viewed as developing the capabilities of people within an organisation in order to improve current and future efficiency, effectiveness and output.

There are many development methods, but the intended outcome is always learning and the application of learning. It is therefore valuable to consider what is really meant by the term 'learning' and how it happens.

LEARNING

Definitions of learning suggest it results in a relatively permanent change in behaviour (French *et al* 2011) and comes about through the acquisition of new knowledge, skills and attitudes (KSA). A useful description of these terms can be found in Gold *et al* (2013, Chapter 5).

However, within this concept of learning there are several caveats which should be considered because they make a difference for the HRD practitioner, three of which are:

Caveat 1: Behaviour change as a result of learning may be neither visible nor sustained.

Employees may, via the process of learning, have changed their capabilities and motivation, but what if the opportunity to use them is missing? Does a lack of visible behaviour change mean that learning has not occurred? For those involved in HRD, this issue of opportunity to use new learning, known as transfer, is a vital part of the process and as such is discussed more fully later in this chapter.

Caveat 2: The change in behaviour as a result of learning may not always be positive or desired.

The concept that all learning is good does not necessarily hold true with adult learners. Employees learn short cuts and poor behaviour when they join an organisation just as quickly as desired behaviours, via informal learning. Formal learning takes place in the context of organised training or learning activities and generates explicit knowledge and skills (overt knowledge and skills that are capable of being shared with a wider audience). Informal learning occurs through daily workplace activities, leading to 'implicit' or 'tacit' knowledge or skills (knowledge and skills taken for granted or unconsciously held in the minds of employees). Burns (2008) reviewed numerous studies and surmised that the majority of workplace learning is in fact informal. The power of informal learning is an important consideration for those involved in organisational HRD: from a positive perspective it presents opportunities to provide timely and cost-effective learning; from a negative perspective it has the power to undermine formal interventions.

Caveat 3: Not all adult learning requires the acquisition of new KSA.

In fact, it could be argued that for the majority of adult learning there is only a requirement for a slight adaptation in existing KSA. For example, an update in technology will probably only require a small amount of new knowledge and it may actually require less skill than the old version, a classic example being the introduction of EPOS till systems in supermarkets, which, it has been argued, deskilled the jobs of cashiers, stock controllers and finance staff. Case Study 10.1 below provides an example of this, where trainers reported that getting existing staff to change what they were doing was more difficult than training new staff from scratch. Similarly, most poor conduct issues are driven by inappropriate attitudes, with the employees having the requisite KSA, ie being perfectly skilled, knowing and able to display the expected behaviour, but choosing not to.

This is important for those who are involved in HRD as changing embedded skills and attitudes can be difficult and more time-consuming, and may require a different approach, than providing new ones.

TELEWEST COMMUNICATIONS

CASE STUDY 10.1

During the 1990s Telewest Communications was one of several companies developing a new cable TV and telephone network in the UK. Telewest was aggressively acquiring franchise areas and digging up the streets to install fibre-optic networks. At the same time, large teams of sales people were cold-calling domestic and business customers in a push to convert existing satellite TV and telephone customers as well as acquire new cable TV customers. Once sales were made, installation teams visited domestic and business premises to complete the installation. Large call centres were also set up, some employing in excess of 300 operators, to manage customer queries and payment operations. In the period from 1993 to 1997 the company grew from 900 employees to over 9,000. As with many start-up high-tech businesses in the 1990s, at the same time as new geographical franchise areas were being developed, the products, services and systems needed to support customers in existing areas were constantly being upgraded and improved. This rapid rise in employee numbers alongside the incessant changes in product, services and systems of work presented enormous challenges for the HR and training functions.

In addition to local technical trainers, a mobile training team was used to both run inductions and basic job training for large numbers of start-up staff in new areas and provide upgrade training for experienced staff in existing areas. Interestingly, trainers reported how much more difficult and time-consuming it was for existing staff to learn new systems compared to new staff, due to embedded KSA.

The central HRD function took responsibility for company-wide training needs analysis (TNA) and design of the training materials, which were delivered locally. Due to the large scale of this undertaking, difficult decisions were made about which employees needed what training, so that only 'must have' needs were addressed with no time or resources for 'added value' or 'nice to have' content (Kearns 2005). Individual tailoring of training was not an option with the 'sheep dip approach' being used (all employees of a certain category being given the same training experience).

Source: Alex Tymon

Questions

1   What are the potential advantages of a training approach such as that used at Telewest?

2   What are the potential disadvantages?

3   Provide three examples of things you have learnt in the last year.

4   What opportunities have you had to use this new learning?

5   How did this learning occur: was it formal or informal?

6   To what extent did you need completely new knowledge, skills or attitudes?

7   To what extent did you only need to adapt existing knowledge, skills or attitudes?

TRAINING, EDUCATION AND DEVELOPMENT

Training, education and development are all methods to enable learning, and are at the disposal of the HRD professional and individual. The definitions of these terms can best be explained using an analogy:

Schools in the UK are required to provide sex and relationships education to children, and whether or not we approve, most of us have a view of what it involves – in essence, the passing on of information, but in a very general way. Most definitions of occupational education concur that it is focused on inputs and therefore has non-specific outcomes. It involves a planned process of providing access to concepts, ideas and knowledge.

However, what if your child was to come home saying, 'We had sex training at school today'? What images could flash through your mind? Such images may be disquieting, because training is very different from occupational education. It is still a formal process but it is focused on outputs not inputs, such as the output of skill development. To quote Holst (2009, p332), 'training is the mastery of action (practice) … it is about building skills, understanding and confidence of people.'

Consider too your reaction if your child said 'We had sex *development* at school today'. What images might be created now? Again they could well be alarming ones. Development is also focused on outputs and implies getting better at something or becoming more advanced. It is the process of growing an individual and preparing them or equipping them for different, better or bigger things.

The interrelationships between these terms are important. It could be argued that training has clear outcomes and adopts a shorter-term perspective compared to development, which has desired outcomes, but these are likely to be less specific than those for training and could adopt a longer-term, nurturing perspective. But this argument could depend upon the organisational context. If a medical consultant takes 13 years to qualify, would this be considered to be training or development, or possibly both? What is probably most important is that training, education and development are all considered tools to be used within HRD in order to facilitate learning.

LEARNING THEORIES OF VALUE TO THE HRD PROFESSIONAL

Many theories are of value when trying to decide the best methods of facilitating learning, from the early behaviorist theories of the 1920s through to more recent theories of cognitive, social and experiential learning and most learning, training and development (LTD) and organisational behaviour textbooks contain accessible chapters on these topics. Illustrative of valuable theories to those charged with facilitating employer-provided training are:

- Hierarchy of learning/cognitive levels (Bloom 1956, Entwhistle 2001), which explain that the deeper the level of learning needed, the more time, effort and investment in training is required.
- Unconscious incompetence to unconscious competence (Howell 1982) informs us that to ensure new skills become second nature to employees, sufficient reinforcement is needed, which again necessitates investment in practice and feedback. If an organisation is not able or willing to provide the necessary level of investment, then the original need for the training should be questioned.
- Learning styles theory (Honey and Mumford 1982, Kolb 1984) is relevant to both learners and trainers, as this asserts we all have preferences for different learning and training methods. A special edition of the journal *Education and Training*, Volume 48 (8/9) provides several articles that explore the uses and criticisms of learning styles.

IDENTIFYING WHEN LEARNING MAY BE NEEDED

The Magic Model (Figure 10.1) is a tool which can be used to identify when it might be necessary for an employee to undergo a learning experience, and therefore it might be prudent to consider carrying out a learning needs analysis (LNA). LNA is a new angle on the traditional process of training needs analysis, which is extensively covered in most training and development textbooks. LNA is the process of identifying a gap in KSA that can and should be filled by a training, education or development intervention.

Figure 10.1 Times when consideration should be given to LNA

Mandatory skills and knowledge are those required by all *new* employees and include induction/orientation, basic job learning to reach competent employee status and legislation-driven learning such as in health and safety. So whenever a new employee comes on board, thought should be given to learning needs analysis.

Adapting to changes in processes, materials, equipment, demand levels etc could all lead to a need for new or amended KSA. So whenever any organisational changes are planned, learning needs analysis should be considered.

Growing into a new role or developing for future career moves will inevitably demand changes and development of KSA. So learning needs analysis should be part and parcel of any career planning activities, either company or individually driven.

Improvements to current work practices and activities may require new or amended KSA. So both day-to-day performance management and the formal review process should include learning needs analysis as standard.

Corrective coaching for shortfalls in performance may require an intervention to increase or refocus KSA. So any poor performance or conduct issues may flag up the need for learning needs analysis.

WHO IS RESPONSIBLE FOR PROVIDING LTD?

Until very recently, it was assumed that employers were responsible for the skills development of employees and, indeed, many organisations took this responsibility seriously and provided comprehensive training and development interventions. Training was something that was 'done to employees' because it was good for the organisation; for example, Budria (2012) reports that employer-provided training positively impacts on job satisfaction (see Chapter 12), which employees implicitly equate to a 17.7 per cent increase in earnings. Traditionally employees expected their employers to provide training and skills development as part of the psychological contract (see Chapter 7).

In some organisations the employer continues to take the lead role, at least for development of skills that the organisation needs, but perhaps not so for skills that are of greater benefit to the employee (organisations might be wary of developing their staff to the extent they become highly attractive to other employers). But the lines are becoming blurred and it is increasingly difficult to be clear where responsibility for skills and career development sits. One way to clarify this might be to establish who benefits most from the skills development and then assign responsibility accordingly.

WHO BENEFITS FROM THE LEARNING?

Knowing who benefits from the learning may also dictate the best methods to use for training and development. Clearly, if the organisation is the main beneficiary, it will be responsible for the training or learning provision, and it is likely to be more formal and structured so that it can be guaranteed that those employees who need the learning receive it. On the other hand, if the employee is the main beneficiary, they must take some responsibility for its provision themselves, and because the learning will be more individual in nature, the development techniques may be unstructured and less formal.

Few organisations would argue that basic job training for new employees and corrective coaching for employees who are underperforming are anything other than a business necessity. Therefore referring to the MAGIC model (Figure 10.1), mandatory KSA and corrective coaching are very clearly in the interests of the organisation if it wants optimal performance from its employees.

Learning for growth, on the other hand, could be viewed as being much more in the interests of the employee, because it will lead to enhanced employment prospects, which could be outside the organisation, even if the organisation will also benefit through more robust succession planning.

Conversely, adapting to change could be viewed as in the interests of both organisation and employee, dependent upon the specifics of their job role. In Case Study 10.1, training call-centre operatives in changes to the customer management system was essential because this was an inherent part of their day-to-day job. However, for installers or sales people this was not essential. Yet changes to the products on offer were considered essential for all employees. Making this distinction led to different training being provided for various employee groups in the first instance, but blanket coverage in the second.

Similarly, training for improvement could benefit both employee and organisation. For example, enabling a call centre operative to be more confident when dealing with irate customers could improve customer satisfaction and company profitability whilst at the same time affording greater job satisfaction for the employee, hence a shared benefit. But getting the same operatives to shorten the call durations would be of benefit to the organisation because this would increase productivity by enabling the operatives to take more calls. Yet for the same reason it could be viewed as a negative for the operatives themselves, if the only reward for efficiency was more calls.

A PARTNERSHIP APPROACH

These examples begin to demonstrate that deciding who benefits from learning is not as straightforward as at first it may seem. As demonstrated in Figure 10.2, mandatory training and corrective coaching are overtly in the interests of the organisation, but they are also covertly in the interests of the employee, as without them their employment is vulnerable. Growth may overtly be in the interests of the employee, but covertly it also benefits the organisation by providing better skilled and potentially more motivated employees.

Figure 10.2 MAGIC model: overt or covert benefit?

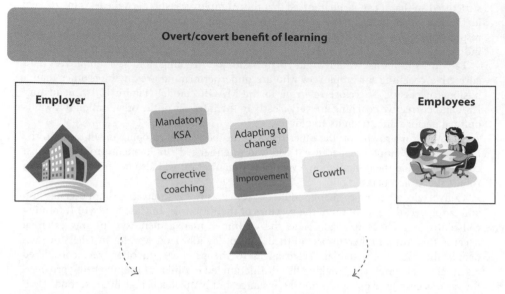

What is becoming increasingly clear is that in the twenty-first century it is unrealistic to expect employers to be totally responsible for HRD activities. It also appears that skills development is much more effective and successful if it is viewed as a partnership approach between the organisation and the learner; this is highlighted by the literature on the move from training to learning, which is discussed later. Case Study 10.2 gives an example of this approach.

 FENMARC PRODUCE LTD

CASE STUDY 10.2

Fenmarc Produce Ltd (a major food supplier to Asda) consider investing and developing its people to be a strategy enabler. It introduced a learning solution called 101 to improve its market position, embed a new company culture and support the change-readiness of the organisation. However, the programme was also the starting point for personal development which focused on the individual. The outcome has been success for the company with profit per employee growing five-fold, but only because

employees have also benefited by increasing their skills and confidence.

Source: HRMID (2007)

Question

1   What training, education and development are provided by your organisation? How does this fit into the MAGIC model? Who benefits from these opportunities or interventions?

FROM TRAINING TO LEARNING

The historical view of training as an activity that is 'done to' an employee is making way for more contemporary approaches which emphasise learning as being initiated and driven by the individual employee. To appreciate this change we need to identify some key phases and concepts which underpin macro-level policy in the UK.

THE SYSTEMATIC TRAINING CYCLE

The Industrial Training Boards, stimulated by the 1964 Industrial Training Act, pushed for an improvement in the quality and quantity of organisational skills training provisions. One of the most heavily promoted tools was the four-stage Systematic Training Cycle (STC). The STC comprises training needs analysis, design, delivery and evaluation, carried out in a systematic way, the intention being to ensure that training provision is both effective and efficient, ie the right things are trained in the most appropriate way. Numerous authors provide detailed descriptions of the four stages (Buckley and Caple 2007, Harrison 2009, Reid *et al* 2007) and the STC is by no means the only systematic model in existence: Cowell *et al* (2006) provide an overview of seven alternative systematic training models.

Despite stringent criticism of the cycle, including the fundamental charges that it is unresponsive to change, slow and costly in terms of resources, and – more generally – cold and clinical, with a basis in scientific management (Rayner and Adam-Smith 2009) the STC is still very much in use in many organisations today. Allen and Swanson point out that although there are many alternatives, 'systematic training is at the core of HRD and is by far the largest HRD investment year after year' (2006, p428). Indeed, there are many examples of organisations that continue to use the STC, achieving some excellent results. The UK Skills website (www.trainingdatabank.com) provides case studies of organisations who have won a National Training Award as recognition of 'exceptional training'. These awards use the STC as a foundation of their judging criteria, which can also be found online: www.nationaltrainingawards.com.

The positive examples could imply that it is not the STC model that is faulty, but the way in which it is used or, rather, misused. There is a wealth of evidence to suggest that few organisations fully use all the stages, with the most poorly completed stages being training needs analysis and evaluation. Gold *et al* (2010) explore why training needs analysis is often not done or not done well, and most textbooks on this topic lament the lack of proper evaluation of training.

Experience of being a judge for the National Training Awards (2009) supports these findings, whereby most entrants were easily able to explain the design and delivery of their learning intervention. However, they were not so clear on the original need for it, and were generally weak on demonstrating value as a result. So it could be argued that the STC is still a valuable tool when used correctly, but there are of course alternatives.

ALTERNATIVES TO SYSTEMATIC TRAINING

It could be argued that most organisations would prefer not to have to provide training: it is not a core activity and requires investment of scarce resources. The alternatives include (McClernon 2006):

- recruiting people who already have the KSA needed
- aligning compensation and reward more closely with performance to improve motivation
- improving communications and performance management to ensure effort is appropriately focused
- redesigning work methods, increasing technology or outsourcing, to reduce or remove the internal need for KSA
- improving the work climate to increase engagement and commitment.

Sutherland (2009) also suggests organisations should make better use of the skills that their employees already have. In his survey more than 50 per cent of employees said their skills were greater than those demanded by their current job.

Supporters of the STC might claim that these activities are not really alternatives, but could in fact be outputs of a thorough training or LNA, yet again suggesting that it is the use or misuse of the STC that is at fault. McGuire and Gubbins (2010) argue that formal learning, such as that supplied by effective use of the STC, is still important in modern organisations and the CIPD (2012i) reports that 56 per cent of organisations use a systematic approach frequently or occasionally. However, even if an organisation uses the STC effectively, there is still likely to be a need for some less formal employee development and learning.

REFLECTIVE ACTIVITY 10.1

Questions

1   How is learning or training needs analysis carried out in your organisation?

2   To what extent does training needs analysis identify alternatives to learning or training interventions?

AWAY FROM SYSTEMATIC TRAINING

In recent years there has been increasing interest in moving away from the 'jug and mug' metaphor for systematic training in which knowledge and skills (from the overflowing jug) are poured into the empty vessel or mug (the learner), towards a more learner-centred approach: the 'sower and seed' philosophy, with learning seen as facilitated growth (McGuire and Gubbins 2010). Research shows that competitive advantage can be gained when individuals are proactive in the learning process (CIPD 2005a, Drucker 2005, Sloman 2007). Beard and Wilson (2006, p4) propose a model called the 'learning combination lock' which highlights the complexity of learning for an individual and the multitude of factors which can affect its success. This model demonstrates how the 'one size fits all' approach of traditional training cannot hope to meet the needs of individual learners. The suggestion therefore is to move from an instructor-led content-based intervention to a self-directed work-based process (CIPD 2005a). This supports the idea of andragogy by Knowles (1990), who speculated that adult learners such as employees within organisations need much more involvement in the learning process for it to be effective.

TOWARDS SELF-DIRECTED LEARNING

Research into self-directed learning attempts to quantify what steps need to be taken to encourage this approach. Of interest to HRD professionals may be the paper by Ellinger (2004), which discusses the implications for integrating self-directed learning into HRD practices. Self-directed learning requires certain organisational aspects, which are likely to be embedded within the culture of the organisation, in order to make success more likely. These include the following (Confessore and Kops 1998, CIPD 2005a, Harrison 2009):

- tolerance for errors and experimentation
- a supportive environment
- using everyday work as an opportunity to learn
- participative leadership and delegation
- a fit with business goals

- open communications
- systems that encourage teamworking
- individual motivation and commitment.

The CIPD has produced a diagnostic tool which could provide the basis for organisations to start the move from training to learning: see www.cipd.co.uk.

DEVELOPING LEARNING AGILITY

Much of the literature also stresses the idea of helping individuals 'learn how to learn' or the concept of ownership for personal development – a recurring theme of this chapter. An analogy for this type of sustainable development could be:

> Give a man a fish and you feed him for a day. Teach a man how to fish and you feed him for life (attributed to Lao Tzu, the founder of Taoism).

If learners can become more adept at learning, or develop learning agility, not only will organisations find it easier to train and develop them, but the individuals themselves will find it easier to embark on the journey of lifelong learning. The twin themes of contribution to organisational effectiveness and personal development have made lifelong learning a topical concept and a theme which is continued later in this chapter. The focus on moving from training to learning leads one to consider the methods of development which might enable this to happen.

CHOICE OF LEARNING AND DEVELOPMENT TECHNIQUES

Choosing development techniques – and the choice is vast – will be influenced by a number of factors, such as organisational culture, resources available and learner-related factors, including learning theories and models, which we discussed earlier in the chapter.

Peter Honey (1998) describes over 100 different techniques in his *Manager's Guide to Workplace Learning* text. Cheetham and Chivers (2001) list almost as many in their paper 'How professionals learn'. Both are useful sources of ideas for those planning development activities. But there is also evidence to show that some techniques are much more widely used than others and some are regarded as being more effective than others.

Interestingly, despite the supposed shift from training to learning, traditional off-job training courses are still widely used, with a CIPD survey (2008b) showing 64 per cent of people had participated in an event of this type in the previous 12 months. However, the same survey showed these courses were not well liked by learners, with only 15 per cent of people ranking them as most appealing while on-job training was most appealing for 46 per cent. Critically, only 19 per cent of respondents in the 2012 survey (CIPD 2012i) regard off-job training as effective, whereas on-job training was thought to be effective by 39 per cent. In this survey, the top spots for effectiveness went to in-house development programmes (52 per cent) and coaching by line managers (46 per cent).

The effectiveness of on-job and in-house methods is almost certainly due to the in-built ability to practise and gain feedback in real time. This links into the learning theory which shows that essential practice and feedback are essential in order for new skills to become unconsciously embedded.

But the situation is more complex. E-learning has long been heralded as the ultimate individualised, learner-centred technique with in-built practice and immediate feedback. But in a CIPD survey only 11 per cent of respondents regarded it as an effective method, with most managers adding that 'it was not a substitute for face to face or classroom learning' (2012i, p10).

REFLECTIVE ACTIVITY 10.2

Who do you want to fly your plane?

An interesting research study by Hendrick (1983) compared the performance levels of both experienced and trainee pilots in a flight simulator. While both groups performed well when normal stick controls were in operation, the experienced pilots made significantly more errors when the stick controls were reversed. When increasing altitude, the experienced pilots made four times as many errors than the trainee pilots.

This study concluded that experience in a task resembled a 'double-edged sword', with lengthy experience resulting in embedded habits. Hendrick concluded that experienced pilots were more vulnerable to error when flying a new type of plane, due to these embedded, and difficult to change, habits.

So who would you prefer to fly your plane and why? The answer may point to complexities and contradictions in the area of learning theory and its practical application.

IMPORTANCE OF THE TRANSFER OF LEARNING

Whatever development technique is selected there is one factor that appears to be essential if it is to be effective: transfer of learning. Indeed, most of us could cite examples of training interventions that were enjoyed by the participants, who later demonstrated changes to their KSA – but with no marked change in job performance. Consider the manager who returns from a two-day management skills workshop brimming with enthusiasm to use new project management techniques or to start coaching and mentoring their team, but within days the enthusiasm is gone and the new techniques put on the back-burner. This could be due to lack of transfer, which Yorks *et al* (1999, p56) tell us 'has long been the Achilles' heel of HRD'. There are multiple reasons for this lack of transfer; time pressures, resource shortages and culture mismatch being just a few. However, probably the biggest issue is related to organisational support and how much the newly trained employee is encouraged to use his or her new knowledge or skill.

Transfer is far more difficult to achieve with traditional systematic training, where trainees undergo a 'one size fits all' intervention, often off-job and therefore not tailored to them and lacking the realism of their everyday work experience. This could be the key to why on-job learning and self-directed learning are regarded as more effective, because they address this issue: learning is completely tailored and is much more likely to take place on-job in real time with in-built practice and feedback.

REFLECTIVE ACTIVITY 10.3

Think about training programmes you have attended. How was learning transfer facilitated?

From your experience of work-based development and training, what methods are employed to assist in translating experiential and other learning into relevant workplace activity?

CAREER AND PROFESSIONAL DEVELOPMENT

The debate about responsibility for learning leads on to a discussion about investment in career and professional development. This is the focus of the rest of this chapter.

WHAT IS A CAREER?

The term 'career', in its most general sense, is interpreted as upward progression through a series of job roles with increasing levels of responsibility or managerial control. In essence, a career is a structured sequence of work experiences that promote employee development and advance organisational capability.

WHAT DOES A CAREER LOOK LIKE?

The concept of a career provides a useful focus for employment and future goals that drive a sense of purpose. There is no doubt that a perspective on career significance is uniquely personal and for some people of resounding meaning: 'careers are what we judge our lives by' (Inkson and Arthur 2001, p48).

By contrast, some individuals attest that they have never had a career, but rather 'a series of bits and pieces', or 'a chapter of accidents'. How can these opposing views be reconciled?

REFLECTIVE ACTIVITY 10.4

Questions

1   How does a career differ from a job?

2   What are the distinctive features of a career?

3   What does a career mean to you?

Individuals often make sense of their employment history by a retrospective construction of career decisions. These career stories may grant coherence to a serendipitous employment experience of different roles or sectors. Media coverage of overnight career success often belies the years spent toiling for recognition. Even Harrison Ford, known for his remarkable good fortune in transitioning from carpenter to leading actor after a chance encounter with the film producer George Lucas, had previously spent 15 years as a cabinet-maker trying to start an acting career.

The rise in different employment contractual relationships (discussed in the introduction) through increasing part-time working, outsourcing and the use of flexible working arrangements, has altered assumptions about careers (Greller 2006, Harrison 2009). Hall (2004) declared the career in terminal decline, yet there is limited evidence of the widespread abandonment of career structures in organisational practice (Sullivan and Baruch 2009, Baruch 2004, 2006). The relevance of career models needs to be questioned in a global economy where a variety of employment patterns emerge, and when contemporary career patterns often transcend occupational and national boundaries.

CONTEMPORARY CAREER MODELS

Three prominent career concepts follow: the traditional career; the boundaryless career; and the self-managed career. These academic constructs provide a useful framework to explore current debates around career development.

TRADITIONAL CAREER

The image of a traditional career is of a pattern of jobs within a single organisation that follow a linear and predetermined path. This is often depicted as a hierarchical ladder that an employee climbs, acquiring greater levels of expertise and managerial accountability (see Figure 10.3). In this model the employer assumes a paternalistic role and employees' self-worth is defined by the organisation (Tams and Arthur 2010, Sullivan and Baruch 2009).

Key characteristics of a traditional career structure are: specific entry criteria linked to education and qualification attainment; a planned and coordinated structure of job experience; and a coherent reward strategy. Reward is provided through the extrinsic acceleration of pay, increased benefits, and role seniority. Additionally, intrinsic rewards flow from public recognition of an individual's promotion and achievement.

Traditional career ladder

Employee success is measured in progressive movement up the career structure that mutually satisfies organisational objectives and individual career growth. Examples of careerists flourishing within a single organisation are Lord Browne, who began work with the oil giant BP as a graduate trainee and rose to become CEO, and Sir Terry Leahy, who joined Tesco as a management trainee and worked his way up to CEO within the supermarket chain prior to leaving in 2010. Such examples indicate the value of company-specific knowledge to career progression, and are a potent indicator of individual worth to the business.

Figure 10.3 Traditional career ladder

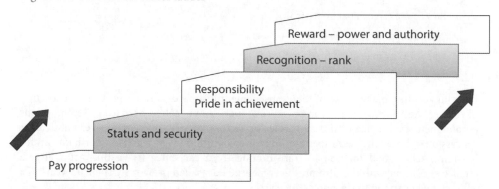

This traditional model is equally valid within the public sector (Baruch 2004). The employer provides relative security of employment and career advancement in exchange for superior performance and firm allegiance to the organisation. However, the removal of many mid-level positions has affected the available rungs in the career ladder.

BOUNDARYLESS CAREER

The unpredictability of lifetime employment has affected expectations of a stable career pattern. DeFillippi and Arthur (1994) introduced the concept of career growth free of organisational restrictions: with no boundaries. The boundaryless career crosses multiple companies and contexts, unlike the traditional career path within a single company. An individual creates a career in various organisations through a process of development along a path of experience (Sullivan and Baruch 2009, Baruch and Rosenstein 1992). The boundaryless career is multidirectional, shaped by opportunity. An individual example is Adam Crozier, who in public interviews has joked that his career path might suggest someone who doesn't quite know what he wants to do. Crozier began employment as a graduate trainee at Mars Pedigree Petfood, and has moved across diverse organisations from the *Daily Telegraph* to Saatchi & Saatchi, to the Football Association, to Royal Mail and to ITV as chief executive. Crozier's industry switching is connected by the transfer of integrated business and change management skills.

SELF-MANAGED CAREER

The self-managed career emphasises the individual as master of his or her own destiny rather than the organisation. Hall (2004) developed the concept of the protean career, so-called as Proteus, the Greek god of the sea, changed form to match the environment. Following the analogy, as the business environment evolves and requirements change, individuals must similarly adapt by renewing their skills and updating their knowledge. A protean career is inevitably characterised by continuous learning. Success is gauged by the individual's vision and values as the career contract is with oneself; an alignment of personal aspirations and work (Hall 2004). Sir Richard Branson, founder of the Virgin Group, is arguably Britain's best-known example of such adaptation. Branson has directed Virgin's evolution from music to airlines, shops, telecoms, drinks and even bridal wear.

Similarly, a portfolio career is one in which an individual makes a deliberate choice of personal independence, working on a variety of contracts with clients and organisations (Handy 1994). The freelancer identifies with clients, groups or collaborators, and this working identity forms a career (Ibarra 2004). The professional with expertise for hire is a free agent, at liberty to showcase skills and competence as saleable commodities (Bridges 1995).

> More than a quarter of all American workers now classify themselves as 'free agents', and half of America's temps are professionals of one kind or another' (*The Economist* 2009).

In this fluid environment an individual needs criteria for effective career management to shape an 'intelligent career' (Baruch 2004, Baruch and Quick 2007). These are framed as open career questions:

- Know why – values, attitudes, internal needs, identity and lifestyle.
- Know how – career competencies: skills, expertise, capabilities, tacit and explicit knowledge.
- Know whom – networking, relationships, how to find the right people.
- Know what – opportunities, threats and requirements.
- Know where – entering, training and advancing.
- Know when – timing of choices and activities.

Another perspective on career is one that sees learning as a collection of knowledge gained from work experiences over time that enables people to adapt their behaviour and career strategy (Tams and Arthur 2010, Sullivan and Baruch 2009, Arthur and Rousseau 1996). This collected learning constitutes a career rather than the biographical succession of work experiences. When asked for his personal career advice, Lord Sugar, the successful entrepreneur, emphasised that accumulated experience is what matters. From this perspective every worker has a career built through successive jobs of his or her working life. Yet there is tension in such a view, because it implies that all individuals are equally capable of deriving skill enrichment from accumulated experience. Individual entrepreneurs such as the easyJet founder, Sir Stelios Haji-Ioannou, demonstrate that some are more skilled than others in making use of their experience.

WHAT IS THE BUSINESS RATIONALE FOR CAREER MANAGEMENT?

The rationale for career management is the effective nurturing of talent, specific company knowledge and the successive deployment of workforce capabilities to best serve the business. Companies such as McDonald's, Walt Disney and the Hilton Group spend considerable time, money and effort turning fresh recruits into loyal company men and women who will internalise and promote organisational values. Although the terms 'career management' and 'development' are often used interchangeably, they are differentiated by career ownership and direction.

Career management is the formal systematic process through which the organisation nurtures the human capital that can provide competitive advantage (Porter 1998). It is marked by managerial interventions such as succession planning, formal mentoring and secondments. Effective career coaching embedded in the performance review process links an individual's development planning to the organisational charting of future resource allocation. Review the CIPD *Guide to Career Management* (King 2004) for further examples of career management.

Organisations invest in employees' education, providing work experiences that expand competences and target development through in-house training and corporate universities. Return on this career investment is assessed against expected career trajectories. For example, in a global bank executive officers' career progress was measured against a predicted speed of reaching branch manager position within a number of years. If this position had not been reached, early severance was encouraged. This demonstrates the organisation's risk management of a career to assess whether an individual remains an increasing asset.

Many organisations need to build expertise through successive job experience and exposure to distinct environments. For example, the medical and legal profession demand intensive training and applied practice to achieve operational competence. Organisational investment in developing pilot skills may be questioned, as technological advances and auto-piloting have diminished individual skill reliance. However, the emergency US Airways jet landing on the New York Hudson River in 2009 dramatically demonstrates the value of an individual pilot's seasoned expertise. The pilot, Chesley Sullenberger, a captain with 29 years' airline experience, saved the lives of all 150 passengers and crew members. By contrast, when the cruise liner Costa Concordia struck rocks in 2012 the evacuation training and leadership capability of the captain Francesco Schettino was severely criticised and charged with a range of offences including manslaughter and abandoning ship.

Although the concept of career management is straightforward, the execution may be more complex. Career oversight is often shared by different business units, managers and mentors, and the locus of control for career management may vary in practice.

REFLECTIVE ACTIVITY 10.5

Consider this employee's view of a career structure: 'The career management is really about who knows who at the moment. There's no real formal structure to the career management' (CIPD 2010b).

Questions

1   What are the career interventions in your organisation?

2   Who develops the career path?

3   What navigates you through the organisational maze?

4   What are the challenges of developing career paths in distinct operating areas?

There is an apparent tension between organisations' promotional use of career opportunity to attract new recruits and the reality of what a promised career delivers. An employment climate affected by recession has further obscured career structures through recruitment and promotion freezes. Read the following example (CIPD 2010b) and consider the implications for an individual employee:

> The career path that we are describing for the future is more come to us, learn some things, gain some skills, go somewhere else, move on and maybe rejoin us later in your career as a senior leading scientist.

This is an opaque route and places the map firmly in the hands of the individual protagonist to chart his or her course. In addition, mergers and acquisitions can affect a maturing career plan that runs counter to the changed requirements of the business. Pressing business demands may include sourcing external expertise to find the right skill sets. Accordingly, commitment may shift from the organisation to the team leader, to the project or to the profession (Grimland *et al* 2012). If employers are ceding control of career management, then increasingly individuals are encouraged to be proactive in their own career development. This echoes the theme of self-directed learning.

Career development marks a shift from directing to enabling development that increases or sustains employees' current productivity. Career development is a critical lever in attracting, engaging and retaining talent. As noted earlier, economic fluctuations demand career resilience (Sullivan and Baruch 2009). Resilience is acquired by a constant updating of skills that enables employees to anticipate change and remain competitive. This assures an individual's employability within the company and outside (Ghoshal *et al* 1999). Positive career development resonates with the need for continual learning, as highlighted in protean and self-managed careers, and summarised in the CIPD model shown in Figure 10.4.

Career development is portrayed as symbiotic, offering the potential for both individual career advancement and the enhancement of organisational capability. The CIPD depicts this as positive career development.

Figure 10.4 Rationale for career development

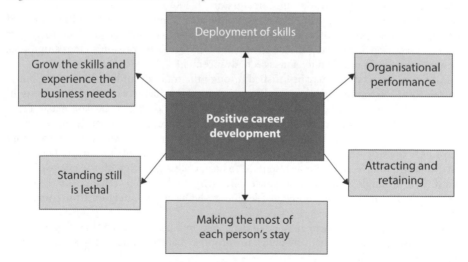

Source: CIPD (2005a)

The extent of the employer's responsibility in providing career development tools, opportunities and funding is debatable. Although it is assumed that HR practitioners will provide career support, this may vary in practice. 'HR departments are, of course, heavily involved in giving career advice and information to individuals, and assessing and advising on their development needs' (CIPD 2009b). Moreover, financial results or conflicting business priorities may overtake development needs. Similarly, line managers differ widely in their competence level as career coaches, and in their enthusiasm for acting as organisational guide. Factors critical for employee career development, support and success are summarised below:

- managerial support
- mentoring guidance
- peer and organisational network support
- organisational investment
- opportunity for extending skills
- inclusive access to development experience
- diversity of staff profile in expected career progress
- harmony of business needs and individual aspirations.

Alternatively, an individual not finding opportunities or support may encounter barriers that limit career growth. Line managers may inhibit career movement, as the employee seeking guidance may become a rival for promotion. Research by the Work Foundation (2009) indicates that access to development and training opportunities is skewed, with managers and professionals five times more likely to receive work-based training than people with no qualification or in an unskilled job.

CAREER DEVELOPMENT STRUCTURES

Career success is in the eye of the beholder, with progression implicit in the psychological contract. Boxall and Purcell (2011) argue that the construct of a deal is in the mind of individual employees and therefore cannot be viewed as contractual. Career success is complex because career aims change over time. Success may be measured in progress consistent with personal aspirations, the achievement of professional excellence or preference for meaningful work (Sullivan and Baruch 2009).

For some, it is the extrinsic reward of power and remuneration; for others, reward through internal feelings of worthiness and achievement (Baruch 2006). Line managers and HR practitioners need to provide clear plans for career progression so that employees are aware of what is required to gain career advancement.

Employee expectations may be satisfied through the trade-off of long journeying hours for the future assurance of career uplift; for example, to achieve partnership status in accountancy firms. Yet the 'big four' accounting firms (Deloitte Touche Tohmatsu, Ernst & Young, KPMG and PricewaterhouseCoopers) all have predominantly male senior partner staffs. Professional women spend more time working flexibly, and have more non-linear career paths. Moreover, although the organisation wants to nurture talent and fast-track potential leaders, it may also need to balance this growth with the intake of fresh blood. For example, the fashion house Givenchy broke from reliance on in-house expertise by hiring the young designer Alexander McQueen to reinvigorate the company's style.

A trust in career fulfilment may be undermined by business survival as organisations are increasingly unable or unwilling to promise career opportunities (Dries and Pepermans 2008, p87).

Career promotion may be a simple case of managerial expediency in response to operational requirements rather than reward for effective performance.

Thus three pertinent questions emerge about career development structures:

- Is there a match between the organisation's needs and the individual's aspirations?
- Is the career framework transparent to all?

● Can the career offer remain valid and affordable for the business?

THE OWNERSHIP OF CAREER DEVELOPMENT

Career ownership revolves around control and direction; and perceptions of career-orientation and control may stem more from individual mindset than external environment (Briscoe and Hall 2006). Yet there is potential ambiguity and competing expectations in the purpose of career development for the organisation and for the individual: can personal growth and development readily transfer to corporate advantage?

International career development may call for distinct approaches in managing across borders. Expatriation is managed according to the organisational strategy for particular expertise; for example, international career structures at the oil company Shell, the Foreign and Commonwealth Office, and Nestlé. Research in international careers has found that the primary motives for going abroad are personal interest, a search for new experiences and an interest in the external environment (Suutari and Brewster 2000). Consequently, there may be a mismatch between individual values and organisational pressure that provoke a career crisis. For example, a BBC journalist may refuse a political assignment in Israel when the individual's interests are focused on social development in Brazil. These individual career aspirations can change with family circumstances, educational requirements, health, financial commitments and personal interests. Moreover, for businesses in recession an increased pressure on developmental budgets may restrict investment in career development to employees identified as talent, and members of a talent pool. For example, BT has a workforce Talent Deal which sets out the expectations of contributions from talent pool members in return for the support they receive in career planning.

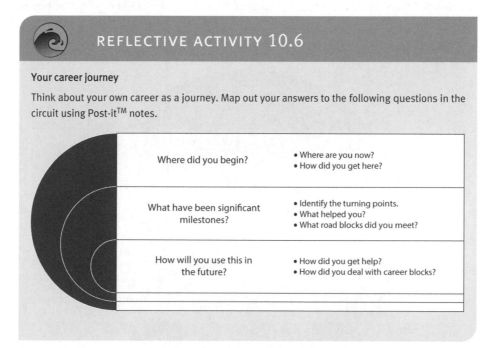

REFLECTIVE ACTIVITY 10.6

Your career journey

Think about your own career as a journey. Map out your answers to the following questions in the circuit using Post-it™ notes.

Where did you begin?	● Where are you now? ● How did you get here?
What have been significant milestones?	● Identify the turning points. ● What helped you? ● What road blocks did you meet?
How will you use this in the future?	● How did you get help? ● How did you deal with career blocks?

A self-managed career demands high levels of self-awareness and personal responsibility (Hall 2004). It also makes significant demands on an individual's ability to adapt in terms of performance and learning, as evidenced in this statement:

> Our graduate scheme will give you everything you need to build the kind of career you want. But it's up to you how it goes. You'll be the one in charge, putting forward your ideas, taking on responsibilities and making choices about how you get the job done (IBM Graduate Scheme 2013).

Certain individuals have a greater tolerance for ambiguity that suits an entrepreneurial approach to career invention. For others, self-directed career management is a burden resulting in mounting stress levels (Cooper 2005). This reveals why many employees wish to keep the traditional psychological contract for the job security that it offers (McDonald *et al* 2005). Workers at Cadbury's chocolate factory in Bourneville may have believed their specific company knowledge and experience would secure future employment until Kraft's takeover undermined such prospects.

Notwithstanding, there is debate as to how much individual development and learning can be effectively harnessed by the organisation, and managed as an organisational resource (Senge 1993). The unpredictability of organisational career paths shifts the emphasis to individuals' personal investment through continuing professional development.

THE CONCEPT OF CONTINUING PROFESSIONAL DEVELOPMENT

Continuing professional development (CPD) has been defined as a constant updating of professional knowledge throughout one's working life by means of systematic, ongoing, self-directed learning (CIPD 2012n). This professional enrichment is depicted in Figure 10.5.

Figure 10.5 Professional expansion

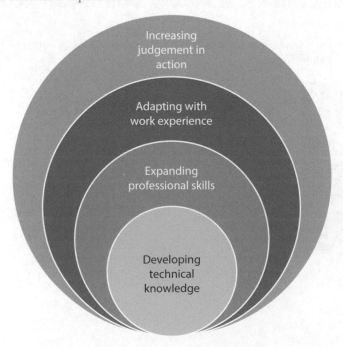

Increasing judgement in action

Adapting with work experience

Expanding professional skills

Developing technical knowledge

UNDERSTANDING CPD

CPD promotes the ongoing attainment of effective job performance through targeting current and emerging development needs. The 'P' in CPD can mean 'personal' as well as 'professional'; the two are often conflated. It can be argued that the product of CPD is essentially 'personal property'. Inkson and Arthur (2001) support the validity of self-interested professional development in what they termed career capitalism, ie the return on investment in a career. The understanding is that by recognising and taking advantage of development opportunities this will lead to career success (Tams and Arthur, 2010, Arthur *et al* 1999, Briscoe and Hall 2006). As a result, an individual who understands the marketplace, and can adapt to what is in demand, can increase the yield on personal capital.

CPD can therefore be seen as a virtuous circle of improvement (see Figure 10.6). We can assume that development momentum is generated by individual and economic self-interest to improve professional capability and performance (Megginson and Whitaker 2007).

However, the tangible evidence of such improvement can be questioned, as many performance reviews witness the annual listing of the same developmental needs. When does the circle devolve into a recurring nightmarish task? Could this be a troubling prospect whereby competencies are acquired that may not have a future demand? British steel-workers formerly employed by the Anglo-Dutch Corus plant may wonder if, in future, their expertise will only be in demand in Asia.

Figure 10.6 Virtuous circle of improvement

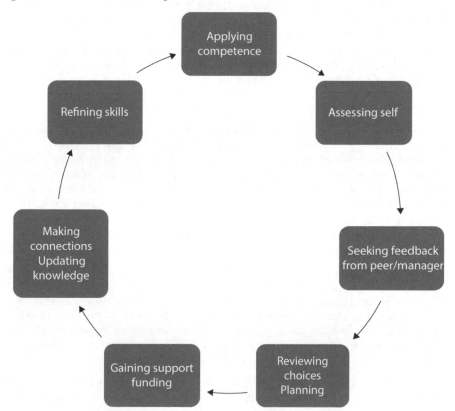

As noted earlier, the Leitch Report (2006) recognised the importance of skills for productivity, and noted that gaps in learning and skills were a collective reason for organisations' failure to compete in global markets. Furthermore, the Department for Innovation, Universities and Skills identified skills and learning gaps as the primary cause for individual lack of participation in economic activity (Gold *et al* 2010). This corroborates CPD as an organisational defensive strategy against the prospect of sector decline or industry changes. In addition, CPD offers the protection of employability for the individual.

REFLECTIVE ACTIVITY 10.7

Questions

1   Provide examples of CPD from your own experience.

2   What has this learning enabled you to do differently?

3   Who, in your opinion, is the prime beneficiary of this development?

EVALUATING CPD

Given organisational investment in training and education, the business will want to harness professional learning to affect improved performance. The Confederation of British Industry's Education and Skills Survey (2012) reported that despite economic pressures 81 per cent of employers plan to maintain or increase their investment in skills to improve productivity. This suggests that CPD practice can support the expansion of skills, knowledge and competence, reinforced by continuous learning as a workforce core competence and performance requirement.

CPD AND PROFESSIONAL BODIES

The revised CIPD Code of Professional Conduct (July 2012c) states the expectation of 'a firm commitment to continuous professional development'. Many professional bodies enforce the practice of CPD as a condition of active membership, and to ensure consumer protection. Professional status is accredited and assures the public of an individual's legitimised expertise. In certain cases CPD is a legal requirement and represents individual professional liability; for example, the Association of Chartered Certified Accountants (ACCA).

Review the following example of CPD from the Royal College of Veterinary Surgeons (Source: www.rcvs.org.uk):

The RCVS Guide to Professional Conduct makes it very clear that veterinary surgeons have a responsibility to ensure that they maintain and continue to develop their professional knowledge and skills. CPD is therefore the personal obligation of all responsible veterinary surgeons and should be seen as the continuous progression of capability and competence. The recommended minimum CPD is 105 hours over three years with an average of 35 hours per year. It is appreciated that most veterinary surgeons will do considerably more than this.

By contrast, the Chartered Management Institute declares a broad approach to CPD (www.managers.org.uk): 'The Institute is not prescriptive as to the content, approach or effort an individual member puts into their development but offers advice and practical support.'

REFLECTIVE ACTIVITY 10.8

Review a range of professional bodies for examples of CPD practice. You might want to look at the Royal Institute of British Architects (RIBA), the Institute of Fisheries Management (IFM) or the Chartered Institute of Environmental Health (CIEH).

Then, in a study group, answer the questions below, then compare your findings on CPD requirements and methods of recording evidence.

Questions

1   What are the advantages of identifying specific CPD categories?

2   Discuss the possible limitations of these approaches.

Table 10.1 gives an example from the Chartered Institute of Plumbing and Heating Engineering (CIPHE) of the requirement for a plumbing engineer to log 30 hours of CPD annually (www.ciphe.org.uk).

Table 10.1 Sample CPD hourly log

CPD category	Maximum hours for CPD claim
Training courses and workshops	30 hours
Conferences and seminars/lectures	14 hours
Attending exhibitions	8 hours
Technical writing	15 hours or 30 for books
Mentoring	20 hours
Private study	8 hours
Qualification studies	30 hours

CPD PRACTICE: STICK OR CARROT?

Two models of CPD are evident in professional bodies: the compulsory approach, or the voluntary. Whilst voluntary practice appeals to members' enlightened self-interest, obligatory practice allows for the audit of CPD records. A survey conducted in 2008 found that 50 per cent of professional bodies made CPD mandatory (*Personnel Today* 2008). CPD was measured by task hours or study units completed, and sanctions included suspension. But 25 per cent of survey respondents stated that they did not measure CPD practice. The resistance to compulsory CPD can denote the balance of professional power; for example, in the medical field (Megginson and Whitaker 2007).

CONSTRAINTS OF CPD

Even if CPD practice and recording is systematic, the outcome and application of such development remains subjective. An inspection framework attempts to judge professional development through quantitative measures. Clocking learning hours and course attendance is easy to verify. Yet exposure to specialist knowledge through conferences may be insufficient for professional advancement in context. Improvement through CPD participation is difficult to evaluate without an assessment of learning.

This highlights an inherent conflict between the demonstration of competence levels and the ongoing need for further development. It is in the interest of the professional body to promote its members' competence, and generate demand for management learning in its role as a provider of professional courses, or as a learning academy (Cervero 2001). There may be little inclination to publicise members' skill gaps or atrophying knowledge. The risk is of CPD deteriorating into a form-filling exercise dominated by process. CPD must be a meaningful account of learning development and skill acquisition beyond a record of attendance at training events. Transforming CPD into a conversation rather than a monologue remains a challenge.

Figure 10.7 Subjective reward of CPD

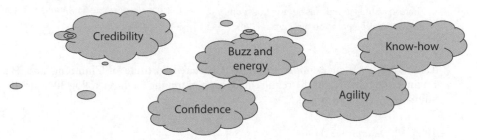

BENEFITS OF CPD

The main benefits of CPD for the individual are updating, increasing competence and enhancing mobility (Sadler-Smith *et al* 2000). Within organisations CPD serves as an auditable record of development activities and agreed development planning. The potential rewards of CPD must be apparent to both the individual and the organisation. For an individual it can expand their options and develop transferable skills (Woodall and Gourlay 2004). The individual incentives for CPD are shown in the thought bubbles of Figure 10.7.

From an organisation's perspective, when seeking to manage its human resources, CPD can cultivate talent and capitalise on exponential learning. Is there then evidence of a convergence of interest for employers and employees in the widespread adoption of CPD?

An expansive concept of CPD provides an alternative to a prescribed, linear career path. Organisations offer structured opportunities for employees to break from daily routine and follow altruistic desires to serve the community. Thus sabbatical leave building classrooms in Cambodia, for example, may coincide with the organisational fulfilment of corporate social responsibility (CSR). Such volunteer work can both satisfy personal brand values and increase an individual's network of connections. Expanding one's social network can be viewed as a resource; getting to know more people fits the career dimension of social capital (Seibert *et al* 2001, Arthur 2008).

Having current skills and knowledge enriches the possibilities of a self-managed career. However, the individual imperative to update skills and acquire qualifications is often a response to job demands that will ensure contract renewal. Despite the heralded benefits of professional development as self-empowering, individuals may be entirely instrumental in learning as they seek to demonstrate career relevance. CPD is increasingly seen as an investment for employment continuity (Rothwell 2005). An individual between jobs needs to acquire marketable experience that will differentiate them from other job candidates, such as herding elephants in Kenya. The individual works on CPD as a personal investment in learning from experience, thereby illustrating learning agility and self-reliance through a colourful CPD portfolio.

The CIPD (2012n) points to continuing professional development as 'an essential part of professional life, not as an optional extra'. Because CPD represents such an integral feature of contemporary working life, it can be illustrated as interconnecting gears within the organisation (Figure 10.8).

Figure 10.8 The dynamics of learning and development

REFLECTIVE ACTIVITY 10.9

How can an organisation maintain the smooth interplay of the three cogs (learning, earning, growing) in this model?

As is evident from this reflective activity, mutual commitment is required to meet the demands of a dynamic economic environment and adapt to constant movement. Learning can increase capability for potential earning. Earning sustains business competitiveness and continuous growing. Growing can expand learning and be life-enhancing.

CASE STUDY 10.3

CAREER DEVELOPMENT IN PRACTICE: A ROADMAP FROM WASHINGTON DC

The US government agency Enduring Defense, based in Washington, DC, recognised employee retention to be an issue. The agency employed over 3,000 staff combining civilians, military personnel and contractor employees. Attracting talented scientists and engineers was not a problem, but holding on to them was challenging. Many specialised staff were frustrated by a slow climb up the agency career pyramid. Some felt that if they couldn't move up, they would move out. As a result they took their cutting-edge technical knowledge and unique skills out of the door.

In the past the agency always agreed to fund staff requests for training and development. Some conferences in Hawaii or Australia appeared to be remote from their departmental job focus. Staff looked at this funding as a networking opportunity for future external consultancy work. Expenditure control and development consistently anchored to mission objectives was a problem.

To address these issues, the agency set up a new corporate university as an umbrella for professional development specifically linked to mission goals. External consultants designed and implemented an organisation-wide competency framework. A set of career guides was rolled out for each function defining job broadbanding and relevant resources for individual development.

Stan Allport worked in the facilities function in charge of logistics. He had attended the career guides roadshow, and was optimistic about his career track. Stan had worked for the US Air Force before joining the agency, and after two tours in Afghanistan felt entitled to protected employment in a steady job.

But when Stan looked through his career guide he didn't find what he wanted. The guide featured employee self-improvement through mentoring and on-the-job projects. There were suggestions for skills updating, continuous learning and knowledge acquisition. Skill proficiency assessments were designed for the line manager and employee to agree on a personal development plan. Stan was disappointed by a lack of specific job vacancies. The guide emphasised employees' development aligned to the organisation's mission, not the plan for his career. Rumour was spreading that the severe restrictions on defense spending meant relocation of the agency to Huntsville, Alabama. This was not in Stan's vision of the future. He knew that his wife Kelly, a doctor at the children's hospital, and twin daughters would never leave the vibrant capital city for a sleepy southern state.

Stan emailed his line manager for an urgent meeting. He wanted to underline to her that the agency had promised him a career when he signed up. This self-improvement was a fuzzy concept; it was too uncertain. Where was the career map? He didn't really want to work on special assignments or extra projects. Stan had done his years of hard graft. It was payback time. Stan really wanted to know when he'd get his next promotion, and how his career was to be mapped out until retirement.

Source: Margaret Mackay

Questions

1   What are the benefits of this development approach from an agency perspective?

| 2 | What are some of the tensions of individual career development in practice? | 3 | If you were Stan's line manager, how would you explain the career guidance? |

CONCLUSION

Learning and effective employee development can maximise opportunities for business survival and success. Managing talent and harvesting dedicated organisational knowledge can be vital. Yet such development activities are often challenged by a dynamic environment.

A single 'one size fits all' approach is unlikely to succeed. If HR is to be effective, it has to be broad, potentially ranging from traditional training provision to harnessing informal learning for both employee career development and organisational advantage. HR has a role to play in raising awareness of the value of learning and enhancing workforce skills. It must also focus on tacit knowledge management and the capture and transfer of unique company-specific skills.

A renewed interest in career management and innovative support for professional development can retain talent and foster engagement. Workplace learning offers mutual benefits for both the organisation and the individual; it increases organisational capability whilst enhancing individual employability. A starting point for HR practitioners is to embrace the concept of lifelong learning, to ensure their own skill sets are current and relevant, thus providing a role model within their organisation.

KEY LEARNING POINTS

- There is a robust business case for investment in employee development to increase competence and ensure organisational competitiveness.
- The impact of the knowledge economy demands continuous learning and skill currency.
- Successful employee and talent development demands a shared approach.
- The emphasis for employee development has shifted from formal training to broader concepts of learning, and values the impact of informal learning.
- Organisations need to proactively support career development to increase motivation and retain talent.
- The individual is increasingly responsible for career orientation and direction.
- CPD is integral to individual learning.

1   How can informal learning be managed in order to capitalise on talent development?

2   How can the HR function address the demands of business leaders who only value formal training?

3   How can HR promote sustained professional development?

4   What is the business rationale for career management?

5   How can line managers address the tension between individual development and organisational needs?

6   How can HR practitioners encourage talent development that embraces a diversity of education and experience?

Gold, J., Holden, R., Iles, P., Stewart, J. and Beardwell, J. (2013) *Human Resource Development, Theory and Practice*. Basingstoke: Palgrave MacMillan. Explore learning theories and how these impact on training, development and CPD.

Megginson, D. and Whitaker, V. (2007) *Continuing Professional Development*. 2nd edition. London: CIPD. Extend strategies for continuous professional development.

Pedler, M., Burgoyne, J. and Boydell, T. (2007) *A Manager's Guide to Self-Development*. 5th edition. Maidenhead: McGraw-Hill. Explore self-development activities to support individual career planning and development.

CHAPTER 11

Managing the Employment Relationship

Derek Adam-Smith and Sally Rumbles

LEARNING OUTCOMES

After reading this chapter, you should be able to:

- specify the importance of the contract of employment and its limitations for the management of employees

- explain differences in how conflict at work is viewed and some of the implications for managerial action

- assess the key implications for managers of recognising trade unions as representatives of employees

- understand the importance of management style and management practice to the effective management of employees

- understand the difference between equal opportunities and diversity

- appreciate the complexity of managing a diverse workforce.

OVERVIEW

The objectives of organisations may be expressed in different ways. In the private sector these typically relate to profitability or market share, while in the public sector account must be taken of budgetary constraints imposed by politicians. Voluntary bodies may express their objectives in terms of service delivery to vulnerable groups in society. All organisations, however, employ people to achieve their objectives irrespective of how they are expressed. Employees also have needs that they want to be met in their work, and expectations about how they will be treated. In this chapter we explore some key features that shape the employment relationship between employers and employees. Some of these elements are determined by employment law, which places constraints on management action. However, there still remains considerable choice in the way that employees may be managed, and this choice is influenced by managers' beliefs and their attitudes towards their staff. One key decision that must be made is whether employees are to be treated in the same way as other organisational resources, or are viewed as a special kind of resource that can provide a competitive advantage. Much contemporary HRM literature is based upon the latter view, and we identify three current themes that are consistent with this perspective: partnership, employee engagement and diversity management. We begin with an overview of the employment relationship and the nature of the contract of employment between the employer and employee.

INTRODUCTION

THE NATURE OF THE EMPLOYMENT RELATIONSHIP

The employment relationship is concerned with the features of the relationship between an employer and an employee, and the ways in which it can be managed. Thus an understanding of employment relations is important for those who are responsible for the effective management of people at work.

In essence, employment relations is concerned with the 'wage–work bargain', ie, what work an employee will do in return for the wages paid by the employer. The term 'wages' refers not just to the pay received, but also to other terms of employment such as holiday entitlement and sick pay. It may also refer to other rewards that the employer may provide, such as subsidised private health insurance and free childcare places. Similarly, 'work' has a wider meaning than the employee's job. Employers have expectations about both the quantity and quality of the work. Some explicitly define specific behavioural characteristics of tasks, particularly in what are called 'customer-facing' jobs. At the fast-food outlet McDonald's employees are expected to acknowledge customers, create a friendly atmosphere, be courteous and have high standards of personal appearance (HRMID 2007). An expectation for the exercise of this type of work has been referred to as 'emotional labour' (Gilmore, in Gilmore and Williams 2012).

THE CONTRACT OF EMPLOYMENT

A useful starting point for our understanding of the terms of the wage–work bargain is through the concept of the contract of employment. Each individual has a contract of employment with his or her employer, and the contract specifies the terms and conditions under which the employee works. However, the nature of the contract of employment is often misunderstood. Very few employees in the UK have a written contract which contains all their terms and conditions of employment in one document: most of us have a contract whose terms can be found in a number of sources. Figure 11.1 depicts some of the main sources of the contract of employment.

When employees refer to their 'written contract of employment' what they often mean is a formal written statement of the main terms of employment. This document is not the contract, as shown in a case heard by the Employment Appeal Tribunal (EAT). In its judgment, the EAT concluded that 'this statement did not constitute a written contract between the parties. It was merely a document that stated the employer's views of the terms' (Sargeant and Lewis 2008, p75).

Figure 11.1 Some possible sources of the contract of employment

Selection interview

Common law terms

Letter of offer of
employment

Job description

Custom and practice

**The contract of
employment**

Employee handbook

Workplace notices

Statutory employment
rights

Written statement of
employment terms

Collective
agreement(s)

The written statement is important, nonetheless, since the Employment Relations Act 1996 requires it to specify the most important terms of employment, including pay, hours of work, holidays and sick pay.

The Act also allows employers to refer employees to other documents that contain these terms, or which provide more details. Thus, the other possible sources shown in Figure 11.1 may need to be examined if we are to have a clearer picture of the terms of the contract.

REFLECTIVE ACTIVITY 11.1

Sources of the contract of employment

Obtain copies of as many of the documents shown in Figure 11.1 as you can, but especially offer letters, written statements and employee handbooks.

Read through these and try to identify examples of statements that refer to

employees' duties or responsibilities, ie what is expected of the employee. Also, identify examples of the pay and other benefits that an employee is entitled to under the contract of employment.

It is common, especially in larger organisations, for the HR department to produce an employee or staff handbook. This often contains details of employees' rights and duties. For example, it might explain what an employee is to do if they are unable to work through illness and what pay they will receive while sick. Similarly, employees who have a work roster may find that their actual times of work are provided by a notice.

Where an organisation uses job descriptions, these include the main duties and responsibilities of an employee: thus they seek to clarify the 'work' element of the wage–work bargain. At the selection interview, there may be discussion about the terms of employment. These may cover both the work expected of an employee and the pay they will receive. For example, a candidate might ask about opportunities for overtime work and be told by the line manager how that is arranged. Although such spoken promises can become terms of the contract, the problem is that it may not be easy to be sure what was said. The avoidance of doubt over the terms of the contract is one of the reasons why legislation requires employers to provide the written statement. Similarly, the need to formalise what is agreed with an employee accounts for HR departments providing letters of employment offers and specifying details in employee handbooks.

However, some terms may still not be written down. Custom and practice refers to possible employment terms that arise because they have operated for some while. For example, an office may have a custom that all workers finish at lunchtime on Christmas Eve, but this has never been written down in any formal documentation. Suppose, then, a manager tells her staff that they will need to work till 17.30, their normal finishing time. Is this lawful? If an employee challenges this decision in a court, it may be decided that the custom is part of the terms of employment.

REFLECTIVE ACTIVITY 11.2

Custom and practice

In the example of custom and practice given in the text about finishing work early on Christmas Eve, what factors do you think the courts might take into account to decide if it was reasonable for the employees to finish at lunchtime?

Other terms may be implied by judges to exist in a contract of employment. These are sometimes referred to as the 'common law terms'. For example, all employees have a duty to use reasonable skill and care in their work. It will be for the courts to decide what is reasonable, but, as we have seen above, job descriptions might be used to specify the standard of work expected of an employee. Another duty of employees is to give faithful and honest service and not commit misconduct. Many organisations will produce a list of disciplinary rules which seek to clarify what this common law term means for employees in reality; these are often included in the employee handbook. The need to set standards of expected behaviour is both good practice and, as we see below, important in unfair dismissal claims. The key point to note, however, is that even if these are not specified in any document, the duties still exist as part of the employee's contract of employment.

Statutory employment rights refer to those that are provided through legislation, emanating from both national and supra-national – eg European Union (EU) – levels. Their purpose is to provide a minimum 'floor of rights' for all employees, and employers cannot offer terms that are worse than those provided by legislation. Some of these relate to specific parts of the wage–work bargain; for example, the UK national minimum wage and the EU Working Time Directive, which was implemented in the UK through the Working Time Regulations. The latter specifies maximum hours of work. Other statutory employment rights are concerned with the way in which employees are managed. These include maternity rights, the right not to be unfairly dismissed (see below), and thus how disciplinary action should be implemented by a manager, and legislation that seeks to prohibit unlawful discrimination on certain grounds, such as race, sex, religion and belief. We explore discrimination in more detail later in the chapter, and also deal with the issue in Chapters 4 and 9.

EMPLOYMENT RIGHTS

For many managers the growth of employment rights has become an accepted part of organisational life. However, there are critics who believe employment regulation is having a damaging impact on UK business's competitive position. This view is illustrated by a recent report undertaken for the Department of Business, Innovation and Skills. The report covers many areas where it suggests that 'employment law and regulation impedes the search for efficiency and competitiveness. It deters small businesses in particular from wanting to take on more employees: as a result they grow more slowly than they otherwise might' (Beecroft 2011, p2). The thrust of the recommendations is seen in two areas: unfair dismissal and exemptions for small businesses. Beecroft argues that if it is not politically acceptable to completely repeal the provisions on unfair dismissal then the legislation should be amended to create compensated no-fault dismissals where an employer could dismiss an employee without giving any reason whilst paying compensation in line with redundancy payments. He also suggests that small businesses employing fewer than 10 employees should be allowed to opt out of a range of regulations, including unfair dismissal, pension auto-enrolment, flexible working requests and flexible parental leave.

The final source of employment terms, shown in Figure 11.2 below, is collective agreements. These can be found in organisations that recognise a trade union or unions, and where terms of employment such as pay and holidays are negotiated between the union and the employer. The outcomes of the negotiations are called collective agreements since they cover the collective group of workers represented by the trade union. A collective agreement normally covers all the employees in a particular occupation or grade, whether or not they are union members. Where unions are recognised, the employer has a relationship with both individual employees and the trade union.

Figure 11.2 The relationship between the contract of employment and collective agreements

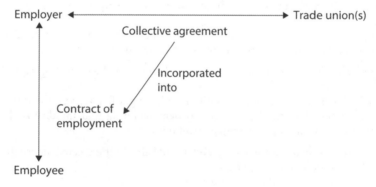

Collective agreements are not normally legally enforceable between the employer and trade union. However, the substantive terms of these agreements – for example, pay and hours – are incorporated into individual contracts of employment. Where an employer has collective agreements with a trade union, these agreements can be an important source of an employee's contractual terms.

THE WAGE–WORK BARGAIN REVISITED

The effective management of the employment relationship requires managers to understand the nature of the contract of employment. In particular, it is important to recognise that the terms of the contract may be found in a number of different sources. However, Williams and Adam-Smith (2010) point out that there are two major problems with viewing the employment relationship simply as a contractual one. First, a contract implies that the two parties come together in a free and equal way. However, those seeking work are clearly in a weaker position than the employer, who has the freedom to offer the job to a number of applicants (see also Chapter 9). Furthermore, once an employee has taken a job, he or she is then required to obey the employer's commands or orders. The second problem with a simple contractual view of the relationship is that it is not possible to specify, at the outset of the relationship, all the obligations of the parties. The contract is thus open-ended, and the relative power of the parties will be important in deciding how the relationship is shaped. Thus, it is also important to recognise that the employment relationship has a power dimension, and that there is potential for differences, or conflict, to emerge in the relationship. Of course, the relationship is also characterised by co-operation between the employer and employees. The latter have an interest in the success of their employer, which will help secure their jobs.

TERMINATION OF THE CONTRACT OF EMPLOYMENT

If an employer terminates the contract of employment, employment legislation allows the employee to claim at an employment tribunal that the dismissal was unfair. Tribunals decide whether the dismissal was fair and reasonable in the circumstances. If the tribunal determines that the dismissal was unfair it can require the employer to reinstate or re-engage the employee, or make an award of financial compensation. In most cases employees will need two years' continuous service before they can make a claim.

The Employment Relations Act (1996) specifies five fair reasons for dismissal:

- misconduct, for example, where an employee breaks company disciplinary rules
- lack of capability, which is concerned with the employee's work performance and is explored in detail in Chapter 12
- redundancy
- statutory bar to employment; for example, where a company driver is disqualified from driving
- some other substantial reason, which might include an employee's refusal to accept changes to their contractual terms in times of business difficulty.

The first two reasons are those that are most closely concerned with managing and leading people.

The employer must show that, in addition to having a fair reason, the dismissal was handled reasonably. This can be achieved by demonstrating that the dismissal followed the principles of natural justice. In employment this means:

- the employee was made aware of the standards of behaviour expected, hence the need to explain these at the start of employment
- the employee was informed of the allegation or complaint
- an investigation was undertaken to establish the facts of the case
- the employee was given an opportunity to explain their view of the case
- the employee was offered the opportunity to be accompanied by a fellow employee or trade union representative
- the penalty was proportionate to the offence
- the employee had the right of appeal to a more senior manager.

In order to effectively manage problems with employee behaviour and demonstrate that they have incorporated the principles of natural justice into their employment practice, organisations draft disciplinary rules and procedures, often including them in employee handbooks.

THE ROLE OF PROCEDURES

The purpose of employment procedures is to create a problem-solving pathway. They allow managers to consider an employee complaint or, in the case of disciplinary action, provide managers with the opportunity to change or correct an employee's behaviour. Formal procedures allow appropriate action to be taken to solve a problem, rather than employees feeling they must express their disagreement with management through other means; for example, by being absent from work or performing below their capability. Procedures seek to ensure that managers deal with employment issues in a fair and consistent way, and allow managers to seek to control or contain conflict in the employment relationship. Grievance and disciplinary procedures are the two most common procedures found in organisations. However, there may be separate procedures covering specific employment matters: capability, to distinguish these issues from those related to conduct; harassment and bullying; equal opportunities; pay grading if a job evaluation scheme is used; and appeals against performance appraisal ratings, especially if this is linked to pay.

The unfair dismissal provisions of employment law have emphasised the importance of formalising disciplinary rules and procedures. The Advisory, Conciliation and Arbitration Service (Acas) has produced a Code of Practice (Acas 2009a) which is taken into account by tribunals hearing unfair dismissal claims. If the tribunal decides that the provisions of the code have not been followed by either the employee or employer, they can adjust any financial awards by up to 25 per cent. Although not having the same status as the code, Acas has also published a guide to handling grievances and disciplinary matters (Acas 2009b). Both publications provide valuable advice to HR managers.

TRADE UNIONS AND COLLECTIVE BARGAINING

The death of ex-UK Prime Minister Baroness Thatcher in 2013 prompted much reflection on her governments' policies on employment relations, some of which were continued by subsequent administrations. Taken together with broader economic and social changes, they have had a significant impact. One interesting example is union membership figures, which have declined significantly in the UK since a peak of some 13 million in 1980. At that time over half of all employees were members of a trade union, and collective agreements set the terms and conditions of about three-quarters of the UK workforce. Overall, some 7 million workers are now union members, which accounts for around 27 per cent of the workforce (Barratt 2009). These figures represent a significant change. Union membership remains particularly strong in the public sector, however, where about two-thirds of employees are members. In the private sector membership is under 20 per cent and mainly confined to larger employers.

As we saw above, collective agreements arrived at through negotiation between trade unions and employers can be a major source of an employee's contractual terms. Collective bargaining refers to the process whereby employers and unions jointly agree the terms and conditions of employees. For the employer, collective bargaining can be an efficient means of determining contractual terms since it does not require negotiation with each individual employee, and can assist in containing the conflict that may arise over employment terms. In addition, since the union has made the agreement, it has an interest in ensuring its members (the employees of the organisation) accept the terms that are agreed. Collective bargaining, then, is a key function of trade unions, and is a process that can provide greater equality of power in the employment relationship.

Collective bargaining is concerned with both parts of the wage–work bargain. It determines important parts of the wage the employee receives. As well as pay, hours and holidays it may cover matters such as overtime and shift premiums, sick pay, redundancy payments, pensions and health insurance (Kersley *et al* 2006). These terms are the economic aspects of the contract, or wages. However, collective bargaining can also determine work issues. For example, as well as redundancy pay, a collective agreement may specify how staff would be selected for redundancy, should that situation arise. In addition, it is not uncommon for there to be collective agreements covering staffing plans, equal opportunities and performance appraisal schemes. Thus, collective bargaining has a managerial aspect, which means that these matters are determined by joint agreement, not by managers alone. This provides an example of how gaps in the open-ended contract may be filled.

As well as collectively bargaining with employers on behalf of employees, trade unions have other functions. They may provide specific services to their members as individuals; for example, legal and financial advice for both work and personal matters. Trade unions in the UK seek to represent their members outside the workplace in wider social matters. This might include lobbying for improved employment legislation such as the introduction of the national minimum wage, and campaigning to improve the employment conditions of migrant workers. One further role of trade unions, important to those managing employment relations, and following the principles of natural justice noted above, trade union officials typically represent their members in formal grievance, disciplinary and similar matters.

REFLECTIVE ACTIVITY 11.3

Find out more information on the role of trade unions. The easiest way to do this is to visit the unions' websites (see www.tuc.org.uk). If your employer recognises a union or unions, this would be a good starting point; if not, perhaps visit the web pages of a union you have recently heard about in the news. For each union, identify how it describes its role and seeks to achieve its objectives, the types of workers it recruits and how many members it has.

CONFLICT AND THE EMPLOYMENT RELATIONSHIP

We have noted the potential for conflict to arise in the employment relationship, so how do managers view the reasons for its existence? Before exploring the answer to this question, undertake Reflective Activity 11.4.

REFLECTIVE ACTIVITY 11.4

Conflict at work

For this activity, you are asked to reflect on each of the four following statements on conflict between employers and employees. For each, identify the values or beliefs of those people who hold this view. Which of these views most closely reflects your own view? Why?

Conflict between an employer and employee is:

- a dysfunctional factor in an otherwise healthy organisation
- largely preventable, provided organisations take a proactive approach to developing policies and practices which take account of employees' needs and expectations from work
- an inherent feature of organisational life, but one that can be largely institutionalised and managed through recognising that differences of interests exist between the two parties

- a reflection of the fundamental divisions and inequalities in the wider society.

Each of the four views in Reflective Activity 11.4 reflects different explanations of the causes of conflict between employers and employees and how they are to be managed. These views are based on 'frames of reference': a term first attributed to Fox (1966, 1974) to distinguish between the beliefs held by managers that influence their approach to the management of employees.

Those who believe that conflict is dysfunctional are characterised as holding a unitary view. Often using the team or family analogy, those with a unitary perspective expect co-operation from their staff since the goals of the organisation and employees are the same: employees must understand and accept their role, and also accept that the leaders of the organisation are best placed to make the important decisions. With its emphasis on co-operation, the unitary view would see conflict as a result of poor communications or, significantly, as the result of troublemakers, like trade union activists, who generate conflict in an otherwise harmonious organisation.

As HRM theory and practice has developed, some authors have coined the term 'neo-unitary' to capture the beliefs that underpin this approach to managing the employment relationship (Farnham and Pimlott 1995). This perspective has much in common with the traditional unitary view in that co-operation and harmony between employers and employees is believed to be the normal state of affairs. However, as the statement in Reflective Activity 11.4 suggests, conflict can be prevented, but only if managers are proactive in developing policies and practices that take account of the needs and expectations of employees. Managers will thus need to utilise the knowledge provided by the Human Relations school of thinking to engender employees' commitment to their work and the organisation's objectives (Edwards 2003).

Those who believe that conflict in the employment relationship is inevitable are said to hold a pluralist perspective. While not disputing that there is scope for co-operation between managers and employees, pluralists point to the differences in interests between employers and employees. For example, employers will naturally wish to minimise wage costs while employees will, equally naturally, wish to maximise their pay. The key concern of pluralists in the employment relationship is to find ways to manage the conflict so that disruption – for example, in the form of strikes – is limited. For those with a pluralist perspective, trade unions are not the cause of conflict. Rather they have a legitimate role in representing one interest group, employees, in the relationship. The task for managers is to build a relationship with trade unions, and develop procedures so that disputes and differences can be resolved through the process of negotiation.

Those holding a Marxist view of conflict see this as the result of workers being exploited in the employment relationship. The development of procedures with trade unions to prevent and resolve expressions of conflict is, at best, only a temporary solution. Conflict, it is argued, will be eliminated only when the distinction between the owners of capital and workers is removed.

MANAGEMENT STYLE AND EMPLOYMENT RELATIONS

The distinction between unitary and pluralist perspectives provides a basis for understanding different management styles. According to Purcell and Ahlstrand (1994, p177), '[management] style implies the existence of a distinctive set of guiding principles, written or otherwise, which set parameters to and signposts for management action regarding the way employees are to be treated...' 'Style', then, describes the choice that is made as to how the employment relationship is to be managed. These authors identify two dimensions of management style: individualism and collectivism.

INDIVIDUALISM

Two broad extremes of individualism can be identified, based on the extent to which managers view employees as individuals with needs and aspirations. Those that are described as having 'high individualism' or an 'investment orientation' towards staff would typically emphasise the following policies and practices:

- employees seen as an important resource
- a focus on internal labour markets
- employee development, appraisal and individual systems of reward
- empowerment.

This management style is based on a neo-unitary view where conflict and differences can be prevented, and – as we will see later – is aimed at generating employee engagement.

In contrast, managers who have a low concern with individual employees, a traditional unitary view, would adopt a 'cost minimisation' approach with the following characteristics:

- labour as a commodity to be bought from, and returned to, the external labour market as economic activity dictates
- an emphasis on numerical flexibility
- limited, if any, training
- tight control over pay.

COLLECTIVISM

Purcell and Ahlstrand (1994) also draw a similar distinction on the collective dimension of management style which seeks to capture the extent to which managers accept that employees have a right to act collectively – for example, by joining a trade union – and are willing to negotiate and consult with employee representatives. At one extreme, typical of the traditional unitary approach, is resistance and hostility towards trade unions. At the other end of the spectrum the relationship sought by management is highly co-operative with the union, and would include: regular consultation with union representatives on strategic plans; extensive information exchange; and the use of joint working parties to manage employment matters. The contemporary term for this approach is 'partnership', and we examine this later in the chapter. Between these extremes lies what Purcell and Ahlstrand (1994) refer to as 'adversarial relations'.

Adversarial relationships may exist in organisations where unions have been recognised by the employer for many years, but where managers would prefer not to have to negotiate with them. The primary concern of managers in these firms will be to protect their right to make decisions without the involvement of unions, sometimes called the 'managerial prerogative' (Storey 1983). Control and stability of the employment relationship, through formally agreed procedures, are important characteristics in such businesses, and the issues on which unions can negotiate are usually carefully and tightly drawn.

PARTNERSHIP AGREEMENTS

We have already noted the importance of collective agreements as a source of employment terms, and that these can be arrived at through either adversarial or co-operative relationships between the employer and trade unions. In recent years there has been increased attention given to partnership agreements between employers and unions, which appear to be the result of a more co-operative approach between the two parties. As Williams and Adam-Smith (2010, p236) note: 'at the heart of partnership working is the notion that it benefits the employer, the recognised union, and the workforce at large too.' However, while pointing out that the concept is 'rather ambiguous', they suggest that studies of such agreements identify some common elements:

- a shared commitment between the employer and trade union to the success of the organisation
- the development of new forms of communication and consultation arrangements
- some form of employer guarantee on job or employment security
- union acceptance of the need for its members to work flexibly.

REFLECTIVE ACTIVITY 11.5

Partnership agreements

List what you believe to be the benefits of partnership agreements to: the employer; the trade union; and the employees of the organisation.

Each of the elements of partnership agreements justifies a little more explanation. The first can be little more than empty rhetoric. However, if it genuinely reflects a greater level of trust between the parties, it may lead to improved employment relations. The development of communication and consultation processes can take different forms. Such processes may, for example, provide for trade unions to be more closely involved in the decision-making processes of the organisations, at least to the extent that union representatives are consulted on those matters that may have an impact on employees. Also, they may provide for representatives of all employees, not just those that are union members, to be informed and involved in business decisions.

The final two elements seek to meet the key needs of the employer and employees. Employees may be reluctant to be more flexible in their working arrangements if they believe that this could put jobs at risk. Thus flexibility comes if the employer is willing to agree to some level of employment security. This need not necessarily be a commitment that employees will keep those specific jobs as a result of organisational change, but that alternative jobs will be available. These two components, then, combine to establish a degree of mutuality in the partnership agreement since each meets the respective key need of the employer and the employee.

As businesses struggle in the difficult economic climate, we have a good opportunity to see how well partnership agreements work in practice. Do they allow the business to survive when faced with poor trading conditions, and provide employees with higher levels of job security than would have been the case without it? Alternatively, are the espoused benefits of partnership working only enjoyed when economic conditions are favourable for organisations? This suggests that the central plank of partnership is the trust needed between the parties in the employment relationship. Without this, partnership is unlikely to succeed.

CASE STUDY 11.1

REGIONAL PAY IN THE PUBLIC SECTOR

As part of its drive to reduce public spending, the coalition government has sought ways to reduce the wage bill in the public sector. It has, for example, made changes to pension entitlements and sought to ensure that annual pay rises are minimised. In a further development, it has raised the possibility of regional pay for parts of the public sector. With few exceptions, most notably an allowance for working in London, employees in local government, the NHS, education and the civil service receive the same rate of pay for their occupation, irrespective of where they are geographically located.

In its submission to the Pay Review Body which sets pay for NHS staff, the Department of Health (DoH) has proposed that there should be a basic rate of pay, set at the minimum level necessary and additional supplements paid in specific geographical areas: what the department calls 'market-facing pay'. This would mean that, for example, nurses, midwives, hospital porters and paramedics working in the North or the Midlands would be paid less than if they worked in the South of England. The DoH argues that this would reflect pay rates in the private sector which vary geographically in line with local labour markets. For example, it is suggested that average earnings in the North-east are 10 per cent lower than the UK average. It claims that this change will lead to more efficient and effective use of NHS funds. The only exception to this proposal would be for highly paid managers in the bodies responsible for delivering the NHS reform programme.

A similar idea has been mooted for some 400,000 civil servants, with a proposition for four geographical pay zones. Here, those working in London would be paid most, employees working in the Bristol to Thames estuary corridor and those in pay 'hotspots' such as Manchester and Birmingham would follow. Those in the South-west, much of the Midlands and North-east would be paid least.

Unions representing the groups of workers who would be affected by these changes have raised a number of arguments against these proposals. They claim that: driving down wages in the provinces would deepen the north–south economic divide and depress economic growth in deprived areas; regional pay could destabilise payment systems; the proposal fails to recognise that delivering public services in deprived areas is often harder work; it would involve expensive bureaucratic controls; the existing scheme can accommodate specific problems like pay 'hotspots'; it could lead to skills shortages in 'low-cost' areas; and that many private sector firms have abandoned regional pay as it was divisive and unworkable. They argue, also, that the proposals are simply about reducing the wages of public sector workers, many of whom are in poorly paid occupations and who had no involvement in creating the financial problems facing the country. In the case of NHS market-facing pay, they point out that the salaries of those senior managers responsible for implementing these changes will not be included in these arrangements.

Questions

1   Are regional pay rates fair for those working in the public sector? Why?

2   Prepare a case that you could present to the trade unions in support of regional pay rates for public sector employees. How would you seek to overcome

their objections outlined in the case study?

3 Assume you are an HR manager working in one of the geographical areas that will have lower pay rates than the rest of the country. Draft a

report which identifies its possible impact on recruitment and retention of staff. What steps could be taken to minimise the impact?

EMPLOYEE ENGAGEMENT

As we pointed out at the start of this chapter, the management of employment relations implicitly includes three current themes. We have referred to the first of these, namely partnership, in the preceding sections. We go on to look at the third of these – diversity management – in greater detail later in this chapter. We now turn to our second theme of employee engagement.

The management of the employment relationship characterised by an 'investment orientation' towards employees is designed to elicit their commitment to the organisation. Where managers are able to achieve an engaged workforce it is claimed that this can lead to both organisational success and employee well-being (MacLeod and Clark 2009). A recent CIPD-commissioned research report (Alfes *et al* 2010, p5) identified engagement as having three dimensions:

- intellectual engagement – thinking about the job and how it might be done better
- affective engagement – positive feelings about doing a job well
- social engagement – actively seeking opportunities to discuss work-related issues.

Where organisations are able to effectively engage their employees on these dimensions, the authors claim that three important outcomes can be identified which can assist organisations in the achievement of their objectives. First, engaged employees are likely to perform better than those who are not. Respondents in the survey claimed to have good levels of job and social skills, were willing to take on extra work and tended to have high ratings in their performance appraisal. Secondly, engaged employees are more likely to be innovative at work. This might include searching out new methods of working, generate enthusiasm for innovative ideas and transform such ideas into meaningful applications. Thirdly, engaged employees are more likely to want to stay with their employer.

How then can organisations generate employee engagement? Holbeche and Matthews (2012) suggest four drivers of engagement:

- Connection. Employees need a sense of identification with, and pride in working for, the employing organisation; there has to be a common purpose and shared values.
- Voice. Managers need to keep employees informed of the organisation's progress and of organisational change, and listen to employees' views so that they feel involved in the business.
- Support. Employees need to be treated as individuals and enabled to do their job; they should feel they are valued and receive a 'fair deal' from their employer, and believe their employer is concerned with their well-being.
- Scope. Work should be purposeful and provide employees with the opportunity for growth and accomplishment; it should allow for autonomy and be underpinned by mutual trust.

Alfes *et al* (2010) came to similar conclusions and highlighted the importance of meaningful work and employee 'voice' to creating an engaged workforce (see also Chapters 8 and 12). Management style is instrumental in fostering employee engagement.

Through communication, managers can help employees place their own work in the context of the organisation's objectives. Similarly, establishing and maintaining effective communication and consultation channels can both reinforce employees' view of the value of their work and enhance social engagement. It is perhaps no surprise, then, that they emphasise the importance of line management style in creating employee engagement. Line managers, it is suggested, are the crucial link between the employer and employees, and their behaviour is central to levels of engagement. Their key tasks in this respect are selecting the correct people for the job, regular communication with their staff, relevant training and development, and ensuring reciprocity of effort and reward.

DIVERSITY AT WORK

INDIVIDUAL DIFFERENCES AND MANAGEMENT STYLES

Management style also affects the way in which managers handle the individual characteristics of employees. We would expect those who have an 'investment orientation' towards employees to take account of individual differences to the benefit of the organisation. Such an approach is analogous with the management of diversity. Before examining the meaning of diversity, we briefly consider the legal provisions on discrimination.

We noted earlier that statutory employment rights are an important source of an employee's terms, and that specific legislation makes for unfair discrimination if it is based on the grounds of sex, race, age, religion and belief, sexual orientation or disability. As we have seen in Chapters 4 and 7, managers regularly discriminate between employees, for example in choosing between job applicants. The legislation prohibits discrimination which has no connection with the work to be done, and distinguishes between direct and indirect discrimination. An example of direct discrimination would be a job advertisement that states that only women can apply for the post. Indirect discrimination arises when a requirement or condition that cannot be justified is applied to a situation where members of one or more of the protected groups cannot comply. An example from the authors' own experience involved a hospitality company that required bar staff to have GCSEs in English language and mathematics. Many of its existing staff, already performing the job competently, did not have this qualification, so it was not a necessary requirement. It was judged unlawful since anyone educated outside England or Wales would not have taken these examinations.

EQUAL OPPORTUNITIES

The concept of equal opportunities underpins many organisational approaches to equality in the UK. These have been developed in response to the legislation introduced by successive UK governments since the mid-1970s to address unfair discrimination in the pursuit, obtaining and retaining of employment, as well as other workplace practices. The result is a legal framework developed around a definition of inequality that draws heavily on the idea of indirect discrimination: 'discriminating against people on grounds that are irrelevant to the jobs they doing or for which they are applying' (Chryssides and Kayle 1996, p89). To reduce disparate treatment by managers, the HR profession has focused on establishing specific procedures to ensure legal compliance and demonstrate equal treatment (Harris 2005). Thus the 'neutral treatment' principle of much anti-discrimination legislation has become the cornerstone of organisational policies and procedures which are designed to achieve sameness of treatment in resourcing decisions (Foster and Harris 2005, p6).

An equal opportunities approach is seen as one of compliance with the law. It typically focuses attention on groups that may be unlawfully discriminated against, and features such initiatives as target-setting, positive action and redressing past discrimination. Its attraction for line managers is that it offers a certain simplicity and ease of application by reducing the scope for exercising discretion and providing the essential means of defending their decisions against claims of less favourable treatment (Wilson and Iles 1999). Its limitation is that it has led HR specialists and operational managers alike to focus on consistency of process or procedural justice, even though consistency is a relative principle, whose pursuit alone will not act as a catalyst for progressive employment practice (Foster and Harris 2005). Relying on a principle of consistency is problematic as it does not require individuals to be treated well – only alike – and allows for situations where all employees are treated equally, but equally badly (Fredman 2001).

In order to meet its EU membership requirements, the UK has expanded its equality legislation to take account of a growing number of specific groups in the workforce. The EU continues to be highly influential in this respect since managing diversity is a key component of the 2009 Lisbon Treaty. In the UK we now have a single Equality Bill, which became law in 2010. This introduced rights that relate to personal circumstances rather than to personal characteristics; for example, parental leave rights. The resultant increased legal complexity has meant that managers need to be aware not only of individual rights, but, as we saw with an 'investment orientation' to employees, a concern with individual needs at work – in other words, a managing diversity approach. Managing diversity in this context is framed as a strategic response arising from demographic change, and is differentiated from equal opportunities on the basis that organisations should focus on the individual rather than the potentially disadvantaged group to which the employee belongs. Thus diversity encompasses a whole range of differences beyond those associated with disadvantage or covered by anti-discrimination legislation (Tomlinson and Schwabenland 2010).

REFLECTIVE ACTIVITY 11.6

Equality and diversity in practice (1)

Research the equality and diversity statements on the websites of the TUC (www.tuc.org.uk), and one or two of the largest trade unions such as Unite (www.unitetheunion.com) or Unison

(www.unison.org.uk). What evidence can you find about their view on equal opportunities? Read the next section on 'the nature of diversity' and research the websites to see if there is any indication of a diversity focus.

THE NATURE OF DIVERSITY

Equal opportunities (EO) initiatives in the UK are aimed at developing a level playing field for disadvantaged groups, but it is claimed that they have failed to achieve the goal of greater organisational inclusion of minorities for two reasons. First, they do not cover adequately all disadvantaged groups, and those that they do (such as women and non-white employees) are treated as homogeneous, often stereotyped, groups. Second, EO fails to generate the involvement and commitment of managers who perceive it simply as a compliance issue (Ahmed 2007). Managing diversity is claimed to overcome these limitations, and to provide a powerful set of arguments with which to mobilise management interest in the needs of members of minority groups (Kandola and Fullerton 1998). At the same time, writers such as Belbin (1991) found that culturally diverse teams were more effective than homogeneous ones, thus providing the basis of a business case for diversity. French (2010) summarises research showing that the performance of multicultural groups at work was typically either much better than that of mono-cultural groups, or significantly worse, highlighting the importance of careful management of such groups, if they are to be effective.

Unlike EO initiatives, a diversity approach recognises that everyone is different even though some may share certain characteristics such as ethnic origin or gender. Diversity therefore consists of visible factors – eg race, age – but also non-visible personal characteristics including background, culture, personality and preferred work style. The diversity argument is founded on the premise that 'harnessing these differences will create a productive environment in which everybody feels valued, where their talents are being fully utilised and in which organisational goals are met' (Kandola and Fullerton 1998, p40). The CIPD defines diversity as 'valuing everyone as an individual – valuing people as employees, customers and clients' (CIPD 2010c, p2). In principle, diversity management encourages the development of more innovative HR policies and practices which offer greater reciprocity in the employment relationship by addressing individual needs. This HR approach appears more relevant to the flexible behaviour required of employees in the less predictable work roles that are a feature of contemporary working life (Foster and Harris 2005). The problem for today's managers then is that there is no single best way of treating employees, because each one will have their own personal needs, values and beliefs.

ORGANISATIONAL BENEFITS OF DIVERSITY

Three main reasons are typically used to justify an organisational approach for making equality and diversity an important management issue:

- the business case
- the impact of the demographic time bomb
- the social justice argument.

The business case for diversity

According to the CIPD (2010c), there are three business reasons for organisations exceeding legal requirements on discrimination, outlined below.

1   *People issues.* Creating an open and inclusive workplace culture in which everyone feels valued helps to recruit and retain good people. People aspire to work for employers with sound employment practices and to feel valued at work. To be competitive, organisations need to derive the best contributions from everyone. Skills shortages and difficulties in filling vacancies are forcing organisations to recruit from more diverse pools and to offer different working arrangements in the 'war for talent'. Managing diversity creates a recruitment pool that improves the chances of getting the right person for the right job. Diversity also creates engaged employees working in a climate of productivity and commitment, with low turnover and sickness absence rates. In turn, creativity and innovation are increased.

2   *Product market competitiveness.* A diverse workforce can help to inform the development of new or enhanced products or services, open up new market opportunities, improve market share and broaden an organisation's customer base.

3   *Corporate reputation.* Healthy businesses flourish in healthy societies and the needs of people, communities and businesses are interrelated. Social exclusion and low economic activity rates limit business markets and their growth. Thus businesses need to consider corporate social responsibility (CSR) in the context of diversity. The overall image of an organisation can be important in attracting and retaining both customers and employees.

Arguably, the business and social justice cases for diversity are complementary, because unless people are treated fairly at work they will feel less committed and may under-perform. Despite many criticisms of the business case, researchers claim that it and social justice arguments can co-exist to produce a case for diversity that is capable of achieving greater social equality. In some organisations – for example, in the voluntary sector – the business case and social justice is largely the same thing (Tomlinson and Schwabenland 2010).

Studies have found that not all HR diversity practices are associated with increased workforce diversity and that attitudes to diversity in large corporations have been, at best, mixed. For example, managers in some organisations have tended to see its value in recruitment and selection, but have not applied it to other working practices. There is also a wide recognition of the supposed value of workforce diversity, but mixed evidence on its impact on business performance. The CIPD (2005b) claims that there is evidence that indicates improved financial performance in organisations which take diversity seriously. However, others argue that there is limited empirical data to prove an association between the outcome of HR diversity practices and improved organisational performance (Shen *et al* 2009). Despite the apparent attractiveness of the business case it appears that organisations still see legislation as the main driver for making changes in practice, and view diversity management as a cost rather than a driver of organisational success. If that is the case, it suggests that arguments for the business case need to be communicated more effectively and its profile raised as a strategic business lever (CIPD 2007c).

 REFLECTIVE ACTIVITY 11.7

Equality and diversity in practice (2)

Research on the Internet the equality and diversity statements of your employer and one or two other employers. What indication do they give as to whether their approach is focused more on equal opportunities or diversity? Identify some examples of the business case for diversity for your chosen organisations.

Demographic changes

The UK workforce is ageing; the proportion of the working population aged between 50 and 64 is at its highest level since the 1970s. This trend is continuing, with predictions that by 2033, 23 per cent of the population will be aged 65 and over with only 16 per cent aged 16 or younger. In addition, there is a sharp tapering of people in the workforce between 30 and 40 years old due to low birth rates in the 1970s, and there are fewer white able-bodied men under 45 years of age (ONS 2010). Put simply, changing demographics mean that if there are fewer white males available for employment, employers need to consider broadening their search for employees. In the view of the then Department of Trade and Industry: '21st century organisations require a flexible, highly skilled workforce, adaptable to change and able to compete in the global marketplace. Employers need to be fishing in the widest possible talent pool to ensure they have access to the breadth and depth of skills available, which meet their business needs' (DTI 2001, p3). The demographic time bomb created by falling birth rates and longer lifespans means that fewer younger people will be employed to provide the taxes to support an ageing population. Even though changes in retirement ages may enable people to have the right to work longer, the statistics predict that proportionately fewer people will be in paid employment.

MANAGING DIVERSITY – HOW TO MOVE EQUALITY FORWARD

One of the main criticisms of managing diversity is that it requires significant resources with no guarantee of success. There is no instant formula for its achievement because it is a complex task and every organisation will approach it differently. The CIPD (2005b, 2007c, 2012j) suggests that, in common with other strategies for employee engagement, it needs to be led from the top of the organisation. Further, it requires systematic management action that moves from minimal legal compliance to a focus on the development of an open workplace culture in which everyone feels valued and can add value. The key is to make managing diversity a mainstream issue, owned by everyone, so that it influences all employment policies, practices and drivers.

The CIPD suggests the following tips for implementing a successful managing diversity strategy:

- ensure that initiatives and policies have the support of senior management
- remember managing diversity is a continuous process, not a one-off initiative
- develop a diversity strategy to support the achievement of business goals which addresses the diverse needs of customers
- focus on fairness and inclusion, ensuring that merit, competence and potential are the basis for people decisions
- review policies and update with changes in law
- address work–life balance needs to the benefit of the organisation and the employee by offering suitable choices and options
- encourage ownership, creating a culture of empowerment so that decisions are not passed up without good reason
- develop guidelines for managers to help them respond flexibly and appropriately to diversity needs
- link diversity management to other initiatives such as Investors in People and quality management
- be aware of the international context and the influence of national cultures on work.

REFLECTIVE ACTIVITY 11.8

How diverse is the UK workforce?

- Unemployment is twice as high among people from ethnic minorities, and there are proportionately more unemployed Chinese, Indian and Black African graduates than white graduates. Interestingly, however, only 12 per cent of white men are in professional occupations, as opposed to 21 per cent of Chinese and Indian men.
- White men have the lowest rate of participation in full-time education between the ages of 16 and 24 (37 per cent) followed by white women (40 per cent).
- 41 per cent of white women in employment work part-time, but only 7 per cent of white men do so, as opposed to 38 per cent of Bangladeshi men.

- Black and Asian people are 2.5 times less likely to have jobs than whites.
- Ethnic minorities account for 8 per cent of the overall population. Because they are relatively younger, it was projected that ethnic minorities would account for half the growth in working population to 2009.
- In the previous decade, the employment rate of the over-50s has risen by almost 25 per cent. The number of people aged over 60 is forecast to rise by 40 per cent in the next 30 years (CIPD 2010c).

Consider the above statistics about diversity and compare them with those in the organisation for which you work. How diverse is your organisation in comparison to these statistics? What initiatives are taken by your employer to encourage diversity; for example, part-time working and flexible hours? What initiatives could your employer consider in future to encourage a more diverse workforce?

The social justice argument has been examined in more detail in Chapter 4. It is essentially an ethically driven approach incorporating CSR. It is often associated with compliance measures directed at disadvantaged groups, target-setting and positive action (Gilmore and Williams 2012). As such, the social justice argument has frequently been linked with equal-opportunities measures targeting groups rather than the individually focused orientation of diversity management.

CASE STUDY 11.2

FORD: DRIVING DIVERSITY AND INCLUSION

'You are unique. That is important to us, and we value the abilities and perspectives all of our employees bring to their work. From the boardroom to the design studio, from the plant floors to the engineering centres, each employee is part of Ford's collective strength as a company. Ford has always taken steps to develop a workforce which reflects the communities in which we do business.

'Today we continue to attract a highly skilled and committed workforce that reflects the diversity within our society. Such variety only helps us better reflect and cater to the needs and requirements of our diverse customer base. Diversity is not only a reality of our workforce, it is a distinct advantage. Ford's comprehensive diversity strategy has helped to create an inclusive environment, which meets the diverse needs of its people and adds value to the business. Our inclusion policies are supported by strong management commitment, robust procedures and effective measurement tools.

'Ford believes in corporate social responsibility and is committed to diversity and inclusion in all aspects of our business, including suppliers,

contractors, and dealerships. All business partners are required to meet the standards outlined in our diversity and dignity at work policies.

'Throughout our history, inclusion has been as much a part of our success as our great products. By choice, Ford is committed to a diverse workplace not simply because it's good for business, but because it is the right thing to do.'

Source: Ford website: www.ford.co.uk/aboutford/fordcareers/whyjoinford/diversity&inclusion [accessed 30 may 2013]

Questions

1 Examine the practicalities of managing a diverse workforce in a traditional production environment like Ford.

2 How might you reconcile the needs of individuals such as workers with caring responsibilities (children or elderly parents) with the needs of a production-line environment?

3 How far should employers adapt workplace practices to accommodate individual needs?

CONCLUSION

The management of the employment relationship is a complex task. Managers have considerable choice in the way in which they structure the relationship, including the extent to which they view employees as a resource, and whether to deal with trade unions as representatives of employees. One key factor that may influence that choice is the market within which the business operates. Employers with tight product or service margins may decide that the costs of investing in employees cannot be afforded. Similarly, they may decide that trade unions will limit flexibility and add to labour costs. It is also important to note that although an investment orientation that includes recognition of individual differences is claimed to improve business performance, there is mixed evidence about the extent of this success.

KEY LEARNING POINTS

- Employment law places some constraints on how managers can treat their employees.
- Beliefs shape management style and influence whether employees are seen as a resource or a factor of production, and whether trade unions are perceived to be legitimate representatives or a source of conflict.
- To achieve a workforce that is trusting of management and committed to the success of the organisation requires managerial initiatives to develop an appropriate culture supported by relevant policies and practices.
- Three contemporary developments which reflect strategies to achieve the commitment of employees are partnership agreements with trade unions, employee engagement and diversity management.
- Discriminatory decisions taken at work need to be made on factors relevant to the work itself and not on personal characteristics such as age, sex, race, etc.
- An equal opportunities approach can be portrayed as one that seeks compliance with legislation, and typically focuses on identifying the groups who are more susceptible to unfair discrimination. It utilises procedures that are designed to meet legal requirements on equal treatment.
- The managing diversity approach focuses on the individual with the aim of creating a work environment where everyone feels valued, where their talents are fully utilised and where organisational goals are met.

REVIEW QUESTIONS

1   With regard to the following scenarios, identify what you consider to be the typical features present in respect of the management of the employment relationship:
    - where employees are seen as a resource that can provide competitive advantage
    - where trade unions are recognised for collective bargaining
    - where employees are viewed as a 'factor of production'.

    If possible, you should draw on your own work experience.

2   What action can an HR manager take to prevent conflict arising within an organisation? If it does arise, what options exist for its resolution?

3   A line manager has asked you to help her understand the importance of the contract of employment, and how far she can rely upon it to ensure she gets the best out of her staff. How would you reply?

4   Evaluate the evidence that managing diversity is good for business using examples from academic sources or from your experience. If you were an HR professional, what arguments could you make to your employer in support of the business case?

5   How might trade unions and other employee representative groups reconcile the needs of their collective body (equal treatment for all) with the needs of individuals (valuing individual needs)?

EXPLORE FURTHER

Gennard, J. and Judge, G. (2010) *Employment Relations*. 5th edition. London: CIPD. This is the CIPD text on the subject.

Gilmore, S. and Williams, S. (eds). (2009) *Human Resource Management*. Oxford: Oxford University Press, Chapters 10 and 11.

Kirton, G. and Greene, A. (2010) *The Dynamics of Managing Diversity: a critical approach*. 3rd edition, Butterworth-Heinemann Oxford.

Konrad, A., Prasad, P. and Pringle, J. (eds) (2006) *A Handbook of Workplace Diversity*. London: Sage.

Williams, S. and Adam-Smith, D. (2010) *Employment Relations: A critical introduction*. 2nd edition. Oxford: Oxford University Press. Takes a thematic approach to the subject area.

WEBSITES

Department for Business, Innovation and Skills (BIS): www.gov.uk/government/organisations/department-for-business-innovation-skills. BIS is the government department responsible for employment policy.

Trades Union Congress: www.tuc.org.uk. The TUC is the umbrella organisation for most of the trade unions in the UK.

Confederation of British Industries: www.cbi.org.uk. The CBI is the national representative body for UK employers.

Advisory, Conciliation and Arbitration Service: www.acas.org.uk. Acas provides a range of impartial advice and publications on employment relations. Its website includes both the code of practice and guide on discipline and grievances.

CIPD website: www.cipd.co.uk. This contains research and other documents on employment relations and managing diversity.

Commission for Equality and Human Rights: www.equalityhumanrights.com. The Commission has responsibility for monitoring the effect of equality legislation.

CHAPTER 12

Performance Management, Motivation and Reward

Alex Tymon and Gary Rees

LEARNING OUTCOMES

After reading this chapter, you should be able to:

- identify the different ways that performance management (PM) can be defined and interpreted by organisations

- understand the assumptions which underpin the application of PM

- recognise the contribution of organisational theory, industrial engineering and behavioural science systems to the development of PM

- understand the relationship between performance, motivation and reward

- evaluate the extent to which PM can assist in improving organisational effectiveness and efficiency

- consider the contribution that HR can make to PM.

OVERVIEW

Organisational effectiveness and efficiency is rarely, if ever, off the management agenda in work organisations, and assumes an even higher priority during times of economic austerity. PM is one process that can enable organisations to produce greater quality of product or service. It is a potentially pivotal topic within the broader managing people area.

However, PM must not be regarded as the universal panacea for improving organisational effectiveness. This chapter places PM in context, and weighs up the pros and cons of adopting PM as a means to improve productivity or service by motivating employees to perform better and, at the same time, considers the arguments for the use of reward as a motivator.

Contemporary issues such as employee engagement and commitment are discussed as part of a focus on motivation theories and approaches, while we keep in view the underlying question of how HR can make a difference in adding value through PM.

INTRODUCTION

There is little doubt that most organisations in the twenty-first century share some common objectives in order to ensure their survival, so that by producing a consistent product and/or service – which raises more in revenue than it costs to provide – they will attract and retain customers and encourage them to keep spending. Not-for-profit organisations share some of these aims, such as the need for consistency and the requirement to minimise costs for the provision of their product or service. What is also beyond doubt is the role of people in helping to meet these objectives. PM is all about managing employees effectively and there is a wealth of research which demonstrates that well-managed employees increase revenues and decrease costs (see, for example, Coombs *et al* (2006) and Subramony (2009), two meta-analytic studies). A very persuasive example from the not-for-profit sector is also provided by West *et al* (2002), who demonstrate the link between PM and patient mortality in hospitals.

The ongoing economic turmoil post-2007 has further increased the spotlight on PM, with questions posed as to the robustness of PM in the light of the 'reward for failure' practices that accompanied the collapse of the banking industry. Wain (2009, p17) cites the CIPD's research, which demonstrated that 92 per cent of its survey thought that closer scrutiny of poor performance accounted for the rising interest in PM.

In this chapter we consider the concept of PM and the theories of motivation that underpin it, along with its implications for managing and leading employees.

WHAT IS PERFORMANCE MANAGEMENT?

There are myriad definitions of PM, but one of the best known is that of Armstrong and Baron (2005), which has been adopted by the CIPD (2012k, p1):

> A process which contributes to the effective management of individuals and teams in order to achieve high levels of organisational performance. As such, it establishes shared understanding about what is to be achieved and an approach to leading and developing people which will ensure that it is achieved.

This definition informs us of two important factors: first, the all-encompassing nature of PM – it has been suggested that all activities within a business should be contributing towards better performance and that managing the performance of employees is 'running the business' (Mohrman and Mohrman 1995); and secondly, the implication that PM can be viewed as a 'continuous process' (Biron *et al* 2011, p1295), involving identifying, measuring and developing employees in line with organisation strategy.

The extent to which PM impacts upon performance is contingent upon the context and the interconnectedness and interlocking of various supporting mechanisms. The ultimate aim is to maximise organisational effectiveness, especially within the ever changing context of the modern organisation (Budworth and Mann 2011).

The all-encompassing nature of PM can be seen by examining the people–performance link. A classic approach is demonstrated by the Boxall and Purcell (2008) AMO model (see Figure 7.3), in which performance is a function of ability, motivation and opportunity. Therefore, the role of the employer, their agent, or the manager has to be to maximise these three elements in order to enhance performance. However, it could be argued that the terminologies adopted by Boxall and Purcell (2011) need to be brought into line with current HR thinking and practice. Incorporating the elements of employee engagement (see Chapter 11) alongside employee commitment and job satisfaction allows us to expand the AMO model and recognise the increased complexity of high performance (see Figure 12.1). The nature of motivation will be discussed in more detail later in this chapter.

In the context of high-performance work organisations (HPWOs), research indicates that the activities presented in Figure 12.1 are representative of those demonstrated by top performing businesses. For example, Jamrog *et al* (2008) found that in a survey of 1,369 organisations, HPWOs have well-established values that are typically well understood by most employees and are key drivers of employee behaviour. They also report that HPWOs are clear about what behaviours employees need to exhibit in order to execute organisational and departmental strategies, and identified that managers need to:

- set clear goals
- understand employees' abilities
- guide and coach employees.

Although the relationship between these management activities and organisational performance is complex, and there are different levels of outcomes dependent on business sector and type of employee, there is evidence to show that PM is interpreted as an investment in staff, which leads to discretionary effort (McClean and Collins 2011).

Figure 12.1 Some of the activities which could maximise ability, motivation, opportunity, satisfaction, commitment and engagement (AMOSCE)

ACE employees: Able, committed and engaged + opportunity, resources and support = High performance

THE STRATEGIC NATURE OF PERFORMANCE MANAGEMENT

The PM process includes the alignment of objectives and performance through measurement, assessment and monitoring. Where there is a gap between objectives and performance, appropriate HR supporting mechanisms are required (Figure 12.2).

Figure 12.2 HR supporting mechanisms

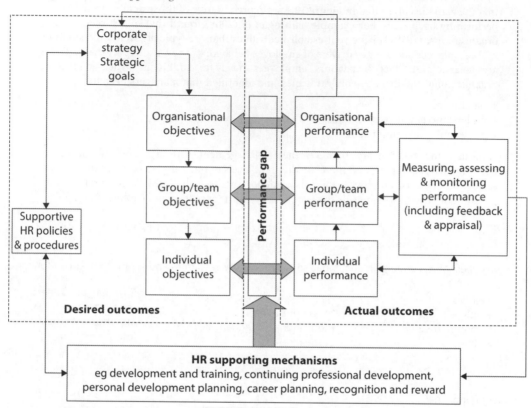

It could therefore be argued that HR as a function can add value through the range of supporting mechanisms that it can provide.

Another method of considering the strategic nature of PM is through the 'balanced scorecard', which attempts to link employee rewards to performance in the areas of finance, customers, internal business processes and innovation, learning and growth. According to Chavan (2009, p396), 'In some instances, companies see the non-financial measures as of such importance that a threshold level of performance is set for each of the non-financials. Only if an individual exceeds these threshold levels can they qualify for performance-related rewards linked to financial performance results.' The importance of organisational culture and vision also has a part to play in how the organisation considers and addresses performance.

PERSPECTIVES ON PERFORMANCE MANAGEMENT

From a managerialist perspective, where the manager has to ensure the most effective and efficient use of resources (including people) in achieving business objectives, PM can be seen as a tool to control and manipulate; very much a top–down process.

The assumption underlying this perspective of PM is that the organisation, in the form of a controlling manager, can make a positive impact upon an individual's work performance. Within this assumption, managers are expected to demonstrate both general management skills as well as skills directly related to the PM process. The latter could include task skills such as objective-setting, understanding technical aspects of the job, monitoring progress and measuring results.

General management skills, in contrast, could include leadership, mentoring, coaching (see Chapter 10) and interpersonal relationships. Managers may demonstrate strong task skills but are often lacking confidence in the softer interpersonal and social skills (Bowles and Coates 1993).

The managerialist perspective also assumes a hierarchy of control, with a direct relationship between manager and subordinate. This is more difficult to achieve in complex organisational structures, such as multi-dimensional matrix structures. For example, a subordinate may report to several different line managers, who are all based in different locations. The control aspect of PM is legitimised through the perceived objectivity of the process. This objectivity then becomes the driving force for achieving performance outputs (Levinson 1970, 1976).

THE ETERNAL TRIANGLE

Herzberg (1968) presents the eternal triangle perspective, whereby there are three general philosophies of personnel (or HR) management: organisational theory; industrial engineering; and behavioural science.

The organisational theorist Weber (1947) believed that human needs are either so irrational or so varied and adjustable that personnel management has to be as pragmatic as the occasion demands. Herzberg cites the example of job design, where, if jobs are organised in a proper manner, the result will be the most efficient job structure, and the most favourable attitudes will follow. Alternatively, within the eternal triangle theory, the industrial engineers (Taylor 1911) believe that humankind is mechanistically orientated and economically motivated, and therefore we need to attune the individual to the most efficient working process. Here we need to design the most appropriate incentive system and design the most appropriate working system for the human machine. Behavioural scientists (eg Schein 1984) focus on group sentiments, the attitudes of individual employees and the organisation's social and psychological climate, with the emphasis on instilling healthy employee attitudes and an appropriate organisational climate. This model illustrates a useful analogy for the use and possible misuse of PM as means to improve performance in organisations.

PERFORMANCE MANAGEMENT AS A PROCESS

PM can also be viewed as a process by looking at the employee lifecycle and the management activities which could contribute to improved performance at each stage. The advantage of this approach is that it can provide guidance to organisations on which activities to introduce and when.

Before recruitment and during the selection process, some of these activities are understood and are embedded in many organisations, others less so. For example, how many organisations provide sufficient information to enable prospective employees to 'self-select' themselves out of the recruitment process thereby potentially saving costs and effort of managing employees who cannot or will not be successful? How many organisations are explicit in looking for employees whose values are aligned to that of the business and are therefore more likely to be committed? How many organisations make the conscious effort to test for potential at the recruitment stage?

During formal induction, when organisations run induction or orientation schemes, to what extent is the robustness of these schemes measured and subsequent action taken? Is there recognition that this is the stage at which employees learn both the formal and informal rules of behaviour and the difference between the overt or stated expectations of the organisation, and the reality of what will be tolerated in practice? A robust induction process can be invaluable in making performance standards and expectations explicit. Research around the 'induction crisis' identifies problems which may manifest themselves in both the short term and long term. For example, the Reed Consulting Survey (2004) demonstrated that 4 per cent of new starters walk out of the job because of poor or non-existent induction programmes, and 93 per cent of the 5,700 respondents in their survey believed that a poor induction had a continuing adverse effect on their productivity at work.

During the probation period, to what extent do line managers appreciate the true value of the probationary period? All too often, it consists of a form-filling exercise initiated by the HR department. The manager signs to say that the new employee should have their position confirmed but without having any idea of how they are actually performing. Then a few months later the manager is complaining that the employee is underperforming, or worse still, are asking HR how they can remove them.

During formal reviews and appraisals, how many managers recognise the value of constant feedback, both positive and developmental? Behaviourist learning theory (Skinner 1953, cited in French *et al* 2011) demonstrates the power of positively reinforcing desired behaviours: employees are much more likely to repeat actions which gain them positive recognition. Positive reinforcement has also been shown to increase employees' 'self-efficacy beliefs', which in turn, increases performance (Bandura 1993). However, there appears to be a blockage against recognising when an employee has performed to standard, a belief that employees should exceed before they receive recognition. A typical comment on supervisor training courses is: 'Why should I recognise an employee who has just reached the standard? That is their job'. But if we employ someone and ask them to reach a certain standard and they do, then this should be recognised and the danger of not doing so is that performance and standards will slide. The power of positive feedback is the theory supporting appreciative inquiry (see below), but many managers appear to spend their time and effort looking for and acting on the 5 per cent of jobs that people do badly, whilst ignoring the 95 per cent that they do effectively.

An excuse sometimes cited for lack of feedback is the idea that people learn from mistakes, and it is certainly true that allowing people to fail can be useful in some circumstances. Control theory (Carver *et al* 2000) indicates that failure can even motivate more than success. Learning organisation theory (Ellinger 2004) suggests that freedom to fail is an important factor to enable an organisation to grow. But there is a lot of difference between giving employees space to experiment accompanied by constructive feedback and abdication management. According to Geal and Johnson (2002, p26):

> What do people learn from mistakes? What not to do, so they need to try something else. But, what else? A manager able and willing to give developmental feedback so they can improve is both necessary and motivating when handled well.

So using the excuse of allowing people to learn from mistakes could be viewed as lazy at best, and at worst could be incredibly costly for the organisation. In summary, the balance between allowing experimentation and providing appropriate feedback needs constant review.

At any time in the employee lifecycle, there may be the need to manage poor performance or conduct. This raises the question of how many managers are able and willing to manage poor performance or conduct in a positive way before it becomes a major issue. An organisation may well have a 'capability and conduct' procedure, which will undoubtedly espouse the wisdom of dealing with performance and conduct issues informally and early. But how many organisations train and support their managers to run these informal 'improving poor performance/poor conduct' discussions?

Table 12.1 Performance management as a process

Employee activity	Timeline and action	Manager/employer activity
Gains knowledge of expectations and culture Self-selects in or out	Before recruitment: Job descriptions, person specifications, adverts, company information	Gives signals of expectations on job performance standards, conduct standards and culture
Demonstrates ability and motivation Conscious or subconscious alignment with values Self-selects in or out	During selection process: Interviews/assessment etc	Tests ability and motivation Checks values alignment Seeks potential
Learns conduct expectations Adapts to the culture	During formal induction/orientation	Formalises conduct expectations, terms and conditions/handbook etc
Learns performance standards Develops knowledge and skills	During mandatory training	Provides standards of job performance Provides knowledge and skills Provides feedback
Becomes a productive employee Adapts to the culture	During probation period	Team briefing and communications Reinforces performance and conduct standards Provides feedback One-to-one reviews Provides ongoing training and coaching
	At any time: Possible poor performance or poor conduct intervention	
Reviews performance Agrees objectives Identifies learning needs Considers aspirations Possibly gains reward	During formal reviews and/or appraisals: Annual or more regularly	Reviews performance Sets objectives Agrees learning needs Identifies potential and aspirations Possible links to reward
Continuous improvement Develops self-feedback mechanisms Achieves potential	Ongoing: Business as usual	Team briefing and communications Reinforces performance and conduct standards Provides feedback One-to-one reviews Ongoing training and coaching

APPRECIATIVE INQUIRY

Drawn from research into positive psychology (Seligman 1998), appreciative inquiry suggests that when employees are encouraged to focus on their strengths, then they are more likely to succeed and enjoy greater job satisfaction (Bryce 2007). For a practical example, see Arkin (2005b).

 PERFORMANCE APPRAISAL AT SODASTREAM

CASE STUDY 12.1

Operating in over 30 countries, SodaStream is the world's largest manufacturer, distributor and marketer of home water carbonation systems. A change in HR personnel led to a project aimed at designing a new appraisal process. Focus groups were carried out to understand issues with the existing scheme and to answer a key question: What are the conditions that can make our performance evaluation process a success? The majority of employees described the existing system as an unpleasant and unhelpful experience; however, they also believed that it was crucial to have a performance appraisal process that was able to: positively energise employees; include follow-up; raise employee motivation; and be short and simple. As a result of this feedback, the HR team at SodaStream commissioned a new process building on the concepts behind appreciative inquiry and positive psychology, which was piloted with 64 employees and 26 managers.

Strength-based performance appraisal (SBPA) – the principles

The goals of the new system were: to improve organisational performance and business results; focus on employees' strengths but without neglecting problems; reflect the double meaning of appreciation, ie valuing good performance and increasing value; and support knowledge management within the organisation. To this end, seven principles were adopted: feed forward; reflected best self-feedback; happiness research;

developing strengths; the 3:1 positive to negative emotion principle; a win-win philosophy; positive organisational core; and collective efficacy.

The SodaStream performance appraisal

The SBPA system at SodaStream contains six steps:

- supervisor–employee meeting including success stories told by the subordinate and enthusiasm stories told by the supervisor
- a joint questionnaire and preparation of reports
- a second supervisor–employee meeting involving a strength-based evaluation discussion looking for new ways to use strengths and agree goals to achieve win-win outcomes
- creation of an organisational strengths map
- a celebration party to recognise strengths
- a follow-up process.

An initial evaluation

Benefits of the new system as reported by subordinates included: increased quality time with managers; a positive experience of performance evaluation; a focus on strengths; goal-setting; increased learning; and better matching of competencies to tasks.

For the organisation, reported benefits included: increased levels of motivation and performance; better goal-setting; improved organisational culture;

increased collaboration; and improved manager–employee relationships.

Source: Bouskila-Yam and Klugar (2011)

Questions

1   How does the SodaStream performance appraisal process

differ from ones you are familiar with?

2   What would need to be in place in an organisation in order to adopt this type of process?

REFLECTIVE ACTIVITY 12.1

Think about an organisation with which you are familiar. Using Table 12.1 as a guide, consider the evidence for a clear PM process being in

place. What evidence exists that it has been implemented in an effective manner?

However, there is more to PM than just the actions involved. Effective PM is not only dependent upon what is done, but also upon how it is done. Purcell *et al* (2003) provide research evidence to support the proposition that no one particular HR practice is critical to organisational success, but rather that good management by line managers, applying various approaches effectively and appropriately according to the context, is the key factor. Committed and capable line managers are, therefore, essential to successful PM (Hutchinson and Purcell 2003). These managers need to know the 'how' of PM as much as the 'what'; ie the answers to questions such as:

1   How can we define performance?

2   Who should define performance?

3   How can we measure performance?

4   What is the link between motivation and performance?

DEFINING PERFORMANCE

For performance to be managed it has to be defined and measured. This demonstrates that what the organisation measures is indicative of what the organisation values (Johnson *et al* 2011).

There is no single, universal definition of performance; it depends very much on the particular perspective adopted. For example, some definitions relate to the organisation and various expectations in terms of outputs:

> Performance should be defined as the outcomes of work because they provide the strongest linkage to the strategic goals of the organisation, customer satisfaction, and economic contributions. (Bernadin *et al* 1995)

Other definitions emphasise behavioural aspects, in addition to outputs or results:

> Performance means both behaviours and results. Behaviours emanate from the performer and transform performance from abstraction to action. Not just the instruments for results, behaviours are also outcomes in their own right – the product of mental and physical effort applied to tasks – and can be judged apart from results. (Brumbach 1988, p389)

WHO DEFINES PERFORMANCE?

It is not only a question of how performance is defined, but also who within the organisation is, or are, responsible for defining performance standards. Often, it is the organisation itself that determines performance and how it will be measured. Performance requirements are often part of a strategic planning process, cascading top–down through the organisation from senior management (Humble 1972). However, this does not have to be the case. Semler (1993) describes a bottom–up approach, where employees at Semco were allowed to set their own performance targets and define appropriate rewards. There is also the possibility of a combined top–down and bottom–up approach, with mutual adjustment of goals and objectives (Nonaka and Takeuchi 1995).

Other stakeholders, such as shareholders, and customers, will have their own views on performance standards or achievements and their views may be contradictory. The parties involved have different perspectives, expectations and experience of performance. For example, shareholders are interested in long-term value of stocks and assets. Middle management may have an interest in protecting and advancing their own position, power and rewards. Customers are increasingly demanding high-quality, customised products and services. In addition, all of these stakeholders may adopt different roles at different times or have multiple, simultaneous roles. Therefore, the agreement of what constitutes effective performance may be difficult to reach.

A more integrated approach may help to overcome some of the problems inherent in defining performance and performance standards. It is generally accepted that involving employees in the setting of objectives and targets is more likely to gain commitment to their achievement. Fundamentally, though, for the organisation to succeed, someone, somewhere needs to combine the targets to ensure that the organisational objectives are indeed being met. This is a line management responsibility, but HR might need to empower and ensure that the process is taking place.

WHAT ASPECTS OF PERFORMANCE CAN BE MEASURED?

What an organisation chooses to measure, and when, depends on the PM framework adopted within the organisational context and on what the organisation values in its employees; for example, to what extent is learning valued as part of the PM process? But a robust PM process typically relies on the setting of definable and measurable goals and targets, which raises challenges as it is impossible to measure all aspects of an employee's performance. For example, how does an organisation measure knowledge-creation, creativity and innovation? PM too often assumes explicit performance measures and cannot always incorporate tacit inputs, throughputs and outputs at individual, group and organisational levels.

Similarly, there are temporal barriers. Performance targets are typically set in time and the timescale might in itself affect accurate measurement. How does one allow for long-term performance improvements and outcomes within an annual appraisal cycle, for example? The critical issue then becomes when we measure and record performance.

In addition there is the challenge of the traditional PM emphasis on the individual, whereas the increasingly interdependent nature of work, and the consequent emphasis on team and groups, makes measurement more challenging. It is not just individual performance that is important, but also the contribution that the individual makes towards group effort, and the combined output of the group as a whole. So team targets are an area that needs to be explored.

An example of these complexities can be seen in a study by Rosen *et al* (2011), who explore the challenges of managing and measuring adaptive performance in teams. This is potentially a very important aspect in the modern business environment; however, it can be difficult to measure behavioural dimensions over time, across groups of employees – as opposed to individuals.

PITFALLS OF DEFINING PERFORMANCE TARGETS

There are many pitfalls with objectives and targets. Reeves (2008) used the term 'targetology' to describe the fixation of the then British government and many organisations with targets. He agrees that targets can be helpful, citing the reduction in hospital waiting times as an example, but he questions the number of targets which are used:

> One or two clear targets can be powerful. A hundred targets is a recipe for confusion, stress and disaster… Just because targets are good, it does not mean that more targets are better.

Hall (2009, p10) argues that 'Focusing organisation and individual activity on what really matters, through the use of targets linked to strategic aims, can be a powerful management "tool" but careful consideration needs to be given to what is targeted, how targets are applied and who targets are applied to.'

Research by Professor Yves Emery (2008) identifies some common issues with both defining targets and attaining them: policy deployment, quality versus quantity targets, goal displacement, individualisation effect, goal override and limited influence. An example of each is provided in Table 12.2.

REFLECTIVE ACTIVITY 12.2

Analyse the targets or objectives that you have been set during a PM process. To what extent do the pitfalls listed in Table 12.2 apply to these? How could your targets be improved upon?

MEASURING PERFORMANCE

The PM process (Table 12.1) shows that measurement or performance review and feedback should be an ongoing activity, so that positive reinforcement or corrective action can be supplied as soon as it is justified. Normal management activities such as walking the floor and one-to-one reviews can enable this measurement to happen and ensure that one of the 'golden rules' of appraisals is followed: 'No surprises', ie anything discussed in a period review or appraisal concerning performance should be expected by both parties. This is important as 'surprised employees become angry employees, and angry employees sue' (Segal 2010 p 76).

Table 12.2 Pitfalls of target definition

Issue	Example
Policy deployment The difficulties of translating strategic goals into meaningful bottom line targets. Not all objectives are easily split and can become meaningless if broken down too much	A common strategic goal, such as 'increase market share', which may well translate into specific objectives for senior managers, but is almost impossible to be a meaningful objective for a back office employee such as a payroll data entry clerk

Issue	Example
Quality versus quantity targets With quantity targets being easier to set and therefore being used in place of quality targets which may be more beneficial	An HR officer may be set a target to ensure 95 per cent of employees who leave the organisation complete an exit interview, a very SMART target. But actually what is really wanted is quality of data from exiting employees about why they are leaving, so that meaningful decisions can be made
Goal displacement Where the measures become seen as the goal	In a call centre the goal may be to improve customer service and one measure of this is to answer calls more quickly. It is easy for employees to 'lose calls' – ie drop them as soon as they are answered – in order to improve the call answering statistics, which actually results in even worse customer service
Individualisation effect Where competing goals set up unintended competition between staff, especially competition for scarce resources	A cable TV sales team may be measured on the number of customers they sign up, and to ensure quality of sales the customers have to stay for a minimum time period of six months. However, the technicians who install the product in the customer's home are measured on speed of install and the quicker the install, the more likely there will be a problem, which in turn leads to customers disconnecting
Goal override Where employees only focus on goal achievement and neglect other important responsibilities. It may become necessary to have a relatively complex measurement system in order to ensure that the 'day job' carries equal weight	A hotel maintenance team may be targeted on the completion of reported repairs and may go flat out to achieve these targets. As a result they may neglect the preventative maintenance jobs, which are a part of their job description, because they are not overtly measured
Limited influence Where employees have very little control over the targets set, or at least perceive this to be the case	In a retail environment where product range, price and advertising are all centrally controlled a shop assistant may easily perceive that they really have very little control over the actual sales that they make and this perception may actually be real. It has also been argued that employees are just the delivery system and that 90 per cent of the impact of their endeavours comes from the system!

Another measurement technique, which is often overlooked, is self-measurement. Although different theorists may argue why, they do mostly conclude that participation in goal-setting can lead to improved performance. The research that supports the idea of autonomy and participation in goal-setting is also well known and includes the work of Herzberg (1968), Hackman and Oldham (1980) and Locke and Latham (1990), to name but a few. For example, Locke (1968) in Hollyforde and Whiddett (2002) identified the value of goals as a motivator and performance enhancer suggesting that specific rather than general goals and participation in goal-setting are important in improving performance. Locke also identifies self-regulation or self-measurement and management as being powerful enablers, an idea supported by Bandura (1993, p128), who states that:

> Most human motivation is cognitively generated. People motivate themselves and guide their actions anticipatorily by the exercise of forethought... Forethought is translated into incentives and appropriate action through self-regulatory mechanisms.

This suggests that self-measurement is an everyday activity.

Latham (2007) provides a useful summary of some of the research around this area, but the message appears to be that although the effects are mediated and moderated by other factors, such as personality, involving employees in goal-setting and facilitating self-feedback can and does result in higher performance. This perhaps provides an argument for the use of more self-appraisal and for developing ways in which employees can access their own feedback on performance.

APPRAISAL AS A PERFORMANCE MANAGEMENT TOOL

The more recent literature (for example, Aguinis 2009), calls for a wide view of PM, including performance planning, assessment and review, identifying that it is more than simply appraisal. But some form of performance appraisal is nearly always incorporated with the aim of improving performance, motivating employees and/or allocating rewards. An honest and accurate assessment of current performance can be a strong driver for further learning, development and performance improvement. As discussed earlier, feedback and the setting of improvement targets can itself be a strong motivator (Locke and Latham 1990), and for there to be equitable distribution of rewards some fair method of comparing contributions between individuals is required. The potential impact of fairness is highlighted by Adams' equity theory – see page 262.

The whole PM system should therefore ensure that employees perceive equity of treatment and fairness, none more so than in the appraisal process and distribution of rewards. This supports the argument that PM and reward policies need to be transparent. The role of perception means that extra attention must be paid to how the process is communicated so as to ensure that the message is clear and universally understood.

However, there is a wealth of evidence that points to negative aspects of performance appraisal and at least three recent books that have called for an end to them (Bouskila-Yam and Kluger 2011). Very careful consideration is therefore needed when choosing a performance appraisal process and planning its implementation.

TYPES OF APPRAISAL

Different types of appraisal include: top–down, self-appraisal, peer appraisal, bottom–up and multi-rater, such as 360-degree and 720-degree feedback. The most common is a top–down approach with the inclusion of self-appraisal, usually as a preparatory activity for the employee. There are many benefits of a multi-rater approach, which in theory will produce a more rounded outcome, but the time and expense involved often rules this out as an option.

Appraisal methods can be divided into two main approaches: those oriented towards results (outputs); and those oriented towards competencies (inputs). Results-oriented appraisal is based on the setting of quantifiable, achievable and time-bounded objectives, most often agreed between manager and subordinate, and geared towards achieving organisational objectives. Competency-oriented appraisal is based on the demonstration of certain key skills and behaviours thought to be associated with high performance. These skills and behaviours, agreed by manager and employee, may also include the use of multi-rater instruments. The trend in recent years is towards combining both results and competency-based approaches in an attempt to deliver the dual benefits of achieving immediate performance targets and supporting longer-term development of key skills and capabilities.

Appraisals and the link to development and reward

PM systems differ in the emphasis they give to rewards or development. The trend is for increasing emphasis on development rather than reward, and de-emphasising the link between PM and pay (Armstrong and Baron 2005). PM and development are overlapping and inter-dependent processes. Performance reviews, whether they are periodic appraisals or continuous day-to-day interactions between managers and employees, provide encouragement for learning and development. Development may take the form of informal training, self-managed learning by the individual employee, coaching by the manager, or more structured training and development interventions. Whatever the form, development is intended to have a direct impact on performance capabilities and can also have a powerful motivational effect (CIPD 2012k).

However, multiple perspectives on appraisals lead to conflicts. Reconciling PM as a developmental process and as a pay decision-making process is not straightforward. Linking performance appraisal to pay reduces the focus on development (Kessler and Purcell 1992). An employee is less likely to highlight a development need if it might be seen as a weakness and therefore detrimentally affect their pay award.

POTENTIAL PITFALLS WHEN EVALUATING EMPLOYEES

Appraisals ask for evaluations to be made, and accordingly there are potential pitfalls, some of which are highlighted below.

Rating scale issues

In appraisal systems where a rating scale is used, there are constant issues with people being unhappy with the 'average' rating. Standard distribution dictates that not everyone will be at the top, some people will be at the bottom and most people will be in the middle. But being rated as 'competent', 'satisfactory', 'C' or '3/5' is unsatisfactory for people who can see 'exceptional', 'A' or '5/5' on the scale.

The Swiss Federal Administration trialled a new system with the following grades:

A++	Far beyond expectations
A+	Beyond expectations
A	Objectives fully reached
B	Objectives partially reached
C	Objectives missed

Although people psychologically still want to be A++, most employees will be rated as an A, which is psychologically better than a C (Emery 2008). However, despite all the research into improving rating scales, there is little evidence that one is better than another, and recent focus has moved onto trying to minimise rater bias (Budworth and Mann 2011).

Appraiser bias

Appraisers all have their own biases. Some have tendencies to rate everyone kindly or everyone harshly, which can raise issues, especially when rewards are linked and comparisons are made with other teams, whose managers have rated differently. In addition, there are those who struggle to differentiate between any employees, wanting something for everyone, known as the 'watering can effect'. Furnham (1997) identified 13 different 'perception errors', which he said could negatively influence an appraisal system. These pitfalls can severely affect an employee's sense of equity and cause dissatisfaction with the system, which in turn is likely to diminish performance.

Furnham's 13 systematic perception errors are:

1   First impressions – rather than how the appraisee has performed.

2   Halo effect – only focusing on one favourable behaviour or quality.

3   Horns effect – contrary to halo effect; a negative rating.

4   Contrast error – comparison with selected employees, often star performers.

5   Same as me – rating appraises highly due to sharing common attributes with appraiser.

6   Different from me – contrary to same as me.

7   Recency effect – judging only recent behaviour, then generalising.

8   Central tendency – rating everyone in the middle of the scale.

9   Leniency in rating – generous to everyone to avoid conflict.

10   Strict rating – consistently strict in appraising performance.

11   Performance dimension error – where two aspects of the appraisal follow, score two distinct qualities the same.

12   Spillover effect – based on previous appraisal.

13   Status effect – giving better ratings to higher-level employees.

Much of the training provided to appraisers attempts to reduce and minimise the impact of these types of rater bias.

Reward pitfalls

Whilst not all formal appraisal systems are overtly linked to rewards, there are many potential issues with appraisal systems being linked to rewards.

Fixed quota systems, where evaluation is based on the amount of reward available and not on actual levels of performance, can lead to meaningless appraisals for employees, especially if the total amount of money available is limited. Evidence suggests that less than 10 per cent of annual salary has a very limited effect on motivating people to higher performance (Emery 2008). In the current economic climate, the question has to be asked as to how many organisations can make budgetary arrangements for this amount of money. If a smaller 'pot' is to be distributed in such a way as to offer more than 10 per cent to some employees, are managers willing or able to differentiate enough between their employees?

Dependent upon organisational structure and context, the practice of team reward may inhibit or adversely affect individual motivation (for further reading, see the CIPD website).

Do employees who are less confident and think they cannot achieve the standards to attain a bonus actually work less hard, so in effect the reward becomes a demotivator? Which leads to a fundamental question: do rewards such as pay and other recognition schemes actually motivate employees at all?

MOTIVATED TO PERFORM?

It must be remembered that PM is, in itself, simply a process. Human beings don't always follow rules and do exactly what they are told. In order to maximise performance by employees themselves, we need to understand the human psyche by considering key aspects such as motivation, commitment and engagement.

MOTIVATION THEORIES

Content and process approaches

Content theories focus on what (outcome or reward) motivates people. Common examples of content theories include: existence-relatedness-growth (ERG) theory (Alderfer), achievement theory (McClelland), two-factor theory (Herzberg), and hierarchy of needs theory (Maslow). In contrast, process theories concentrate on how people are motivated, or the cognitive process used to connect effort with outcomes or reward. Goal-setting theory (Locke 1968) is an example of a process theory, as are equity theory (Adams) and expectancy theory (Vroom), which are both discussed below. For an in-depth treatment of content and process motivation theories, see Mullins (2013). Effective management interventions combine both content and process motivation theories as they are complementary not opposites (Hollyforde and Whiddett 2002).

Equity theory

Adams' (1965) equity theory contends that employees consider the inputs, eg abilities and effort they bring to work, in relation to the outputs (perceived rewards they gain as a result), and then go on to compare the ratio of these two factors with referent others, through the use of the distributive justice concept (see Chapter 4).

A perceived injustice motivates the individual to take action – they can increase or decrease their inputs, or seek to increase or decrease the inputs of others. Alternatively, they can seek to change the outputs for either themselves or others. In extreme circumstances they may choose to leave the organisation. Leaving the organisation may also include psychological withdrawal, eg turning up for work but spending all day on Facebook. It is important to note the critical part that perception plays in equity theory, so the injustice may not be perceived by others (Mullins 2013).

All through the twentieth century, theorists argued about the capacity of money to motivate employees towards greater performance (Latham 2007). Money, or what it can supply (money can be a status symbol or a sign of recognition), appears in all of the 'content' theories of motivation and therefore it is implied that money is a motivator (see 'Reflection theory' below). Barber and Bretz (2000) suggest that money is among the most important factors for people when deciding on a job.

REFLECTIVE ACTIVITY 12.3

Think about yourself and talk to others you know. What was it that made you and they think about looking for a new job?

This activity may give some insight into the complexity of the question as to whether money is a motivator. One only has to consider the 70,000 'games-makers' who volunteered to work during the Olympics and Paralympics of 2012 to recognise that money is not always the single motivator. These people were driven by other factors, and whilst without doubt some were driven by extrinsic drivers such as social or status needs, for many, the motivation would have been intrinsic, such as a sense of achievement or development and growth.

EXPECTANCY THEORY

A process theory of motivation seeks to explain the cognitive process of how an individual is motivated to increase performance. A common example by Vroom (1964) is explained through the formula:

$$F = E \times I \times V$$

F is the force of motivation, ie how much effort will be applied ('how hard I am willing to work').

E is expectancy, ie the belief that extra effort will result in better performance ('if I work harder, my output will increase').

I is instrumentality, ie the belief that better performance will lead to a reward ('if my output increases, I will get a reward').

V is valence, the perceived value of the reward ('how much I want the reward').

Valence links back to content theories of motivation, which these tell us that individuals are motivated by a multitude of factors (needs and wants), including money, but also security, affiliation, power, achievement, status, growth and more.

Source: Buchanan and Huczynski (2010)

REFLECTIVE ACTIVITY 12.4

Why is pay important to an individual member? Does pay provide the mirror by which an employee reflects images of power, status, value and succession? The meaning that pay holds is largely deduced from employees' personal characteristics (values), pay level (relative to others) and the level of familiarity the person experiences with the pay system (pay system knowledge). These meanings are expected to influence employee outcomes such as satisfaction, motivation and performance (Thiery 2001, in Salimaki *et al* 2009).

This view is supported by anecdotal evidence of practitioners pointing to exit interview data and proclaiming that lack of money is the reason for demotivated people leaving an organisation. However, more detailed analysis may produce a different picture. People who have decided to leave an organisation may well quote the 'bigger and better' pay packet as the reason for joining a new organisation, but if a different exit interview question is asked – 'What made you start looking for another job to start with?'– then other factors begin to emerge. People become dissatisfied and demotivated with jobs due to poor management, lack of opportunities and boredom. Therefore HR responding to management requests to match pay offers from competitors in order to retain employees seldom works, especially in the longer term.

The importance of intrinsic motivation

The resurgence of interest in intrinsic factors such as meaning, purpose, spirituality and commitment and, more recently, engagement, has emphasised the importance of work as a motivator in the organisation (Fox 1994, Lockwood 2007, Meyer and Herscovitch 2001). Intrinsic motivation is the spontaneous satisfaction individuals derive from the activity itself. Extrinsic motivation, in contrast, requires tangible or verbal rewards (Ankil and Palliam 2012). Intrinsic motivation can lead to more engaged and committed employees and the four most critical intrinsic rewards are: a sense of meaning and purpose; a sense of choice; a sense of competence; and a sense of progress (Chalofsky and Krishna 2009). In terms of meaningfulness, people with the highest levels of productivity and fulfilment view themselves as inseparable from their work, intrinsically motivated by the work itself and professionally committed to and engaged with the organisation (Chalofsky and Krishna, ibid).

So, there is evidence to suggest money can reduce the effectiveness of intrinsic motivation and there are circumstances when it appears not to. The deciding factor, as is so often the case, is not what is done, but how it is done. Even if money is a motivational factor, it is commonly linked to equity theory (as discussed earlier in this chapter), ie employees compare their rewards with colleagues and if they perceive unfair treatment, they are motivated to act. Transparency in how rewards such as pay are implemented is therefore very important. In addition, expectancy theories of motivation (see below) also provide potential guidelines on implementation of reward policies and practice.

Commitment and job satisfaction

Defined by Koster (2011, p2838) as: 'the decision to participate', organisational commitment can be seen as the psychological bond between an individual and an organisation. Meyer and Herscovitch (2001) concluded that employees can be committed to different targets; including their occupation, team or manager in addition to or in place of their organisation. The positive benefits of increased employee commitment are well documented and include: increased performance outcomes; enhanced organisational citizenship behaviours; and reduced labour turnover (see, for example, Meyer *et al* 2002). Meyer and Allen (1991) expanded the concept of commitment to explain why it leads to positive outcomes, outlining three components: affective commitment – emotional attachment to the target; normative commitment – moral obligation to the target; and continuance commitment – a perceived lack of choice on whether to leave the organisation. Mayfield and Mayfield (2012) argue that affective commitment is the most powerful of the three components.

Job satisfaction, a more established concept, deals with how a person feels about their job or work experience (Locke 1976). High levels of job satisfaction are not thought to increase performance directly; however, job satisfaction has been shown to increase commitment, reduce grievances, lower labour turnover and contribute to engagement. Hackman and Oldham's (1980) job characteristics model in French *et al* (2011) links five job characteristics – skill variety, task identity, task significance, autonomy and feedback – with positive psychological states (see also Chapter 8). This model provides a platform for linking meaningful jobs with higher levels of job satisfaction.

THE LINKS BETWEEN REWARD AND PERFORMANCE

The topic of reward is in itself a significant area for research and debate. For further in-depth discussions, please see the Explore Further section on page 272, Perkins and White.

PAY AND INTRINSIC MOTIVATION

According to Kuvaas (2006), the link between pay and performance is mediated and moderated by employees' personal levels of intrinsic motivation. It is suggested that money, an extrinsic motivator, may actually decrease long-term intrinsic motivation and so have a detrimental effect on performance.

Two conflicting meta-analyses were published in 2001, both trying to establish the link between extrinsic rewards and intrinsic motivation, and the results are mixed. According to Deci *et al* (2001), the use of rewards as a motivational strategy is a risky proposition, as this disengages interest and self-regulation. Cameron *et al* (2001) counteracted this by stating that rewards are not harmful to motivation to perform a task (see Latham (2007) for a summary of the debate). Interestingly, recent evidence from a multiple employer study showed that performance-related pay (PRP) was positively related to intrinsic motivation, which can shape the workforce. Employees for whom PRP is a motivator will self-select to work in organisations which offer this benefit (Fang and Gerhart 2012).

PERFORMANCE-RELATED REWARD – EXPECTANCY THEORY IN ACTION

A classic use of expectancy theory is to define and execute a performance-related reward scheme, in order to improve short-term performance. An example could be an attempt to increase sales of sports shoes in a sports shop in the lead up to Christmas: the employer wants to increase the amount of effort (force) that employees will put in. For this to work employees need:

- A belief that putting in extra effort, talking to customers, learning about stock, etc will result in making extra sales. So they need training, goal-setting and feedback to this effect (expectancy).
- A belief that the extra sales they make will be recognised by their manager and result in a reward. This could be extra pay, prizes, recognition, promotion, a permanent contract, time off, more interesting work, etc. There needs to be a system for individuals to record their sales that actually result in the promised reward being given (instrumentality).
- A belief that the reward is worth having to them. This is a good reason to offer a choice of rewards if possible (valence).

Is performance-related pay right for your organisation?

As both performance and motivation are affected by many factors, PRP (or any other intervention) cannot be linked in a causal manner. Williams (1998, p173) argues that managers' and employees' views need to be considered in order to analyse the effect of PRP on motivation and performance. Whilst the debate around PRP continues, it is worth considering some of the operational difficulties that have been associated with reward practice.

The following set of questions has been raised by Williams (1998, p176) and adapted to fit the categories provided.

With regard to organisational culture, teams and individual attitudes to PRP:

- Is PRP appropriate to all organisations?
- Is there a climate of trust (particularly in line managers – subordinate relations)?
- What effect does PRP have on team and co-operative building?

- Does a focus on individual performance lead employees to place self-interest ahead of those of the organisation generally?
- Does PRP create divisiveness?
- Does PRP encourage short-termism?

He similarly raises questions about the PM process itself:

- What criteria should be used for measuring performance? Outputs? Inputs? Both?
- Can individual performance be measured objectively and fairly?
- Can performance be defined comprehensively?
- Do line managers have the willingness and ability required to operate PRP?
- How much of performance is within the individual's control?
- How should average performers be treated?

Questions related to the value of rewards also need to be addressed:

- What amount of pay constitutes a significant increase in the eyes of employees?
- Will PRP diminish the value of intrinsic rewards?

It may be relatively simple to provide an answer to each of these individual questions. However, when considered together, the complexity of linking PRP to performance becomes much more evident. Thus simple, prescriptive solutions cannot be found.

So the question of whether money is a motivator that can lead to improved performance is a very complex one and the answer is by no means clear (Latham 2007). At best, it can be said that there is a connection between money and satisfaction which may under certain circumstances increase commitment and perhaps performance.

More important is the fact that all employees will be motivated by different factors, as highlighted by the 'content theories'. The effective manager will recognise this and work towards helping employees gain maximum motivation at work, using the principles of expectancy theories and equity theory to make this happen.

 TOTAL REWARD AT ARUP

CASE STUDY 12.2

Arup is a global design and engineering consultancy. The company employs around 10,500 people in 37 countries, around half of whom are based in the UK. At Arup, which is employee-owned, the reward package includes a global profit-sharing scheme as well as a range of other benefits.

Although the organisation did not formally publish a total reward policy until 2007, Arup has been practising a total reward strategy for much longer, and offers online total reward statements to its employees around the world. Tony Hatton-Gore, director, group remuneration and benefits, joined Arup in 2001. At that time, there was an awareness of total reward within the organisation and, soon

afterwards, Arup decided to adopt this approach.

There were three key reasons behind the decision to introduce total reward statements:

- total reward statements were seen as an effective way to ensure staff understood the make-up and the value of their employment package
- in line with its values of honest and fair dealings with staff, and in the interests of transparency, Arup wanted people to understand what was available within the organisation as an employee-owned firm
- as an engineering and design consultancy, the organisation wanted to take a holistic 'total design' approach to reward.

Total reward statements

Hatton-Gore explains that although there are some elements of the benefits package – such as the global profit-share scheme and global retirement policy – that are determined centrally, the benefits vary by country, and are based on the company values in combination with what Arup needs to compete in the local labour markets.

The total reward statements are tailored for each individual employee. They include details of salary, profit-share payments and in some cases more than 20 items to which the employee is entitled. The items included are mainly those on which a value can be placed, and these are totalled to give a monetary value for the overall employment package.

Other benefits, such as holiday allowance or the availability of flu vaccinations, are included on the statement but not given a cash value. Hatton-Gore notes that some of the benefits listed on the statement are included because the organisation wants to make sure that employees are aware of what is available: for example, the employee assistance programme. He says: 'We have not attempted to put a monetary value on these things.'

However, while training and development opportunities are viewed as part of the employment package, these are not included on the total reward statement. Hatton-Gore explains that reward in a monetary sense is just one part of what working for the organisation is about; the career and personal development opportunities, and the chance to work on interesting projects, are part of the overall experience rather than another element in the reward list.

Arup's formal total reward policy combines both the monetary and the non-monetary benefits of working for the organisation. The policy was published in a company magazine when it was formally launched in 2007, and is also available to employees via the intranet.

Hatton-Gore says if somebody finds a way to put a value on some of the other, less tangible, elements of the employment package – such as career opportunities – this would be a 'very interesting idea', but says it is a challenge that has not yet been cracked.

Source: Sharp (2009)

www.XpertHR.co.uk

Questions

1   To what extent can Arup's total reward strategy be truly transparent?

2   How will this reward approach be received across all 37 countries? What happens after PM?

If a standard formal appraisal interview occurs with the appraisee, a range of actions or options is available to superiors and subordinates alike. As we have suggested already, there may be a portfolio of approaches that interact within the PM process, such as 360-degree feedback, self-appraisal, upward appraisal, coaching and mentoring interventions.

Companies may operate a system of forced ranking, or forced distribution, whereby groups of employees are compared against each other and ranked from best to worst, instead of being judged against independent performance standards. Although this approach is more common with appraising managers, it can be applied to any area of work. Employees who are placed in the lowest category (for example, the lowest 5 per cent) may be dismissed from the organisation or given a fixed time to improve their current performance to the expected organisational standards. Conversely, the top-performing employees may be provided with significant learning opportunities, career growth and perhaps significant financial and personal rewards (Boyle 2001).

HOW CAN PERFORMANCE BE IMPROVED?

Dependent upon the source(s) of the performance problem, the organisation needs to decide on the type and scope of problem intervention. There may need to be consideration of the macro-level issues affecting the broader organisational context, or attention given to micro-level, individual issues.

Some of the techniques available include:

- learning
- development
- training
- coaching and mentoring
- team-building
- culture change programmes
- reward schemes
- structure, process, systems, job redesign, etc
- management approach.

ARGUMENTS AGAINST THE USE OF PERFORMANCE MANAGEMENT

There is increasing evidence that PM can have a positive impact on organisational performance (Armstrong 2000, Molleman and Timmerman 2003). However, evidence is not universally positive (Furnham 2004, Hazard 2004, Morgan 2006). Some studies suggest performance appraisal and pay to be the least effective HR policies, as perceived by the employees (Hutchinson and Purcell 2003). Pulakos (2009) reports that more than two-thirds of employees are dissatisfied with their PM system and believe it has no impact on improving their performance. This mixed picture may exist for multiple reasons: the spectrum of different PM approaches adopted across organisations; the issues of implementation, ie what may be right, but the how is neglected; and the difficulties of proving cause and effect between the use of high-performance working practices (HPWPs) and improved organisational performance (see, for example, Guest 1997, Koster 2011). So PM should not be regarded as a simple 'best practice' solution. Rather than adopting mechanistic, off-the-shelf approaches or processes, organisations need to ensure their PM approach and processes are implemented in a way that suits their context, giving due consideration to organisational culture (Haines and St-Onge 2012).

MEASUREMENT AT WHAT COST?

PM is not without potentially significant costs in terms of staff time and administration. Not only are implementation costs to be considered, but also the long-term maintenance costs of any PM system once established. To what extent do organisations consider the total costs of the PM system versus the impacts, both positive and negative, on performance outcomes? An example would be the internal focus of systems within the automotive manufacturing industry, where the needs of customers were ignored to the long-term harm of the organisation. Organisations may assume that a PM system will have a positive impact, but any improvement needs to be offset against the often substantial costs of running the system itself.

THE ROLE OF HR AND BEST PRACTICE WITHIN PM

Research suggests that world-leading companies adopt a more strategic approach to PM as opposed to a tactical one, and this linking of daily operations to strategy translates into increased employee commitment, engagement and performance (Biron *et al* 2011). Therefore, although HR should support line managers in the implementation of PM processes, success is dependent on full involvement of senior managers within the organisation, requiring them to 'walk the talk', so that employees receive clear signals that this is important. Without this, PM can easily become a painful and negative form-filling exercise, with HR bullying and nagging line managers to complete what they see as a time-wasting process. Therefore perhaps the most important role for HR in PM is working with senior management to facilitate commitment so that they can model the required behaviours.

HR also has a key role in designing, communicating and training the PM process and there are interesting ideas emerging about how to improve this: for example, aligning the process to employment engagement strategies (see Gruman and Saks 2011). In this way, HR managers can demonstrate the 'thinking performer' skills expected of the HR business partner. Another interesting stream of research looks at PM from the employee perspective (see, for example, Buchner 2007), a valuable route for the increasing number of less hierarchical organisations employing knowledge workers.

Other important contributions that HR can make include: facilitating communication and training for both appraisers and appraisees, as this enables a more inclusive and positive process; communication of company strategy, which will lead to individual objectives; and helping employees see how their own values align with those of the organisation in order to build commitment and engagement.

CRITICAL REFLECTION

Global competition places greater pressure on the cost of employment (by driving costs down), with arguably employees expected to work harder and be more productive (output driven). Underlying this is the expectation that employees work longer hours, beyond their stated contracts of employment. Assuming that PM lies primarily within the remit of line managers, how can the HR function work with line managers to ensure that employees are not overworked, to the point that employee burnout may emerge within departments or divisions?

CONCLUSION

The employment relationship continues to change in differing organisational contexts and climates. Performance remains at the centre of organisational strategies and plans, but what is expected of employees in terms of outputs has perhaps heightened. Talent management and developing future leaders remain key issues for organisations and these are undoubtedly (if not sometimes, subtly) linked to PM.

From an HRM and HRD perspective, the emphasis should be on developing people rather than on the job itself. However, the challenge for employers may be in retaining employees for the duration of their most productive work (while they add value) and no longer. The choice of a global talent pool remains attractive for some organisations, but the reality for most organisations remains the need to drive down (not simply control) the cost of employment, with many public services in the UK enduring a pay freeze over the last few years, manufacturing companies competing on cost with the rest of the world.

The HR (and HRD) strategy has to encompass all aspects affecting performance, at contextual, organisational, team and individual level. To do this, it has to be part of the main business strategy, closely aligned to organisational culture and supported by appropriate mechanisms – such as organisational structure, HR policies and procedures – and be strongly aligned to the HRD strategy.

More flexible and fluid arrangements will be necessary, within which there is a greater appreciation of the subjective, tacit, multi-stakeholder aspects of performance. From a more strategic perspective, the resource-based view of HR (Boxall 1996, Boxall and Purcell 2003) suggests ways in which organisations can build upon unique clusters or 'bundles' of human and technical resources in order to improve levels of performance and thereby achieve competitive advantage in the marketplace. The agility highlighted by Dyer and Shafer (1999) and adapted by Boxall and Purcell (2003) may provide an insight as to how organisations can use PM within a bundle of HR activities.

The HRD strategy could also be enhanced to incorporate ways in which HRD and HRD professionals can assist in motivating employees (Buchner 2007), and move away from what is 'being done' to employees and move towards how the employees can grow in their capabilities, skills and competences.

PM may contribute to the success of the firm, but the vital issue is how the talents of employees can be retained, developed and utilised so as to add value to the organisation. Whilst we may concentrate on the output measurement from PM and deal with its consequences, the question to be answered is 'How do we increase performance?' The answer may take us back to developing and nurturing the organisation's greatest asset – employees: a theme we developed in Chapter 10.

KEY LEARNING POINTS

- PM is only a process. The perspective that senior management adopts will impact significantly on how the process is implemented and the consequences of the process followed through.
- Emphasis needs to be placed upon the employees' expectations throughout the whole PM and appraisal process. These expectations may link to the psychological contract and organisational culture influences.
- When it comes to setting performance targets, there is a strong requirement to readjust to contextual changes and maintain a realistic perspective, or the targets themselves may negatively impact upon performance.
- The question of who defines performance is a critical part of the PM process. The relationship between the appraiser and appraisee needs to be clearly defined and professionally maintained.
- There needs to be a sensitive and pragmatic balance of PM, motivation and reward systems to affect appropriate performance outcomes.
- Managers (including HR professionals) need to understand not just what motivates employees, but why they are motivated.

REVIEW QUESTIONS

1   Critically assess the role and contribution that HR makes to the PM process.

2   What motivates you at work, and how would you classify these motivators in terms of content and process theories?

3   To what extent is 360-degree feedback a fad that is unsustainable as a true and workable practice (in relation to manager–employee interactions)?

4   Do you believe that everything surrounding and including PM places too much emphasis upon the individual, at the expense of teams, divisions, organisational cultures, etc?

CASE STUDY 12.3

 JOHN LEWIS PARTNERSHIP

Highly praised and much loved, the John Lewis Partnership (JLP) has more than 80,000 partners in the best-known and arguably most successful example of employee ownership in the UK.

The partners (all permanent employees) co-own 276 Waitrose supermarkets and 36 John Lewis stores, an online and catalogue business, a production unit and even a farm. The workforce is retail-dominated, but also comprises distribution workers, head office staff and specialist buying, IT and finance functions. The workforce is stable, with lower turnover than its competitors and longer service. People who join JLP tend to go on to build careers through the organisation.

Andrew Clark, head of reward, is in no doubt that JLP's success is down to its partners and the competitive advantage they bring. They are, he says, 'what differentiates us from other organisations'. One of Clark's key priorities, however, is to further unlock the competitive advantage of partners to ensure JLP retains its successful position and, although this is an HR issue generally, he is certain that reward has a central role to play.

A key part of the reward strategy is pay and benefits positioning and Clark, along with the partnership council, has thought very carefully about where JLP positions itself in the market and how it rewards good performance through its PRP approach rather than reward basic levels of performance. JLP now pays above national minimum wage across the country regardless of local conditions that may allow them to pay minimum rates. And while there is, says Clark, pressure to be market-leading on recruitment rates, this is not the approach JLP has decided to take. While some competitors may pay slightly higher starting rates, there is often very minimal pay progression beyond that point, whereas at JLP, through individual performance-driven progression, partners can, over time, achieve earning rates substantially ahead of their starting pay. So for Clark it is about being competitive on base pay, market-leading on benefits, but being really distinctive on overall earning potential. By way of illustration, he says:

'What we want is to be distinctive on rewarding excellent performers and to allow earning potential without having to be promoted. So if we've got an excellent furniture saleswoman who is of real value to the business, why shouldn't we be paying her a really great rate? Why should she need to go and be a section manager somewhere else, when actually her skills are best suited to her job and she can really drive her own earning potential?'

Getting these 'nuts and bolts' of pay right, says Clark, is the 'rock of solidity' underpinning the whole employee value proposition. In his view, if partners are paid right, they understand it, and if they think their pay is fair, consistent and equitable, this allows the organisation and partners to move on to discuss other things – from developing the benefits proposition to engagement and high performance.

As well as getting base pay positioned right and pay progression driving individual performance, JLP's total reward package is pretty exceptional. Although it was lower in 2011, the universal partnership bonus was still 14 per cent of salary (the equivalent of more than seven weeks' pay). There are a vast array of benefits on offer, from store discounts, subsidised holidays and leisure activities to life assurance and a final-salary pension scheme. Innovative ways of presenting total reward statements – using QR codes so partners can access them via their smartphones, for example – are reaching those partners who may not engage with benefits through traditional media. Ultimately, though, Clark is unequivocal about the bigger picture: 'Customers keep coming back to us because of our partners. That is the key focus for the business, for HR and for reward.'

What JLP is executing in its reward strategy is all about putting the partners at the centre of this hugely successful business.

Source: CIPD (2012l)

Question

1   How does the concept of a 'partner' possibly change the employment relationship and attitude towards rewards?

EXPLORE FURTHER

Armstrong, M. and Baron, A. (2005) *Managing Performance: Performance management in action*. London: CIPD. Remains the frontrunner of PM texts. Particularly useful on the 'how to' approaches.

Buytendijk, F. (2008) *Performance Leadership: The next practices to motivate your people, align stakeholders, and lead your industry*. McGraw-Hill Professional. This text provides a broader perspective on PM and is strong on highlighting its pitfalls.

Cokins, G. (2004) *Performance Management: Finding the missing pieces (to close the intelligence gap)*. New York: Wiley and SAS Business Series. This text provides a pragmatic approach to PM and introduces a range of techniques and approaches that HR professionals should find both interesting and useful.

Hutchinson, S. (2013) *Performance Management: Theory and practice*. London: CIPD Publications.

Perkins, S.J. and White, G. (2011) *Reward Management: Alternatives, Consequences and Context*. London: CIPD.

Read the latest edition of the CIPD Annual Reward Survey for insights as to what is changing and what is remaining the same in relation to benefits and rewards available and adopted.

PART 5

CONCLUSION

CHAPTER 13

Summary Themes and Future Trends

Gary Rees and Ray French

LEARNING OUTCOMES

After reading this chapter, you should be able to:

- identify some of the key challenges and themes impacting on HR

- indicate some possible future HR developments

- highlight key research findings that impact upon HR (this learning outcome is embedded throughout the chapter).

OVERVIEW

The purpose of this final chapter is to highlight recurrent themes in our book in order to identify the key challenges facing those who lead, manage and develop people in the contemporary workplace. As we have seen, responsibility in this area may fall to a designated HR function. In some cases, though – for example, in many smaller organisations – line managers take the leading role in managing workers. An alternative model is to outsource this activity to specialist providers. We noted at several points throughout the book that this outsourcing model has become increasingly prevalent. In reality, a combination of line and HR expertise is required in many situations in order to effectively manage people at work. In Chapter 2 we examined the possible shape of HR activity – ie, who carries out the work? – in greater detail.

In conclusion, though, whoever undertakes the people management role will be required to operate in a pressured situation. Based on consistent trends over the past 20 years, they will almost certainly be faced with competing demands to secure high worker performance leading to perceived added value, while at the same time securing employee engagement. As we noted at the very start of the book, managing people within such a demanding context is no easy task. We look again at key external developments facing HR in this final chapter, together with suggestions for effective people management in a challenging era.

How can we most effectively lead, manage and develop people? While we counsel against regarding the latest fad (whatever that may be) as a panacea, there is a need to evaluate major contemporary research in HRM and HRD as well as valid theories and models in areas such as motivation and how people learn. Sometimes these models highlight central findings which have remained valid over many decades, while in other cases recent research points to new and developing insights. The challenge for students, and of course managers, is to appreciate what is changing and what is enduring in this subject area. In this chapter we highlight findings and theories which can help aspiring and existing managers.

The chapter concludes with a look at the possible future of HR with reference to recent research such as the CIPD (2010a) 'next generation' report.

As the core book for CIPD's Leading, Managing and Developing People module, we trust that this chapter will serve as a useful revision tool for both students and tutors. Please also refer to www.cipd.co.uk for additional resources.

INTRODUCTION

In this book we have examined a very wide range of topics. The breadth of coverage reflects the all-encompassing nature of leading, managing and developing people. When examining the management of employees we have considered the nature of the employment relationship (Chapter 11), recruitment and selection (Chapter 9), training and development (Chapter 10) and performance management and reward (Chapter 12). There are, in short, many different and varied aspects to employing workers – although in Chapters 2 and 3 we saw how such disparate threads might be subsumed within a strategic focus or 'bundles' of connected policies.

Beyond the specific subdivisions of HR work listed above, we have also stressed the broader importance and role of leadership as an activity (Chapter 5). Linked with leadership are the ethical and professional aspects of leading and managing people (Chapter 4).

We have also argued that the ways in which people are managed are influenced in a most profound way by wider economic, political and social developments. The drive for flexibility (Chapters 7 and 8), emanating from work organisations – and externally from national governments and supra-national bodies – has been particularly influential in this regard. Increasingly, flexibility becomes part of the mindset of employees too and we have shown how the desire for, or even expectation of, flexible working can impact on workers' psychological contracts. Managing flexible work arrangements sensitively and efficiently brings a new focus to HR.

It is also necessary to consider the role and place of HR within organisations as all the topical knowledge and cutting-edge skills possessed by managers would be ineffective if HR does not have a defined role and status within a workplace. Only if this role and status exists can those who manage people have a positive influence on organisations' people management strategies, policies and practices.

We have seen how HR can be both a specialist and 'line' role and how it has developed from a support administrative function focused on compliance to, in many cases, a fully integrated business partner role.

In view of the broad topic coverage of this book, implicit in the subject area, we will select particular areas for further scrutiny in this final chapter.

Although key external factors facing HR are numerous and ever-changing we have highlighted the concept of globalisation and its potentially wide impact on employment, both in terms of creating clusters of key knowledge workers but also the continued presence of more routine work and standardised workers. We also focus on the role of macroeconomic factors, specifically the economic downturn which began in 2008, on managing people in different contexts such as the private and public sectors, drawing on material presented in Chapter 3.

We also return to look at particular themes which are threaded through the book. It is increasingly a routine part of HR managers' life to work with a diverse workforce and we summarise issues surrounding diversity raised in previous sections, particularly Chapters 4 and 11. The theme of conflict is also revisited, because although types of conflict may ebb and flow with time, some degree of conflict is inevitable within workplaces. Conflict is by no means a negative phenomenon and can be managed to drive up organisational performance. We deal also with the phenomenon of outsourcing and the sensitive areas this flags up for HR.

One overriding important theme is change. In Chapter 6 we concluded that it is vital to plan, communicate and execute change successfully if a business was to survive. Organisations may wish to change or, alternatively, are compelled to, due to altered legal obligations or some other changing external driver. As change is ultimately about people, HR in partnership with line managers has a key role in change management. In this chapter we identify some important changing trends as they affect people management. However, what is more important than identifying specific examples of change is the recognition that HR managers need to have a positive attitude or mindset towards change *per se*, given the inherently changing nature of leading, managing and developing people.

HR CONTEMPORARY CHALLENGES

GLOBALISATION AND TALENT CLUSTERS

All organisations need to confront the key issues emanating from the external environment. In the early twenty-first century one key environmental factor is globalisation, powered by the strategic aim of companies to seek out new market opportunities, while attempting to use changes in the environment to their advantage. Such an evolutionary trend reflects better communication and accessibility provided by the Internet, development of sophisticated and standardised software (so-called 'microsoftisation'), improvements in infrastructure, and decades of tough competition necessitating cost-cutting in all sectors. As these trends evolve, all organisations become challenged to achieve sustainability in their marketplaces.

In essence, globalisation is underpinned by profoundly important economic, socio-cultural, technological and political factors. It is a deep-rooted phenomenon which has impacted on business in different but always important ways and is predicted to evolve – paradoxically in unpredictable ways – in future.

Linstead *et al* (2009) characterise globalisation as an increased blurring of boundaries of all sorts including those between nation states, economies, industries and work organisations. A sense of greater interconnectedness between different parts of the world has implications for all aspects of business. For our purposes, though, we can identify two: first, the pressure to drive down employment costs in the face of significant overseas competition; and second, freer movement of workers across the globe resulting in a more diverse workforce.

Profound consequences for HR can follow. For example, some private sector organisations in Western economies have recognised the lower cost-base of other economies such as India and responded by relocating particular business operations there. This is by no means an inevitable process. Bawden (2009) notes how companies including BT, Powergen, Santander and Orange have repatriated call centre jobs back to the UK from India in recent years.

However, there has been a clear trend since the mid-1990s to relocate white-collar jobs from the UK to emerging and developing economies.

At the same time, much routine manufacturing work has similarly been outsourced or otherwise moved to developing countries like China. One can predict that these emerging economies, built on relatively low-cost provision, will themselves develop as the cycles of wealth creation and increased opportunity begin to take their course.

KNOWLEDGE WORKERS

What are the implications of such trends for the HR manager? French (2010) notes that one consequence of globalisation has been the concentration of clusters of world-class expertise in particular sectors by location. Thus we find high-technology clusters in Silicon Valley in northern California, parts of Japan and Cambridge in the UK. Much of the net inflow of workers to London (170,000 in 2006 alone), prior to the 'credit crunch' of 2008, can be attributed to the status of London as a magnet for talent and world-class cities continue to welcome in talented workers. In 2013, Mayor Boris Johnson stressed the need for London to attract 'the brightest entrepreneurial minds', noting that a new development in Canary Wharf was well placed to 'foster just the talent we need to future-proof the capital's technology and financial sectors' (Wood 2013). Who would take the lead in fostering such talent and what is HR's role?

In Chapter 8 we recorded the view that an upskilling of the UK's workforce could be accompanied by a workforce desiring greater autonomy and control in their jobs; see Hutton (2004).

The term 'knowledge workers' has come to denote people engaged in non-repetitive results-oriented work, who require continuous learning and the exercise of creativity (see Bratton and Gold 2007). It is argued that the demands of such high-level employees can be dealt with more effectively by those organisations which lead and manage workers in imaginative ways and develop them to a very high level of competence.

REFLECTIVE ACTIVITY 13.1

Traditionally, financial indicators have been the only measure of performance that really mattered. Profitability, earnings-per-share and return-on-capital-employed, among others, were considered to be the best barometers of business performance.

Some businesses, especially knowledge-based firms, are now recognising that short-term financial metrics provide a poor indication of organisational health. Current profitability provides no clue to future performance, financial or otherwise. If customer satisfaction, in terms of quality and delivery, is low, for example, then consumers will search for alternatives.

The primacy of financial measures has given way to a basket of performance indicators – including quality, customer satisfaction and employee satisfaction – as organisations grapple with the ever-changing environment in which they operate.

It is no longer good enough to manage tangible assets efficiently; the effectiveness of intangible assets must also be added to the equation. The bulk of intangible assets are knowledge-based, including the competence of staff and feedback from customers. Importantly, and unlike conventional tangible assets, knowledge grows when it is shared.

The growth of predominantly knowledge-based organisations – that is, businesses whose activities are based principally on the expertise, skills and creativity of their staff rather than on the physical production of goods – has raised the importance of measuring the so-called invisible factors that determine corporate success or otherwise.

As Margareta Barchan, chief executive of Celemi, the Swedish-owned global consultancy specialising in corporate learning tools, has explained: 'As a knowledge-based business, we at Celemi realised early on that our financial statement did not represent the true value of our firm. Where was it reflected that we were a team of highly skilled professionals who provided effective service to our clients? Where would a stakeholder be able to assess the value of the unique learning processes that we were creating for our clients? Where did we account

for the value of our loyal and growing customer base?'	1	To what extent have Celemi added value to their business?

As we saw in Chapter 9, the concepts involved in recruiting, retaining and retraining knowledge workers have changed considerably in recent years. Less emphasis is placed on recruiting and training knowledge workers for specific jobs because jobs are changing so quickly. Instead, employees are recruited and developed who can contribute in a flexible way to an organisation's future. If HR adopts more of a fit-the-job-to-the-person (FJP) approach, as opposed taking an FPJ (fit-the-person-to-the-job) stance, there may be additional benefits in terms of performance and future performance.

Perhaps HR needs to be more innovative in terms of capturing talent, and then nurturing it. The extent to which HR adopts a risk-averse approach by following standardised processes and not 'thinking beyond the box' could result in the loss of talent. Emphasis needs to be placed upon seeking talent, with contribution to performance – a key criteria for recruitment and selection, not just in the job/role being filled following a prescriptive process, including possible avoidance of legislative malpractice and concerns over potential discriminatory practice.

Getting the best from knowledge workers is dependent on their having the autonomy and discretion to contribute to their maximum ability. Clearly, this can be risky for the organisation and requires a certain level of trust and more subtle (and probably informal) forms of performance management. A full system thus comprises hired, empowered and bright, well-managed knowledge workers with managers who have commensurate skills and abilities. If the whole system does not work from a process point of view, however, sustainability and the high-performance working ideal is lost.

Whilst there are many challenges facing HR, as we have seen throughout the book, there has been a recent preoccupation with managing 'high-end', multi-skilled, highly qualified, high-contributing talent. However, not all jobs are prescribed as high end, and inevitably, many workers and managers will occupy 'standard' jobs, and in some cases, what could be deemed 'dirty' jobs.

Concepts such as knowledge management, knowledge workers, talent, talent pipeline and talent management may be commonplace in many organisations. To what extent these terminologies are rhetoric rather than reality may come down to definition.

MANAGING ROUTINE WORK AND THE 'STANDARDISED' WORKER

Much HR literature – for example, Harrison and Kessels (2003) and Holbeche (2008b) – focuses on achieving the best from knowledge workers. As the authors of several chapters have pointed out, in so doing we can be in danger of ignoring the less glamorous, often worse-paid staff who occupy more routine functions. Some would argue, especially from a total quality view, that all jobs can be treated as holding knowledge and all staff should be seen as knowledge workers, and this is probably true. For the most part, however, our rhetoric fails to meet that reality, and in many instances standardised jobs are, potentially, just that.

Beardwell and Claydon (2010) indicates that the term 'talent' has typically been used to identify individuals who make a difference to organisational performance. As such this could, and arguably should, refer to all employees, in addition to the more specific connotation of key positions that are important to fill for an organisation. In summary, talent management is a broad term referring to all important workers and roles which are pivotally important to organisational success.

Certain tasks (such as serving at a food counter) have been through the mill of cost-cutting. Sections of employment have very often been deskilled, to the point where workers feel alienated from their tasks (see Chapter 8). These workers experience pressures different from those of the uncertainties connected to knowledge workers, which include the pressure from high-volume repetitive work with little control and the associated dangers of work intensification.

Managing standardised workers is usually more straightforward because the tangible outputs are measurable (Chapter 12). In reality, one is often looking to neutralise or minimise the damage that can be caused by staff not bothering (consciously or unconsciously) to undertake routine tasks effectively. In such instances a person–job fit approach (Chapter 8) is appropriate in order to align expectations on both sides of the employment relationship. Clearly, this strategy has consequences for the psychological contract, which was discussed in Chapter 7.

While performance management of standardised workers might be straightforward (because their tasks are straightforward), reward is not. In Chapter 12 Tymon and Rees described wages as an important aspect of reward, up to a point. For many standardised workers, wages are of high importance. However, an organisation must ensure that it does not create an escalating cost-drain from year-on-year wage increases at high levels because these are difficult to correct at a later stage.

Traditionally, HR is mainly associated with FPJ, where a standardised procedure includes a job description, person specification and a set of guiding rules and principles around matching the 'best' candidate to a job. To recruit and retain standardised staff, the 'cocktail' of benefits has to be thought through carefully to match the needs of a targeted set of available staff. Simple financial rewards can be used in an uncomplicated contract that has supervisors who are strong in 'management' using conventional performance management processes.

Alternatively, one might try to cut the wage bill and offer other types of inducements, such as prospects of internal development and promotion (used commonly by media companies), a strong sense of positive-value culture (illustrated by the supermarket Asda in Chapter 9), or promote positive aspects of the work – as is commonly seen in parts of the voluntary sector, where the nature of a job-holder's contribution makes a difference to vulnerable people. The 'leadership' aspect of our text would be more important if such non-wage angles were adopted in order to provide proximal reinforcement of the offer.

Regarding leadership in such contexts (Chapter 5), it is likely that selection of managers who deal mainly with standardised workers will depend on strength in management with leadership (at a high level) being less crucial. However, managers who are in this situation really do need to have skills in leading, managing and developing people. The importance of focusing effort on business objectives and the need for a clear direction and purpose is crucial in order to ensure that the managing and leading of staff has a clear aim, and thus provides the basis for performance management. Staff will detect any absence of a clear direction, and its lack will undermine efforts of leading (nowhere?) and managing (for what purpose?). This presents a fundamentally important but difficult task.

MANAGING DURING ECONOMIC HARDSHIP

It could be argued that HR faces heightened challenges during an economic recession (see the McDonald's case study in Chapter 1). In 2007 much of the world began to experience the onset of an economic downturn, fuelled by a crisis in sub-prime mortgage lending in the USA. In itself the ensuing crisis demonstrated the interconnectedness of national economies as the crisis rapidly took hold in diverse parts of the planet. There were documented job cuts in many sectors. Indeed, many businesses failed in the course of the recession, leading to job losses in companies with progressive HR policies and practices swept away in the economic and financial maelstrom. When this edition was written in 2013 the UK economy was still 'flatlining'. However, there is evidence that many organisations have reconsidered their HR policies during the downturn while attempting to maintain their overall strategic focus. The CIPD (2009c, p2) thus quoted a corporate HR leader from a financial services group:

> Our talent management initiatives are robust and believed to add value to the organisation. We therefore believe that the attraction and retention of talent is even more important in the current economic environment than it has been at any time in the past.

The CIPD (2009a) presented findings from a research study carried out among a sample of 705 members who held senior roles across the private, public and third (not-for-profit) sectors. Some findings resulting from reduced budgets were perhaps predictable with concerns regarding employee development initiatives, coupled with the macro-level economic situation impacting on pay and recruitment and selection – with many respondents reporting a shift of focus from recruitment to employee retention.

The impact of economic recession has also resulted in some more innovative strategic refocusing according to this report. Findings include:

- Organisations focusing more of their time on engaging, motivating, retaining and fully using the skills of existing employees.
- Recognition of increasing opportunities to recruit talent discarded by competitors.
- As noted earlier, renewed scrutiny on talent management systems and processes.
- More honest and frequent communications between managers and other employees, with greater individual understanding of the situation faced by the business.
- Reconsideration of pay and reward, with more creative thinking about non-financial rewards.
- Greater emphasis on ethical leaders who are able to lead and motivate in both bad and good times.

REFLECTIVE ACTIVITY 13.2

The HR Outlook CIPD report (2012b) took a fresh look at HR priorities. In this study 68 per cent of respondents reported that managing performance was a strong area of focus. However, in the report, the public sector is shown as more likely to be focusing on managing change and cultural transformation, workforce planning, employee well-being and organisational restructuring rather than the private sector, which is more focused on engagement, staff retention and talent management.

Consider what factors could underpin this apparent divide between the public and private sectors, and how the role of HR may differ within these particular contexts.

TURBULENCE AND HARDSHIP IN THE PUBLIC SECTOR

We saw in Chapter 3 that while differences in HR between the private and public sectors may not be great in many instances, the high proportion of staff costs in many public sector institutions meant that HR had a fundamental role in determining expenditure levels. In 2010 all the main political parties in the UK set out policies intended to reduce costs, at the very least by asking the same staff to do more. Few expected the years following 2010 to be anything other than tough and this has been borne out by measures introduced by the coalition government.

In 1992 a leading HR academic, John Storey, published a scheme which differentiated between traditional personnel management/industrial relations (IR) and the emerging term HRM. Storey provided 27 points of difference which would locate the characteristics of personnel/IR and HRM in relation to each other. Such differences included beliefs and assumptions, strategic aspects and key levers exhibited by both traditions.

Storey's scheme identified the following points. While in the personnel/IR model the manager would be preoccupied with developing and enforcing contractual obligations, in HR there was a move to get employees to go beyond contract. The HR role was seen as transformational as opposed to transactional (see Chapter 5 for a summary of these terms). There was also a difference in that HRM was concerned to foster a greater link between performance and reward in contrast to highly regulated pay. It can be argued that the personnel/IR tradition as outlined here is strongly reminiscent of the way in which people were managed in the public sector. The flagging up of the HRM alternative opened the way to a reconsideration of how people were to be led, managed and developed in the sector.

In the same period (from roughly 1990), a revolution occurred within UK local government and public service providers. Political agendas comprising reduction in taxes (local and national) together with advances in transparency and public audit resulted in generational change in the sector. UK governments of all political persuasions have consistently rewarded those organisations which do well and public service providers are now used to a variety of league tables. Such processes increase expectation to perform in ever-spiralling demands. The more recent downturns in global and local economies have, as indicated earlier, squeezed the public sector still further as governments seek to balance expenditure.

Such pressures have changed the nature of leadership and management in the sector. Hospitals and universities now attract a different type of chief executive from what was expected 20 years ago. The same is true of most of the public sector and the expanding voluntary sector. Top leaders now need to 'drive' the organisation in more senses than one: steering has always been a function, but chief executives are pressing the accelerator for change and achievement as never before.

One can conclude that linked developments in the academic and political spheres led to a situation whereby the nature of people management in the UK public sector was reviewed and in many cases took on a new direction emphasising a performance focus combined with an attempt to engage workers and to derive added value from employees. The HR function itself came under pressure with new roles evolving and a need to demonstrate relevance in terms of performance, together with cost savings and efficiencies.

REFLECTIVE ACTIVITY 13.3

In Chapter 1 we referred to the attempts by Wychavon District Council to put overall management principles into effect through policies and styles designed to engender employee engagement. Among the council's stated strategic management principles were:

- adopt an entrepreneurial, not municipal, culture
- apply good performance management as a cornerstone of the council's management

- invest to save where there are robust cases to do so
- focus on resident and customer satisfaction as a principal objective
- continually develop and challenge to remain excellent.

Wychavon Council's objectives could only be achieved by a change in organisational culture. Refer back to Chapter 1 and summarise the ways in which it sought to engage its employees in this change programme.

Question

1   What type of leadership would be most appropriate in such a situation? Give

reasons for your conclusion, with reference to material set out in Chapter 5.

KEY THEMES

Having outlined some of the key external factors confronting those who manage people in organisations, we now turn to identify some of the important themes contained within this book which, we have argued, underpin people management in contemporary workplaces.

MANAGING DIVERSITY

How organisations approach and manage diversity – introduced in Chapter 4, and explored in greater depth in Chapter 11 – will be a 'differentiator' for the future. It is much easier, and tempting, to hire similar people who get on easily. A homogeneous workforce might be thought to be an easy means of avoiding the 'diversity issue'. However, there is much evidence suggesting that enhancing diversity within groups and teams has a potential pay-off in terms of performance; see Belbin (1993).

Notwithstanding this classic finding from the field of social psychology, it is also true that a diverse workforce needs careful managing if the benefits of diversity are to be secured. In examining the specific case of cultural diversity, French (2010) recorded the consensus view of research in this area – namely, that multicultural work teams will either perform much better than mono-cultural groups or much worse. So the key to securing performance is good management. Surowiecki (2004) made a similar point in highlighting the potential wisdom of crowds. He noted, for example, that if one wanted to guess the weight of an ox, the average of a crowd's guesses would always give the best estimate. The more diverse the crowd, the more accurate they would be.

Surowiecki also recognised, however, that if a high-performing team were left to their own devices, they may come to feel invincible and hence vulnerable to making blatant mistakes. This is an important finding reminiscent of the notion of 'groupthink' (Janis 1982). A seemingly excellent work team, or trouble-free work environment more generally, should never be taken for granted, therefore, and both their outcomes and processes should be monitored with a view to swift intervention if problems are signalled.

So we see that managing diversity is a challenging activity offering both the promise of enhanced worker performance while at the same time containing in-built dangers. More generally, the recent findings outlined above point to another key theme within this book: namely, the need to review evidence and to be open to new research insights.

In view of persistent global economic and social trends, it remains unlikely that any sector can survive without embracing diversity, depending on the level of supply of specific workers. Where there are staff shortages, finding homogeneous workers will require either specialised recruitment and selection (Chapter 9), selective internal promotion through learning, training and development (Chapter 10), or increasing rewards (Chapter 12).

We have also suggested that diversity can be a source of competitive advantage (see the Ford case study in Chapter 11), despite the caveats in the last but one paragraph. It is hard to see how an organisation can only partially adopt the changes needed to cope with a diverse organisation and still remain effective. For example, if current trends continue, the UK and other markets with high employment levels will continue to be net importers of skilled workers, with most entrants having a diverse range of backgrounds. Organisations which learn how to take advantage of new pools of talent – wherever they come from – have potential for differentiation.

MANAGING DIFFICULTY

We conclude this section of the chapter by highlighting several further areas which can prove problematic for those engaged in HR, together with some suggestions for overcoming problems.

Hand-in-hand with diversity come the effort and challenge involved in managing the inevitable conflicting interests that difference produces – which can lead to actual conflict. The effective manager will ensure that any ensuing problems are limited to constructive and task-related conflicts (see Chapter 11) and do not degenerate into damaging interpersonal disputes. As we have suggested, diverse groups can produce innovative and smart solutions that provide (differentiated) competitive advantage. To be successful such staff will need context- or contingency-based leadership styles (Chapter 5) rather than one-best-way. Managers who can cope with such demands will have to be recruited or developed.

 SOCIAL MEDIA AT NOKIA

CASE STUDY 13.1

In February 2011, it looked like things couldn't get any worse for Nokia, the Finnish mobile phone company. The now famous 'burning platform' blog post by CEO Stephen Elop (which many at first thought to be a leaked internal memo) rapidly went viral, with millions of people reading his painfully frank thoughts on where the company was going wrong, how it had missed out on market share and that it had to decide whether to 'plunge into icy waters' or perish.

Matthew Hanwell, Nokia's community and social media HR director, remembers it well: 'I was angry,' he says. 'It's a great metaphor for where we are, but we actually knew all of this already. That said, it was a wake-up call for the company in terms of saying: "We have some very difficult decisions to make now, which way are we going to go?"'

What Nokia's detractors at the time probably didn't know was that Hanwell, alongside teams from IT and other parts of the business, had already started work some months before on encouraging employees to have a more open and honest dialogue. A project known as 'Reconnecting Nokia' had commenced six months prior to Elop joining the company in September 2010. Central to this was the use of social media. This encapsulated a portfolio of internal social networking platforms, including a Facebook-type tool known as SocialCast, whereby people can post questions, 'follow' each other, rate videos and share ideas.

The idea was to lower the barriers to participation in the wider company dialogue and improve employee engagement at a time when the company's fortunes seemed to be uncertain. 'If you invite participation, rather than broadcasting everything to employees, you lower the threshold to people providing ideas,' explains Hanwell. 'Those who are able to participate and interact are generally more engaged in what they are doing.'

Openness and honesty

Social media is also central to the new leadership values of openness and honesty at the company. On his first day at Nokia, new CEO Elop posted in one of the social media forums, saying: 'Imagine we're having a cup of coffee together. What would you say that we need to change, what must we keep and what do you think that I might miss?' The response was immense, with some threads on the discussion attracting hundreds of posts.

But where some executives might treat this feedback as a box-ticking exercise, Elop started a dialogue about some of the things that had been said. 'We knew that he was listening because he was responding to some of the comments in that social media thread. And, better than that, he would at every opportunity stand up at a "town hall" meeting and reference these conversations that he had been having online. It was very powerful,' says Hanwell.

Using social media to bring employees together was not new at Nokia, however. It had introduced an employee forum known as 'Jazz Cafe' in 2001, but, over time, a raft of new forums, wikis and blogs had been introduced without any of them becoming truly effective. Ensuring that employees know where to go to access intelligence has been crucial in how social media has helped to turn Nokia's fortunes around. 'We decided that if we were going to create a social media culture in Nokia we should have a portfolio,' explains Hanwell. 'We wanted something where, in the same way you don't have to think before you send an email or start a PowerPoint presentation, people would not have to think where to go to interact in a certain way.' SocialCast now has approaching 30,000 users across the organisation.

Role of technology

Having had 'a foot in both camps', as Hanwell describes his career, helps him understand the role of technology in improving employee collaboration. His background is in technology, having

worked in HR and enterprise resource planning systems implementation before joining Nokia in 1999 to roll out its global HR software system. He 'officially' joined the HR function in 2000, but admits that he is 'fascinated by the balance between technology and people'. 'How do you get people to use technology really well, how do you get the most out of that investment?' he asks.

His job title is a highly unusual one for an HR professional, but one he believes to be forward-thinking. 'I had this responsibility for creating a community way of working and working out how we get communities to come together in Nokia. Social media would enable all of that to happen, so I was given this title,' says Hanwell. The sponsor for social media at Nokia is its head of HR, Juha Akras.

Fear around social media

'In my opinion, HR needs to be much more involved in [social media] and take a much stronger role in it going forward,' he adds. 'It affects the way people collaborate and the extent to which they come together. That's an HR issue.' However, he recognises that there is considerable fear around embracing social media (on the *Personnel Today* website) in the HR community. 'The analogy I always use is swimming – if you can't swim, if you've never learnt to swim, being confronted with a piece of deep water is pretty frightening,' he explains. 'The digital natives will dive straight in, but some people are afraid to even dip their toe in the water. If you don't actually try it, you'll never understand the benefits of it.'

But while social media is helping Nokia to overcome the issues that have hampered its success in the past few years – silo working, a failure to innovate quickly enough and not recognising how the market for mobile phones had changed – Hanwell appreciates that it is not a 'silver bullet' that is going to make everything right.

'But it does give you a sense of openness and participation so you can understand and debate what's wrong,' he says. 'The discussion we had about how Nokia should change told us what we already knew as a company, but perhaps before we had not been able to utilise that intelligence, because we had no way of accessing those conversations. If every individual had sent an email, nobody else would have been able to know what was being said.'

New strategy

When the company announced its new strategy, days after the 'burning platform' post made headlines in February 2011, Hanwell and his team precreated a number of groups within SocialCast so conversations about the new strategy could take place. Every opportunity is taken to embed openness and discussion into employees' working lives. Social media is also being used to help employees affected by the changes at the company, for example by redundancy, to discuss those changes with colleagues and share the burden.

It might seem counterintuitive to place social media at the heart of Nokia's future strategy when there is so much it needs to achieve to claw back a share of this fast-changing market, but Hanwell and the other leaders at the company do not doubt its role. 'We find people get more done, and better things done, as a result of being better connected,' he says. It is difficult to argue with that.

Questions

1   What went wrong at Nokia, and why?

2   What actions should Hanwell have taken to have ensured a better outcome for social media usage at Nokia?

There is evidence that an increasing number of organisations have outsourced activities, for example to subcontractors in order to concentrate on their own core capabilities (Child 2005). In an important sense outsourcing has become normal and accepted practice within the notion of flexibility and its associated benefits; see Chapter 7. Subcontractors, offering a better price than can be generated internally, might be using legitimate means (such as economies of scale) in their cost-cutting, but they might not. How far the contracting organisation should (and does) investigate the terms and conditions of subcontracted workers is an area ripe for investigation as the structure of our economy changes. HR is likely to be at the forefront when such investigations do become routine. They will have to be well placed in terms of their investigating skills and extend their understanding of all aspects of managing and leading people beyond the legal issues into the ethical dimensions of employment; see Chapter 4.

ENDURING THEORIES AND MODELS FOR LEADING, MANAGING AND DEVELOPING PEOPLE

CONTINGENCY APPROACHES

Which concepts and models are especially relevant when leading, managing and developing people? One important insight is that there are few universally applicable principles and prescriptions. Throughout this book we find numerous examples of policy measures which can work very well – but only in particular situations. A contingency perspective provides the guiding philosophy that the best way to organise and manage –

in this case lead, manage and develop people – will all depend on the particular circumstances. This insight is itself not new as several British and American studies, which concluded that organisations should be designed and structured according to their size or technology employed or the turbulence they encountered in their market, are now five decades old; see Burns and Stalker (1961) and Lawrence and Lorsch (1967). So a contingency approach to business and management is part of mainstream thought. Returning to the area of leading, managing and developing people in the early twenty-first century, we find examples of the continuing value of the essential contingency insight in this book.

In Chapter 3 we saw how HR practices and their delivery could themselves vary according to the organisational context. Charlotte Rayner and Liza Howe-Walsh note, for example, that the recruitment and retention of volunteer workers in the third sector (charitable and voluntary organisations) was especially tough, together with funding and reward of employees. Meanwhile the particular circumstances surrounding small and medium-sized enterprises (SMEs) led to much HR work being outsourced. Growing organisations also faced specific issues with Greiner's (1972) model of crises in such organisations pointing to possible variances in how people were managed. We saw, finally, how the field of international HRM was associated with specific strategic decisions; eg whether to adopt an ethnocentric or global approach to managing people and the use of particular methods, such as mentoring for expatriate managers.

In Chapter 5 on leadership, we again saw how some academics (see Hersey *et al* (2001) and Kreitner (2001)) found that particular leadership styles would be more appropriate in some situations than others. Gill Christy suggests in her chapter that contingency perspectives remain highly relevant for the exercise of leadership in modern organisations. She concludes that the contingency perspective should inform training of leadership and management skills and that leadership might change hands in response to changed circumstances.

Contingency perspectives form the main thrust of the conclusions to Chapters 8 and 9, with the implication that principles of, and actual practices in, job design and recruitment and selection respectively could and should alter according to the situation. In Chapter 10, Alex Tymon and Margaret Mackay find value in applying the contingency principle to the area of developing employees. They indicate that the choice of learning and development techniques is strongly influenced by contingent factors such as prevailing organisational culture, resources available and learner-related factors. In Chapter 12 Alex Tymon and Gary Rees conclude that what an organisation chooses to measure within its performance management policies (an important underpinning factor) will depend on the organisational context; for example, what, deep down, it really values in its employees. In this chapter we also encounter expectancy theories of motivation which show how individual workers evaluate the link between effort, performance and reward, thereby suggesting that workers might vary considerably in terms of what motivates them and how.

ENDURING PRINCIPLES

While contingency theory is undoubtedly alive and kicking in the field of people management, we do not wish to suggest that effective leadership, management and development of people can be attained by adopting a pure 'pick and mix' of those strategies and practices which we diagnose as fitting a situation at any one time. To do so would be both simplistic and misleading, since there are undoubtedly core principles and insights which should inform managers no matter what situation they find themselves in. We set out below some of these enduring principles which have been associated with successful management over a long period.

There is a need first to ensure that all people management initiatives are seen to add value to an organisation. In Chapter 3 we presented findings of research by Truss and Gill (2009), who noted that HR was perceived as adding value if it delivered services reliably and on time. Stronger performance was correlated with a strong sense of identity and purpose amongst HR practitioners. A CIPD report (2010a) found that high-achieving HR departments were embedded in the core business of their organisations. So, in summary, the success of any policy initiative, as applied to leading, managing and developing people, will be dependent on other key managers' perceptions of how it adds value and also their pre-formed views on the credibility of the people who put forward that initiative. It is also important to employ measures and techniques which are valid – see our discussion of recruitment and selection techniques in Chapter 9 – and also relevant, as shown by the necessity of transferring learning to the workplace in Chapter 10.

In Chapters 4 and 11 we saw how the management of people was influenced by employment law, so there is a need always to ensure that existing and new measures are compliant with both national and supra-national (eg EU) legal frameworks. The effective management of the employment relationship, as set out in the first part of Chapter 11, underpins the work of all those involved in managing people. Managers' perception of this relationship should ideally go beyond ensuring minimum legal compliance. If the relationship is characterised by a proactive investment orientation towards employees, we saw that it is more likely to result in employee engagement and organisational success. This long-standing conclusion has been reinforced more recently by MacLeod and Clark (2009) and Alfes *et al* (2010).

Workers' perceptions of how they are treated continue to influence their sense of identity with the employing organisation and motivation to their work. In Chapter 12 we saw how performance management must be carried out in a fair and equitable way; for example, in an appraisal process. Performance management and reward policies should be transparent and understandable. Equity theory dates from the work of Adams (1965) and continues to receive support; see Hollyforde and Whiddett (2002). If workers perceive an injustice when they compare their own inputs and outputs – eg effort and reward – with those of others, the resultant unpleasant feeling will motivate them to take action. In Chapter 7 Simon Turner reviewed the concept of the psychological contract, which again indicates that we all make a mental comparison between inputs and outcomes at work and that a balanced state is desirable in this regard. In Chapter 4, Charlotte Rayner and Richard Christy began their discussion of ethics and professionalism by emphasising that human beings are special and can reasonably demand to be treated in certain ways by employers. They go on to conclude that managers have an important role to play in terms of acting with integrity, going beyond that which is required by the law. There is no more enduringly important and relevant principle in leading, managing and developing people than that of fair treatment.

THE FUTURE OF HR?

HR remains under threat from forces that may intend to reduce or possibly eradicate it in the near future. There will continue to be the need for an HR function, but in what guise it exists and how it operates has scope to change dramatically. The nature of communication around the globe will continue to change the ways that organisations operate. Both internal and external communication patterns will change, but what is more significant is the speed at which communication now travels. This was witnessed in March 2012 in the UK when Francis Maude, a government minister, suggested that people should top up their spare petrol cans in preparation for a potential strike by petroleum distribution companies. The result was catastrophic in terms of petrol stations running out of fuel due to panic buying by motorists. Closely allied to this is the use of social media at work. A CIPD report (2013d, p3) found that 'Social media has profound implications when applied to organisations, because it is changing the way that people interact at work and even the nature of the employment relationship.'

In a CIPD (2012m, p21) research report it is argued that 'within organisations, openness and transparency will be the vital business characteristics that will make all the difference in the coming years'. The question remains as to whether this proposition is sustainable. With transparency comes trust, and perhaps an assessment of the openness of the line manager role, as well as the HR role. In future years, employment contracts may change by adopting a shorter, more transient type of arrangement. The concept of trust may become a higher-level priority for both organisations and employees, as may the constant renegotiation of the employment relationship (CIPD 2012m).

A great deal of work in HR has been undertaken under the guise of 'employee engagement' (see Chapter 11), often referred to as the 'new motivation'. Another angle on this concept is that engagement may be the new 'retention', whereby employers seek to retain their valued employees. Whilst trust may be an important element here, remaining employed may be reward itself during times of economic recession.

In a recent CIPD survey (CIPD 2012b), 60 per cent of higher-earning HR professionals prioritise business issues over what matters to HR compared to one-third for lower-earning HR professionals. Perhaps the concept of the HR business partner is finally taking root, but whether this is beneficial is still to be seen. Aligned with the concept of trust is visibility, where senior managers in particular need to be more visible (face-to-face and virtually), and adopt a collaborative (two-way communication) approach (CIPD 2012m). In 2009, Sullivan *et al* from the Work Foundation argued that the employment relationship, together with the employer–employee relationship, trust and employer branding and segmentation are critical areas for the future of HR. All of these areas remain critical in the near future. The ultimate office for corporate social responsibility should not only lie within the HR function, but should be part of the DNA of HR (CIPD 2013a).

Ultimately HR holding high office may not be sufficient to maintain its standing in organisations. The point of reference may change from the organisation and from the manager to the employee. 'The future of work will be influenced by more networked ways of operating. Firms are more likely to manage people whom they don't employ directly. This fundamentally challenges how we define an "employee" and has massive impact upon our profession – we need to rethink how we view what an employee is' (Kinnie *et al* 2012, p3).It is vital that HR embraces and relishes its leadership role in organisations.

CONCLUSION

We began this book by stating that leading, managing and developing people is a tough topic. It is not possible to manage people effectively by adhering to a checklist. One size definitely does not fit all. Managing people is hard work, which requires thought, care and considerable attention to detail in every interaction and decision made. The sheer breadth of sub-topics covered by the chapters in this book is impressive, and expertise is developing in all areas. The ideas presented in this book provide the reader with a wide set of options to take into their own work environment. The 'basics' are needed to survive, but with changes to people's psychological contracts and changes in employee expectations, the 'basics' are likely to become more complex and demanding.

This text is being written at a time when it is widely acknowledged that change is a constant feature of our work context and all sectors are under pressure to produce results within a negative economic environment. The resource-based view of organisations, summarised by Pilbeam and Corbridge (2010), has helped in placing people centre-stage in the achievement of competitive advantage. Mobilising this potential should be a fundamental task in leading, managing and developing people. More recent concepts such as engagement, openness, visibility and honesty may take a higher profile within organisations, permeating through HR, line managers and employees.

Solutions are increasingly geared to process (how we do things) rather than content (what we do). This trend is reflected in all chapters, and provides a considerably more sophisticated challenge than previously.

Leading, managing and developing people is demanding due to the inherently problematic nature of people as resources, taken together with a challenging external context. The other side of the coin is that it is also rewarding on a whole range of levels for practising or aspiring HR managers. Leading, managing and developing people can be a source of fulfilment even when it involves taking tough decisions. Helping employees to fulfil their potential can be the most rewarding task within any workplace.

EXPLORE FURTHER

Throughout this book we have stressed the importance of keeping abreast of current research. Indeed this is one important theme within the CIPD Leading, Managing and Developing People unit. You are recommended to search appropriate websites in order to be aware of emerging reports and data surveys. Suitable websites include those listed below:

- Chartered Institute of Personnel and Development: www.cipd.co.uk
- CIPD magazine: www.peoplemanagement.co.uk
- Institute for Employment Studies: www.employment-studies.co.uk
- International Labour Organization: www.ilo.org
- Department of Business, Innovation and Skills: www.bis.gov.uk
- Office of National Statistics: www.ons.gov.uk
- European Union Employment and Social Affairs: ec.europa.eu/social/home.jsp
- Chartered Institute of Management: www.managers.org.uk
- Trades Union Congress: www.tuc.org.uk
- *Independent* newspaper: www.independent.co.uk
- *Daily Telegraph* newspaper: www.telegraph.co.uk
- The BBC: www.bbc.co.uk/news
- CNN business news: www.cnn.com/business

References

Acas. (2009a) *Code of Practice 1: Disciplinary and Grievance Procedures*. London: Acas.

Acas. (2009b) *Discipline and Grievances at Work: The ACAS Guide*. London: Acas.

Acas. (2010) *How to Manage Change: ACAS Guidelines*. January 2010. Available at: www.acas.org.uk [accessed 12 April 2013].

Adair, J. (1983) *Effective Leadership*. London: Pan Books.

Adair, J. (2003) *The Inspirational Leader: How to motivate, encourage and achieve success*. London: Kogan Page.

Adams, J.S. (1965) 'Inequality in Social Exchange', in Berkowitz, L. (ed.) *Advances in Experimental Social Psychology*. New York: Academic Press.

Adler, P.S. (1999) 'The emancipatory significance of Taylorism', in Cunha, M.P.F. and Marques, C.A. (eds) *Readings in Organisation Science – Organisational Change in a Changing Context*. Lisbon: Instituto Superior de Psicologia Aplicada.

Aguilar, F.J. (1967) *Scanning the business environment*. New York: Macmillan.

Aguinis, H. (2009) *Performance management*. 2nd edition. New Jersey: Pearson Prentice Hall.

Ahmed, S. (2007) The language of diversity. *Ethnic and Racial Studies*. Vol. 30, No. 2, pp235–56.

Alfes, K., Truss, C., Soane, E.C., Rees, C. and Gatenby, M. (2010) *Creating an Engaged Workforce: Findings from the Kingston Employee Engagement Consortium Project*. London: CIPD.

Alimo-Metcalfe, B. (1995) An investigation of female and male constructs of leadership and empowerment. *Women in Management Review*. Vol. 10, No. 2, pp3–8.

Allen, M.R. and Wright, P. (2007) 'Strategic management and HRM' in Boxall, P., Purcell, J. and Wright, P. (eds) *The Oxford Handbook of Human Resource Management*. Oxford: Oxford University Press.

Allen, W.C. and Swanson, R.A. (2006) Systematic Training - Straightforward and Effective, *in Advances in Developing Human Resources*. Vol. 8, No. 4, pp427-429.

Allio, R.J. (2008) C.K. Prahalad heralds a new era of innovation. *Strategy and Leadership*, Vol. 36, No. 6, pp11–14.

Alvesson, M. and Willmott, H. (2000) Identity regulation as organizational control: producing the appropriate individual. [Electronic version.] *Journal of Management Studies*, Vol. 39, No. 5, pp619–644.

Anderson, N., Born, M. and Cunningham-Snell, D. (2001) 'Recruitment and selection: applicant perspectives and outcomes', in Anderson, N., Ones, D. and Sinangil, H.K. (eds)

Handbook of Industrial Work and Organizational Psychology, Vol. 1. London/New York: Sage.

Anderson, V. (2007) *The Value of Learning: From return on investment to return on expectation.* London: CIPD.

Anderson, V. and Boocock, G. (2002) Small firms and internationalisation: learning to manage and managing to learn. *Human Resource Management Journal.* Vol. 12, No. 3, pp5–24.

Anderson, V. and Skinner, D. (1999) Organisational learning in practice: how do SMEs learn to operate internationally? *Human Resource Development International.* Vol. 2, No. 3, pp235–258.

Anell, B. and Wilson, T. (2000) The flexible firm and the flexible co-worker. *Journal of Workplace Learning: Employee Counselling Today.* Vol. 12, No. 4, pp165–170.

Ankil, E. and Palliam, R. (2012) Enabling a motivated workforce: exploring the sources of motivation. *Development and Learning in Organizations.* Vol. 26, No. 2, pp7–10.

Argyris, C. (1960) *Understanding Organizational Behaviour.* London: Tavistock.

Arkin, A. (2005a) Power play. *People Management.* Vol. 11, No. 5, pp40–42.

Arkin, A. (2005b) Mr Bright Side. *People Management.* May, pp28-30.

Armstrong, M. (2000) *Performance Management Practice: Key Practices and Practical Guidelines.* London: Kogan Page.

Armstrong, M. and Baron, A. (2005) *Managing Performance: Performance management in action.* London: CIPD.

Arnold, J. (1996) The psychological contract: a concept in need of close scrutiny? *European Journal of Work and Organisational Psychology.* Vol. 5, No. 4, pp511–520.

Arnold, J., Cooper, C.L. and Robertson, I.T. (2005) *Work Psychology: Understanding human behaviour in the workplace.* 4th edition. Harlow: FT/Prentice Hall.

Arnold, J., Cooper, C.L. and Robertson, I.T. (2010) *Work Psychology: Understanding human behaviour in the workplace.* 5th edition. Harlow: FT/Prentice Hall.

Arrata, P., Despierre, A. and Kumra, G. (2007) Building an effective change team. *McKinsey Quarterly*, November.

Arthur, J. (1994) Effects of human resources systems on manufacturing performance and turnover. *Academy of Management Journal.* Vol. 37, No. 3, pp670–687.

Arthur, M. (2008) Examining Contemporary Careers: A Call for Interdisciplinary Enquiry. *Human Relations.* Vol. 61, No. 2, pp163–186.

Arthur, M.B., Inkson, K. and Pringle, J.K. (1999) *The New Careers: Individual Action and Economic Change.* London: Sage.

Arthur, M. and Rousseau, D. (1996) *The Boundaryless Career: A new employment principle for a new organisational era.* Oxford: Oxford University Press.

Ashford, S. and DeRue, S. (2012) Developing as a Leader: The Power of Mindful Engagement. *Organzational Dynamics.* Vol. 41, No. 2, pp146–154.

Aston, L. (2013) Time to Address the Engagement Deficit. *People Management.* 7 January. Available at: www.cipd.co.uk/pm/peoplemanagement/b/weblog/archive/2013/01/07/time-to-address-the-engagement-deficit.aspx [accessed 18 June 2013].

Atkinson, C. (2002) Career management and the changing psychological contract. *Career Development International.* Vol. 7, No.1, pp14–23.

Atkinson, J. (1984) Manpower strategies for flexible organisations. *Personnel Management.* August, pp28–31.

Avolio, B.J., Kahai, S. and Dodge, G.E. (2000) E-leadership: implications for theory, research and practice. *The Leadership Quarterly.* Vol. 11, No. 4, pp615–668.

Avolio, B., Walumbwa, F. and Weber, T. (2009) Leadership: current theories, research and future directions. *Annual Review of Psychology.* Vol. 60, pp421–449.

Backhaus, K. (2003) Importance of person-organisation fit to job-seekers. *Career Development International.* Vol. 8, No. 1, pp221–226.

Bakan, I., Suseno, Y., Pinnington, A. and Money, A. (2004) The influence of financial participation and participation in decision-making on employee job attitudes. *International Journal of Human Resource Management.* Vol. 15, No. 3, pp587–596.

Baker, K. (2009) Whitehall HR business partners get skills refresher to deal with cuts. *Personnel Today.* 17 November. Accessed through XpertHR, 27 April 2010.

Ballantyne, I. (2009) 'Recruiting and selecting staff in organizations', in Gilmore, S. and Williams, S. (eds) *Human Resource Management.* Oxford: Oxford University Press.

Balogun, J., Gleadle, P., Hope Hailey, V. and Willmott, H. (2005) Managing change across boundaries: boundary-shaking practices. *British Journal of Management.* Vol. 16, pp261–278.

Bandura, A. (1993) Perceived self-efficacy in cognitive development and functioning. *Educational Psychologist.* Vol. 28, No. 2, pp117–148.

Barber, A. and Bretz, R. (2000) 'Compensation, attraction and retention', in Rynes, S.L. and Gerhart, B. (eds) *Compensation in Organisations.* San Francisco, CA: Jossey-Bass.

Barney, J.B. and Hesterly, W.S. (2008) *Strategic Management and Competitive Advantage.* 2nd edition. Harlow: Pearson/Prentice Hall.

Barratt, C. (2009) *Trade Union Membership 2008.* London: Department for Business, Enterprise and Regulatory Reform.

Baruch, Y. (2004) The desert generation. *Personnel Review.* Vol. 33, No. 2, pp241–256.

Baruch, Y. (2006) Career development in organisations and beyond: balancing traditional and contemporary viewpoints. *Human Resource Management Review.* Vol. 16, No. 2, pp125–128.

Baruch, Y. and Rosenstein, E. (1992) Career planning and managing in high tech organisations. *International Journal of Human Resource Management.* Vol. 3, No. 3, pp477–496.

Bass, B.M. (1985) *Leadership and Performance Beyond Expectations.* New York: Free Press.

Bawden, T. (2009) BT returns call-centre jobs to Britain from India. *The Times,* 16 July.

BBC Radio 4. (2008) Interview with Professor Joseph Nye, *The Today Programme,* broadcast on 23 April.

Beard, C.M. and Wilson, J.P. (2006) *Experiential Learning: A Best Practice Guide for Trainers and Educators.* London: Kogan Page.

Beardwell, J. and Claydon, T. (2010) *Human Resource Management: A contemporary approach.* 6th edition. Harlow: FT/Prentice Hall.

Beaumont, P. and Harris, R. (2002) Examining white-collar downsizing as a cause of change in the psychological contract: some UK evidence. *Employee Relations.* Vol. 24, No. 4, pp378–388.

Becker, B. and Huselid, M.A. (2006) Strategic human resource management: where do we go from here? *Journal of Management.* Vol. 32, No. 6, pp898–925.

Beecroft, A. (2011) *Report on Employment Law.* www.bis.gov.uk/policies/ employmentmatters/employmentlawreview/reportbyadrianbeecroft [accessed 26 November 2012].

Beer, M. and Spector, B. (1989) 'Corporate-wide transformations in human resource management', in Walton, R.E. and Lawrence, P.R. (eds) *Human Resource Management, Trends and Challenges.* Boston, MA: Harvard University School Press.

Beer, M., Spector, B., Lawrence, P.R., Mills, D.Q. and Walton, R.R. (1984) *Managing Human Assets.* New York: Simon & Schuster, Free Press.

Belbin, M.R. (1990) *Team Roles at Work.* Oxford: Butterworth-Heinemann.

Belbin, M.R. (1991) *Management Teams – Why They Succeed or Fail.* Oxford: Butterworth.

Belbin, M.R. (1993) *Team Roles at Work.* Oxford: Butterworth-Heinemann.

Bentley, R. (2008) Where did the business partner model go wrong? *Personnel Today.* 31 March. Accessed through XpertHR, 27 April 2010.

Bergman, S. (2012) Open thread: what are the best methods to recruit staff? *The Guardian.* 22 November.

Bernadin, H.K., Kane, J.S. and Ross, S. (1995) 'Performance appraisal design, development and implementation', in Ferris, G.R., Rosen, S.D. and Barnum, D.J. (eds) *Handbook of Human Resource Management.* Cambridge, MA: Blackwell.

Bersin and Associates. (2011) *U.K. Talent Acquisition Factbook 2011: Benchmarks and Trends in Spending, Staffing and Key Recruiting Metrics.* Report.

Berry, M. (2007) Cadbury-Schweppes launches UK graduate recruitment campaign with a new online chatroom. *Personnel Today.* 7 November. Available at: www.personneltoday.com [accessed 16 May 2008].

Biggs, D. and Swailes, S. (2006) Relations, commitment and satisfaction in agency workers and permanent workers. *Employee Relations.* Vol. 28, No. 2, pp130–143.

Biron, M., Farndale, E. and Pauuwe, J. (2011) Performance Management Effectiveness: Lessons from World Leading Firms. *International Journal of Human Resource Management.* Vol. 22, No. 6, pp1294–1311.

Bjorkman, I. and Yuan, L. (1999) The management of human resources in Chinese-Western joint ventures. *Journal of World Business.* Vol. 34, No. 2, pp1–19.

Blake, R.R. and McCanse, A.A. (1991) *Leadership Dilemmas – Grid Solutions.* Houston: Gulf Publishing.

Blake, R.R. and Mouton J.S. (1964) *The Managerial Grid.* London: Gulf Publications.

Blanchard, P.N. and Thacker, J.W. (2004) *Effective Training: Systems, strategies and practices.* New Jersey: Pearson/Prentice Hall.

Bloisi, W., Cook, C.W. and Hunsaker, P.I. (2003) *Management and Organisational Behaviour.* London: McGraw-Hill.

Bloisi, W., Cook, C.W. and Hunsaker, P.I. (2007) *Management and Organisational Behaviour.* 2nd edition. London: McGraw-Hill.

Bloom, B.S. (ed.) (1956) *Taxonomy of Educational Objectives Handbook 1: Cognitive Domain.* New York: Longman.

Blyton, P. and Morris, J. (1992) 'HRM and the limits of flexibility', in Blyton, P. and Morris, J. (eds) *Reassessing Human Resource Management.* London: Sage.

Boatright, J.R. (2000) *Ethics and the Conduct of Business.* 3rd edition. London: Prentice Hall.

Bollaert, H. and Petit, V. (2010) Beyond the dark side of executive psychology: current research and new directions. *European Management Journal* (in press): doi:10.1016/j.emj. 2010.01.001.

Bond, R. (2004) Call centre is 'my dream job'. BBC News website, 14 April.

Boselie, P., Brewster, C. and Paauwe, J. (2009) In search of balance – managing the dualities of HRM. *Personnel Review.* Vol. 38, No. 5, pp461–471.

Bouskila-Yam, O. and Kluger, A. (2011) Strength-based performance appraisal and goal setting. *Human Resource Management Review.* Vol. 21, No. 2, pp137–147.

Bowen, D.E. and Ostroff, C. (2004) Understanding HRM-firm performance linkages: the role of 'strength' of the HRM system. *Academy of Management Review.* Vol. 29, pp203–221.

Bowles, M.L. and Coates, G. (1993) Image and substance: the management of performance as rhetoric or reality? *Personnel Review.* Vol. 22, No. 2, pp3–21.

Boxall, P. (1996) The strategic HRM debate and the resource-based view of the firm. *Human Resource Management Journal.* Vol. 6, No. 3, pp59–75.

Boxall, P. and Purcell, J. (2000) Strategic human resource management: where have we come from and where should we be going? *International Journal of Management Review.* Vol. 2, No. 2, pp 183–203.

Boxall, P. and Purcell, J. (2003) *Strategy and Human Resource Management.* Basingstoke: Palgrave Macmillan.

Boxall, P. and Purcell, J. (2008) *Strategy and Human Resource Management.* 2nd edition. Basingstoke: Palgrave Macmillan.

Boxall, P. and Purcell, J. (2011) *Strategy and Human Resource Management.* 3rd edition. Basingstoke: Palgrave Macmillan.

Boyle, M. (2001) Performance reviews: perilous curves ahead. *Fortune Europe.* Vol. 143, No. 11.

Bradshaw, D. (1985) Transferable intellectual and personal skills. *Oxford Review of Education.* Vol. 11, No. 2, pp201–216.

Bramley, P. (1996) *Evaluating Training Effectiveness.* Maidenhead: McGraw-Hill.

Bratton, J. and Gold, J. (2007) *Human Resource Management Theory and Practice.* 4th edition. Basingstoke: Palgrave Macmillan.

Bratton, J. and Gold, J. (2012) *Human Resource Management Theory and Practice.* 5th edition. Basingstoke: Palgrave Macmillan.

Braverman, H. (1974) *Labour and Monopoly Capital: The degradation of work in the twentieth century.* New York: Monthly Review Press.

Brech, E.F.L. (1975) *Principles and Practice of Management.* 3rd edition. Harlow: Longman.

Bridge, S. (2007) What's the future of HR? *Times Online,* 7 February.

Bridges, W. (1995) *JobShift: How to prosper in a workplace without jobs.* London: Nicholas Brealey.

Briscoe, J. and Hall, D. (2006) The interplay of boundaryless and Protean careers: combinations and implications. *Journal of Vocational Behaviour.* Vol. 69, pp4–18.

Brockett, J. (2010) See HR as a professional services firm, says Ulrich. *People Management.* 25 March, p11.

Brown, D. and Armstrong, M. (1999) *Paying for Contribution.* London: Kogan Page.

Brown, M. (2012) George Entwistle Deserves His £450,000 BBC Payoff. *The Guardian.* 29 November. Available at: www.guardian.co.uk [accessed 18 December 2012].

Brumbach, G.B. (1988) Some ideas, issues and predictions about performance management. *Public Personnel Management.* Winter, pp387–402.

Bryce, V. (2007) Give me strength. *People Management.* 8 February, p7.

Buchanan, D. and Badham, R. (1999) *Power, Politics and Organizational Change: Winning the turf war game.* London: Sage.

Buchanan, D. and Boddy, D. (1992) *The Expertise of the Change Agent.* London: Prentice Hall.

Buchanan, D. and Huczynski, A. (2007) *Organizational Behaviour.* 6th edition. London: FT/Prentice Hall.

Buchanan, D. and Huczynski, A. (2010) *Organizational Behaviour.* 7th edition. London: FT/Prentice Hall.

Buchanan, D.A. and Wilson, B. (1996) 'Next patient please: the operating theatres problem at Leicester General Hospital NHS Trust', in J. Storey (ed.) *Cases in Human Resource and Change Management.* Oxford: Blackwell Business.

Buchner, T.W. (2007) Performance management theory: a look from the performer's perspective with implications for HRD. *Human Resource Development International.* Vol. 10, No. 1, pp59–73.

Buckley, R. and Caple, J. (2007) *The Theory and Practice of Training.* London: Kogan Page.

Budria, S. (2012) The Shadow Value of Employer-Provided Training. *Journal of Economic Psychology.* Vol. 33, No. 3, pp494–514.

Budworth, M. and Mann, S. (2011) Performance management: Where do we go from here? *Human Resource Management Review.* Vol. 21, pp81–84.

Burnes, B. (2004) *Managing Change,* 4th edition. Harlow: FT/Prentice Hall.

Burns, J. (2008) Informal learning and transfer of learning: how new trade and industrial teachers perceive their professional growth and development. *Career and Technical Education Research.* Vol. 33, pp3–24.

Burns, T. and Stalker, G.M. (1961) *The Management of Innovation.* London: Tavistock.

Burns, T. and Stalker, G.M. (1994) *The Management of Innovation.* 3rd edition. Oxford: Oxford University Press.

Caldwell, R. (2008) HR business partner competency models: re-contextualising effectiveness. *Human Resource Management Journal.* Vol. 18, No. 3, pp275–293.

Caldwell, S.D. (2013) Are change readiness strategies overrated? A commentary on boundary conditions. *Journal of Change Management.* Vol. 13, No. 1, pp 19–35.

Caligiuri, P., Lepak, D. and Bonache, J. (2010) *Managing the Global Workforce.* Chichester: Wiley.

Cameron, J., Banko, K.M. and Pierce, W.D. (2001) Pervasive negative effects of rewards in intrinsic motivation: the myth continues. *The Behaviour Analyst.* Vol. 24, pp1–44.

Cantrell, S. and Benton, J.M. (2007) The five essential practices of a talent multiplier. *Business Strategy Series.* Vol. 8, No. 5, pp358–364.

Carnall, C. (2003) *Managing Change in Organizations*. 4th edition. Harlow: FT/Prentice-Hall.

Carver, C., Sutton, S. and Scheier, F. (2000) Action, emotion and personality: emerging conceptual integration. *Personality and Social Psychology Bulletin*. Vol. 26, pp741–751.

Cassell, C., Nadin, S. and Gray, M. (2002) Exploring human resource management practices in small and medium-sized enterprises. *Personnel Review*. Vol. 31, No. 6, pp671–692.

Caulkin, S. (2003) How to catch a rising star. *The Observer* Business pages, 9 November, p15.

CBI. (2009) Education and Skills Survey. Available at: www.cbi.org.uk/ndbs/content.nsf/b80e12d0cd1cd37c802567bb00491cbf/e83f616f81370ce880256dc60047ede9 [accessed 29 April 2010].

CBI. (2012) Education and Skills Survey. Available at: www.cbi.org.uk [accessed 4 June 2013].

Cervero, R. (2001) Continuing Professional Education in Transition 1981–2000. *International Journal of Lifelong Education*. Vol. 20, No. 1/2, pp16–30.

Chalofsky, N. and Krishna, V. (2009) Meaningfulness, commitment and engagement: the intersection of a deeper level of intrinsic motivation. *Advances in Developing Human Resources*. Vol. 11, pp189–203.

Chaudhry, A., Coyle-Shapiro, J. and Wayne, S. (2011) A Longitudinal Study of the Impact of Organizational Change on Transactional, Relational, and Balanced Psychological Contracts. *Journal of Leadership & Organizational Studies*. Vol. 18, No. 2, pp247–259.

Chaudhry, A., Wayne, S. and Schalk, R. (2011) A Sensemaking Model of Employee Evaluation of Psychological Change Fulfilment: How and When Do Employees Respond to Change? *The Journal of Applied Behavioural Science*. Vol. 45, No. 4, pp498-520.

Chavan, M. (2009) 'The balanced scorecard: a new challenge', in *Journal of Management Development*. Vol. 28, No. 5, pp393–406.

Cheetham, G. and Chivers, G. (2001) How professionals learn in practice: an investigation of informal learning amongst people working in professions. *Journal of European Industrial Training*. Vol. 25, pp250–88.

Chhokar, J.S., Brodbeck, F.C. and House, R.J. (eds) (2007) *Culture and Leadership Across the World*. New Jersey: Lawrence Erlbaum Associates.

Child, J. (1972) Organizational Structure, Environment and Performance: The Role of Strategic Choice. *Sociology*. Vol. 6, pp1-22.

Child, J. (2005) *Organisation*. Oxford: Blackwell.

Cho, Y., Cho, E. and McLean, G.N. (2009) HRD's role in knowledge management, advances in developing human resources. OnlineFirst, published 14 July 2009 as doi: 10.1177/1523422309337719.

Chryssides, G. and Kayle, J. (1996) *Essentials of Business Ethics*. Maidenhead: McGraw-Hill.

CIPD. (2003a) *Maximising Employee Potential and Business Performance: The role of high-performance working*. Report. London: CIPD.

CIPD. (2003b) *Reward Management 2003: A survey of policy and practice*. London: CIPD.

CIPD. (2003c) *People and Performance in Knowledge-Intensive Firms*. London: CIPD.

CIPD. (2004a) *Human Capital Reporting: An Internal Perspective*. London: CIPD.

CIPD. (2004b) *High-performance working*. Factsheet, revised February. London: CIPD.

CIPD. (2004c) *Graphology*. Factsheet. London: CIPD.

CIPD. (2005a) *Training to learning*. Change agenda. London: CIPD.

CIPD. (2005b) *Managing Diversity: People make the difference at work – but everyone is different*. London: CIPD.

CIPD. (2006) *Diversity: An overview*. Factsheet. Available online at: www.cipd.co.uk/subjects/dvsequl/general/divover.htm?Issrchres=1 [accessed 8 May 2008].

CIPD. (2007a) *Leadership and Management Standards*. Available at: www.cipd.co.uk [accessed 21 April 2008].

CIPD. (2007b) *Annual Survey Report: Recruitment, Retention and Turnover*. London: CIPD.

CIPD. (2007c) *Diversity in Business: a Focus for Progress*. Survey report. London: CIPD.

CIPD. (2008a) *Smart Working: The Impact of Work Organisation and Job Design*. Research Insight. London: CIPD.

CIPD. (2008b) *Annual Survey Report: Recruitment, Retention and Turnover*. London: CIPD.

CIPD. (2009a) *Employee Outlook*. Quarterly survey report. London: CIPD. Available online at: www.cipd.co.uk/surveys [accessed 20 March 2010].

CIPD. (2009b) *Organisation Development*. Factsheet. London: CIPD.

CIPD. (2010a) *HR Business Partnering*. Factsheet. London: CIPD.

CIPD. (2010b) *Learning and Talent Development*. Report. London: CIPD.

CIPD. (2010c) *Diversity: An overview*. Factsheet. London: CIPD.

CIPD. (2012a) *HR and its role in innovation, Part 1, November 2012: Innovative forms of organising: Networked working*. London: CIPD.

CIPD. (2012b) *CIPD HR Outlook: Views of Our Profession 2012–13*. Available at: www.cipd.co.uk/hroutlook

CIPD. (2012c) Code of Professional Conduct. Available at: www.cipd.co.uk

CIPD. (2012d) *CIPD Unveils Evidence Highlighting the Solid Business Case Supporting an Extension of Rights to request Flexible Working*. Available at: www.cipd.co.uk.

CIPD. (2012e) *The Psychological Contract*. Factsheet. July 2012. London: CIPD.

CIPD. (2012f) *Managing for Sustainable Employee Engagement: Developing a Behavioural Framework*. London: CIPD.

CIPD. (2012g) *Resourcing and Talent Planning Annual Survey Report 2012*. London: CIPD.

CIPD. (2012h) *Competence and competency frameworks*. Factsheet. Available at: www.cipd.co.uk/hr-resources/factsheet/competency-frameworks [accessed 20 December 2012].

CIPD. (2012i) *Learning and Talent Development*. Survey report. London: CIPD.

CIPD. (2012j) *Game On! How to Keep Diversity Progress on Track*. Policy report. London: CIPD.

CIPD. (2012k) *Performance Management: An Overview*. Factsheet. London: CIPD.

CIPD. (2012l) *Reward Management*. Annual survey report. London: CIPD.

CIPD. (2012m) *Where has all the trust gone?* Research Report. March 2012. London: CIPD.

CIPD. (2012n) *What is CPD?* Factsheet.

CIPD. (2013a) *The role of HR in corporate responsibility*. Research report. February 2013. London: CIPD.

CIPD. (2013b) *HR Outsourcing*. Factsheet. London: CIPD.

CIPD. (2013c) *Learning and Talent Development*. London: CIPD.

CIPD. (2013d) *Social media and employee voice – the current landscape*. Research report. March 2013. London: CIPD.

Clark, J. (1993) 'Full flexibility and self-supervision in an automated factory', in Clark, J. (ed.) *Human Resource Management and Technical Change*. London: Sage.

Clarke, C. and Pratt, S. (1985) Leadership's four-part progress. *Management Today*. March, pp84–86.

Clegg, S., Kornberger, M. and Pitsis, T. (2008) *Managing and Organisations*. London: Sage.

Clegg, S., Kornberger, M. and Pitsis, T. (2011) *Managing and Organisations*. 3rd edition. London: Sage.

Cohen, T.R., Panter, A.T. and Turan, N. (2012) Guilt Proneness and Moral Character. *Current Directions in Psychological Science*. Vol. 21, No. 5, pp355–359.

Collings, D.G., Scullion, H. and Dowling, P.J. (2006) Global staffing: a review and thematic research agenda. *International Journal of Human Resource Management*. Vol. 20, No. 6, pp1253–1272.

Confessore, S.J. and Kops, W.J. (1998) Self-directed learning and the learning organisation: examining the connection between the individual and the learning environment. *Human Resource Development Quarterly*. Vol. 9, pp365–375.

Conger, J. (1999) Charisma and how to grow it. *Management Today.* December, pp78–81.

Conger, J. (2002) Danger of delusion. *Financial Times.* 29 November.

Coombs, J., Liu, Y., Hall, A. and Ketchen, D. (2006) How much do high-performance work practices matter? A meta-analysis of their effects on organizational performance. *Personnel Psychology.* Vol. 59, No. 3, pp501–528.

Cooper, C. (2005) The future of work: careers, stress and wellbeing. *Career Development International,* Vol. 10, pp396–399.

Cowell, C., Hopkins, P.C., McWhorter, R. and Jorden, D.L. (2006) *Advances in Developing Human Resources.* Vol. 8, No. 4, pp460–475.

Coyle-Shapiro, J. and Kessler, I. (2000) Consequences of the psychological contract for the employment relationship: a large-scale survey. *Journal of Management Studies.* Vol. 37, No. 7, p903.

Crail, M. (2007) Online recruitment delivers more applicants and wins vote of most employers. *Personnel Today.* 20 November. Available online at: www.personneltoday.com [accessed 16 May 2008].

Crane, A. and Matten, D. (2010) *Business Ethics.* 3rd edition. Oxford: Oxford University Press.

Crook, C. (2005) The good company. *The Economist.* 22 January, pp3–4.

Crush, P. (2013) Parental Leave Mums v Dads. *People Management.* 8 January.

Csikszentmihalyi, M. (1990) *Flow: The psychology of optimal experience.* New York: Harper Perennial.

Cully, M., Woodland, S. and O'Reilly, A. (1999) *Britain at Work, as depicted by the 1998 Workplace Employee Relations Survey.* London: Routledge.

Cunningham, I. (2008) 'A race to the bottom? Exploring variations in employment conditions in the voluntary sector.' in *Public Administration.* Vol. 86, No. 4, pp1033–1053.

Daft, R.L. Murphy, J. and Willmott, H. (2010) *Organization Theory and Design.* Andover: Cengage.

Dany, F., Guedri, Z. and Hatt, F. (2008) New insights into the link between HRM integration and organizational performance: the moderating role of influence distribution between HRM specialists and line managers. *International Journal of Human Resource Management.* Vol. 19, No. 11, pp2095–2112.

Davenport, T.H. (1993) *Process Innovation: Re-engineering work through information technology.* Boston, MA: Harvard Business School Press.

Davies, M.E. (2013) *Women on Boards.* Cranfield, Bedford: Cranfield School of Management.

Day, D. and Sin, H.P. (2011) Longitudinal Tests of an Integrative Model of Leader Development: Charting and Understanding Development Trajectories. *The Leadership Quarterly.* Vol. 22, No. 3, pp545–560.

DCSF [Department for Children, Schools and Families] (2009) *14–19 Briefing: Making change happen.* www.dcsf.gov.uk/14-19.

DCSF [Department for Children, Schools and Families] (2009) *Quality, Choice and Aspiration.* Report.

Deci, E.L., Ryan, M. and Koestner, R. (2001) The pervasive negative effects of rewards on intrinsic motivation: response to Cameron. *Review of Educational Research.* Vol. 71, pp43–51.

DeFillippi, R. and Arthur, M. (1994) The boundaryless career: a competency-based prospective. *Journal of Organisational Behaviour.* Vol. 15, No. 4, pp307–324.

De Gama, N., McKenna, S. and Pettica-Harris, A. (2012) Ethics and HRM: Theoretical and Conceptual Analysis. *Journal of Business Ethics.* Vol. 111, No. 1, pp97–108.

Deloitte. (2009) *Shaping Up: Evolving the HR function for the 21st century.* New York/London: Deloitte MCS Limited.

deMenezes, L. and Kelliher, C. (2011) Flexible Working and Performance: A Systematic Review of the Evidence for a Business Case. *International Journal of Management Reviews.* Vol. 13, No. 4, pp452–474.

Devanna, M.A., Fombrun, C.J. and Tichy, N.M. (1984) 'A framework for strategic human resource management', in Fombrun, C.J., Tichy, M.M. and Devanna, M.A. (eds) *Strategic Human Resource Management.* New York: John Wiley.

De Vos, A. and Meganck, A. (2009) What HR managers do versus what employees value. *Personnel Review.* Vol. 38, No. 1, pp45–60.

De Wit, B. and Meyer, R. (2004) *Strategy: Process, content and theory.* 3rd edition. London: Thomson Publishing.

Dimbleby, D. (2012) The BBC Has Throttled Itself With Its Own Bureaucracy. *Daily Telegraph.* 12 November. Available at: www.telegraph.co.uk [accessed 18 December 2012].

Donaldson, T. and Preston, L. (1995) The stakeholder theory of the corporation: concepts, evidence and implications. *Academy of Management Review.* Vol. 5, pp265–269.

Dowling. P.J., Festing, M. and Engle, A.D. (2008) *International Human Resource Management.* 5th edition. London: Thomson.

Doz, Y.L. and Prahalad, C.K. (1988) 'A process model of strategic redirection in large complex firms: the case of multinational corporations', in A.M. Pettigrew (ed.) *The Management of Strategic Change.* Oxford: Blackwell.

Dries, N. and Pepermans, R. (2008) Real high-potential careers. *Personnel Review.* Vol. 37, No. 1, pp85–108.

Drucker, P.F. (1989) *The Practice of Management.* Heinemann Professional.

Drucker, P.F. (1993) *Post-Capitalist Society.* Oxford: Butterworth-Heinemann.

Drucker, P.F. (2005) 'Managing Oneself', in *Harvard Business Review.* Vol. 8, No. 1, pp100-109.

DTI. (2001) *Diversity Best Practice in the Corporate World: A guide for business.* London: Department of Trade and Industry, Women and Equality Unit.

DTI. (2005) *High Performance Work Practices: Linking strategy and skills to performance outcomes.* London: DTI in association with the CIPD.

Dyer, L. and Shafer, R. (1999) 'Creating organizational agility: implications for strategic human resource management', in Wright, P., Dyer, L. and Boudreau, J. (eds) *Research in Personnel and Human Resource Management* (Supplement 4: Strategic human resources management in the twenty-first century). Stamford, CT: JAI Press.

The Economist. (2009) Talent on tap: the fashion for hiring temps has reached the executive suite. 10 December.

Education and Training. (2006) Vol. 48, No. 8/9.

Edwards, P. (2003) 'The employment relationship and the field of industrial relations', in Edwards, P. (ed.) *Industrial Relations.* 4th edition. Oxford: Blackwell.

Egan, J. (2009) *HR Roles and Responsibilities.* IRS Employment Review survey (2nd edition, January). Available at: www.xperthr.co.uk/searchresults.aspx?s=egan [accessed on 8 June 2010].

Eglin, R. (2004) Cash is not king in holding on to staff. *Sunday Times* Appointments. 15 February, p7.

Eikhof, D.R., Warhurst, C. and Haunschild, A. (2007) Introduction: What work? What life? What balance? Critical reflections on the work-life balance debate. *Employee Relations.* Vol. 29, No. 4, pp325–333.

Ellesworth, R.E. (2002) *Leading with Purpose: The new corporate realities.* Palo Alto, CA: Stanford University Press.

Ellinger, A. (2004) The concept of self-directed learning and its implications for human resource. *Advances in Developing Human Resources.* Vol. 6, p158.

Elliott, L. (2004) Job flexibility can tie you up in knots. *Guardian Weekly.* 25–31 March, p16.

Emery, Y. (2004) Rewarding civil service performance through team bonuses: findings, analysis and recommendations. *International Review of Administrative Sciences.* Vol. 70, No. 1, pp157–168.

Emery, Y. (2008) Lecture presentation at Portsmouth University, based upon three research articles by Emery, Y. and Glauque, D. (2005) *Paradoxes de la gestion publique.* Paris: L'Harmattan.

Emery, Y. and Gonin, F. (2007) *Dynamiser la gestion des resources humaines.* Lausanne: Presses polytechniques et universitaires romandes.

Engle, A.D., Dowling, P.J. and Festing, M. (2008) Globalisation of SMEs and implications for international human resource management research and practice. *European Journal of International Management.* Vol. 2, No. 2, pp153–169.

Entwistle, N. (2001) Styles of Learning and Approaches to Studying in Higher Education. *Kybernetes.* Vol. 30, No. 5, pp593–603.

Evans, J. (2008) Leaders need to be humble, not heroes. *People Management*. 17 April. Available at: www.peoplemanagement.co.uk [accessed 5 December 2012].

Evans, P., Pucik, V. and Bjorkman, I. (2012) *The Global Challenge: International Human Resource Management*. 2nd edition. London: McGraw-Hill.

Fang, M. and Gerhart, B. (2012). Does pay for performance diminish intrinsic interest? *The International Journal of Human Resource Management*. Vol. 23, No. 6, pp1176–1196.

Farndale, E. and Brewster, C. (2005) In search of legitimacy: personnel, management associations worldwide. *Human Resource Management Journal*. Vol. 15, No. 3, pp33–48.

Farndale, E., Pauuwe, J., Morris, S.S., Stahl, G., Stiles, P., Trevor, J. and Wright, P. (2010) Context-bound Configurations of Corporate HR Functions Across the Globe. *Human Resource Management*. Vol. 49, No. 1, pp45-66.

Farnham, D. and Pimlott, J. (1995) *Understanding Industrial Relations*. 4th edition. London: Cassell.

Farnham, D. and Stevens, A. (2000) Developing and implementing competence-based recruitment and selection in a social services department. *International Journal of Public Sector Management*. Vol. 13, No. 4, pp369–382.

Fayol, H. (1949) *General and Industrial Management*. London: Pitman.

Festing, M. (2007) Globalisation of SMEs and implications for international human resource management research and practice. *International Journal of Globalisation and Small Business*. Vol. 2, No. 1, pp5–18.

Fincham, R. and Rhodes, P. (2005) *Principles of Organizational Behaviour*. Oxford: Oxford University Press.

Fitzgerald, C. and Howe-Walsh, L. (2008) Self-initiated expatriates: an interpretative phenomenological analysis of professional female expatriates. *International Journal of Business and Management*. Vol. 21, No. 3, pp156–175.

Fletcher, C. (2007) *Appraisal, Feedback and Development: Making performance review work*. 4th edition. London: Taylor & Francis.

Fletcher, C. and Williams, R. (1996) Performance management, job satisfaction and organisational commitment. *British Journal of Management*. Vol. 7, pp169–179.

Fombrun, C.J., Tichy, M.M. and Devanna, M.A. (eds) (1984) *Strategic Human Resource Management*. New York: John Wiley.

Foot, M. and Hook, C. (2005) *Introducing Human Resource Management*. 4th edition. Harlow: FT/Prentice Hall.

Foot, M. and Hook, C. (2011) *Introducing Human Resource Management*. 6th edition. Harlow: FT/Prentice Hall.

Foote, D. (2001) The question of ethical hypocrisy in human resource management in the UK and Irish charity sectors. *Journal of Business Ethics*. Vol. 34, pp25–38.

Foster, C. and Harris, L. (2005) Easy to say, difficult to do: diversity management in retail. *Human Resource Management Journal*. Vol. 15, No. 3, pp4–17.

Fournier, V. (1999) The appeal to 'professionalism' as a disciplinary mechanism. *The Sociological Review*. Vol. 47, No. 2, pp280–307.

Fox, A. (1966) *Industrial Sociology and Industrial Relations*. Research Paper No. 3. Royal Commission on Trade Unions and Employers' Associations. London: HMSO.

Fox, A. (1974) *Beyond Contract: Work, power and trust relations*. London: Faber & Faber.

Fox, M. (1994) *The Reinvention of Work: A new vision of livelihood for our time*. New York: HarperCollins.

Frahm, J. and Brown, K. (2005) First steps: linking change communication to change receptivity. *Journal of Organisational Change Management*. Vol. 20, No. 3, pp370–387.

Francis, H. and Keegan, A. (2006) The changing face of HRM: in search of balance. *Human Resource Management Journal*. Vol. 16, No. 3, pp231–249.

Frank, E. (1991) The UK's Management Charter Initiative: The First Three Years. *Journal of European Industrial Training*. Vol. 17, No. 1, pp9-11.

Fredman, S. (2001) Equality: a new generation? *Industrial Law Journal*, Vol. 30, No. 2, pp145–168.

Freer, T. (2011) Social media gaming – a recipe for employer brand success. *Strategic HR Review*. Vol. 11, No. 1, pp13–17.

Freifeld, L. (2009) Brain sells. *Training*. Vol. 46, No. 6, p9.

French, J. and Raven, B. (1968) 'The bases of social power', in Cartwright, D. and Zander, A. (eds) *Group Dynamics: Research and theory*. London: Harper & Row.

French, R. (2010) *Cross-Cultural Management in Work Organisations*. 2nd edition. London: CIPD.

French, R., Rayner, C., Rees, G. and Rumbles, S. (2008) *Organisational Behaviour*. Chichester: Wiley.

French, R., Rayner, C., Rees, G. and Rumbles, S. (2011) *Organisational Behaviour*. 2nd edition. Chichester: John Wiley & Sons.

French, W.L. and Bell, C.H. (1999) *Organizational Development: Behavioural science interventions for organizational improvement*. 6th edition. Upper Saddle River, NJ: Prentice Hall.

French, W.L., Kast, F.E. and Rosenzweig, J.E. (1985) *Understanding Human Behaviour in Organizations*. London: Harper & Row.

Friedman, M. (1970) The social responsibility of business is to increase its profits. *New York Times* Magazine. 13 September, p32ff.

Furnham, A. (1997) *The Psychology of Behaviour at Work*. Hove: Psychology Press, Taylor & Francis.

Furnham, A. (2004) Performance management systems. *European Business Journal*. Vol. 16, No. 2, pp83–94.

Furnham, A. (2005) Where egos dare. *People Management.* Vol. 11, No. 3, pp40–42.

Garcia, M.F., Posthuma, R.A. and Colella, A. (2008) Fit perceptions and the employment interview: the role of similarity, liking and expectations. *Journal of Occupational and Organizational Psychology.* Vol. 81, No. 2, pp173–189.

Geal, M. and Johnson, B. (2002) Management performance: a glimpse of the blindingly obvious. *Training Journal.* October, pp24–27.

Gershon Efficiency Review (2004) Available at: www.hm-treasury.gov.uk/ spend_sr04_index.htm [accessed on 29 April 2010].

Ghoshal, S., Bartlett, C. and Moran, P. (1999) A new manifesto for management. *Sloan Management Review.* Vol. 40, No. 3, pp9–22.

Giles, C., Guha, K. and Atkins, R. (2010) At the sharp end – the failings of flexibility. *Financial Times.* 22 January. Available at: www.ft.com [accessed 1 February 2010].

Gilliland, S.W. (1993) The perceived fairness of selection systems: an organizational justice perspective. *Academy of Management Review.* Vol. 18, pp694–734.

Gilmore, S. (2009) 'Conclusions', in Gilmore, S. and Williams, S. (eds) *Human Resource Management.* Oxford: Oxford University Press.

Gilmore, S. (2012), 'Introducing Human Resource Management', in Gilmore, S. and Williams, S. *Human Resource Management.* Oxford: Oxford University Press.

Gilmore, S.E. and Williams, S. (2003) Constructing the HR professional: a critical analysis of the Chartered Institute of Personnel and Development's professional project. Third International Critical Management Studies Conference. Lancaster University Management School.

Gilmore, S. and Williams, S. (2007) Conceptualising the 'personnel professional': a critical analysis of the Chartered Institute of Personnel and Development's professional qualification scheme. *Personnel Review.* Vol. 36, No. 3, pp398–414.

Gilmore, S. and Williams, S. (eds) (2009) *Human Resource Management.* Oxford: Oxford University Press.

Gilmore, S. and Williams, S. (2012) *Human Resource Management.* 2nd edition. Oxford: Oxford University Press.

Gioia, D.A. and Thomas, J.B. (1996) Identity, image and issue interpretation: sense making during strategic change in academia. *Administrative Science Quarterly.* Vol. 41, pp370–403.

Glen, C. (2006) Key skills retention and motivation: the war for talent still rages and retention is the high ground. *Industrial and Commercial Training,* Vol. 38, No. 1, pp37–45.

Glover, L. and Butler, P. (2012) 'High-Performance Work Systems, Partnerships and the Working Lives of HR Professionals', in *Human Resource Management Journal.* Vol. 22, No. 2, pp199-215.

GMAC. (2008) www.expatica.co.uk/hr/story/Reporting-on-global-relocation-trends-in-2008.html [accessed 5 June 2013].

Gold, J., Holden, R., Iles, P., Stewart, J. and Beardwell, J. (2010) *Human Resource Development: Theory and practice.* Basingstoke: Palgrave Macmillan.

Gold, J., Holden, R., Iles, P., Stewart, J. and Beardwell, J. (2013) *Human Resource Development: Theory and Practice.* 3rd edition. Basingstoke: Palgrave Macmillan.

Goldthorpe, J.H., Lockwood, D., Bechhofer, F. and Platt, J. (1968) *The Affluent Worker: Attitudes and behaviour.* Cambridge: Cambridge University Press.

Gould-Williams, J. (2003) The importance of HR practices and workplace trust in achieving superior performance: a study of public sector organizations. *International Journal of Human Resource Management.* Vol. 14, No. 1, pp28–54.

Gratton, L. (2000) *Living Strategy: Putting people at the heart of corporate purpose.* Harlow: FT/Prentice Hall.

Greenleaf, R. (1977) *Servant Leadership: A Journey into the Nature of Legitimate Power and Greatness.* New York: Paulist Press.

Greiner, L. (1972) Evolution and revolution as organizations grow. *Harvard Business Review.* July–August. Available at: 78.63.254.76/Organizations.pdf, [accessed 4 June 2013].

Greller, M. (2006) Hours invested in professional development during late career as a function of career motivation and satisfaction. *Career Development International.* Vol. 11, No. 6, pp544–559.

Grey, C. (2009) *A Very Short, Fairly Interesting and Reasonably Cheap Book About Studying Organizations.* 2nd edition. London: Sage.

Grey, C. (2013) *A Very Short, Fairly Interesting and Reasonably Cheap Book About Studying Organizations.* 3rd edition. London: Sage.

Grimland, S., Vigoda-Carot, E. and Baruch, Y. (2012) Career Attitudes and Success of Managers: the Impact of Chance Event, Protean and Traditional Careers. *The International Journal of Human Resource Management.* Vol. 23, No. 6, pp1074–1094.

Grint, K. (1997) *Fuzzy Management.* Oxford: Oxford University Press.

Gruman, J. and Saks, A. (2011). Performance management and employee engagement. *Human Resource Management Review.* Vol. 21, pp123–136.

Grundy, T. (1993) *Managing Strategic Change.* London: Kogan Page.

Gubbins, C. and Garavan, T.N. (2009) Understanding the HRD role in MNCs: the imperatives of social capital and networking. *Human Resource Development Review.* Vol. 8, pp245–275.

Guest, D. (1997) Human resource management and performance: a review of the research agenda. *International Journal of Human Resource Management.* Vol. 8, No. 3, pp263–276.

Guest, D. (1998) Is the psychological contract worth taking seriously? *Journal of Organizational Behaviour.* Vol. 19, pp649–664.

Guest, D. (2004) Flexible employment contracts, the psychological contract and employee outcomes: an analysis and review of the evidence. *International Journal of Management Reviews.* Vol. 5/6, No. 1, pp1–19.

Guest, D.E. and Conway, N. (2002) *Pressure at Work and the Psychological Contract.* London: CIPD.

Guest, D.E. and Woodrow, C. (2012) Exploring the Boundaries of Human Resource Managers' Responsibilities. *Journal of Business Ethics.* Vol. 111, No. 1, pp109–119.

Hackman, J.R. and Oldham, G.R. (1980) *Work Redesign.* New York: Addison-Wesley.

Haines III, V. and St-Onge, S. (2012) Performance management effectiveness: practices or context? *The International Journal of Human Resources Management.* Vol. 26, No. 6, pp1158–1175.

Hakim, C. (2011) *Feminist Myths and Magic Medicine: The Flawed Thinking Behind Calls for Further Equality Legislation.* Centre For Policy Studies. Available at: eprints.lse.ac.uk/36488/1/Feminist_myths_and_magic_medicine_the_flawed_thinking_behind_calls_for_further_equality_legislation_(lsero).pdf [accessed 5 June 2013].

Hall, D. (1996) *The Career Is Dead, Long Live the Career.* San Francisco, CA: Jossey-Bass.

Hall, D. (2004) The Protean Career: A Quarter-Century Journey. *Journal of Vocational Behaviour.* Vol. 65, No. 1, pp1–13.

Hall, D. (2009) 'How Smart are Targets?' in *HR Bulletin: Research and Practice.* Vol. 4, pp8-10.

Hammer, M. and Champy, J. (1993) *Re-engineering the Corporation: A manifesto for business revolution.* London: Nicholas Brealey.

Handy, C. (1976) *Understanding Organisations.* London: Penguin Books.

Handy, C. (1989) *The Age of Unreason.* London: Business Books.

Handy, C. (1994) *The Empty Raincoat: Making sense of the future.* London: Hutchinson.

Hanlon, G. (1998) Professionalism as enterprise: service class politics and the redefinition of professionalism. [Electronic version.] *Sociology.* Vol. 32, No. 43.

Hardy, C. (1994) *Managing Strategic Action: Mobilizing change – concepts, readings and cases.* London: Sage.

Hardy, C. (1996) Understanding power: bringing about strategic change. *British Journal of Management.* Vol. 7 (special issue), ppS3–S16.

Harrington, S., Rayner, C. and Warren, S. (2012) Too Hot to Handle? Trust and Human Resource Practitioners' Implementation of Anti-Bullying Policies. *Human Resource Management Journal.* Vol. 22, No. 4, pp392–408.

Harris, L. (2005) 'Employment law and human resourcing strategies', in Leopold, J., Harris, L. and Watson, T.J. (eds) *The Strategic Managing of Human Resources.* Harlow: Pearson Education.

Harrison, R. and Kessels, J. (2003) *Human Resource Development in a Knowledge Economy.* Basingstoke: Palgrave Macmillan.

Harrison, R. (2005) *Learning and Development.* 3rd edition. London: CIPD.

Harrison, R. (2009) *Learning and Development.* 5th edition. London: CIPD.

Harry, W. and Collings, D. (2012) 'Localisation, Societies, Organisations and Employees', in Stahl, G.K, Mendenhall, M.E. and Oddou, G.R. *Readings and Cases in International Human Resource Management and Organisational Behaviour.* 5th edition. London: Routledge.

Hasson, J. (2007) Blogging for talent. *HR Magazine.* Vol. 52, No. 10, pp65–68.

Hays-Thomas, R. (2004) 'Why now? The contemporary focus on managing diversity', in Stockdale, M.S. and Crosby, F.J. (eds) *The Psychology and Management of Workplace Diversity.* Oxford: Blackwell.

Hazard, P. (2004) Tackling Performance Management Barriers. *Strategic HR Review.* Vol. 3, pp3–7.

Heenan, D. and Perlmutter, H. (1979) *Multinational Organizational Development: A social architecture perspective.* Reading, MA: Addison-Wesley.

Henderson, S. (1997) Black swans don't fly double loops: the limits of the learning organisation. *The Learning Organisation.* Vol. 4, No. 3, pp99–105.

Hendrick, H. (1983) Pilot Performance Under Reversed Control Stick Conditions. *Journal of Applied Psychology.* Vol. 56, No. 4, pp297–301.

Hendry, C. (1995) *Human Resource Management.* Oxford: Butterworth-Heinemann.

Heneman, R.L. (1992) *Merit Pay: Linking pay increases to performance ratings.* Reading, MA: Addison-Wesley.

Hersey, P., Blanchard, K. and Johnson, D. (2001) *Management of Organisational Behaviour: Leading human resources.* 8th edition. London: Prentice Hall.

Herzberg, F. (1968) One more time: how do you motivate your employees? *Harvard Business Review.* January–February, pp109–120.

Hiltrop, J.-M. (1996) Managing the changing psychological contract. *Employee Relations.* Vol. 18, No. 1, pp36–49.

Hobson, J. (2009) Bullying in the workplace. *Personnel Today.* 5 March.

Hofstede, G. (1991) *Cultures and Organizations.* Maidenhead: McGraw-Hill.

Hofstede, G. (2001) *Culture's Consequences: Comparing values, behaviours, institutions and organizations across nations.* London: Sage.

Holbeche L. (2008a) *Aligning Human Resources and Business Strategy.* Oxford: Butterworth-Heinemann.

Holbeche, L. (2008b) Where is Leadership Going? *Impact.* Issue 22, February, pp16–17.

Holbeche, L. (2013) Chapter 13 'The Future of HR' in Rees, G. and Smith, P.E. (eds) *Strategic Human Resource Management: An International Perspective.* London: Sage.

Holbeche, L. and Matthews, G. (2012) *ENGAGED: Unleashing your organisation's potential through employee engagement.* Chichester: Wiley/Josey Bass.

Holden, N. (2002) *Cross-Cultural Management: A knowledge management perspective.* Harlow: Pearson.

Hollyforde, S. and Whiddett, S. (2002) *The Motivation Handbook.* London: CIPD.

Holst, J.D. (2009) Conceptualizing training in the radical adult education tradition. *Adult Education Quarterly.* Vol. 59, No. 4, pp318–334.

Honey, P. (1998) *101 Ways to Develop Your People Without Really Trying: A manager's guide to work-based learning.* Maidenhead: Peter Honey Publications.

Honey, P. and Mumford, A. (1982) *The Manual of Learning Styles.* Maidenhead: Peter Honey Publications.

Howell, W.S. (1982) *The Empathetic Communicator.* University of Minnesota: Wadsworth Publishing.

Howe-Walsh, L.J. and Schyns, B. (2010) Self-initiated expatriates: implications for HRM. *International Journal of Human Resource Management.* Vol. 21, No. 2, pp260–273.

HR-inform. (2012) *Does an Organisation Have to Hold a Christmas Party for its staff?* Available at: www.cipd.co.uk/pm/peoplemanagement/p/paymentgateway.aspx?returnURL=/pm/peoplemanagement/b/weblog/archive/2012/11/06/does-an-organisation-have-to-hold-an-annual-christmas-party-for-its-staff-2012-11.aspx&blogid=2&postid=96710 [accessed 5 June 2013].

HRMID. (2007) McDonald's serves up better customer care and lower employee turnover: Two-stage training for more than 4,000 staff. *Human Resource Management International Digest.* Vol. 15, No. 1, pp23–26.

Huczynski, A. and Buchanan, D. (2007) *Organisational Behaviour: An introductory text.* 6th edition. Harlow: Pearson Education.

Huczynski, A. and Buchanan, D. (2010) *Organisational Behaviour: An introductory text.* 7th edition. Harlow: Pearson Education.

Huczynski, A. and Buchanan, D. (2013) *Organisational Behaviour.* 8th edition. Harlow: Pearson Education.

Hughes, M. (2006) *Change Management: A critical perspective.* London: CIPD.

Humble, J. (1972) *Management by Objectives.* London: Management Publications.

Hunt, B. (2007) Managing equality and cultural diversity in the health workforce. *Journal of Clinical Nursing.* Vol. 16, pp2252–2259.

Huselid, M.A. (1995) The impact of human resource management practices on turnover, productivity and corporate financial performance. *Academy of Management Journal.* Vol. 38, pp635–672.

Hutchinson, S. and Purcell, J. (2003) *Bringing Policies to Life: The vital role of front-line managers in people management.* London: CIPD.

Hutton, W. (2004) Got those old blue-collar blues. *The Observer.* 22 August.

Huws, U. and O'Keefe, B. (2008) EMCC company network - Managing change in EU cross-border mergers and acquisitions - Case example: Impress: Meeting company goals through strategic acquisitions. Available at: www.eurofound.europa.eu/publications/htmlfiles/ef08043.htm [accessed 11 July 2013].

Ibarra, H. (2004) *Working Identity: Unconventional strategies for reinventing your career.* Boston, MA: Harvard Business School Press.

IBM. (2013) IBM Graduate Scheme. Available at: www-05.ibm.com/employment/uk/graduate-programmes/index.shtml [accessed January 2013].

IDS. (2006) *Online Recruitment.* IDS study 819. April. London: Incomes Data Services.

Iles, P., Forster, A. and Tinline, G. (1996) The changing relationships between work commitment, personal flexibility and employability: an evaluation of a field experiment in executive development. *Journal of Managerial Psychology.* Vol. 11, No. 8, pp18–34.

Inkson, K. and Arthur, M. (2001) How to be a successful career capitalist. *Organisational Dynamics.* Vol. 30, No. 1, pp48–61.

IRS. (2000) Measuring intangible assets. *IRS Management Review.* Issue 19. Available at: www.xperthr.co.uk/article/6106/measuring-span-span-classhighlightintangible-span-span-classhighlightassets.aspx [accessed 4 June 2013].

IRS. (2008) Line managers' role in people management. *IRS Employment Review.* Issue 894. Available at: www.xperthr.co.uk/article/84008/survey--line-managers-role-in-people-management.aspx [accessed 11 July 2013].

IRS. (2009) IRS flexible working survey 2009: availability, take-up and impact. *IRS Employment Review.* Issue 92. Available at: www.xperthr.co.uk/article/93627/irs-flexible-working-survey-2009--availability,-take-up-and-impact.aspx [accessed 11 July 2013].

IRS. (2010) Evaluation of training: the 2010 IRS survey. *IRS Employment Review.* Available at: www.xperthr.co.uk/article/100298/evaluation-span-of-span-classhighlighttraining--the-2010-irs-survey.aspx [accessed 11 July 2013].

Jamrog, J.J., Vickers, M., Overholt, M.H. and Morrison, C.L. (2008) High-performance organizations: finding the elements of excellence. *People and Strategy, The Human Resource Planning Society Journal.* Vol. 31, No. 1, pp29–38.

Janis, I.L. (1972) *Victims of Groupthink.* Boston, MA: Houghton Mifflin.

Janis, I.L. (1982) *Groupthink: Psychological studies on policy decisions and fiascos.* New York: Free Press.

Jarrett, T. (2011) *The Equality Act 2010 and Positive Action.* Standard Note SN/BT/6093. London: House of Commons Library.

Jehn, K. (1994) Enhancing effectiveness: an investigation of advantages and disadvantages of value-based intragroup conflict optimising performance by conflict stimulation. *International Journal of Conflict Management.* Vol. 5, No. 3, pp223–238.

Jenner, S. and Taylor, S. (2007) *Employer branding – fad or the future for HR?* Research Insight Paper. London: CIPD.

Johnson, G. and Scholes, K. (2002) *Exploring Corporate Strategy.* 6th edition. London: FT/Pitman.

Johnson, G., Scholes, K. and Whittington, R. (2007) *Exploring Corporate Strategy; Texts and cases.* 7th edition. London: FT/Pitman.

Johnson, G., Scholes, K. and Whittington, R. (2011) *Exploring Corporate Strategy.* 8th edition. London: FT/Pitman.

Jones, T.W. (1995) Performance management in a changing context. *Human Resource Management.* Fall, pp425–442.

Judge, T.A. and Cable, D.M. (1997) Applicant personality, organisational culture and organisation attraction. *Personnel Psychology.* Vol. 50, No. 2, pp359–394.

Judge, W.Q., Naoumova, I. and Douglas, T. (2009) Organizational capacity for change and firm performance in a transitional economy. *International Journal of Human Resource Management.* Vol. 20, No. 8, pp1737–1752.

Kakabadse, A., Myers, A., McMahon, T. and Spony, G. (1997) 'Top Management Styles in Europe: Implications for Business and Cross National Teams', in Grint, T. *Leadership: Classicals, Contemporary and Critical Approaches.* Oxford: Oxford University Press.

Kandola, R. and Fullerton, J. (1998) *Diversity in Action: Managing the mosaic.* 2nd edition. London: CIPD.

Kang, D. and Stewart, J. (2007) Leader-member exchange (LMX) theory of leadership and HRD. *Leadership and Organization Development Journal.* Vol. 28, No. 6, pp531–551.

Katou, A.A. and Budhwar, P.S. (2009) Causal relationship between HRM policies and performance: evidence from the Greek manufacturing sector. *European Management Journal.* Vol. 28, pp25–39.

Kearns, P. (2005) *Evaluating the ROI from learning: how to develop value-based training.* London: CIPD.

Kelliher, C. and Anderson, D. (2010) Doing more with less? Flexible working practices and the intensification of work. *Human Relations.* Vol. 63, No. 1, pp83–106.

Kersley, B., Alpin, C., Forth, J., Bryson, A., Bewley, H., Dix, G. and Oxenbridge, S. (2006) *Inside the Workplace: Findings from the 2004 Workplace Employment Relations Survey.* London: Routledge.

Kessler, I. and Purcell, J. (1992) Performance-related pay: objectives and application. *Human Resource Management Journal.* Vol. 2, No. 3, pp6–33.

Khapova, S. and Arthur, M. (2011) Interdisciplinary approaches to contemporary career studies. *Human Relations.* Vol. 64, No. 1, pp3–17.

Kiessling, T. and Harvey, M. (2005) Strategic global human resource management research in the twenty-first century: an endorsement of the mixed-method research methodology. *International Journal of Human Resource Management.* Vol. 16, No. 1, pp22–45.

King, Z. (2004) *Guide to Career Management.* London: CIPD.

Kinnie, N., Swart, J., Hope-Hailey, V. and van Rossenberg, Y. (2012) *Innovative forms of organizing: Networked working in HR and its role in innovation, Part 1.* Report. November. London: CIPD.

Kinnie, N., Swart, J., Kund, M., Morris, S., Snell, S. and Kang, S.C. (2006) *Managing people and knowledge development in professional service firms.* London: CIPD.

Kissler, G. (1994) The new employment contract. *Human Resource Management.* Vol. 33, No. 3, pp335–352.

Knowles, M. (1990) *The Adult Learner: A neglected species.* London: Gulf Publications.

Kolb, D.A. (1984) *Experiential Learning as a Source of Learning and Development.* Eaglewood Cliffs: Prentice Hall.

Koster, F. (2011) Able, willing, and knowing: the effects of HR practices on commitment and effort in 26 European countries. *The International Journal of Human Resource Management.* Vol. 22, No. 14, pp2835–2851.

Kotter, J.P. (1996) *Leading Change.* Boston, MA: Harvard Business School Press.

Kotter, J.P. (1999) *What Leaders Really Do.* Boston, MA: Harvard Business School Press.

Kreitner, R. (2001) *Management.* 6th edition. Boston, MA: Houghton Mifflin.

Kreitner, R. and Kinicki, A. (2001) *Organisational Behaviour.* 5th edition. New York: McGraw-Hill.

Kreitner, R. Kinicki, A. and Buelens, M. (2002) *Organizational Behaviour.* 2nd edition. New York: McGraw-Hill.

Kremer, W. (2012) Why Feeling Guilty may Make You a Better Boss. BBC News Magazine. Available at: www.bbc.co.uk/news/magazine-20257373 [accessed 13 December 2012].

Kuvaas, B. (2006) Performance appraisal satisfaction and employee outcomes: mediating and moderating roles of work motivation. *International Journal of Human Resource Management.* Vol. 17, No. 3, pp504–522.

Ladkin, D. (2008) Leading Beautifully: How Mastery, Congruence and Purpose Create the Aesthetic of Embodied Leadership Practice. *The Leadership Quarterly.* Vol. 19, No. 1, pp31–41.

Ladkin, D. and Taylor, S. (2009) Enacting the True Self: Towards a Theory of Embodied Authentic Leadership. *The Leadership Quarterly.* Vol. 21, No. 1, p64–74.

Lashley, C. (1995) Towards an understanding of employee empowerment in hospitality services. *International Journal of Contemporary Hospitality Management.* Vol. 7, No.1, pp27–32.

Latham, G. (2007) *Work Motivation: History, theory, research and practice.* London: Sage.

Lawler, E. (2009) The knowing-doing gap. *Conference Board Review,* Vol. 46, Issue 3, May/June, p29.

Lawrence, P. and Lorsch, J. (1967) *Organisation and Environment.* Boston, MA: Harvard Business School Press.

Leach, D. and Wall, T. (2004) *What is Job Design?* Sheffield: Institute of Work Psychology.

Leanna, C. and Barry, B. (2000) Stability and change as simultaneous experiences in organizational life. *Academy of Management Review*, Vol. 25, No. 4, pp75–9.

Legge, K. (2000) 'HRM in a Critical Analysis', in Storey, J. (ed.) *Human Resource Management: a Critical Text.* London: Thomson.

Legge, K. (2005) *Human Resource Management: Rhetorics and realities.* 2nd edition. Basingstoke: Palgrave Macmillan.

Leitch, S. (2006) *Review of Skills: Prosperity for all in the global economy – world-class skills.* Final Report. Norwich: HMSO. Available at: www.hm-treasury.gov.uk/leitch [accessed November 2009].

Lessem, R. (1989) *Global Management Principles.* Harlow: Prentice Hall.

Levinson, H. (1970) Management by whose objectives? *Harvard Business Review.* July–August, pp125–134.

Levinson, H. (1976) Appraisal of what performance? *Harvard Business Review.* July–August, pp30–46.

Lewin, D. (2001) IR and HR perspectives on workplace conflict: what can each learn from the other? *Human Resource Management Review.* Vol. 11, No. 4, pp453–85.

Lewin, K. (1947) Frontiers in group dynamics. *Human Relations.* Vol. 1, pp5–42.

Lewin, K. (1951) *Field Theory in Social Science.* New York/London: Harper & Row.

Linstead, S., Fullop, L. and Lilley, S. (2009) *Management and Organisation: A critical text.* 2nd edition. Basingstoke: Palgrave Macmillan.

Lloyd, M. and Maguire, S. (2002) The possibility horizon. *Journal of Change Management.* Vol. 3, No. 2, pp149–157.

Locke, E.A. (1968) Towards a Theory of Motivation and Incentives. *Organizational Behaviour and Human Performance.* Vol. 3, No. 2, pp157-189.

Locke, E.A. (1976) The nature and causes of job satisfaction. In M.D. Dunnette (ed.) *Handbook of industrial and organizational psychology.* Chicago: Rand McNally. pp1297–1349.

Locke, E.A. and Latham, G.P. (1990) *A Theory of Goal-Setting and Task Performance.* Englewood Cliffs, NJ: Prentice Hall.

Lockwood, N.R. (2007) *Leveraging employee engagement for competitive advantage: HR's strategic role.* Alexandria, VA: Society for Human Resource Management.

Lowry, C. (2006) HR Managers as Ethical Decision Makers: Mapping the Terrain. *Asia Pacific Journal of Human Resource Management.* Vol. 44, No. 20, pp211–221.

Lupton, T. (1991) Organisational change: top-down or bottom-up management? *Personnel Review.* Vol. 20, No. 3, pp4–10.

MacDonald, D.J. and Makin, P.J. (2000) The psychological contract, organisational commitment and job satisfaction of temporary staff. *Leadership and Organization Development Journal.* Vol. 21, No. 2, pp84–91.

Mackie, J.L. (1977) *Ethics – Inventing Right and Wrong.* Harmondsworth: Penguin.

Macleod, D. and Clark, N. (2009) *Engaging for Success: Enhancing performance through employee engagement.* London: Office of Public Sector Management.

Maguire, H. (2002) Psychological contracts: are they still relevant? *Career Development International.* Vol. 7, No. 3, pp167–180.

Mahoney, J. (1994) 'How to be ethical: ethics resource management', in Harvey, B. (ed.) *Business Ethics – A European Approach.* Hemel Hempstead: Prentice Hall.

Mammam, A., Akuratiyagamage, V.W. and Rees, C.J. (2006) Managerial perceptions of the role of the human resource function in Sri Lanka: a comparative study of local, foreign-owned and joint venture companies. *International Journal of Human Resource Management.* Vol. 17, pp2009–2020.

Marchington, M., Carroll, M., Grimshaw, D. and Pass, S. (2009) *Managing People in Networked Organizations.* London: CIPD.

Marchington, M., Grimshaw, D., Rubery, J. and Willmott, H. (2005) *Fragmenting Work: Blurring organizational boundaries and disordering hierarchies.* Oxford: Oxford University Press.

Marchington, M., Rubery, J. and Grimshaw, D. (2011) *Alignment, integration and consistency in HRM across multi employer networks.* London: CIPD.

Marchington, M., Vincent, S., and Cooke, F.L. (2005) 'The role of boundary-spanning agents in inter-organizational contracting', in M. Marchington, D. Grimshaw, J. Rubery and H. Willmott (eds) *Fragmenting Work: Blurring organizational boundaries and disordering hierarchies.* Oxford: Oxford University Press.

Marks, A. (2001) Developing a multiple foci conceptualization of the psychological contract. *Employee Relations.* Vol. 23, No. 5, pp454–469.

Marks & Spencer. (2008) *About Plan A.* Company website: plana.marksandspencer.com [accessed 18 April 2008].

Marris, P. (1986) *Loss and Change.* 2nd edition. London: Routledge & Kegan Paul.

Marsden, D. and French, S. (1998) *What a Performance: Performance-related pay in the public services.* London: Centre for Economic Performance.

Martin, G. (2012) *Lens on Talent, a collection of Next Generation HR Thought pieces. Part 2, August.* London: CIPD.

Mayfield, M. and Mayfield, J. (2012) Logo leadership: breathing life into loyalty and putting meaning back into work. *Development and Learning in Organizations.* Vol. 26, No. 2, pp11–15.

Mayon-White, B. (1993) 'Problem-solving in small groups: team members as agents of change', in Mabey, C. and Mayon-White, B. (eds) *Managing Change.* 2nd edition. Buckingham: Open University/Paul Chapman Publishing.

McCalman, J. and Paton, R.A. (1992) *Change Management.* London: Paul Chapman Publishing.

McClean, E. and Collins, C. (2011) High-commitment HR practices, employee effort, and firm performance: Investigating the effects of HR practices across employee groups within professional services firms. *Human Resource Management.* Vol. 50, No. 3, pp341–363.

McClernon, T. (2006) Rivals to systematic training. *Advances in Developing Human Resources.* Vol. 8, No. 4, pp442–459.

McCracken, M. and Wallace, M. (2000) Towards a redefinition of strategic HRD. *Journal of European Industrial Training.* Vol. 24, No. 5, pp281–290.

McDonald, P., Brown, K. and Bradley, L. (2005) Have traditional career paths given way to Protean ones? Evidence from senior managers in the Australian public sector. *Career Development International.* Vol. 10, No. 2, pp109–129.

McGuire, D. and Gubbins, C. (2010) The Slow Death of Formal Learning: A Polemic. *Human Resources Development Review.* Vol. 9, No. 30, pp249–265.

McLellan, D. (ed.) (2000) *Karl Marx: Selected Writings.* Oxford: Oxford University Press.

Megginson, D. and Whitaker, V. (2007) *Continuing Professional Development.* 2nd edition. London: CIPD.

Mercer Survey. (2008/9) Available at: www.employeebenefits.co.uk/item/7971/23/319/3 [accessed 4 June 2013].

Meyer, J.P. and Allen, N.J. (1991) A three-component conceptualization or organizational commitment. *Human Resource Management Review.* Vol. 1, pp61–89.

Meyer, J.P. and Herscovitch, L. (2001) Commitment in the workplace: towards a general model. *Human Resources Management Review.* Vol. 11, pp299–326.

Meyer, J.P and Herscovitch, L. (2002) 'Commitment to organizational change: extension of a three-component model', in *Journal of Applied Psychology.* Vol. 87, No. 3, pp474-487.

Miller, D. (2004) Building sustainable change capability. *Industrial and Commercial Training.* Vol. 36, No. 1, pp9–12.

Mills, C. (2010) HMRC running out of time to regain its sense of purpose. *The Times*, 14 January.

Millward, N., Bryson, A. and Forth, J. (2000) 'All change at work: British employment relations 1980–1998 as portrayed by the Workplace Industrial Relations Series', in Blyton, P. and Turnbull, P. (eds) *The Dynamics of Employee Relations.* 3rd edition. Basingstoke: Palgrave Macmillan.

Mitchell, L. (2009) David Fairhurst interview in *Managing People.* 30 July. Available at: www.hrzone.co.uk.

Mohrman, A.M. and Mohrman, S.A. (1995) Performance management is 'running the business'. *Compensation and Benefits Review.* July–August, pp69–75.

Molleman, E. and Timmerman, H. (2003) Performance Management When Innovation and Learning Become Critical Performance Indicators. *Personnel Review.* Vol. 32, No. 1, pp93–113.

Morgan, R. (2006) Making the Most of Performance Management Systems. *Compensation and Benefits Review.* Vol. 38, pp22–27.

Morris, S.S., Wright, P., Trevor, J., Stiles, P., Stahl, G., Paauwe, J. and Farndale, E. (2009) 'Global Challenges to Replicating HR: the Role of People, Processes and Systems', in *Human Resource Management.* Vol. 48, No. 6, pp973-995.

Mullins, L.J. (2007) *Management and Organisational Behaviour.* 8th edition. Harlow: FT/Prentice Hall.

Mullins, L. (2010) *Management and Organisational Behaviour.* 9th edition. Harlow: FT/Prentice Hall.

Mullins, L.J. (2013) *Management and Organisational Behaviour.* 10th edition. Harlow: Prentice Hall.

Mumford, E. (1995) Contracts, complexity and contradictions: the changing employment relationship. *Personnel Review.* Vol. 24, No. 8, pp54–70.

Murphy, N. (2008a) Line manager's role in people management. *IRS Employment Review* survey, Issue 894, 3 April. Available at: www.xperthr.co.uk/article/84008/survey--line-span-span-classhighlightmanagers-span-span-classhighlightrole-span-in-people-span-classhighlightmanagement.aspx?searchwords=murphy_2008_line_managers_role [accessed on 8 June 2010].

Murphy, N. (2008b) HR roles and responsibilities. *IRS Employment Review* survey. Available at: www.xperthr.co.uk/searchresults.aspx?s=murphy_2010 [accessed on 8 June 2010].

Murphy, N. (2008c) Trends in recruitment methods in 2006 and 2007. *IRS Employment Review*, Issue 893. Available at: www.xperthr.co.uk [accessed 16 May 2008].

Murray-West, R. (2002) Sunderland car workers are Europe's most productive. *Daily Telegraph*, 9 July.

Needle, D. (2004) *Business in Context.* 4th edition. London: Thomson Learning.

Needle, D. (2010) *Business in Context.* 5th edition. Andover: Cengage.

Nelson, D. and Bergman, D. (2013) Bangladesh dispatch: the miracle of Rana Plaza gives way to grief as body count rises. *Daily Telegraph*, 25 April.

Nelson, L. (2003) A case study in organisational change: implications for theory. *The Learning Organization.* Vol. 10, No. 1, pp18–30.

Nijssen, M. and Paauwe, J. (2012) 'HRM in Turbulent Times: How to Achieve Agility', in *International Journal of Human Resource Management.* Vol. 23, No. 16, pp3315-3335.

Nonaka, I. and Takeuchi, H. (1995) *The Knowledge-Creating Company.* Oxford: Oxford University Press.

Noon, M. and Blyton, P. (2002) *The Realities of Work.* 2nd edition. Basingstoke: Palgrave Macmillan.

Nye, J. (2008) *The Powers to Lead: Soft, hard, and smart.* Oxford University Press.

ONS. (2010) Office for National Statistics. Available at: www.statistics.gov.uk [accessed 24 March 2010].

Open University. (1985) Block 1. *Managing and Messy Problems.* Course T244. *Managing in Organizations.* Milton Keynes: Open University.

Paauwe, J. (2009) HRM and performance: achievements, methodological issues and prospects. *Journal of Management Studies.* Vol. 46, No. 1, pp129–142.

Paauwe, J. and Boselie, P. (2005) HRM and performance: what next? *Human Resource Management Journal.* Vol. 15, pp68–83.

Paton, G. (2010) Exploited work experience students forced to make tea. *Daily Telegraph,* 11 January.

Paton, R.A. and McCalman, J. (2000) *Change Management: Guide to effective implementation.* 2nd edition. London: Sage.

Patterson, M., West, M., Lawthorn, R. and Nickell, S. (1997) *Impact of People Management Practices on Business Performance.* Issues in People Management, No. 22. London: Institute for Personnel and Development.

Peacock, L. (2010) Abercrombie & Fitch adverts run risk of discrimination claims. *Personnel Today.* Available at: www.personneltoday.com/articles/11/02/2010/54093/abercrombie.htm [accessed 24 May 2013].

Perkin, H. (1989) *The Rise of Professional Society – England since 1880.* London: Routledge.

Perkins, S.J. and Shortland, S.M. (2006) *Strategic International Human Resource Management.* 2nd edition. London: Kogan Page.

Perkins, S.J. and White. G. (2011) *Reward Management: Alternatives, Consequences and Context.* London: CIPD.

Perlmutter, H.V. (1969) The tortuous evolutions of the multinational corporation. *Columbia Journal of World Business.* January–February, pp9–18.

Perry, E. and Kulik, C.T. (2008) The devolution of HR to the line: implications for perceptions of people management effectiveness. *International Journal of Human Resource Management.* Vol. 19, No. 2, pp262–273.

Perry, M. (2001) Flexibility pays. *Accountancy Age.* 6 December, pp15–18; reprinted (2002) in *Human Resource Management International Digest.* Vol. 10, No. 4, pp13–15.

Personnel Today. (2008) Survey reports continued growth in CPD importance. Available at: www.personneltoday.com/articles/04/09/2008/47385/survey-reports-continued-growth-in-cpd-importance.htm [accessed 25 July 2013].

Personnel Today. (2012) Jo Faragher, HR needs to invest in its own development, says report. Available at: www.personneltoday.com/articles/13/07/2012/58663/hr-needs-to-invest-in-its-own-development-says-report.htm [accessed 24 May 2013].

Peston, R. (2007) *Rose Goes Green in Pursuit of Profit*. BBC News website, 15 January. Available at: news.bbc.co.uk [accessed 18 April 2008].

Peters, T.J. (1999) *The Brand You 50; Or: Fifty ways to transform yourself from an 'employee' into a brand that shouts distinction, commitment, and passion!* New York: Knopf Publishing.

Pettigrew, A. (1985) *The Awakening Giant: Continuity and change at ICI*. Oxford: Blackwell.

Pettigrew, A. and Whipp, R. (1993) 'Understanding the environment', in Mabey, C. and Mayon-White, B. (eds) *Managing Change*. 2nd edition. London: Paul Chapman Publishing.

Pilbeam, S. and Corbridge, M. (2006) *People Resourcing: Contemporary HRM in Practice*. 3rd edition. Harlow: FT/Prentice Hall.

Pilbeam, S. and Corbridge, M. (2010) *People Resourcing and Talent Planning: HRM in Practice*. 4th edition. Harlow: FT/Prentice Hall.

Pitcher, G. (2008) Backlash against HR business partner model. *Personnel Today*, 29 January.

Plummer, K. (2010) *Sociology: The Basics*. Abingdon: Routledge.

Pollert, A. (1991) 'The orthodoxy of flexibility', in Pollert, A. (ed.) *Farewell to Flexibility?* Oxford: Blackwell.

Pollitt, D. (2003) Shift-pattern switch improves staff turnover and recruitment at Seeboard. *Human Resource Management International Digest*. Vol. 11, No. 1, pp12–14.

Porter, M. (1985) *Competitive Advantage: Creating and sustaining superior performance*. New York: Free Press.

Porter, M. (1998) *Competitive Strategy: Techniques for analyzing industries and competitors*. New York: Free Press.

Porter, M.E. and Kramer, M.R. (2006) Strategy and society: the link between competitive advantage and corporate social responsibility. *Harvard Business Review*. Vol. 84, No. 12, pp78–92.

Povah, L. and Sobczak, K. (2010) A Context-oriented Approach to Leader Selection: A Strategy for Uncertain Times. *People Strategy*. Vol. 33, No. 4, pp40–47.

Preece, D. (2012) 'HRM in an Organizational Context', in Gilmore, S. and Williams, S. (eds) *Human Resource Management*. 2nd edition. Oxford: Oxford University Press.

Price, A. (2004) *Human Resource Management in a Business Context*. 2nd edition. London: Thomson.

Price, D. (ed.) (2009) *Principles and Practice of Change*. Basingstoke: Palgrave Macmillan.

PricewaterhouseCoopers. (2012) *PwC Survey of Global Mobility Policies.* Available at: www.pwc.com/us/en/hr-management/publications/global-mobility-policies-survey-summary.jhtml [accessed 25 July 2013].

Priem, R.L. and Butler, J.E. (2001) Is the resource-based theory a useful perspective for strategic management research? *Academy of Management Review.* Vol. 26, No. 1, pp22–40.

Pugh, D.S. and Hickson, D.J. (1976) *Organizational Structure in Its Context.* Farnborough: Saxon House.

Pulakos, E. (2009). *Performance management: A new approach for driving business results.* Malden, MA: Wiley-Blackwell.

Purcell, J. and Ahlstrand, B. (1994) *Human Resource Management in the Multi-Divisional Company.* Oxford: Oxford University Press.

Purcell, J. and Hutchinson, S. (2007) Front-line managers as agents in the HRM performance causal chain: theory, analysis and evidence. *Human Resource Management Journal.* Vol. 17, No. 1, pp3–20.

Purcell, J., Kinnie, N., Hutchinson, S., Rayton, B. and Swart, J. (2003) *Understanding the People and Performance Link: Understanding the Black Box.* London: CIPD.

Rajan, A. (2002) Meaning of Leadership in 2002. *Professional Manager*, March, p33.

Rao, T.V. and Varghese, S. (2008) Trends and challenges of developing human capital in India. *Human Resource Development International.* Vol. 12, No. 1, pp15–34.

Rayner, C. and Adam-Smith, D. (eds) (2009) *Managing and Leading People.* London: CIPD.

Rayner, G. and Swinford, S. (2013) Chaos and Faffing at BBC as Jimmy Savile Scandal Detonated. *Daily Telegraph.* 22 February. Available at: www.telegraph.co.uk [accessed 22 April 2013].

Reed Consulting survey (2004) Available at: www.reedpressoffice.co.uk/docs/Employee %20Attrition.pdf [accessed 4 June 2013].

Rees, D. and McBain, R. (2004) *People Management.* Basingstoke: Palgrave Macmillan.

Rees, G. and Smith, P.E. (eds) (2014) *Strategic Human Resource Management: An International Perspective.* London: Sage.

Reeves, N. (2012) JT (formerly Jersey Telecom), Leadership Development Initiative. *People Management.* Available at: www.peoplemanagement.co.uk/pm/articles/2012/09/jt-formerly-jersey-telecom-leadership-development-initiative.htm [accessed 19 December 2012].

Reeves, R. (2008) The trouble with targets. *Management Today.* 8 January. Available at: www.managementtoday.co.uk/news/774435/the-trouble-with-targets [accessed 5 June 2013].

Reid, M., Barrington, H. and Brown, M. (2007) *Human Resource Development.* 7th edition. London: CIPD.

Robbins, S. (1993) *Organisational Behaviour: Concepts, controversies and applications*. 6th edition. Englewood Cliffs, NJ: Prentice Hall.

Rodrigues, C.A. (1988) Identifying the right leader for the right situation. *Personnel Today*. September, pp43–46.

Rodwell, J.J., Noblet, A.J., Stean, P., Osborne, S. and Allisey, A.F. (2008) Investigating people management issues in a third sector health care organisation – an inductive approach. *Australian Journal of Advanced Nursing*. Vol. 27, No. 2, pp55–62.

Rollinson, D. (2008) *Organisational Behaviour and Analysis: An integrated approach*. 4th edition. Harlow: FT/Prentice Hall.

Rose, S. (2007) Back in fashion: how we're reviving a British icon. *Harvard Business Review*. May, pp51–58.

Rosen, M., Bedwell, W., Wildman, J., Fritzsche, B., Salas, E. and Burke, C. (2011) Managing adaptive performance in teams; Guiding principles and behavioral markers for measurement. *Human Resource Management Review*. Vol. 21, No. 2, pp107–122.

Rosener, J. (1990) Ways women lead. *Harvard Business Review*, November–December, pp. 119–25.

Rosenfeld, R. and Wilson, D. (1999) *Managing Organisations: Texts, readings and cases*. 2nd edition. London: McGraw-Hill.

Rothwell, A. (2005) How HR professionals rate 'continuing professional development'. *Human Resource Management Journal*. Vol. 15, No. 3, pp18–32.

Rousseau, D. (1995) *Psychological Contracts in Organizations: Understanding written and unwritten agreements*. London: Sage.

Sabbagh, D. (2012) George Entwistle: 23 Years Getting to the Top of the BBC. Gone in 54 Days. *The Observer*. 10 November. Available at: www.guardian.co.uk [accessed 18 December 2012].

Sadler-Smith, E., Allinson, C. and Hayes, J. (2000) Learning preferences and cognitive style: some implications for continuing professional development. *Management Learning*. Vol. 31, No. 2, pp239–256.

Salimaki, A., Hakonen, A. and Heneman, R. (2009) Managers generate meaning for pay. *Journal of Managerial Psychology*. Vol. 24, No. 2, pp161–177.

Sargeant, M. and Lewis, D. (2008) *Employment Law*. 4th edition. Harlow: Pearson.

Saunders, M.N.K. and Thornhill, A. (2006) Forced employment contract change and the psychological contract. *Employee Relations*. Vol. 28, No. 5, pp449–467.

Schaumberg, R. and Flynn, F. (2012) Uneasy Lies the Head That Wears the Crown; The Link Between Guilt Proneness and Leadership. *Journal of Personality and Social Psychology*. Vol. 103, No. 2, pp327–342.

Schein, E. (1978) *Career Dynamics: Matching the individual and organisational needs*. Reading, MA: Addison-Wesley.

Schein, E. (1984) Coming to a new awareness of organizational culture. *Sloan Management Review.* Vol. 25, No. 2, pp3–16.

Schuler, R.S., Dowling, P. E. and De Cieri, H. (1993) An integrative framework of strategic international human resource management. *Journal of Management.* Vol. 19, No. 2, pp419–59.

Searle, R. (2003) *Selection and Recruitment: A critical text.* Milton Keynes: Palgrave Macmillan in association with the Open University.

Searle, R.H. and Skinner, D. (2011) New Agendas and Perspectives. In Searle, R.H. and Skinner, D. (eds) *Trust and Human Resource Management.* Cheltenham: Edward Elgar Publishing, pp340–343.

Sears, L. (2010) *Next Generation HR: Time for change – towards a next generation HR.* London: CIPD.

Segal, J. (2010). Performance management blunders. *HR Magazine.* November, pp75–78.

Seibert, S., Kraimer, M. and Linden, R. (2001) A Social Capital Theory of Career Success. *Academy of Management Journal.* Vol. 44, No. 2, pp219–237.

Seligman, M. (1998) *Learned Optimism.* New York, NY: Simon & Schuster.

Semler, R. (1993) *Maverick: The success story behind the world's most unusual workplace.* London: Arrow Books.

Senge, P. (1993) *The Fifth Discipline: The Art and Practice of the Learning Organisation.* New York: Random House.

Senior, B. and Swailes, S. (2010) *Organisational Change.* 4th edition. Harlow: FT/Prentice Hall.

Sennett, R. (1998) *The Corrosion of Character: The personal consequences of work in the new capitalism.* London: Norton.

Sharp, R. (2009) Total reward at Arup. *IRS Employment Review.* Issue 916, 19 February.

Shen, J., Chandra, A., D'Netto, B. and Monga, M. (2009) Managing diversity through human resource management: an international perspective and conceptual framework. *International Journal of Human Resource Management.* Vol. 20, No. 2, pp235–251.

Sirkin, H.L, Keenan, P. and Jackson, A. (2005) The Hard Side of Change Management. *Harvard Business Review.* Vol. 83, No. 10, pp108-118.

Simpson, S. (2010) *Volcano Update: Seven things employers should be doing.* 22 April. Available at: www.personneltoday.com [accessed 23 April 2010].

Sloman, M. (2007) *The Changing World of the Trainer.* London: Routledge.

Sparrow, P.R. (2005) 'Global human resource management', in Shams, M. and Jackson, P. (eds) *Developments in Work and Organizational Psychology: Implications for international business.* London, New York and Amsterdam: Elsevier.

Sparrow, P.R. (2012) Globalising the international mobility function: the role of emerging markets, flexibility and strategic delivery models. *International Journal of Human Resource Management*. Vol. 23, No. 12, pp2404–2427.

Springett, N. (2002) The impact of corporate purpose on strategy, organisations and financial performance. *Human Resources and Employment Review*. Vol. 2, No. 2, pp117–124.

Springett, N. (2004)'Corporate Purpose as the Basis of Moral Leadership of the Firm', in *Strategic Change*. Vol. 13, No. 6, pp297-307.

Stahl, G.K., Bjorkman, I., Farndale, E., Morris, S.S., Paauwe, J., Stiles, P., Trevor, J. and Wright, P. (2012) 'Six principles of Effective Global Talent Management', in *MIT Sloan Management Review*. Vol. 53, No. 2, pp25-32.

Sternberg, E. (2000) *Just Business*. 2nd edition. Oxford: Oxford University Press.

Stevens, M. (2013) Employers are from Mars, Young People are from Venus. *People Management*. Available at: www.cipd.co.uk/pm/peoplemanagement/b/weblog/archive/2013/04/25/employers-are-from-mars-young-people-are-from-venus.aspx [accessed 25 April 2013].

Stewart, J. and McGoldrick, J. (eds) (1996) *Human Resource Development: Perspectives, strategies and practice*. London: Pitman.

Storey, J. (1983) *Managerial Prerogatives and the Question of Control*. London: Routledge.

Storey, J. (1989) 'From personnel management to human resource management', in Storey, J. (ed.) *New Perspectives on Human Resource Management*. London: Routledge.

Storey, J. (1992) *Developments in the Management of Human Resources*. Oxford: Blackwell.

Storey, J. (1995) *Human Resource Management: A critical text*. London: Routledge.

Strack, R., Caye, J., Leicht, M., Villis, U., Bohm, H. and McDonnell, M. (2007) *The Future of HR in Europe: Key challenges through 2015*. London: Boston Consulting Group.

Subramony, M. (2009) A Meta-analytic investigation of the relationship between HRM bundles and firm performance. *Human Resource Management*. Vol. 48, No. 5, pp745–768.

Suff, R. (2008) Business partnering at the AA. *IRS Employment Review*, Issue 908.

Suff, R. (2012a) Recruiting and selecting graduates: 2012 XpertHR survey. *IRS Employment Review*. Available at: www.xperthr.co.uk/article/114836/recruiting-span-and-span-classhighlightselecting-span-span-classhighlightgraduates--2012-xperthr-survey.aspx?searchwords=recruiting+and+selecting+graduates [accessed 28 November 2012].

Suff, R. (2012b) XpertHR recruitment trends survey 2012: activity picks up. *IRS Employment Review*. Available at: www.xperthr.co.uk/article/112441/xperthr-recruitment-span-span-classhighlighttrends-span-span-classhighlightsurvey-2012--activity-picks-up.aspx?searchwords=recruitment+trends+survey [accessed 21 March 2012].

Suff, R (2013a) *Using corporate websites for recruitment: 2013 XpertHR survey*. Available at: www.xpertHR.co.uk/article/115260/usingcorporatewebsitesforrecruitment [accessed 30 January 2013].

Suff, R (2013b) *Using job boards for recruitment: 2013 XpertHR survey*. Available at: www.xpertHR.co.uk/articleusingjobboardsforrecruitment [accessed 30 January 2013].

Sullivan, J., Wong, W. Adusumilli, D., Alder, A., Blazey, L., Huggett, M. and Parkin, J. (2009) *Deal or no deal? An exploration of the modern employment relationship. The future of HR Working Paper*. London: The Work Foundation.

Sullivan, S. (1999) The changing nature of careers: a review and research agenda. *Journal of Management*, Vol. 25, No. 3, pp457–484.

Sullivan, S. and Baruch, Y. (2009) Advances in Career Theory and Research: A Critical Review and Agenda for Future Exploration. *Journal of Management*. Vol. 35, No. 6, p1542.

Surowiecki, J. (2004) *The Wisdom of Crowds*. New York: Doubleday.

Sutherland, J. (2009) WERS Report. Training and employee use of skills in Scotland: some evidence. *Fraser Economic Commentary*. Vol. 33, No. 1, pp60–64

Suutari, V. and Brewster, C. (2000) Making their own way: international experience through self-initiated foreign assignments. *Journal of World Business*. Vol. 35, No. 4, pp417–436.

Swart, J., Kinnie, N., Rabinowitz, J., Lund, M., Snell, S., Morris, S. and Kang, S.C. (2007) *Managing across boundaries: human resource management beyond the firm*. London: CIPD.

Takeuchi, R., Lepak, D and Swart, J. (2011) 'How organizations evaluate and maintain fit of human capital with their needs', in Burton-Jones, A. and Spencer, J.C. (eds) *Oxford Handbook of Human Capital*. Oxford: Oxford University Press.

Tamkin, P., Barber, L. and Hirsh, W. (1995) *Personal Development Plans: Case studies of practice*. Brighton: Institute for Employment Studies.

Tams, S. and Arthur, M. (2010) New directions for boundaryless careers: Agency and Interdependence in a Changing World. *Journal of Organizational Behaviour*. Vol. 31, No. 5, pp629–646.

Tan, V. and Tiong, T.N. (2005) Change management in times of economic uncertainty. *Singapore Management Review*. Vol. 27, No. 1, pp49–68.

Tannenbaum, R. and Schmidt, W.H. (1973) How to choose a leadership pattern. *Harvard Business Review*. May–June, pp162–180.

Taylor, F.W. (1911) *Principles of Scientific Management*. New York: Harper.

Taylor, R. (2002) The future of work–life balance. *Human Resource Management International Digest*. Vol. 10, No. 4, pp13–15.

Tesco. (2008) Tesco.com website [accessed 13 September 2004; 16 February 2005; 4 May 2008].

Tharenou, P. (2008) 'Self-initiated careers', in Baugh, S.G. and Sullivan, S.E. (eds) *Maintaining Focus Energy and Options Over the Career.* Charlotte, NC: Information Age Publishing

Thomas, R.M. (2001) *Recent Theories of Human Development.* Thousand Oaks, CA: Sage.

Thomas, R. (2009) 'The business environment of human resource management', in Gilmore, S. and Williams, S. (eds) *Human Resource Management.* Oxford: Oxford University Press.

Thomson, P. (2008) The business benefits of flexible working. *Strategic HR Review.* Vol. 7, No. 2, pp17–22.

Thompson, P. and McHugh, D. (2009) *Work Organisations: A critical approach.* 4th edition. Basingstoke: Palgrave Macmillan.

Tomlinson, F. and Schwabenland, C. (2010) Reconciling competing discourses of diversity? The UK non-profit sector between social justice and the business case. *Organisation.* Vol. 17, pp101–121.

Torrington, D., Hall, L. and Taylor, S. (2002) *Human Resource Management.* 5th edition. Harlow: FT/Prentice Hall.

Torrington, D., Hall, L. and Taylor, D. (2008) *Human Resource Management.* 7th edition. Harlow: FT/Prentice Hall.

Townsend, R. (1981) *Up the Organisation.* Greenwich, CT: Fawcett.

Toynbee, P. (2008) MPs must fulfil Labour's pledge to low paid and temporary workers. *The Guardian.* 23 February, p33.

Training Magazine. (2012) *Training Magazine Ranks 2012 Top 125 Organizations.* Available at: www.trainingmag.com [accessed 17 January 2013].

Truss, C. and Gill, J. (2009) Managing the HR function: the role of social capital. *Personnel Review.* Vol. 38, No. 6, pp674–695.

Truss, C., Soane, E. and Edwards, C. (2006) *Working life: employee attitudes and engagement 2006.* Research report. London: CIPD.

UKCES. (2009) *National Employer Skills Survey 2009.* Key Findings Report. March. London: UK Commission for Employment and Skills.

UKCES. (2012) *National Employers Skills Survey 2011.* Available at: www.ukces.org.uk/publications/er46-employer-skills-survey-2011-england-results [accessed 2 May 2013].

Ulrich, D. (1997) *Human Resource Champions: The next agenda for adding value and delivering results.* Boston, MA: Harvard Business School Press.

Ulrich, D. and Brockbank, W. (2005) *The HR Value Proposition.* Boston, MA: Harvard Business School Press.

Ulrich, D. and Smallwood, N. (2004) Capitalizing on Capabilities. *Harvard Business Review.* Vol. 82, No. 6, pp119–127.

Ulrich, D., Younger, J. and Brockbank, W. (2008) The twenty-first-century HR organization. *Human Resource Management.* Vol. 47, No. 4, pp829–850.

Van Buren, H.J., Greenwood, M. and Sheehen, C. (2011) Strategic Human Resource Management and the Decline of Employee Focus. *Human Resource Management Review.* Vol. 21, No. 30, pp209–219.

Van Dierendonck, D. (2010) Servant Leadership: A Review and Synthesis. *Journal of Management.* Vol. 37, No. 4, pp1228–1261.

Vilanova, M., Lozano, M. and Arenas, D. (2009) Exploring the nature of the relationship between CSR and competitiveness. *Journal of Business Ethics.* Vol. 87, pp57–69.

Von Bergen, C.W., Soper, B. and Parnell, J.A. (2005) Workplace diversity and organisational performance. *Equal Opportunities International.* Vol. 24, No. 3/4, pp1–16.

Vroom, V. (1964) *Work and Motivation.* New York: John Wiley.

Wahrenburg, M., Hackethal, A., Friedrich, L. and Gellrich, T. (2006) Strategic decisions regarding the vertical integration of human resource organizations: evidence for an integrated HR model for the financial services and non-financial services industry in Germany, Austria and Switzerland. *International Journal of Human Resource Management.* Vol. 17, No. 10, pp1726–1771.

Wain, D. (2009) Command performance. *People Management,* 5 November.

Wainwright, S., Clark, J. and Griffith, M. (2006) *The UK voluntary sector almanac.* London: NVCVO Publications.

Walumbwa, F., Avolio, B.J., Gardner, W.L, Wernsing, T. and Peterson, S. (2008) Authentic leadership: development and validation of a theory-based measure. *Journal of Management.* Vol. 34, No. 1, pp89–126.

Wang, C., Indridason, T. and Saunders, M. (2010) Affective and continuance commitment in public private partnership. *Employee Relations.* Vol. 32, No. 4, pp396–417.

Wang, G.G. and Sun, J.Y. (2009) Clarifying the boundaries of human resource development. *Human Resource Development International.* Vol. 12, No. 1, pp93–103.

Wang, D. and Shyu, C. (2008) Will the strategic fit between business and HRM strategy influence HRM effectiveness and organizational performance? *International Journal of Manpower.* Vol. 29, No. 2, pp92–110.

Warech, M. and Tracey, J.B. (2004) Evaluating the impact of human resources: identifying what matters. *Cornell Hotel and Restaurant Administration Quarterly.* Vol. 45, pp76–87.

Warren, C. (2009) HR and OD 'should be one and the same'. *People Management,* 20 November.

Waterman, R., Waterman, J. and Collard, B. (1994) Toward a career resilient workforce. *Harvard Business Review.* July–August, pp87–95.

Watson, T.J. (2006) *Organising and Managing Work.* 2nd edition. Harlow: FT/PrenticeHall.

Watson, T.J. (2012) *Sociology Work and Organisation.* 6th edition. Abingdon: Routledge.

Weber, M. (1947) *The Theory of Social and Economic Organization* (translated by Henderson, A.M. and Parsons, T.). Oxford: Oxford University Press.

West, M., Borril, C., Dawson, J., Scully, J., Carter, M., Anelay, S., Patterson, M. and Waring, J. (2002) The link between the management of employees and patient mortality in acute hospitals. *International Journal of Human Resource Management.* Vol. 13, No. 8, pp1299–1310.

White Paper (1999) archive.cabinetoffice.gov.uk/moderngov/download/modgov.pdf [accessed 27 January 2010].

Whitford, A. (2003) *Why You Can't Ignore Internet Recruitment: One-stop guide.* Reed Business Information. Available online at: www.xperthr.co.uk [accessed 16 May 2008].

Wight, G. (2007) Bending the rules: Surrey County Council embraces flexible working. *Development and Learning in Organizations.* Vol. 21, No. 4, pp20–21.

Wignall, A. (2004) Work in progress. *The Guardian.* 21 September.

Wiley, C. (2000) Ethical standards for human resource management professionals: a comparative analysis of five major codes. *Journal of Business Ethics.* Vol. 25, pp93–114.

William, N. (2008) Competency-based interviews and online psychometric tests are best for choosing candidates. *Personnel Today,* 10 March. [accessed online 7 May 2008].

Williams, R.S. (1998) *Performance Management: Perspectives on employee performance.* London: International Thomson Business Press.

Williams, S. and Adam-Smith, D. (2010) *Contemporary Employment Relations: A critical introduction.* 2nd edition. Oxford: Oxford University Press.

Wilson, E. and Iles, P. (1999) Managing diversity – an employment and service delivery challenge. *International Journal of Public Sector Management.* Vol. 12, No. 1, pp27–48.

Wilson, F.L. (2006) *Organizational Behaviour and Work: A critical introduction.* 2nd edition. Oxford: Oxford University Press.

Wolff, C. (2008) Wychavon District Council: staff engagement proved vital to success. *IRS Employment Review.* Issue 909. 17 November.

Wood, A. (2013) *Boris Johnson Opens Level 39 at Canary Wharf.* Available at: www.techcitynews.com [accessed 3 May 2013].

Wood, J., Zeffane, R., Fromholtz, M., Wiesner, R. and Creed, A. (2010) *Organisational Behaviour.* 2nd edition (Australasia). Milton, Queensland: John Wiley & Sons.

Woodall, J. and Gourlay, S. (2004) The relationship between professional learning and continuing professional development in the United Kingdom. In Woodall, J., Lee, M. and Stewart, J. (eds) *New frontiers in HRD.* London: Routledge.

Woodall, J., Scott-Jackson, W., Newham, T. and Gurney, M. (2009) Managing the decision to outsource human resources. *Personnel Review.* Vol. 38, No. 3, pp236–52.

Woods, D. (2011) UK talent acquisition costs rise to £5,311 per hire, compared to £2,226 in US. *HR Magazine.* Available at: www.hrmagazine.co.uk [accessed 30 January 2013].

Woodward, J. (1965) *Organisation and Technology.* Oxford: Oxford University Press.

Workforce Management. (2004) Available at: www.workforce.com/section/09/feature/23/85/39/index.html [accessed 30 April 2010].

Work Foundation. (2003) *The Missing Link: From productivity to performance.* Work and enterprise panel of inquiry. London: The Work Foundation.

Work Foundation. (2009) *Quality People Management for Quality Outcomes: The future of HR review on evidence on people management.* Report. July.

Wright, C. (2008) Reinventing human resource management: business partners, internal consultants and the limits of professionalization. *Human Relations.* Vol. 61, No. 8, pp1063–1086.

Wright, P.M. and Haggerty, J.J. (2005) Missing variables in theories of strategic human resource management: time, cause and individuals. *Management Review.* Vol. 16, pp164–173.

Wright, P.M. and McMahan, G. (1992) Theoretical perspectives for strategic human resources management. *Journal of Management.* Vol. 18, No. 2, pp295–320.

Xpert HR. (2008) International HR: the People Agenda. *Personnel Today.* 24 November 2008.

Xpert HR. (2012) How employers align HR with the business: 2012 XpertHR survey. *Employment Review.* 30 July 2012.

Yorks, L., Lamm, S. and O'Neil, J. (1999) Transfer of learning from Action Learning programs to the organizational setting. *Advances in Developing Human Resources.* Vol. 1, p56.

Yukl, G. (2006) *Leadership in Organisations.* 6th edition. London: Prentice Hall.

Yukl, G. (2009) *Leadership in Organizations.* 7th edition. Harlow: Pearson International.

Zigurs, I. (2003) Leadership in virtual teams: oxymoron or opportunity? *Organizational Dynamics.* Vol. 31, No. 4, pp339–351.

Index